Renewing OUR **HOPE**

"Barron's fans well know the reservoirs of thought and learning he draws, so effortlessly, upon. Here we trace the waters to their source: his charism as a scholar and teacher. This is the Bishop at his reflective, ruminative best. More gripping than Grisham!"

"More than almost any person I know, Bishop Barron lives to ponder and savor the things of God. And in meditating passionately upon the Gospel, he takes delight in reasoned argument and in the power of a memorable turn of phrase. Ever attuned to the real-world purchase of doctrine, he can be said to embody St. Paul's dictum: 'Test everything; hold fast to what is good.' For those engaged in the mission of thinking with the Gospel and bearing it to the world, this book will be a beacon."

Renewing
OUR HOPE

ESSAYS FOR THE NEW EVANGELIZATION

ROBERT BARRON

Foreword by
Archbishop Christophe Pierre, Apostolic Nuncio

THE CATHOLIC UNIVERSITY OF AMERICA PRESS
Washington, DC

 The paper used in this publication meets the minimum requirements of American
National Standards for Information Science—Permanence of Paper for Printed
Library Materials, ANSI Z39.48–1984.
∞

Cataloging-in-Publication data available from the Library of Congress.
ISBN 978-08132-3305-5.

Contents

Foreword

There is no doubt about it: Bishop Robert Barron, Auxiliary Bishop of Los Angeles, is a gifted communicator of the 'Good News.' The Word on Fire apostolate, together with series such as *Catholicism* and *Pivotal Players*, have made him a household name in the United States. Engaging believers and nonbelievers alike, whether young people, professionals at Google, legislators in Congress, or anyone who comes across his YouTube videos, Bishop Barron has been perfecting the art of communicating the best of Catholicism.

Bishop Barron possesses the gift of taking complex ideas and simplifying them, providing examples from contemporary culture, art, or the lives of the saints to connect to the lives of the men and women of our day. He has evangelized through the new media and has taken up the call of the last three popes to be engaged in the New Evangelization.

Such a capacity is rooted in a deep intellectual formation. For two decades as a seminary professor and rector at the University of St. Mary of the Lake (Mundelein Seminary), he shaped and formed the minds and spiritual lives of many priests who are serving in parishes in the United States and around the world. Always a critic of 'dumbed-down Catholicism,' Bishop Barron displays his intellectual gifts in *Renewing Our Hope: Essays for the New Evangelization*.

In July 2017, Bishop Barron experienced what many of us have experienced: a delayed flight and a missed connection. As such, he could not be present at the Convocation of Catholic Leaders held in Orlando, Florida. He was forced to deliver his keynote address from a studio via satellite. Listening to Bishop Barron tackle the phenomenon of the 'nones'—those who profess no religion—in the context of the New Evangelization, I heard him identify and critique three obstacles, which are at the same time, opportunities for evangelization: scientism, the 'm'eh' culture (i.e., relativism), and the culture of self-invention.

In this collection of essays, we find Bishop Barron not only addressing the need to evangelize the 'nones,' but also engaged in theological discourse on complex subjects such as the divine simplicity of God. His aim is always evangelization. He brings forth for the reader the richness and relevance of the Tradition, most especially St. Thomas Aquinas. Saint Thomas, for Bishop Barron, is not a man of the past, but a theologian, philosopher, and saint who can engage with today's culture, offering an intellectual response to ideologies like scientism and relativism, offering objectivity as an antidote for the culture of self-invention, and offering a path for dialogue with modern philosophers like Jacques Derrida on the dilemma of the gift. Barron demonstrates how the theological tradition is relevant for today.

Nor does Barron restrict himself to St. Thomas. In this volume, we find him reflecting again on the impact of Hans Urs von Balthasar. The Swiss theologian's aesthetics are often referenced by Barron in his popular works, but here we find in the fifth chapter, "How Von Balthasar Changed My Mind," an account of his shift from Rahner to Balthasar. Barron's references to Balthasar in this work and others are a reminder that if the Church is to evangelize today, it will be through the force of attraction, the attractiveness of Christ and the beauty of the faith. People are naturally drawn to the beautiful, good, and the true. By offering the reader sound theology, Barron draws the reader to encounter the One who is the Good, the Beautiful One, and who is the Way, Truth, and Life.

It is precisely from sound theological principles that authentic pastoral practice flows, and, at times and in turn, pastoral experience informs and refines our articulation of principles. It is for this reason that Pope Francis has emphasized the realities of people's concrete situations; it is there that the Word of God and good theology must penetrate. Theology cannot remain abstract; it must lead others to encounter the Mystery of God, who can change our lives, open new horizons, and give us direction. Two essays—"Looking for the Nones" and "Evangelizing the Nones"—are examples of the type of practical theology called for by Pope Francis.

Barron is not afraid to engage the theology of Pope Francis in these essays, offering the reader an exposure to the Holy Father's meditations on the virtues, which are nourished and nurtured within the family. St. Thomas's treatment of the virtues is often ignored in moral theology, but it is essential for Christian living. The Holy Father too recognizes that it is within the family that the person matures in virtue, developing a *habitus*. It is within this lens that Barron believes we should try to understand *Amoris Laetitia*. Nor is Barron afraid to engage the Jesuit thinker Gaston Fessard, who with Guardini influenced Pope Francis, leading to the articulation of his four principles found in *Evangelii Gaudium*.

In a world marked by advancing secularism, some Catholics believe that it is better to retreat from the culture rather than to engage it. In the essays presented here, Bishop Barron offers a different response; rather than retreat, we must take confidence in the power of the Gospel to engage and purify the culture with the best that Catholicism has to offer. The dialectic between Revelation and culture finds expression in this work in an address Barron gave to the American Congress in 2019 entitled "Liberalism and Catholicism—Why the Disconnect?" and in a lecture given in 2018 in Denver entitled "Relativism and Its Discontents."

I was pleased to receive this volume. It is an example of scholarship by a bishop who is, at the same time, an accomplished theologian. It seems to me that the Church in the United States and its efforts to carry out the New Evangelization could greatly benefit from a theologically engaged episcopate. In *Renewing Our Hope: Essays for the New Evangelization*, Bishop Barron offers us some insights not merely into the obstacles to the faith but also into the opportunities offered for the proclamation of the Gospel. After all, what is proclaimed is not mere words but the Word, who is the Person of Jesus Christ who offers us salvation.

Archbishop Christophe Pierre
Apostolic Nuncio

Preface by Bishop Robert Barron

All of the articles and speeches in this book were composed during the past five years, which is to say, the time when I have been involved primarily in ecclesial administration, as Rector of Mundelein Seminary and subsequently as Auxiliary Bishop in the Archdiocese of Los Angeles. For the previous twenty years, I had been a full-time academic, teaching primarily at Mundelein, but also at a number of other institutions as a visiting scholar. In those two decades, I wrote nearly a dozen books and numerous articles on different aspects of theology and spirituality. Though I have been more recently preoccupied with pastoral leadership, and hence unable to do the sort of sustained research that I had managed to do previously, I have tried to keep my hand in the game, accepting invitations to speak at conferences or to contribute to collections and journals. I must say that having the opportunity, during this period as rector and bishop, to return to my books and to the intellectual arena has always been a source of great joy to me.

Anyone who has followed my work over the years will recognize a number of familiar themes and preoccupations in this collection, including the theology of God, the opportunities and perils in the field of evangelization, and the transition from a more Rahnerian to a more Balthasarian approach to theology. But he or she will notice new emphases as well: the contribution of Pope Francis to the theological conversation, the need for renewal in the life of seminaries, the dangers posed by a Nietzschean program of self-invention, and the Christological import of some recent cinema. Throughout my entire career as a theological writer, I have tried to follow the lead of my mentor Francis Cardinal George, who was, of course, a sharp critic of what he took to be dysfunctional elements within contemporary society, but who also thought that one could never effectively evangelize a culture that one did not love.[1]

The first part of this collection includes a number of presentations that I gave concerning the so-called 'nones,' or religiously unaffiliated, whose numbers have increased exponentially during the past decade. I will not rehearse the details of those articles here, but suffice it to say that I have become convinced that the dramatic rise of the 'nones' is, at least in part, the bitter fruit of a decision that Church leaders took in the immediate wake of the Second Vatican Council to dumb down our presentation of the faith. Survey after survey tells us that those who have disaffiliated from religion have done so because they don't believe in the teachings proposed by classical Christianity. Armies of them have been argued into the position of nonbelief or agnosticism by the aggressive evangelism of the new atheists. In order to respond to this properly intellectual crisis, bishops, priests, catechists, apologists, and evangelists have to pick up their theological game in a serious way.

The essays presented in the second section of this book represent attempts to affect just that sort of renewal. Chapter six on the divine simplicity was originally presented at an academic symposium that I participated in with the Protestant philosopher and apologist William Lane Craig. Though I deeply admire the deft manner in which Craig engaged the new atheists (indeed, he was one of the all too few Christian thinkers able to argue rings around Christopher Hitchens and Sam Harris), I take strong exception to his dismissal of the doctrine of the divine simplicity. In the course of my intervention, I contend that God's simplicity is a cardinal teaching of Christianity, an insight on which so many other doctrines—Incarnation, creation, sacramentality—turn. In point of fact, this conviction provides the theoretical matrix for the article on the *aporia* of the gift, which I presented at the University of St. Thomas Aquinas in Rome. Apart from the divine simplicity, I maintain, it is indeed impossible to avoid the dilemmas surrounding God's capacity to give

---

1. Cardinal Francis George, *The Difference God Makes: A Catholic Vision of Faith, Communion, and Culture* (New York: The Crossroad Publishing Company, 2009), 27–28.

authentic gifts. Therefore, a theology of grace collapses if we bracket the classical understanding of God's nature as utterly self-sufficient. Chapter nine on Pope Francis and Gaston Fessard was presented originally as a paper at a conference on the Pope's often-overlooked intellectual formation. While many might acknowledge the influence of Guardini on the young Jorge Mario Bergoglio, almost no one, even in academe, realizes how profoundly marked he was by Fessard's Hegelian-Ignatian reading of history.

As someone who came of age, attended seminary, and exercised his priesthood in the wake of the Second Vatican Council, I have been, naturally enough, preoccupied with issues of ecclesiology, which is the focus of the book's third part. Unquestionably, the greatest threat to the Church in the last twenty-five years has been the clerical sex abuse scandal, which I have described as a diabolical masterpiece. It has long concerned me that, though we have examined the crisis from the legal, institutional, and psychological points of view, we have been derelict in using the interpretive key that should prove most illuminating—namely, the Word of God. This I attempt to redress in chapter ten on looking at the sexual abuse scandal with Biblical eyes, an essay first given five years ago as part of a symposium in Rome on the scandals.

Chapter twelve concerning the *imago Dei*, given as a talk at the World Meeting of Families in Philadelphia in 2015, is my attempt to unpack the implications of the priest-prophet-king baptismal anthropology articulated at Vatican II and still, in my judgment, largely unappreciated and unrealized on the ground. The Church is, finally, the community of the baptized sent out to sanctify, instruct, and govern the world in accordance with the mind of Christ.

With the pieces in the fourth and final section, we come full circle, for the topics broached there are relevant to the re-evangelization of those who have become disaffiliated from the Church. The first chapter covers Pope Francis's post-synodal apostolic exhortation *Amoris Laetitia*. In this article, originally a talk given at the World Meeting of Families in Dublin in 2018, I argue that the Pope's meditations on education in virtue, which takes place within the family, provides the most adequate hermeneutical lens for reading the whole of the exhortation, and especially the controverted eighth chapter. Chapter fifteen, a brief analysis of liberalism and

Catholicism (given originally to members of Congress in Washington, DC, in 2019) attempts to show both the points of contact and the conflicts between classical Catholicism and the dominant *Weltanschauung* (worldview) in the secular culture. Until we understand both what is positive and negative in liberalism, we will not be able to engage the minds of those who have so thoroughly embraced it. One of the negative consequences of the liberal worldview—though not, I would argue, essential to it—is an ethical and intellectual relativism, which has indeed deeply undermined the Church's mission. This I address in chapter sixteen, "Relativism and Its Discontents," offered originally as the Archbishop's Lecture in Denver in 2018. Finally, I examine a number of Christ figures that have been featured in recent cinema. A part of my evangelical strategy over the past twenty years has been to search out *semina verbi* (seeds of the Word) in both the high and the popular culture, and there are a surprising number of these seeds in films. I have found that, in approaching the 'nones,' the employment of the winsome, less threatening transcendental of the beautiful is a promising method.

May I say, as I conclude, that I am particularly grateful that the Catholic University of America Press is bringing out this collection, for my years at Catholic University, under the tutelage of such magnificent teachers as Thomas Prufer, John Wippel, and Robert Sokolowski, profoundly shaped both the content and style of my thinking. I would be delighted if my readers might appreciate this book as a humble *homage* to those who formed both my mind and heart long ago at Catholic University.

Acknowledgments

The author would like to gratefully acknowledge the permission granted by prior publishers of his work, which is here used with permission and all rights reserved.

Chapter 5: "How Von Balthasar Changed My Mind" was previously published as "A Reflection on Christ, Theological Method, and Freedom," in *How Balthasar Changed My Mind*, ed. Rodney A. Howsare and Larry S. Chapp, 9–25 (New York: The Crossroad Publishing Company, 2008). Copyright © Rodney A. Howsare and Larry S. Chapp. Reprinted by arrangement with The Crossroad Publishing Company. www.crossroadpublishing.com

Chapter 9: "Gaston Fessard and the Intellectual Formation of Pope Francis" was previously published as "Gaston Fessard and Pope Francis" in *Discovering Pope Francis: The Roots of Jorge Mario Bergoglio's Thinking*, ed. Brian Y. Lee and Thomas L. Knoebel, 114–129 (Collegeville, MN: Liturgical Press Academic, 2019).

Chapter 11: "*Optatam Totius* and the Renewal of the Priesthood" was previously published in *The Reception of Vatican II*, eds. Matthew Lamb and Matthew Levering, 191–207 (New York: Oxford University Press, 2017). © Oxford University Press. Reproduced with permission of the Licensor through PLSclear.

Chapter 17: "Christ in Cinema: The Evangelical Power of the Beautiful" was previously published under the same name in *The Oxford Handbook of Christology*, ed. Francesca Aran Murphy, 475–487 (Oxford: Oxford University Press, 2015). © Oxford University Press. Reproduced with permission of the Licensor through PLSclear.

Part 1
RENEWING OUR **MISSION**

CHAPTER 1

LOOKING FOR THE NONES

A nyone who has followed my work over the past many years knows that I've been deeply concerned about evangelization, especially of young adults. We have all been chagrined by the disturbing statistics regarding the 'nones'—namely, those who claim no religious affiliation. To give just one figure, fully fifty percent of those brought up in the Catholic Church, who are thirty or younger, have left the Church, and indeed many have renounced any sort of religion.[1] Pope Francis, in the General Congregation speech that, according to most observers, gained him the papacy, spoke famously of a Church that goes out from itself to the margins,[2] but what too few have noticed is that he specified, not simply the economic peripheries, but the existential peripheries as well. He desired an outreach to those who are, for a variety of reasons, alienated from God and who have, consequently, lost a sense of meaning and transcendent purpose.

Soon after his election, the Pope sat down for an interview with a fellow Jesuit in the course of which he identified the Church as a

---

1. Pew Research Center, "America's Changing Religious Landscape: Chapter 2" (May 12, 2015). https://www.pewforum.org/2015/05/12/chapter-2-religious-switching-and-intermarriage.

2. Nicole Winfield, "Pope's 2013 Stump Speech to Cardinals a Blueprint for Papacy," *APNews.com* (March 17, 2017), https://apnews.com/0d2ce8c37582475bb506 5b16caca6c3b.

field hospital.[3] What almost every commentator focused on is the merciful attitude of the Church implicit in that image, but what almost every commentator overlooked is the Pope's dire assessment of the spiritual condition of many people in our culture that is also implicit in that image. Francis spoke, not of a clinic where mild infections are addressed, but rather of a hospital situated close to a battlefield, where those who have suffered huge and life-threatening wounds stagger or are carried for treatment. Bring these two Franciscan insights together and you have a clear though sobering account of the present situation of many in the West, especially among the young. Armies of twenty- and thirty-somethings are in acute danger and require immediate and substantive treatment, precisely because they have lost their spiritual bearings.

At the same time, anyone who works in this field realizes that, behind the very questions that even the most aggressively antireligious young people pose is a spiritual hunger and fascination. I have sometimes teased my fiercely atheist or agnostic interlocutors on the Web that they are 'secret Herods.' Just as the ancient Galilean tetrarch loved to listen to the prophet whom he had thrown in jail (Mk 6:20), so many self-proclaimed enemies of religion attend ardently to the pronouncements of a religious figure, coming over and again to my site to comment, to critique, and to mock. I can't help but see this stubborn refusal to give up as a manifestation of the soul's passion for God.

To my mind, all of these insights have been confirmed by the most recent work of Christian Smith and his colleagues at Notre Dame. In their study *Understanding Former Young Catholics: Findings from a National Study of American Emerging Adults*, they don't simply count the number of 'nones,' they speak of them in some depth, seeking to understand their attitudes, questions, convictions, and perspectives. Their study makes for fascinating, though somewhat depressing, reading.[4] What I hope to make clear in this essay is that the situation

---

3. Antonio Spadaro, "Interview with Pope Francis" (August 19, 2013). Available at vatican.va. All Vatican documents in this book are available at vatican.va unless otherwise noted.

4. Nicolette Manglos-Weber and Christian Smith, *Understanding Former Young Catholics: Findings from a National Study of American Emerging Adults* (Notre Dame, IN: University of Notre Dame Press, 2014).

of young former Catholics is something of an indictment of the educational and catechetical strategies employed for the past fifty years. At the same time, it represents a kind of *kairos*, a privileged moment to connect with young people, and a call to action for those who want to reach them with the Gospel.

Smith presents his findings under seven major headings. I will only treat those that have a more immediate theological or catechetical implication. But I will take advantage of his basic architecture to structure this essay.

Former Catholics Still (Mostly) Believe in and Interact with (Some Version of) God

In some ways, I am most concerned about his first finding—namely, that many former Catholics believe in some version of God—not because I disagree with it, but because it might be used as pretext for concluding that things really aren't that bad. I can hear many people saying, 'Well, if these young people still believe in God, they can't be so lost.' I think that a careful attention to what these young believers actually say will temper our optimism a tad. Smith maintains that "staunch atheism is still fairly uncommon among Americans, and the same holds true for formerly Catholic emerging adults."[5] But when we listen to the rather superficial and intellectually vapid accounts of God offered by young former Catholics, we'd almost, I daresay, prefer a robust atheism! At least it would give us more traction for a constructive conversation.

One young woman, Sara, was asked if she had any religious beliefs and responded, "'I don't think so, but sometimes when I look at things, I'm like, God will work it out.' She laughed. 'I sometimes feel that certain things happen for a reason, you know, some higher being. You see those Hallmark cards—When one door closes, another opens, or God is saving this for bigger things—and I'm like, alright!'" While serving in the Navy, she came to admire the chaplains, and this led her to the conviction that "'God's gonna take care of this. And I was like, I wanna fall back on God.'"[6] Now, once again,

---

5. Manglos-Weber and Smith, *Understanding Former Young Catholics*, 6.
6. Ibid.

we shouldn't overlook the authentic spiritual sense and perception
that informs these formulations, but we also can't help but notice
the juvenile level of articulation and the fundamentally self-absorbed
quality of the spirituality: God is there primarily to solve one's personal problems. I think it is fair to say that even the most cursory
reading of the Bible would show that God never simply 'solves the
problems' of Israel, nor does he guarantee that those who follow him
will avoid suffering; just the contrary. Another young man, Joe, who
identifies as an agnostic, admitted that he prays occasionally, but he's
not at all sure to whom the prayer is directed: "Maybe the Universe,
maybe the big white man with the bushy beard."[7] In other words,
he embraces either the crudest form of pantheism or the most naïve
type of anthropomorphism. That there is a rationally compelling
biblical alternative to these options does not seem to occur to him.

Smith tells us, furthermore, that most former Catholics, if they
believe in God, don't see God as a "personal being" and are unwill-
ing to "commit to any clear view of God at this time in their lives."[8]
Do you see why I say that this 'belief' in God among the former
Catholic nones is hardly ground for optimism? We stand, it should be
clear, at a distant remove from anything even vaguely resembling a
biblical view of the Creator God or the God and Father of our Lord
Jesus Christ. If the goal of evangelization is to cultivate in people a
real friendship with the Son of God, this sort of vague spirituality is
hardly a promising starting point.

To be sure, even these deeply inadequate articulations at the
very least reveal, as I indicated above, the hunger for God, the fascination with him that endures even in the face of inadequate catechesis and deep confusion. I have found in my own evangelical work
with young people that the Augustinian anthropology—"For Thou
hast made us for Thyself and our hearts are restless till they rest in
Thee"[9]—still provides a good deal of traction. People instinctively
know that none of the goods of this world finally satisfy the longing for joy that is hardwired into them. Tapping into this delicious

---

7. Ibid.

8. Manglos-Weber and Smith, *Understanding Former Young Catholics*, 8.

9. St. Augustine, *Confessions*, 2nd ed., trans. F. J. Sheed (Indianapolis: Hackett Publishing Company, Inc., 2006), 3.

dissatisfaction, if I can riff on a theme of C. S. Lewis, is central to any program of evangelization of the young. But once again, this vague longing or spiritual sensibility should never be construed as somehow 'enough.' The same Augustine who spoke of the universal hunger for God also said that religion in the generic sense is to be sharply distinguished from true religion.

Uncomfortable with Statements about Who or What God Is

This leads neatly to Smith's next category. Younger former Catholics, in common with most people in their age bracket, seem to be uneasy with any strong statements made regarding theology. To a large degree, this is a function of the relativism that holds sway practically everywhere today. Many would readily speak of 'my truth and your truth,' but would be uncomfortable indeed with any talk of *the* truth. I have termed this the 'M'eh' culture, the culture of 'whatever.' As Smith puts it in his summary report, "What works for one person might not work for someone else," and consequently "very few if any general statements can or should be made about God, faith, or morality."[10]

As Dr. Smith suggests, this relativism seems to have a particular authority when it comes to matters religious. One former Catholic commented, "I'm so okay with the uncertainty. I think uncertainty is beautiful. I think the most beautiful works of art are the ones that lead you to asking questions as opposed to those trying to supply answers to what something is."[11] Furthermore, "the essence of spirituality is being comfortable with questions."[12] Permit me to say that I think young people have actually intuited something central to the Catholic intellectual tradition here; namely, the conviction that no statement about God is ever completely adequate. As St. Augustine famously put it, *Si comprehendis, non est Deus* ("If you comprehend him, he is not God" or "If you can grasp it, it isn't God").[13] There is, quite

---

10. Manglos-Weber and Smith, *Understanding Former Young Catholics,* 8.

11. Ibid.

12. Manglos-Weber and Smith, *Understanding Former Young Catholics,* 9.

13. St. Augustine, *Essential Sermons,* trans. Edmund Hill, The Works of Saint Augustine: A Translation for the 21st Century, Part III-Homilies (Hyde Park, NY: New City Press, 2007), Sermon 117.5, pg. 197 (PL 38, 673).

properly, always an element of indeterminacy in even the best of our theological formulations. However, I have come to recognize that this almost complete romanticization of the quest, especially among the young, goes hand in hand with the relativism just noted, for to make a decision, either morally or intellectually, is to make a definitive claim, one that excludes all others.

To use the terminology of Bernard Lonergan, the romanticization of the quest keeps us locked at the second stage of the epistemic process—namely, the intelligent exploration of hypotheses and likely scenarios that follow upon careful observation of the relevant data.[14] But this romanticization precludes the next and decisive step of being reasonable, which is to say, deciding among the various hypotheses which one is actually correct, which of the many bright ideas is in fact the right idea. And a failure to come to the third step means that one never arrives at the fourth level, which is the responsible acting out of the implications of one's judgment. Lonergan helps us to see why the suspension of the process at the second stage is so attractive to so many: it precludes real responsibility. In the measure that I cannot or will not decide, I can remain uncommitted. When we see this in the religious context, we notice just how debilitating it is, for it means irresponsibility in regard to the highest and most important things.

And though it seems to imitate the curiosity and open-endedness of the sciences, it actually stands athwart the real method of the physical sciences. The formation of hypotheses leads to the conducting of experiments, which lead finally to the making of judgments, many of which have become what we term 'settled science.' It is decidedly not the case that biology, chemistry, physics, and psychology remain permanently open-ended, always privileging question over answer. No responsible cosmologist thinks we should be open to the suggestion that the sun revolves around the earth; and no intelligent biologist holds that seven-day creationists should be included around the table of conversation. Uncertainty can indeed be beautiful, but only as a propaedeutic to deeper understanding. As G. K. Chesterton said, the open mind is something like the open mouth,

---

14. For a brief summary, see Bernard Lonergan, SJ, *Method in Theology* (Toronto: University of Toronto Press, 2003 reprint), 14–15.

designed to bite down on something solid.[15] I wonder whether a route of access to young people who valorize the sciences is to show how the total romanticizing of the quest and of uncertainty is repugnant to real scientific achievement.

Former Catholics Live in Religiously Diverse Families and Friendship Networks

Even the most casual survey of Western culture today would reveal that diversity is radically valorized. I see this against the backdrop of the oldest issue in philosophy, which is to say, the problem of the one and the many. For a variety of reasons that I won't explore now, we have swung dramatically to the 'many' side of this famous divide. Though the culture insists again and again on the positive elements of diversity, it rarely if ever appreciates diversity's shadow side—and the opposite is true of unity. If I might use Paul Tillich's categories, we consistently stress individualization rather than participation, dynamics rather than form, freedom rather than destiny.[16] But if Tillich is correct, any one-sided emphasis in regard to these polarities conduces almost inevitably to crisis and collapse. In point of fact, many features of our political culture today indicate an exaggerated reaction formation in the direction of participation, form, and destiny.

What the uncritical valorization of diversity looks like in the religious context is an allergy to anything that smacks of orthodoxy or settled belief. Here is how Smith sums up the attitude: "to believe in only one religion or profess only one version of God implies, in the minds of many emerging adults, that these other people are in error or will be judged by God."[17] A practical implication is that "religion gets talked about at home much less since it has the potential

---

15. G. K. Chesterton, "Illustrated London News" (October 10, 1908), in *Collected Works*, vol. XXVIII (San Francisco: Ignatius Press, 1987), 196; Chesterton, *Autobiography* (New York: Sheed & Ward, 1936), 229.

16. Paul Tillich, *Systematic Theology*, vol. 1 (Chicago: The University of Chicago Press, 1951), 174–178, 178–182, 182–186.

17. Manglos-Weber and Smith, *Understanding Former Young Catholics*, 10.

to be a source of conflict."[18] But evangelization, rather than, say, more abstract forms of religious speech or investigation, is directed to conversion. The evangelist, perforce, is a convinced believer, and he wants those who hear him to become convinced believers. And so evangelization stands in an at least awkward relationship with the etiquette of diversity and acceptance. Time and again, in both the high and the popular culture, we confront the stereotype of the religious advocate as aggressive, intolerant, and at the limit, violent. I recall an event several years ago in Chicago, soon after Cardinal George named me as his vicar for evangelization. At a Jewish-Catholic dialogue, one of the Jewish participants commented that when he hears the word 'evangelization,' he thinks immediately of genocide. I obviously understood (and understand) the altogether legitimate moral indignation that gave rise to that association in his mind, but I also grasped (and grasp) that he was telling any prospective evangelist, in no uncertain terms, to cease and desist.

This point of view is bolstered by the reduction of religion to morality—a tendency rampant in the West today. I might construe this, by the way, as the almost total victory of Immanuel Kant's understanding of religion as ethics. For the great eighteenth-century philosopher, every other aspect of religious belief and practice—liturgy, prayer, dogma, sacraments, veneration of saints, and so on—is reducible to bringing an adept into accord with the demands of the categorical imperative.[19] To put the Kantian perspective into more contemporary language, as long as 'being a good person' is all that finally matters, then why worry about doctrinal differences? Or, as one of Smith's young people put it: "You have your beliefs and I have mine, and does it really matter in the long run?"[20]

I wonder whether we might make some progress here by proposing an analogy with other areas of interest. Let us consider first the political arena. I doubt whether you'd find many people who would blithely remark that 'it doesn't really matter which political opinions you hold, as long as deep down you're a nice person.' How

---

18. Ibid.

19. See Immanuel Kant, *Religion within the Limits of Reason Alone* (New York: Harper Torchbooks, 1960).

20. Manglos-Weber and Smith, *Understanding Former Young Catholics,* 11.

many would calmly say, 'You know, I'm a Democrat, and you're a Republican, but as long as we're decent people, who am I to tell you how to think?' Most people I know feel that there is an at least relatively correct political point of view and they are ready, willing, and eager to defend it through argument and to convert their inter-locutors. In regard to this dimension of life, they seem little con-cerned that their opponents would feel condemned or excluded if they sought to correct their assumptions. If such a situation obtains in regard to politics, why would or should such a bland indifferent-ism obtain in regard to religion? Or consider the arena of sports. I sincerely doubt that an avid golfer, eager to draw a friend into the adventure of that most difficult of games, would blithely say, 'Well, swing the club any way you want. It doesn't really matter, as long as you have a positive attitude.' Fully acknowledging that each player will develop a distinctive swing, an experienced golfer would never-theless insist on some very objective features that characterize a suc-cessful striking of the ball. But again, regarding religion, an almost complete subjectivization is permitted to hold sway.

There appears to be an underlying though rarely averred to assumption that only two options exist in regard to religious claims: bland toleration or violence. What I would like to suggest is that a lively third option exists—namely, real religious argument. One need not do violence to one's opponent nor compel her to change her mind; nor does one have to withdraw into mere toleration or intellec-tual indifferentism. One can marshal evidence, form hypotheses, cite authorities, make illuminating analogies, and draw conclusions. In a word, one can make arguments when discussing religion. And contra Kant, it matters very much what we believe in regard to doctrine, for ethical imperatives are grounded, finally, in certain metaphysi-cal and anthropological convictions. Just as flowers will eventually wither once they are removed from the plant that sustains them, so ethical principles will indeed evanesce once they are dissociated from a doctrinal framework.

I cannot think of a better model for the making of religious argument within a pluralistic context than St. Thomas Aquinas. Even the most casual acquaintance with Aquinas's writings reveals that he is remarkably inclusive in his engagement of a wide variety of religious viewpoints. In fact, the spirit of the University of Paris in

the thirteenth century was not altogether different from the pluralistic atmosphere of our time. A wide variety of viewpoints, philosophies, and religious attitudes were on offer. In the course of his public
disputations and writings, Aquinas dialogues with a range of Christian thinkers with whom he has disagreements, some quite serious—
Origen, Pseudo-Dionysius, and Tertullian, to name a few—and with
a plethora of non-Christian figures—Plato, Aristotle, Cicero, Moses
Maimonides, Averroes, Avicenna, and others. In his writings, we find a
veritable seminar where diverse viewpoints are entertained, but always
in a respectful manner. One of the distinctive marks of Aquinas's style
was the formulation of his opponents' arguments in a manner pithier
and more convincing than they themselves could manage.

Nevertheless, the purpose of the Aquinas conversation is to
come to religious truth. He is not satisfied that a lively, respectful
exchange of views took place. He wants that dialogue to yield clarity
in regard to the question at hand. In a similar way, Cardinal George
often commented that the Church is not a debating society, but an
evangelical engine.[21] A final point in regard to Aquinas: one crucial condition for the possibility of his intellectual achievement was
a community of friends who thought religious conversation was of
highest value. In contrast, Smith reports that "former Catholics are
also distinct in that more of them report that none of their close
friends is at all religious."[22] No interest and no convicted conversation
partners spell the end of fruitful religious dialogue and argument.

Former Catholics Tend to Describe Religious Faith as Illogical or Unscientific

In a Pew Forum Study from 2016, one of the reasons that young
people gave for abandoning religion and belief is that both are at
odds with science.[23] I confront this problem on a daily basis in my

---

21. Cardinal Francis George, *The Difference God Makes: A Catholic Vision of Faith, Communion, and Culture* (New York: The Crossroad Publishing Company, 2009), 164–165.

22. Manglos-Weber and Smith, *Understanding Former Young Catholics,* 11.

23. Pew Research Center and Michael Lipka, "Why America's 'Nones' Left Religion Behind" (August 24, 2016). https://www.pewresearch.org/fact-tank /2016/08/24/why-americas-nones-left-religion-behind.

own evangelical work. I found particularly striking Smith's statistics, which indicate that, among former Catholics, fully three quarters agree or strongly agree with the statement that ultimately the teachings of science and religion conflict with each other.[24]

In my experience, it is clear that armies of young people have internalized the new atheists' characterization of religious claims as so much pre-scientific nonsense, 'Bronze Age mythology,' the musings of ignorant people who barely understood the physical dynamics of the universe, and so forth. Christopher Hitchens, Richard Dawkins, Sam Harris, Daniel Dennett, and, on a more popular level, Bill Maher, regularly hold religious faith up for just this sort of ridicule. Smith's interviews confirm my intuition: "Jordan is confident in his atheism because he sees no good scientific proof for the Christian God—no more than, say, Thor the comic book hero or Vishnu the Hindu deity."[25] Jordan also shares what he takes to be unanswerable intellectual objections to theistic belief: "If God is omnipotent, can he create something that he can't lift?"[26] And if the principle that everything comes from something else holds, then what caused God? Smith shows that even those young people who cultivate some belief in God nevertheless apologize for it sheepishly, as though it is something they ought to have grown out of by now: "I know it's not scientific, but…" says one of his interlocutors. Another, when asked whether "God is an explanation for the unexplainable," said with a laugh, "Yeah, but it's very unscientific." Still another, in a remark that would have warmed the heart of Ludwig Feuerbach, commented when asked whether her beliefs about religion are unreasonable, "Yeah. Just because they're like things to fall back on, you know." [27]

Perhaps a first observation to make is that scientism does indeed hold sway in our culture, especially among the rising generation. By this term I mean the reduction of all knowledge to the scientific form of knowledge. What can be known through the scientific method, that is to say, through empirical investigation, the formation and

24. Manglos-Weber and Smith, *Understanding Former Young Catholics*, 15.

25. Manglos-Weber and Smith, *Understanding Former Young Catholics*, 14.

26. Ibid.

27. Manglos-Weber and Smith, *Understanding Former Young Catholics*, 17.

testing of hypotheses, experimentation and the drawing of conclusions is identified, quite simply, with the real. The obvious success of the physical sciences in the mastery of nature and the massive usefulness of their attendant technologies have made this a plausible position for many. Whereas philosophies and religions seem mired in endless and irresolvable disputes, the sciences do indeed have predictive power. Hence, on scientistic grounds, any other claim to rational insight is invalid; the alternative to the physical sciences is simply nonsense.

There is much that could be said against this point of view.[28] I would only point out, first, that scientism is self-refuting in the measure that the scientific method as such could never yield the conclusion that nonscientific forms of reasoning are invalid. Where precisely did one empirically verify this? How precisely did one perform an experiment to test its legitimacy? Secondly, in a fundamental sense, religion and science cannot be in conflict, even in principle, for God is not an item in the universe, but rather the ground of the universe's being, the reason why there is something rather than nothing. God is not one competitive cause among many, nor is he one more item within the nexus of conditioned things. Hence the methods appropriate to the sciences could never be adequate to adjudicating issues regarding God one way or the other.

This is not to say, of course, that there aren't rational paths to God. It is my conviction that every catechist, evangelist, and apologist ought to have a compelling argument for God's existence at his or her fingertips. Although young people today have little acquaintance with philosophy—or at least with some non-relativist or non-nihilist version of it—it might be good to introduce them to a nonscientific but deeply rational approach to God. I have had a good deal of success with a modified version of the argument from contingency, a classical argument for God's existence. The starting point is irrefutable: contingent or non-necessary things exist. If someone balks even at this, you can ask them whether they had parents, whether they eat and drink, and whether they breathe oxygen. A contingent thing requires extrinsic causes. Now, are those causes themselves contingent or are they self-explanatory? If they are contingent, we must

---

28. See chapter two, "Evangelizing the Nones," 28–29, for more on this subject.

search for their extrinsic causes. This process cannot go on indefi-
nitely; otherwise, we have not met the demand of the principle of
sufficient reason. We must come, finally, to some reality whose very
nature is to be, whose essence and existence coincide.[29] A particular
advantage of this demonstration is that it clearly concludes to the
existence of a reality that is not one more item within the physical
universe, but rather the creator and ground of the finite world.

Relatedly, we have to get to work on communicating the proper
understanding of the word 'faith.' On Bill Maher's program *Real
Time* one night, I saw a prominent evangelical activist, an intelligent
man, sparring with the host. Maher said, "Now, you're a man of
faith, which means you're someone who accepts fantastic things on
the basis of no evidence." To my infinite surprise and chagrin, the
man simply nodded his assent! Authentically construed, faith is never
infra-rational but supra-rational. That is to say, it hasn't a thing in
common with superstition or credulity or naiveté. It is decidedly not
the acceptance of claims on the basis of no evidence. I much prefer
John Henry Newman's characterization of faith as "the reasoning
of a religious mind."[30] Religious minds empirically observe, form
hypotheses, test them in various ways, and marshal evidence. They
are just reasoning about different things, or better, a different dimension of reality.

The process by which one comes to know another person well,
even intimately, provides a remarkably apt analogy to the relation
between reason and faith in regard to knowing God. When one
wants to find out about another person, he first engages in a good
deal of rational investigation. He makes his own observations; he
speaks with others who know the person in question; he does a Google search, perhaps even a background check. Eventually, he meets
the prospective friend and does his own direct sizing-up: observing,
listening, musing. But at a decisive moment, if the friendship has

---

29. For a classical version of this, see Thomas Aquinas, *Summa theologiae Prima
Pars 1–49*, trans. Fr. Laurence Shapcote, Latin/English Translation Series (Lander, WY:
The Aquinas Institute for the Study of Sacred Doctrine, 2012), I, q. 2, a. 3.

30. John Henry Newman, "Sermon XI, The Nature of Faith in Relation to Reason," in *Fifteen Sermons Preached Before the University of Oxford Between A.D. 1826 and 1843*,
ed. James David Earnest and Gerard Tracey (Oxford: Oxford University Press, 2006),
no. 1, 143.

deepened sufficiently, the interlocutor will reveal something about himself that one could never have known by any rational means. He will speak his heart. At this point, one has to make a decision whether to believe what has been revealed. If sufficient trust has been built up, one accepts, one acquiesces, one chooses to believe. Something very similar obtains in regard to knowing the Creator. One investigates the matter rationally, examines arguments for God's existence, asks and answers question after question, and interrogates those who already believe. But at the propitious moment, one considers what God has revealed about himself in the biblical witness. One then chooses whether to believe; one makes the decision for faith. But what should be clear is that this hasn't a thing to do with naïve credulity or accepting wild propositions on the basis of no evidence. Rather, the act of faith rests upon and is conditioned by reason. Oliver Wendell Holmes Jr. once wrote, "The only simplicity for which I would give a straw is that which is on the other side of the complex."[31]

Much of the supposed conflict between religion and science is tied up, of course, with naïve approaches to the Bible. As long as one holds that the Bible, especially the opening chapters of the book of Genesis, are trading in physics and cosmology, in the contemporary sense of those terms, then the scriptural account will seem simply primitive. Key to the resolution of this problem, therefore, is an introduction to nonliteralistic strategies of biblical reading, which have been on offer in the life of the Church from the patristic period on. We might also keep in mind Fr. George Coyne's simple observation that since the last book of the Bible was written around the year 100, and the modern scientific method was developed only in the sixteenth century, it is simply impossible that the Bible could contain 'science' in the modern sense of the term.[32]

Another step, this one more positive, is to show that the modern physical sciences emerged precisely out of a theological thought matrix, hardly surprising, since they were born in and through

---

31. Oliver Wendell Holmes, Jr., *Holmes-Pollock Letters: The Correspondence of Mr. Justice Holmes and Sir Frederick Pollock 1874–1932*, vol. 1, edited by Mark DeWolfe Howe (Cambridge, MA: Harvard University Press, 1942), 109.

32. See Fr. Coyne's interview with Bill Maher for the movie *Religulous* (2008), available online at https://www.youtube.com/watch?v=xRnA4S8xrlY.

Church-sponsored universities. The first assumption that undergirds the sciences is that the world of nature is distinct from God. As long as nature is divinized or sacralized, it cannot be the object of investigation and experimentation; rather, it is worshipped or revered. The second requisite assumption is that the world of nature is, in its entirety, intelligible. Any scientist, in any discipline, must commence her work with the presumption that the reality she goes out to meet is marked by an intelligible pattern. This is true for the physicist, the chemist, the biologist, the psychologist—for any scientist. But both of these assumptions are grounded in a more fundamental theological commitment—namely, the doctrine of creation. If the world is a creature of God, then it is not divine and it can, hence, be analyzed. And if the world is a creature of God, who necessarily acts in an intelligent way, it must be marked, in every nook and cranny, by intelligibility. The young Joseph Ratzinger made this argument in his *Introduction to Christianity*: universal intelligibility points to the existence of a grounding and creating Intelligence. Therefore, properly construed, religion and science are not only compatible but, in a way, mutually implicative.[33]

Having made these clarifications, let me conclude this section with a more general observation. These comments about the irrationality of Catholic faith break my heart and prompt a *cri de coeur*. One of the distinctive marks of Catholicism across the centuries has been a commitment to the intellectual articulation of the faith. The mainstream of the tradition has not sided with Tertullian's observation about Athens having nothing to do with Jerusalem;[34] we have not accepted Luther's excoriation of reason as "the devil's whore."[35] John Henry Newman said that one of the surest signs that the faith is developing properly is that Catholics stubbornly think about the data of revelation.[36] Mary, treasuring the events

---

33. Joseph Ratzinger, *Introduction to Christianity*, trans. J. R. Foster and Michael J. Miller (San Francisco: Ignatius Press, 2004), 152–155.

34. Tertullian, "On Prescription Against Heretics," trans. Alexander Roberts and James Donaldson, in *The Ante-Nicene Fathers*, vol. 3, *The Writings of the Fathers down to A.D. 325* (Grand Rapids, MI: William B. Eerdmans Publishing Company, 1963), 246.

35. Martin Luther, *Tischreden*, ed. K. Aland (Stuttgart: P. Reclam, 1981), 43.

36. John Henry Newman, "Sermon XV: The Theory of Developments in Religious Doctrine," in *Fifteen Sermons*, no. 18–19, pp. 220–221.

of salvation history in her heart, turning them over in a meditative spirit, is, for Newman, the model of theologizing.[37]

However, over the past several decades, at least in the West, there has been an extraordinary dumbing down of the faith, an option, again and again, for the experiential and the emotional over the intellectual. Some of this was due to the victory of Schleiermacher's "experiential-expressivism" (to use a phrase from George Lindbeck) in the years after the Council, mediated through the heroes of liberal theology.[38] But much of it was due to a failure at the catechetical level, a stubborn insistence that religion is not something that young people ought to be thinking about seriously. Other priorities—community, the sharing of feelings, a commitment to social justice—all outweighed the importance of theology. Why do our high school students, in Catholic schools, read Shakespeare in English class, Einstein in physics class, Virgil in Latin class—but elementary books in religion? If young people can handle Shakespeare, Einstein, and Virgil, why in the world couldn't they handle Augustine, Aquinas, and Chesterton? Why in so many of our religious education programs and Confirmation preparation programs is there little focused study of the Creed, or no apologetic engagement with the objections to the faith which are on offer so widely in our culture? The dumbing down of Catholicism has been, I don't hesitate to say, a pastoral disaster of the first order. And we can see the effects of it clearly in study after study.

Vocational Discernment

All of the aforesaid provides a sobering but clarifying background to the consideration of the main theme of the recent synod—namely, vocational discernment among the young. The call of God is one of the most fundamental biblical categories. God's great rescue operation commences with the summoning of Abram. After a disastrous period during which human beings listened to their own voices and produced calamity after calamity, as we see in chapters four through

37. John Henry Newman, "Sermon XV," in *Fifteen Sermons*, no. 1–4, pp. 210–212.

38. Friedrich Schleiermacher, *The Christian Faith*, ed. H. R. MacKintosh and J. S. Stewart (Edinburgh: T&T Clark, 1986), no. 15, pg. 76; George Lindbeck, *The Nature of Doctrine* (Philadelphia, PA: The Westminster Press, 1984), 31.

eleven of Genesis, we hear finally of someone who listened to the voice of God. Abram was called out of his home country and his former way of life and worship and called into the desert so as to sojourn to a new country and a new form of worship. This vocation of Abram sets the tone for the rest of the biblical revelation. Israel is called out of something old and toward something new.

This is the sense of the *qahal* in Hebrew, the convocation or the assembly. (*Synagoga* typically translates the term in Greek.) In the New Testament, the term *ekklesia* carries much the same sense, derived as it is from *ek* and *kalein* (to call out from). Israel is a people called out from the world and into right relationship with God. The Church, which is the new Israel, is similarly called out from the *kosmos* (the world) and into the body of Christ, an entirely new way of thinking, behaving, and seeing. "May that same mind be in you which was in Christ Jesus" (Phil 2:5), the Apostle urges the church of Philippi. The one who has heard the call of God moves into the capacious space of the 'theo-drama' (if I can borrow a term of Hans Urs von Balthasar) and out of the narrow confines of the ego-drama.[39] Paul expresses this idea with characteristic vigor: "There is a power already at work in you that can do infinitely more than you can ask or imagine" (Eph 3:20). In his inaugural address in the Gospel of Mark, Jesus speaks of *metanoia*, which carries a very similar sense: going beyond the mind that you have (*meta nous*) (Mk 1:15).

What we have been exploring together are some of the many factors that are making the vocational call hard to hear for many young people today. How do I know that the voice of God is not just a wish-fulfilling fantasy? How can I believe something that seems to stand athwart scientific reason? How can I follow one truth to the exclusion of all others? Would accepting the demands of God not lead to violence? In a way, we find ourselves in a cultural situation analogous to that which held sway in the time of Eli and Samuel: the word of God is exceptionally hard to hear, and even when we manage to hear it we don't recognize it as God's voice (1 Sm 3). What do our young people need today? They need elders to assume the role of Eli, those who can hear the voice of God in the call for justice and

---

39. See Hans Urs von Balthasar, *Theo-Drama: Theological Dramatic Theology*, 5 vols. (San Francisco, CA: Ignatius Press, 1988–1998).

equality, in the radical contingency of the world, in the narratives of the Bible, in the definitive teaching of the Church, and in the beauty of the saints.

Might I make a suggestion in closing? As I just suggested, many young people are animated by a deep desire to affect social justice and to foster inclusion and equality. Where does this desire come from? And where finally does it lead? Why should the individual human being matter so much? Why should we be concerned with people halfway across the world, whose sufferings will never directly touch us? We have some sense of the inviolable dignity of the individual human being. But where does that come from? It certainly wasn't widely held in the classical world. It has certainly not been universally held in modern society. It finds absolutely no ground in the assumption that human beings are simply chance products of a blind evolutionary process. Thomas Jefferson helps us to see the answer: human beings are "endowed by their Creator with certain unalienable Rights, that among these are Life, Liberty, and the pursuit of Happiness."[40] The operative word here is 'Creator.' Finally, it is only belief in God that satisfactorily explains the passion for justice, inclusion, and equality.

Can we elders today play the role of Eli vis-à-vis Samuel and help our young people understand that the voice they hear calling them is, in point of fact, the voice of God?

---

40. Thomas Jefferson, "The Declaration of Independence," in *Basic Documents in American History*, ed. Richard B. Morris, The Anvil Series, (Malabar, FL: Krieger Publishing Company, 1965), 27.

CHAPTER 2

EVANGELIZING THE NONES

Cardinal Francis George consistently maintained that Vatican II is best construed as a missionary council, whose purpose was not so much to clarify disputed matters of doctrine as to facilitate the carrying of the *lumen* of Christ to the *gentes* of the modern world.[1] Hans Urs von Balthasar, in a programmatic text from the 1950s, spoke of the "razing of the bastions"—that is to say, knocking down the high medieval walls behind which the riches of the Church were sequestered.[2] Paul VI not only brought this evangelical council to a successful completion; he also penned a text that would provide the marching orders for the next five decades of the Church's life— namely, *Evangelii Nuntiandi*, the central argument of which is that the Church, by its very nature, is missionary.

At the synod of bishops on evangelization that preceded the publication of *Evangelii Nuntiandi*, the Archbishop of Krakow, Karol Wojtyła, was actively engaged. Hence it is no surprise that, upon becoming Pope three years later, John Paul II would make the New Evangelization central to his magisterium and pastoral practice. Benedict XVI, who as a young man was a major player at John XXIII's Council and who served for twenty years as John Paul's chief doctrinal officer, enthusiastically pursued the program of his

---

1. Cardinal Francis George, *A Godly Humanism: Clarifying the Hope that Lies Within*, (Washington, DC: The Catholic University of America Press, 2015), 98. See Vatican Council II, *Lumen Gentium* [The Light of the Nations] (November 21, 1964).

2. Hans Urs von Balthasar, *Razing the Bastions* (San Francisco: Ignatius Press, 1993). The original German publication was in 1952.

predecessor. And Pope Francis, who as Cardinal Bergoglio presided over the writing of the remarkably evangelical Aparecida Document of 2007, has continued in the path of his predecessors with the apostolic exhortation *Evangelii Gaudium,* whose title explicitly evokes *Evangelii Nuntiandi,* a text which Francis has called "the greatest pastoral document that has ever been written to this day."[3] All of which is to say that an evangelization "new in ardor, method, and expression"[4] has been and continues to be the governing preoccupation of the Church Catholic.

That it is needed especially now in our country has been borne out by some recent and deeply disturbing statistics. By far the fastest growing 'religious' group in the United States is the 'nones'—that is, those who claim no religious affiliation. In the latest Pew Forum survey, fully twenty-six percent of the country—approximately 60,000,000 people—say that they have no formal religion, and the increase in this regard is nothing short of startling.[5] In 1972, only seven percent of the country would self-identify as a 'none,'[6] and in the last ten years, the number has gone from seventeen percent to the current twenty-six percent. When we focus on young people, the picture becomes even more bleak. Fully forty percent of those classed as millennials (born 1981 to 1996) are 'nones,'[7] and among Catholics in that age group, fully fifty percent have left the Church. This means that every other Catholic child baptized or confirmed these last thirty years now no longer participates in the life of the Church. I do realize that these statistics are, in many ways, an unnerving commentary on the ineffectiveness of our evangelical strategies, despite all of the encouragement from popes, councils, and encyclicals. But

---

3. Pope Francis, *Address of Pope Francis to Participants in the Pilgrimage from the Diocese of Brescia* (June 22, 2013).

4. Pope John Paul II, "Address to the Assembly of CELAM" (March 9, 1983), §3: *AAS* 75 (1983), 778.

5. Pew Research Center, "In U.S., Decline of Christianity Continues at Rapid Pace: An Update on America's Changing Religious Landscape" (October 17, 2019). https://www.pewforum.org/2019/10/17/in-u-s-decline-of-christianity-continues-at-rapid-pace.

6. Pew Research Center, "'Nones' on the Rise" (October 9, 2012). https://www.pewforum.org/2012/10/09/nones-on-the-rise.

7. Pew Research Center, "In U.S., Decline of Christianity."

to focus on the present situation, they are certainly a wake-up call for teachers, catechists, evangelists, apologists, priests, and bishops. In the course of this presentation, I would like to propose a number of paths that an effective evangelization should follow. My suggestions are born, not only of theoretical musing, but also from nearly fifteen years of practical experience evangelizing 'nones,' atheists, agnostics, and seekers who dwell in the shadowy but fascinating space of the virtual world, our version of Paul's Areopagus (Acts 17:16–34).

Commencing with Beauty

In his great theological triptych, Hans Urs von Balthasar purposely reversed the Kantian arrangement of the transcendentals. Whereas Kant had moved from the true (*Critique of Pure Reason*) to the good (*Critique of Practical Reason*), to the beautiful (*Critique of Judgment*), Balthasar turned this around, commencing with the beautiful (*The Glory of the Lord*), moving through the good (*The Theo-drama*), and ending with the true (*The Theo-logic*). As Balthasar ably demonstrated, the beautiful has been a theme in classical Christian theology at least from the time of Pseudo-Dionysius, but typically it had taken a subordinate position to the good and especially the true. Balthasar intuited something in the middle of the twentieth century, just as the postmodern critique was getting underway—namely, that initiating the theological project with truth or goodness tends to be a nonstarter, since relativism and skepticism in regard to those transcendentals were powerful indeed. If such subjectivism and relativism were strong in the fifties of the last century, they have become overwhelming at the beginning of the twenty-first century; Ratzinger's "dictatorship of relativism" is now taken for granted.[8] Any claim to know objective truth or any attempt to propose objective goodness tend to be met now with incredulity at best and fierce defensiveness at worst: 'Who are you to tell me how to think or how to behave?' But there is something less threatening, more winsome, about the beautiful.

Balthasar was deeply influenced by Paul Claudel, who famously experienced a reversion to Catholicism on Christmas Day 1886,

---

8. Joseph Ratzinger, *Mass Pro Eligendo Romano Pontifice: Homily of his Eminence Card. Joseph Ratzinger, Dean of the College of Cardinals* (April 18, 2005).

while he was standing in Notre Dame Cathedral gazing at the North Rose Window and listening to sung vespers.[9] It was not argumentation that brought him to renewed faith, but a visceral experience of the beautiful. We find a very similar dynamic in what I consider the finest Catholic novel of the twentieth century, Evelyn Waugh's *Brideshead Revisited*. Charles Ryder, the narrator of the story, is a skeptic, a professed agnostic, convinced that religion is more or less outmoded mythology and a function of "the province of 'complexes' and 'inhibitions'."[10] But he finds himself drawn by the physical beauty of his Oxford companion Sebastian, who in turn leads him to his family home, a country estate called Brideshead. St. Paul referred to Christ as Head of his Bride the Church, and thus the stately manor is evocative of the Church in its various dimensions. Recalling his first summer sojourn at Brideshead, Charles remarks, "It was an aesthetic education to live within those walls."[11] So it is that many people across the centuries have been initially led to the Gospel along the aesthetic path. As the novel progresses, we see Charles drawn into the moral world of the house and finally, after a long struggle, into acceptance of the truth that it represents. The Balthasarian rhythm, from the beautiful to the good to the true, is on clear display.

Now why precisely should this work? How does the beautiful evangelize? Following Dietrich von Hildebrand, we should say that the truly beautiful is an objective value, to be sharply distinguished from what is merely subjectively satisfying.[12] This means that the beautiful does not merely entertain; rather, it invades, chooses, and changes the one to whom it deigns to appear. It is not absorbed into subjectivity; it re-arranges and re-directs subjectivity, sending it on a trajectory toward the open sea of the Beautiful itself. I am taking this image, of course, from the Diotima speech in Plato's *Symposium*, according to which the particular beautiful thing opens the mind to

---

9. Louis Chaigne, *Paul Claudel: The Man and the Mystic*, trans. Pierre de Fontnouvelle (New York: Appleton-Century-Crofts, Inc., 1961), 47–50.

10. Evelyn Waugh, *Brideshead Revisited* (New York: Back Bay Books, 1945), 86. This passage does not appear in the later 1973 edition.

11. Waugh, *Brideshead Revisited*, 80.

12. Dietrich von Hildebrand, *Christian Ethics* (New York: David McKay Company, Inc., 1953), 34–63.

a consideration of ever-higher forms of beauty conducing finally to the source and ground of all Beauty, the form of the beautiful.[13] It is this very trajectory that James Joyce illustrates in the famous strand scene from *A Portrait of the Artist as a Young Man*. After taking in the beauty of the girl who stands knee-deep in the sea off the shore, Joyce's Stephen Daedalus follows her gaze out to the open ocean and then sighs, "Heavenly God!"[14]

Therefore, in our radically relativistic time, it does seem advisable to commence the evangelical process with the winsome attractiveness of the beautiful, and thank God, Catholicism has plenty to offer in this regard. As Ewert Cousins pointed out, part of Catholicism's genius is that it never "threw anything out."[15] Accordingly, there is a 'grandma's attic' quality to the Church. At our best, from the time of John Damascene onward, the Catholic tradition has resisted the iconoclastic temptation, and thus we have Chartres Cathedral, the Sainte Chapelle, the Sistine Chapel Ceiling, the haunting icons of the East, Dante, Mozart, and the miraculous image of Our Lady of Guadalupe. This last reference is a reminder that evangelically compelling beauty does not exist merely at the rarified level, but at the popular level as well. John Paul II obviously had a deep appreciation for the finest of the fine arts, but he also had a sure feel for forms of popular devotion and religiosity. The same can be said of Pope Francis, who loves German opera but who has also developed a spirituality that draws from the wells of the devotional lives and piety of ordinary believers: processions, relics, statues, and images of the saints. Of course, as John Paul in particular realized, the Church is most beautiful in her saints. Just as we might instruct a young person in a given sport by showing examples of the greatest practitioners of that game, so we show the nature of Christianity best, perhaps, in its heroes.

---

13. Plato, *Symposium* in *Complete Works*, ed. John M. Cooper, trans. Alexander Nehamas and Paul Woodruff (Indianapolis: Hackett Publishing Company, 1997), 211a–212c, pp. 493–494.

14. James Joyce, *A Portrait of the Artist as a Young Man*, Oxford World's Classics (Oxford: Oxford University Press, 2000), 144.

15. Ewert Cousins, private conversation with the author. See Robert Barron, *Bridging the Great Divide* (Lanham, MD/Oxford: Rowman & Littlefield Publishers, 2004), 79.

Stop Dumbing Down the Faith

John Henry Newman said that one of the principal indicators that
Christianity is properly developing and not falling into corruption
is that its representatives are stubbornly thinking about the data
of revelation.[16] For the great English convert, Mary, treasuring the
events of salvation history in her heart, is the model of a faith that
is consistently and seriously *quaerens intellectum* (seeking understanding). At its best, the Catholic tradition has resisted Tertullian's suggestion that Jerusalem should have nothing to do with Athens.[17]
Instead, it has treasured figures from Irenaeus to Thomas Aquinas
to Joseph Ratzinger who have insisted that the dialogue between
faith and reason is indispensable to the evangelizing mission of
the Church.

In the middle of the twentieth century, there was an extraordinary renaissance of Catholic intellectualism across a variety of lit-
erary disciplines. One thinks of Waugh, Graham Greene, Thomas
Merton, Flannery O'Connor, Georges Bernanos, Balthasar, Fulton
Sheen, Dorothy Day, and many others. Furthermore, the documents of Vatican II were produced by the cream of the intellectual
crop of mid-twentieth-century Catholic philosophy and theology:
Henri de Lubac, Jean Daniélou, Ratzinger, Yves Congar, and Karl
Rahner, to name just a few. And yet, in the years following the
Council, a debilitating anti-intellectualism came to hold sway in
the Church, at least in the West. I know this, by the way, not from
books of sociology, but from very direct experience, for I came of
age precisely in this period. To make the faith accessible through
appeals to common experience and to emotion was the preferred
catechetical method, and within a properly theological context,
the experientialism of Schleiermacher and his disciples was all
the rage. Accordingly, during this 'banners and balloons' period,

---

16. John Henry Newman, "Sermon XV: The Theory of Developments in Reli-
gious Doctrine," in *Fifteen Sermons Preached Before the University of Oxford Between A.D. 1826
and 1843*, ed. James David Earnest and Gerard Tracey (Oxford: Oxford University
Press, 2006), no. 1–4, pp. 210–212.

17. Tertullian, "On Prescription Against Heretics," trans. Alexander Roberts
and James Donaldson, in *The Ante-Nicene Fathers: The Writings of the Fathers down to A.D.
325*, vol. 3 (Grand Rapids, MI: William B. Eerdmans Publishing Company, 1963), 246.

biblical distinctiveness and theological precision were, to state it mildly, underplayed. Some years ago, the late Cardinal George showed me his fourth-grade religion book from the 1940s. My jaw dropped at the complexity, intellectual rigor, and technical vocabulary on offer, especially in comparison to the texts that my generation read for religious instruction.

The dumbing down of the faith has been a pastoral disaster, significantly contributing to the mass exodus of two generations from the Church. A childish, intellectually shallow religion simply cannot stand in the face of the trials of life and the questions of an adult mind. One of the most deleterious consequences of this anti-intellectualism was an almost total compromising of the apologetic art within the context of evangelization. My generation was indoctrinated to consider apologetics as too rationalistic, anti-Protestant, arrogant, hostile to the culture, and defensive. This indoctrination was accompanied by a naïve embrace of the wider culture, as though reading the 'signs of the times' was tantamount to accommodation. 'The world sets the agenda for the Church' was a typically wrong-headed watchword of that time. When significant segments of the culture turned dramatically against the faith following the events of September 11 and in the wake of the sex abuse scandals, we were left in most cases defenseless against our enemies. For evidence of this, witness the pathetic performance of the vast majority of Christian spokespeople against the sharpest of the new atheists. One of the very few happy exceptions is William Lane Craig, an evangelical who draws intelligently indeed from the Catholic philosophical tradition.

What is desperately needed, if the work of evangelization is to move forward, is a new apologetics. Drawing on years of frontline engagement with a skeptical culture, I would identify five major areas of focus: the doctrine of God, the interpretation of the Bible, theodicy, religion in relation to violence, and religion in relation to science. I will say more about the theology of God below, but for now I would like to concentrate on the last issue, for in that Pew Forum Study I referenced in chapter one, it was listed as a major reason why people, especially young people, are leaving their childhood religion, including Christian churches.[18] It is sadly becoming an axiomatic assumption among many that religious faith is simply incompatible with a scientific worldview. As philosophy at the university level has degenerated into deconstruction, relativism, and nihilism, and as literary study has devolved into political correctness, trigger warnings, and the uncovering of microaggressions, the hard physical sciences remain, in the minds of many young people, the sole reliable bearers of truth about the world. And overwhelming numbers of them have bought the critique offered by the scientific establishment that religion is, at best, a primitive and now outmoded version of science. Read Daniel Dennett, Stephen Hawking, Sam Harris, Lawrence Krauss, and Richard Dawkins if you want the details. I can testify from direct engagement with the contemporary culture that the disciples of these figures are thick on the ground, and mind you, these young devotees have not been hugged into atheism; they have been argued into it. We have to argue them back to our position.

The most fundamental problem in this regard is scientism, the reduction of all knowledge to the scientific form of knowledge. The smashing success of the physical sciences and their attendant technologies have, understandably enough, beguiled the young into thinking that the scientific method is the only legitimate route to truth and that anything lying outside their purview is tantamount to nonsense or fantasy. As Cardinal George once observed, the effective disappearance of philosophy as a mediating discipline between science and religion has had a deleterious effect on epistemology in general.[19] When philosophy was construed as a legitimate bearer of truth, people saw that a discipline could be nonscientific and yet altogether rational. Given the self-destruction of philosophy, religion seemed, *a fortiori*, relegated to the shadows of irrationality and superstition. Scientism is, in point of fact, a rather silly position to hold, for it is operationally self-refuting. It can in no way be proven through the scientific method that the scientific method is the sole route of access to truth. Moreover, as I have frequently endeavored to show in my

---

18. Pew Research Center and Michael Lipka, "Why America's 'Nones' Left Religion Behind" (August 24, 2016). https://www.pewresearch.org/fact -tank/2016/08/24/why-americas-nones-left-religion-behind.

19. Cardinal Francis George, *A Godly Humanism*, 15.

apologetic work, people readily, though without averring to it consciously, accept drama, painting, literature, and philosophy as not only diverting, but also as truth-bearing. Though they are anything but scientific texts, *Hamlet*, the *Symposium*, and *The Wasteland* teach truths about the world, destiny, and human psychology that could not be known in any other way.

I have also found a good amount of traction demonstrating that the modern physical sciences emerged when and where they did precisely because of a Christian thought matrix. As a number of theorists have maintained, two assumptions are essential to the development of the sciences—namely, that the world is not divine (and hence can be investigated and analyzed rather than worshipped) and that the universe is intelligible (and hence in correspondence with an inquiring intelligence). Both of these assumptions are corollaries of the properly theological doctrine of creation, which insists that the world is other than God and that it is endowed in every dimension with intelligibility, since it was thought into being by a personal God. Ratzinger says that this connection is signaled by the word "recognition," literally re-cognition, implying that every act of knowledge is a re-thinking of what had been antecedently thought by a higher intelligence.[20] If this last point is true, then religion is not only compatible with science; in a real sense, it is the condition for the possibility of science. I believe that the addressing of this issue should be priority one for a new apologetics.

Tell the Great Story of Israel

N. T. Wright has argued that most of the Christology of the past two hundred years, both Protestant and Catholic, has been largely Marcionite in form—that is to say, developed in almost complete abstraction from the Old Testament.[21] Consider Schleiermacher's presentation of Jesus as the human being with a constantly potent God-consciousness, or Kant's account of the archetype of the person

---

20. Cited by Vincent Twomey, *Pope Benedict XVI: The Conscience of Our Age* (San Francisco: Ignatius Press, 2007), 125–126, from Joseph Ratzinger, *Wahrheit, Werte, Macht: Prüfsteine der pluralistischen Gesellschaft* (Freiburg im Breisgau: Herder, 1993), 51–52.

21. N. T. Wright, *Jesus and the Victory of God*, vol. 2 of *Christian Origins and the Question of God* (Minneapolis: Fortress Press, 1996), 25–27.

perfectly pleasing to God, or Rudolf Bultmann's paragon of the existential choice, or Paul Tillich's appearance of the new being under the conditions of estrangement,[22] or Rahner's insistence that Christology is fully-realized anthropology.[23] All of these approaches—fascinating as they might be in themselves—are intelligible apart from the dense texture of Old Testament revelation and expectation. But when Jesus is presented in this manner, he devolves in short order into a sage, an exemplar of moral virtue, or a teacher of timeless truths. But evangelization—the declaration of good *news*—has precious little to do with any of this. It has to do with the startling announcement that the story of Israel has come to its climax, or to state it a bit differently, that the promises made to Israel have been fulfilled. Not to get Israel, therefore, is not to understand why in the world Jesus represents such good news.

To develop this idea fully would require a number of books, but allow me to unfold it according to two simple motifs: priesthood and kingship. On Genesis's poetic telling, the world comes forth from the Creator in the manner of a liturgical procession, each element following the previous one in stately order. At the close of the procession is the human being, who functions, therefore, as the high priest of the chorus of praise. It is absolutely no accident that every creature mentioned in the Genesis account—planets, the sun, the moon, the earth itself, the animals that move upon the earth—were, at one time or other, worshipped as deities. By placing them in the liturgical procession and ordering them to the praise of the Creator, the author of Genesis was effectively demoting them but also giving them their proper orientation in relation to God.[24] The early Jewish commentators, as well as the Church Fathers who followed them in this regard, appreciated Adam prior to the Fall as the first priest and the Garden as a kind of primordial

---

22. Paul Tillich, *Systematic Theology*, vol. 2 (Chicago: The University of Chicago Press, 1957), 177.

23. Karl Rahner, *Foundations of Christian Faith: An Introduction to the Idea of Christianity*, trans. William V. Dych (New York, NY: The Crossroad Publishing Company, 1978), 195–203.

24. John Bergsma and Brant Pitre, *A Catholic Introduction to the Bible*, vol. 1, *The Old Testament* (San Francisco: Ignatius Press, 2018), 96.

Temple.[25] Walking in easy harmony with God, Adam was naturally in the stance of *adoratio* (literally 'mouth-to-mouth') vis-à-vis God, all of his energies properly aligned to the Creator. What this right praise produced was order, first within the person of Adam and then in the world around him, cult cultivating the culture, to paraphrase Dorothy Day and Peter Maurin.[26] Again, both the intertestamental sages and the Church Fathers came together in understanding the divine permission to eat of all of the trees of the Garden (save one) as an invitation to engage in philosophy, politics, the arts, conversation, science, and so on. Therefore, the right ordering of these enterprises is contingent upon the right praise (orthodoxy) of the one who enters into them.

In light of this reading, we can see that the Fall involved a compromising of the priestly identity of the human race. Grasping at the tree of the knowledge of good and evil, Adam and Eve arrogated to themselves the prerogatives of godliness, which is to say, the privilege of determining the good, the true, and the beautiful. This 'will to power' amounted to the suspension of right praise and hence conduced toward the disintegration of the self and the society. The antagonism, not only between Adam and Eve ("the woman you put here with me" made me do it [Gn 3:12]) but also between humanity and nature ("The snake tricked me, so I ate it" [Gn 3:13]), symbolically suggest that the harmonization of all elements of creation through the rightly-ordered priesthood of Adam has been fatally compromised.

Now Adam prior to the Fall was not only interpreted as priest but also as king, more precisely a king on the march, for his purpose was not only to cultivate the Garden but to expand its borders outward, making the whole world a place where God is correctly

---

25. For example, see Philo of Alexandria, *On the Creation of the Cosmos According to Moses*, trans. David T. Runia, Philo of Alexandria Commentary Series 1 (Leiden: Brill, 2001), §55, pg. 70; St. Ambrose, *Hexaemeron, Paradise, and Cain and Abel*, trans. John J. Savage, The Fathers of the Church: A New Translation 42 (Washington, DC: The Catholic University of America Press, 1961), 70.

26. Peter Maurin, "Building Churches," in *Easy Essays* (Eugene, OR: Wipf and Stock Publishers, 2003), 28–29; "The Way to Fight Communism: Irish Scholars," in *Easy Essays*, 142; "Irish Culture," in *Easy Essays*, 206; See also Dorothy Day and Francis J. Sicius, *Peter Maurin: Apostle to the World* (Maryknoll, NY: Orbis Books, 2004), 91.

praised. Under this rubric, we can understand the Fall as a failure in kingship. Compromised in his basic identity, Adam was no longer able to defend the Garden, much less to increase its empire. Consequently, he and Eve were expelled from paradise, and we shouldn't read this as arbitrary divine punishment, but rather as spiritual physics. From the loss of priestly and kingly identity follows, as night follows day, the loss of the Garden. The Fall, of course, is described in the third chapter of Genesis, and it is most instructive to read the ensuing chapters, for they constitute an extraordinarily concentrated account of permutations and combinations of dysfunction that follow from the original disintegration. We find stories of corruption, violence, envy, murder, imperialistic machination, and cruelty. St. Augustine did not miss the biblical identification of the fratricidal Cain as the founder of cities, seeing in this the skewing of the political order that ought to have followed from right kingship, and he practically delighted in the echo of this in the story of the founding of Rome by a similar fratricide.[27]

God's answer to all of this, on the biblical reading, was a rescue operation, precisely in the form of a holy people who would listen to his voice, learn to praise him correctly, and draw all the nations to right order through the splendor of their way of life. After creation, the Fall, and the consequences of the Fall, are described in chapters one through eleven, chapter twelve of Genesis introduces us to Abraham, the father of Israel, the father of faith. This new Adam figure is the progenitor of a priestly and a kingly people. He and his descendants, from Isaac and Jacob, through David and Solomon, to Isaiah and Ezekiel, would attempt, through the disciplines of Torah, temple worship, prophetic speech, kingly rule, and sacred covenant, to restore a properly ordered humanity. The coming together of the priestly and kingly offices is perhaps nowhere better expressed than in the exuberant dance of King David, wearing the ephod of a priest, before the Ark of the Covenant, which contained the tablets of the Law (2 Sm 6:14). But the priests of Israel tended to fall into corruption and run after false gods; and the kings of Israel, time and again, betrayed their office. Even the greatest king, David, was an adulterer

---

27. St. Augustine, *The City of God*, ed. Marcus Dods (New York: Random House, 1950), XV.5, pp. 482–483.

and a murderer. Much of this dissolution is summed up in Ezekiel's devastating vision, recounted in the tenth chapter of his prophetic book, of the *Shekinah* (the glory) of Yahweh leaving his Temple and moving toward the east, away from Israel. But the enduring hope of Israel is expressed in that same prophet's prediction that one day the glory of the Lord would return to his Temple and on that day water would flow forth from the side of the building for the renewal of creation (Ezek 43:1–9; Ezek 47:1–12).

All of this—and I am but touching on highlights in the most cursory way—is the necessary background for understanding the good news regarding Jesus Christ. The New Testament writers and kerygmatic preachers of the first century consistently presented Jesus, not according to a philosophical system, but *kata ta grapha* (according to the writings). In a word, they interpreted him against the loamy background of Israel, its identity, its failure, and its aspiration. Accordingly, they saw him as priest and as king and hence, as Paul so clearly stated, as the new Adam (see Rm 5:14; 1 Cor 15:45). When Matthew arranges the genealogy of Jesus according to three groups of fourteen generations, he was declaring Christ as the new David, for fourteen is the number that corresponds, in the Hebrew custom, to the name *Dawid*.

All four Gospels compel us to see Jesus through the lens of John the Baptist, and this means the lens of Temple and priesthood, for John was the son of a priest and he was performing the rituals of an alternate Temple in the desert. When Jesus comes, John cries, "Behold, the Lamb of God" (Jn 1:29), signaling that Christ was, above all, the one to be sacrificed. In accord with this hermeneutic, Jesus says, in reference to himself, "something greater than the temple is here" (Mt 12:6), and he performs the great ministries of teaching, healing, and forgiving that were customarily carried out by the temple priesthood. At the climax of his life, he comes to the Jerusalem Temple and announces that if "this temple" is torn down, he will in three days rebuild it, referring, John helpfully tells us, to the temple of his body (Jn 2:19–21). The night before he dies, Jesus identifies the Passover bread with his body, which will be "given away," and the Passover wine with his blood that will be poured out like the blood of lambs sacrificed in the Temple (Mk 14:22–24). This trajectory ends on the cross, properly interpreted not simply as a Roman execution but as the carrying out of the definitive act of right praise. When the Roman soldier pierces the Lord's side, blood and water flow forth (Jn 19:34), and no first-century Jew would have failed to see the fulfillment of Ezekiel's prophecy that when the *Shekinah* of Yahweh would return to his Temple, water would flow forth from its side for the renewal of a new Garden of Eden (Ezek 47:1). Therefore, to evangelize is to announce that the priestly identity of the holy people Israel has been realized in a manner beyond all expectations, that Mt. Zion, the place of the crucifixion, has indeed finally become the place to where all the tribes go up, the tribes of the Lord, to join together in right praise of the true God.

All of the Gospels, moreover, insist that Jesus' essential message was of a kingdom. In Mark's version of Christ's inaugural address, the Lord says, "This is the time of fulfillment. The kingdom of God is at hand. Repent, and believe in the gospel" (Mk 1:15). If the kingdom has come, then the King, the new David, must have arrived, and this indeed is what Jesus announces regarding himself. And in line with all of Israel's kings, this ultimate king will fight, and indeed he does, from the moment of his birth: against Herod and all Jerusalem, against the scribes and Pharisees, against those who seek to stone him and destroy him, and against the demons themselves. At the climax of his life, the whole panoply of evil comes at him: hatred, cruelty, violence, injustice, stupidity, and institutional corruption. On the cross he fights, but not in the worldly manner, meeting fire with fire, but rather swallowing all of it up in the divine mercy. The victory would be complete when the risen Jesus would say to those who had abandoned and betrayed him, *Shalom,* "Peace be with you" (Jn 20:21). What the first believers came to understand was that God's love is greater than anything that is in the world, and therefore they were willing to hold up the cross, which was meant to terrify Rome's enemies into submission, as a sort of taunt. One might distill the earliest kerygmatic preaching as 'Caesar killed him, but God raised him up.' This made Pontius Pilate, in a delicious irony, the first evangelist, for he had put over the cross a sign, in the three major languages of that time and place, "Jesus the Nazorean, the King of the Jews" (Jn 19:19). Any first-century Jew would have understood that the King of the Jews would be, by extension, the King of all the world, and this is precisely why Rabbi Sha'ul, once he met the risen Jesus and became the Apostle Paul, conceived the mission to tell the world that it had a new King. Hence his constant message *Iesous Kyrios*, Jesus is Lord, meant as an ironic challenge to the oft-used phrase *Kaiser Kyrios*, Caesar is Lord, landed him frequently in jail, for the authorities knew exactly what Paul meant. Once again, this evangelical claim, and its accompanying mission, make not a lick of sense apart from the story of Israel.

A few years ago, the daughter of one of my Word on Fire colleagues came to our office. Her mother said, "Tell Fr. Barron how much you know about *Star Wars*." With that, the eight-year-old girl launched into a stunningly detailed account of the *Star Wars* narrative, involving subplots, extremely minor characters, and thematic trajectories. As she was unfolding her tale, all I could think of were the myriad educators whom I have heard over the years assuring me that young people could not possibly take in the complexities, convoluted plot twists, and strange names found in the Scriptures. I don't know, but I don't think Methusalah and Habbakuk are really any more puzzling than Obi-Wan Kenobi and Lando Calrissian—and this eight-year-old hadn't the slightest problem remembering those latter two or how they fit into George Lucas's narrative. If we want our evangelization efforts to succeed, we have to learn again how to tell the story of Israel—especially to our young people—in a compelling way.

Emphasize the God of the Burning Bush

There is nothing really new in the arguments of the new atheists. They are borrowed from Feuerbach, Marx, Freud, Nietzsche, and Sartre. And what all the atheists, new and old, have in common is a mistaken notion of God, for to a person they construe God as one being among many, an item within the nexus of conditioned things. The roots of this misconception are deep and tangled, stretching back to antiquity, but I would put a good deal of the blame for the present form of the problem on the transition from an analogical to a univocal conception of being, on display in Duns Scotus and especially in William of Ockham.[28] On Thomas Aquinas's analogical interpretation, God is not one item, however impressive, in the genus of existing things. Indeed, Thomas insists that God is not an individual and is not to be categorized in any genus, even that most generic of genera, the genus of being.[29] God is not so much *ens summum* (highest being) as *ipsum esse subsistens* (subsistent being itself).[30] But if, as Scotus and Ockham would have it, being is a univocal term, then God and creatures can be considered under the same ontological rubric, and they do indeed belong to an identical genus. This means, in consequence, that God, though he might be described as infinite, is one being among many, an individual alongside other individuals. Ockham stated the principle with admirable economy of expression: *Praeter illas partes absolutas nulla res est* ("outside of these absolute parts, there is nothing real").[31]

I realize that this might seem the very archetype of pointless medieval hairsplitting, but on this point hinges a great deal indeed. On the analogical reading, all of finite reality participates in the fullness of the *actus essendi* (act of being) of God, and hence God and creation cannot be construed as rivals, since they don't compete for space, as it were, on the same ontological grid. But on the univocal reading, God and creation are competitive, and a zero-sum game does obtain in their regard. The Protestant Reformers were massively shaped by the nominalist view that came up from Ockham, and they therefore inherited this competitive understanding of the God/world relationship, which is evident in so much of their speculation concerning justification, grace, and providence: if God is to

---

28. Blessed John Duns Scotus, *On Being and Cognition*, ed. and trans. John van den Bercken (New York: Fordham University Press, 2016), I, d. 3, p. 1, q. 2, nn. 20–70, pp. 45–70. For secondary literature, see Matthew C. Menges, *The Concept of Univocity Regarding the Predication of God and Creature According to William Ockham* (St. Bonaventure, NY: Franciscan Institute, 1952).

29. St. Thomas Aquinas, *Summa theologiae*, I, q. 13, a. 5.

30. Aquinas, *Summa Contra Gentiles: Book Three, Providence, Part 1*, trans. Vernon J. Bourke (Notre Dame, IN: University of Notre Dame Press, 1975), III.19; *Summa theologiae*, I, q. 4, a. 2; q. 11, a. 4.

31. William of Ockham, *Scriptum in Librum Primum Sententiarum: Ordinatio (Dist. XIX-XLVIII)* in *Opera Theologica*, vol. IV (St. Bonaventure, NY: The Franciscan Institute, 1977), d. 30, q. 1, pg. 317.

get all of the glory, the world has to be emptied out of glory; if grace is to be fully honored, nature has to be denigrated; and if salvation is all God's work, cooperation with grace has to be denied. When this notion of God became widespread in Europe after the Reformation, it provoked a powerful counterreaction, which one can see in almost all of the major philosophical figures of early modernity. The threatening God must be explained away (as in Spinoza), fundamentally identified with human consciousness (as in Hegel), internalized as the ground of the will (as in Kant), or shunted off to the sidelines (as in most forms of Deism). In time, the God of late-medieval nominalism is ushered completely off the stage by an impatient atheism that sees him (quite correctly, in fact) as a menace to human flourishing. Thus Ludwig Feuerbach could argue that *"Das Nein zu Gott ist das Ja zum Menschen,"* ("The no to God is the yes to man"), and every single atheist since has followed him.[32] Mikhail Bakunin, a Russian revolutionary anarchist, also in the nineteenth century, summed up the exasperation with the competitive God in a pithy syllogism: "If God is, man is a slave; now, man can and must be free; then, God does not exist."[33] And Christopher Hitchens has echoed the Feuerbach view, observing that believing in God is like accepting permanent citizenship in a cosmic version of North Korea.[34]

I find in my work of evangelization that the competitive God still haunts the imaginations of most people today, especially the young, and this is certainly one reason why the new atheists have found such a receptive audience. We who would evangelize simply have to become better theologians—that is to say, articulators of the truth about who God is. I would suggest that the best biblical image for God is the burning bush—on fire, but not consumed—which appeared to Moses. The closer the true God comes to a creature, the more radiant and beautiful that creature becomes. It is not destroyed, nor is it obligated to give way; rather, it becomes the very best version

32. This paraphrase of Feuerbach comes from Walter Kasper, *The God of Jesus Christ* (New York: Continuum Books, T&T Clark International, 2012), 29; see also Walter Kasper, *Der Gott Jesu Christi* (Mainz: Matthias-Grünewald-Verlag, 1982), 45.

33. Mikhail Bakunin, *God and the State*, trans. Benjamin Tucker (New York: Mother Earth Publishing Association, 1916), 25.

34. Rudyard Griffiths, ed., *Hitchens vs. Blair: Be it Resolved Religion is a Force for Good in the World: The Munk Debates* (Toronto: House of Anansi Press Inc., 2011), 8.

of itself. This is not just fine poetry; it is accurate metaphysics. We can find this truth on display in the narratives concerning David, Saul, and Samuel, wherein God definitively acts, but not interruptively. Rather, he works precisely through the ordinary dynamics of psychology and politics. Nowhere is the God of the burning bush more fully on display than in the Incarnation, that event by which God becomes a creature without ceasing to be God or undermining the integrity of the creature he becomes. It is most instructive to note how the formula of the Council of Chalcedon—two natures in one person—held off an extremism of the right (monophysitism), an extremism of the left (Nestorianism), and, if I can put it this way, an extremism of the middle (Arianism). 'Fully divine and fully human' is intelligible only within a metaphysical framework of noncompetition. Feuerbach felt obligated to say no to the Ockhamist God, but St. Irenaeus, who had the biblical idea of God in his bones, could say, *Gloria Dei homo vivens* (The glory of God is a human being fully alive).[35]

Michael Buckley argued many years ago in his seminal *The Origins of Modern Atheism* that one of the conditions for the possibility of the emergence of an aggressive atheism these last two centuries is that Christians had become remarkably inept at articulating what they mean by the word 'God.'[36] In light of my experience in the evangelical front lines, I would maintain that his observation remains of singular relevance today.

Conclusion: Engage in Radical Witness

I have spoken so far of the beautiful and the true. Might I close by saying a word about the third transcendental? One of the better-known one-liners from the ancient Church is the observation made by Tertullian of the followers of Jesus: "Look how they [the Christians] love one another."[37] There is little doubt that one of the

---

35. St. Irenaeus of Lyons, *Against Heresies*, IV.20.7. In *Irenaeus on the Christian Faith: A Condensation of* Against Heresies, trans. and ed. James R. Payton, Jr. (Eugene, OR: Pickwick Publications, 2011), 116.

36. Michael J. Buckley, *At the Origins of Modern Atheism* (New Haven, CT: Yale University Press, 1987), 38–39, 41, 332–333, 358–363.

37. Tertullian, *Apology*, trans. T. R. Glover, The Loeb Classical Library (London: William Heinemann Ltd, 1931), 39.7, pg. 177.

principal reasons that the Christian Church grew within the context of the Roman Empire was the witness of its adepts, especially their willingness to care for the suffering of those around them, including those who were not members of their community. So out of step with the tribalism and elitism of the time, this practice led many to embrace the faith. We find something very similar in the example of the Desert Fathers, beginning with Antony. Their lifestyle of simplicity, poverty, and trust in God's providence brought armies of young men and women to the desert, and the life of Antony, composed by the great Athanasius of Alexandria, had a galvanizing effect on some of the best and brightest of the fourth and fifth centuries, including Augustine himself.[38] For example, it is said that the young Gregory Thaumaturgos came to Origen seeking to understand Christian doctrine, and the great teacher said, "First come and share our life, and then you will understand our doctrine."

In the sixth century, when the order of Rome had definitively collapsed, monastic communities commenced to form in the West, the best known that of Benedict and his brothers. Prayer, poverty, simplicity of life, and confidence in providence were, once more, the hallmarks of this form of life. It is, of course, a commonplace to observe that these communities served not only to evangelize Europe but to restore its civilization as well. Something very similar happened in the thirteenth century, during a time of significant clerical and institutional corruption. Both Dominic and Francis opted to return to evangelical basics and thereby served to revitalize the mission of the Church. After the French Revolution, when the Church was threatened with extinction in Western Europe, many great missionary orders arose: the Oblates of Mary Immaculate, the Congregation of Holy Cross, and the Marianists, among others. The twentieth century, the time of greatest persecution in the history of the Church, witnessed the rise of Opus Dei, Communion and Liberation, Focolare, as well as the stunning example of St. Teresa of Calcutta and her Missionaries of Charity.

Especially in light of the sex abuse scandals of recent years and the emergence of an aggressive new atheism, the recovery of a

---

38. Athanasius, "Life of Antony," in *Early Christian Lives*, trans. Carolinne White (London: Penguin Books, 1998), 3–70.

radical form of the Christian life is essential to the task of evangelization. We must regain our moral and spiritual credibility, and this happens, as it always does, through a back-to-basics evangelicalism. In its most elemental form, Christianity is not a set of ideas, but rather a friendship with the Son of God, a friendship so powerful and transforming that Christians up and down the ages could say, with St. Paul, "It is no longer I who live, but Christ who lives in me" (Gal 2:20). When it is radically internalized in this Pauline way, the friendship with Jesus fills the mind, fires the heart, awakens the will, and changes the body. And then, it sends us on mission.

As I trust I have made sufficiently clear, I believe that the time we are passing through represents a crisis in the life of the Church. But it is also an opportunity, a *kairos*. The rapid rise of secularism, the emergence of the nones, and the explicit attacks of the new atheists have served to rouse the Christian churches to a new attention and a new commitment to action. The last decade has witnessed an explosion in apologetics, in Scripture studies, and in fundamental theology—to a degree within the academy, but much more thoroughly at the grassroots level. And these new apologists and evangelists have seized the same means so often employed by the enemies of the faith—namely, the internet, YouTube, and social media. To give just one example of this revival, there is more sophisticated discussion of the classical arguments for God's existence on the Internet than I have seen in my lifetime within the academy.

The dialogue with the culture, "scrutinizing the signs of the times,"[39] has been, since the Council, perhaps the principal preoccupation of the Church. But far too often, the conversation has been one-sided, the Church straining to make itself understandable to the culture, and the culture making precious little effort to reciprocate. Perhaps the very hostility of the culture today is compelling the Church to revisit the treasure house of its own tradition: the Bible, the saints, art and architecture, and metaphysics, for instance. And perhaps it is serving as a summons to an army of smart and spiritually alert catechists, evangelists, and witnesses willing to give their lives to the great task before them.

---

39. Vatican Council II, Pastoral Constitution *Gaudium et Spes* (December 7, 1965), §4.

CHAPTER 3

THOMAS AQUINAS AND THE NEW EVANGELIZATION

Commencement Address for the Dominican School of Theology in Washington, DC

I should like to begin by paying tribute to the Dominican Fathers, who have played such a decisive role in my own development as a Christian, a priest, and a theologian. I have often told the story of my awakening to the faith under the influence of Fr. Thomas Paulsen, a young (at the time) Dominican friar teaching at Fenwick High School outside of Chicago. One warm spring afternoon in 1974, Fr. Paulsen laid out the fundamentals of Thomas Aquinas's argument from causality for God's existence, and his lecture was, for me anyway, like the ringing of a bell, like a clap of thunder. It gave me a sense of the *reality* of God that I have never lost, and it set me on a path that I have never really left, and that has led me to where I stand right now. Another of my teachers at Fenwick, Fr. Joseph Hren, explained the rudiments of Latin to me when I was fourteen, and his instruction was the opening of a door to a world that I have loved and explored ever since. Many other Dominicans have inspired me over the years, but I would like especially to reference Fr. Paul Murray, whose writings and personal style seem to sum up the Dominican way. You have honored me by this invitation; may I take the opportunity to thank you for what your Order has meant to me.

The last three Popes have been summoning the Church to engage in a New Evangelization, and the motivation for that summons has come clearly from the documents of the Second Vatican Council, which, as my mentor Cardinal Francis George often said, ought to be construed primarily as a missionary council.[1] Like the 'old' evangelization, the New Evangelization involves the proclamation of the Lordship of Jesus Christ, but its novelty consists, as John Paul II specified, "in ardor, method, and expression."[2] To speak of the first two characteristics would be subject matter for another presentation, but I should like, for our purposes here, to speak of the last, "novelty in expression," and I should like to do so with the help of the Church's Common Doctor.

For the past twenty-five years, I have been engaging in theological writing and discourse, and for the last twelve years or so, I have focused on the specific issue of evangelizing the culture. I have done this through academic research and writing, but also through more popular writing and through social media. In the process, I have encountered a number of typical objections to the faith, and I would like, in this chapter, to address just two of them, with the help of St. Thomas Aquinas: theological method and the doctrine of God.

Assimilation vs. Correlation

One of the principal causes of the present enervation of religion in the West, and one of the major reasons why people respond less and less to Christianity, is the dominance of the correlational or 'experiential-expressivist' method in theology.[3] The roots of this approach, of course, stretch back to the period just after the devastating European wars of religion in the late sixteenth and early seventeenth centuries. Unable to resolve their disputes through appeal to reason,

---

1. Cardinal Francis George, *A Godly Humanism: Clarifying the Hope that Lies Within*, (Washington, DC: The Catholic University of America Press, 2015), 98.

2. Pope John Paul II, "Address to the Assembly of CELAM" (March 9, 1983), §3: *AAS* 75 (1983), 778.

3. George Lindbeck, *The Nature of Doctrine* (Philadelphia, PA: The Westminster Press, 1984), 31.

Protestants and Catholics had recourse to violence—and their battles nearly brought Europe to its knees.

In the wake of this terror, many of the best and brightest European intellectuals— Spinoza, Leibniz, Kant, Hegel, Schleiermacher, and the like—attempted to articulate a version of the Christian religion that was universal in scope, standing beyond the particularities of revelation and grounded in common experience. Thus, for Spinoza, authentically rational religion flows from an intuition of the oneness of being: *Deus, sive natura* (God, or Nature);[4] for Kant, it comes forth from the demand of the categorical imperative, discovered at the root of the will itself;[5] for Schleiermacher, it proceeds from the uniquely textured "feeling of absolute dependence."[6] From these experiential and universal starting points, the great modern philosophers then interpreted the data of revelation, accepting what was in line with the experiential ground and rejecting, or radically re-configuring, what was out of step with it. In this, they all followed Descartes, who taught that all objective claims—whether regarding God or the world—had to be brought before the bar of the *cogito* for adjudication.

The experiential method of the modern philosophers massively influenced the major Christian theologians of both the nineteenth and twentieth centuries. Rudolf Otto commences his project, not with the objectivities of revelation, but with the sense of the *mysterium tremendum.*[7] Paul Tillich takes, in the modern manner, "ultimate concern" as his starting point,[8] adapting for a post-Freudian audience the

4. Baruch Spinoza, *Ethics*, vol. 1 of *The Collected Works of Spinoza*, trans. Edwin Curley (Princeton: Princeton University Press, 1985), Part IV, Preface, 544.

5. Immanuel Kant, *Groundwork of the Metaphysics of Morals: A German–English Edition*, ed. and trans. Mary Gregor and Jens Timmermann (Cambridge: Cambridge University Press, 2011) 33, 61–109.

6. Friedrich Schleiermacher, *The Christian Faith*, vol. 1, trans. Terrence N. Tice, Catherine L. Kelsey, and Edwina Lawler (Louisville, KY: Westminster John Knox Press, 2016), §4.4, pg. 24; §5.1, pg. 27; §5.3, pg. 31; §8.2, pg. 52; §8.4, pg. 56.

7. Rudolph Otto, *The Idea of the Holy: An Inquiry into the Non-Rational Factor in the Idea of the Divine and its Relation to the Rational*, trans. John W. Harvey (London: Oxford University Press, 1970), 12–30, 186.

8. Paul Tillich, *Systematic Theology*, vol. 1 (Chicago: University of Chicago Press, 1967): 8–12, 211–213.

"sense and taste for the infinite" of Schleiermacher;[9] and he characterizes his method as one of correlation—that is, setting in conversation the questions that arise from experience and the answers that appear in revelation. Karl Rahner writes not a *Dogmatik* but a *Grundkurs des Glaubens*, deliberately calling to mind Schleiermacher's *Christliche Glaube*, which itself was a conscious departure from the dogmatics produced by the Old Protestantism that preceded him. In line with subjectivizing sensibilities, Rahner proposes the experience of absolute mystery as the starting point and criterion for his meditations on Christian revelation. In more recent years, David Tracy commences his project with the "limit experiences" that are common to all human beings.[10] In all these instances, the logic and strategy remain remarkably consistent: test the claims of dogma at the bar of common human experience.

Now problems with this method abound, but I should like to draw attention to what I take to be its fundamental flaw—namely, the positioning of revelation by a criterion extrinsic to itself. Such a move stands athwart the structuring logic of the New Testament, whereby Christ the Logos is that in which all things inhere and in terms of which all things are understood. For the details, I would recommend a careful reading of both the prologue to the Johannine Gospel and the opening chapter of Paul to the Colossians. The implication of these high claims is that Jesus cannot be interpreted from a point of vantage higher than or outside of himself. For those who navigate the Schleiermacher Autobahn, experience becomes the measure of Christ and not vice versa. Karl Barth's way of stating this problem was that the method of correlation would work admirably well in Paradise before the Fall or in Heaven, when the questions we ask would be altogether fitting and appropriate. But in the fallen world, our questions are themselves skewed and misguided, and therefore the answers that we get are misleading. As any reader of the Platonic dialogues realizes, the one who poses the questions always

---

9. Friedrich Schleiermacher, "Explanations of the Second Speech," in *On Religion: Speeches to its Cultured Despisers*, trans. John Oman, (New York: Harper and Brothers, Publishers, 1958), 103. This was a translation of the third German edition of the work.

10. David Tracy, *The Analogical Imagination: Christian Theology and the Culture of Pluralism* (New York: The Crossroad Publishing Company, 1981), 160–161.

determines the flow and nature of the conversation; therefore, if the questions are dysfunctional, the answers will likewise be dysfunctional.

The consistent exercise of this method within Catholic theology for the past seventy years or more has produced, on the ground, what I have termed "beige Catholicism,"[11] which is to say a Catholicism whose distinctive colors have faded and which has devolved into a flattened out simulacrum of the environing culture, a Catholicism unsure of itself, "adrift," in Peter Steinfels's apt phrase.[12] What has prevented critics of the correlational style from speaking out more clearly is the fear that the abandonment of this method would result in a sterile sectarianism, an ecclesial retreat from the culture repugnant to the stated ideals of Vatican II. But this is so much nonsense. There is not a binary option between correlationism and sectarianism—though this is often argued by advocates of the liberal method. I would advocate the method followed by John Henry Newman, which I would describe as assimilationist. Newman speaks of the power of assimilation as one of the clearest signs of a living idea.[13] Like a healthy organism that roams the countryside, taking in what it can and resisting what it must in order to survive, a healthy idea assimilates from its environment what coheres with it, even as it rejects what is repugnant to its integrity. An animal neither retreats utterly from its environment nor becomes completely adapted to it (in fact, either state of affairs would be tantamount to the animal's death); rather, it plays a subtle game of assimilation and rejection, which presumes that its own integrity is the measure of what it takes in and resists. Accordingly, the Church can and should reach out to the world, but not in the liberal manner. It should remain light on its feet, willing to move and react appropriately; neither fully embracing or fully resisting; open and closed, depending on the circumstances; a culture lover and a culture warrior.

---

11. Robert Barron, *Bridging the Great Divide: Musings of a Post-Liberal, Post-Conservative Evangelical Catholic* (Lanham, MD/Oxford: Rowman & Littlefield Publishers, Inc., 2004), 11–21; *Exploring Catholic Theology: Essays on God, Liturgy, and Evangelization* (Grand Rapids, MI: Baker Academic, 2015), 204–207.

12. Peter Steinfels, *A People Adrift: The Crisis of the Roman Catholic Church in America* (New York: Simon & Schuster, 2003).

13. John Henry Newman, *An Essay on the Development of Christian Doctrine*, 6th ed. (Notre Dame, IN: University of Notre Dame Press, 1989), V.III.1–5, pp. 185–189.

I would like to demonstrate now that this assimilationist method was indeed the method followed by Thomas Aquinas in his work of relating revelation to culture. To do so I recommend we turn to a consideration of the opening question of the *Summa theologiae* in which (if I may be permitted a more modern usage) the 'method' of Aquinas is clarified. The hinge issue is the relationship between philosophy and theology, or more precisely, how and whether theology ought to use philosophy in its work of articulating sacred doctrine. To be sure, many major figures at the time thought that Aquinas's use of Aristotelian philosophy was illegitimate, amounting to a compromising of the primacy of biblical revelation, indeed a positioning of theology by secular reason.[14] Therefore, this first question of the *Summa theologiae* was by no means of merely academic interest for Aquinas.[15]

In the opening article of question one, Aquinas holds off the kind of reductive rationalism that was afoot in his own time (Latin Averroism) but that would become rampant in the modern period. He wonders whether there is a need for *sacra doctrina* beyond the discipline of philosophy.[16] The second objector maintains that, since philosophy treats of being *qua* being, there can be literally nothing that stands outside of its purview, including God and the things of God. Here the objector anticipates Heidegger by seven centuries, who said that whatever God is, he is a being of some kind and hence would fall under the consideration of philosophy.[17] In his *respondeo*, Aquinas clarifies that revelation and the science that considers it are necessary precisely because the human being is directed to an end that surpasses what unaided reason can grasp.[18] This is the first statement in the *Summa* of the problem that would vex so many thinkers up and down the ages, especially in the twentieth century, regarding

---

14. For instance, Henry of Ghent, the most prominent member of the Paris theology faculty after Thomas's death in 1274, participated in a commission called by the bishop of Paris in 1277 that condemned 219 propositions associated with Aristotelianism, including some defended by Thomas. See John F. Wippel, "Thomas Aquinas and the Condemnation of 1277," *The Modern Schoolman* 72, no. 2/3 (1995): 233–272.

15. St. Thomas Aquinas, *Summa theologiae*, I, q. 1.

16. *Summa theologiae*, I, q. 1, a. 1.

17. *Summa theologiae*, I, q. 1, a. 1, ad. 2. See Ben Vedder, *Heidegger's Philosophy of Religion: From God to the gods* (Pittsburgh: Duquesne University Press, 2007), 37.

18. *Summa theologiae*, I, q. 1, a. 1, *respondeo*.

the play of nature and grace. The paradox is that we seem naturally to desire something that is properly beyond our natural powers to attain. For our purposes, it is fascinating to note how Aquinas holds off an easy philosophical rationalism and how he effectively destabilizes the knowing subject, assuring that he is never entirely in control of the situation.

In article two, Aquinas wonders whether theology or sacred doctrine qualifies as a science.[19] In answer, he famously distinguishes between two types of science, those that are derived from the principles of reason itself and those that are subalternate to higher sciences, as music, for example, is subalternate to arithmetic. Theology (*sacra doctrina*) is a subalternate science, since its principles are derived, not from the light of natural reason, but from the 'science' or knowledge that God has of himself and that the saints have of God. In a word, it is a manner of knowing grounded necessarily in prayer, taking its form and content, not primarily from reason, but from a kind of contemplation. One of the objections has it that philosophy is a higher science than theology since the latter seems to depend upon the former.[20] Aquinas clarifies in response that theology depends upon philosophy, not in the sense that it derives its principles from it, but only in the measure that it can use it to communicate its truths to the fallen mind, which requires a sort of *manuductio* (leading by the hand) in order to acquire even a minimal understanding of theology's deliverances.

What becomes clear in this densely-textured first question of the *Summa* is that Aquinas will not be fitting the faith into any pre-existing philosophical system, much less conforming it to ordinary human experience; rather, he will be using elements of Aristotelian philosophy in order better to explicate the faith to a contemporary academic audience. In a word, he is not the least bit interested in bending theology to Aristotle. If anything, he will bend Aristotle to the contents of revelation. One of my great professors at Catholic University, Dr. Thomas Prufer, told us that Aquinas speaks 'a fractured Aristotle-ese.' A very good example of this peculiar usage is the almost Zen-like manner in which Aquinas characterizes creation in the *De potentia Dei*: that which receives the act of creation is itself

---

19. *Summa theologiae*, I, q. 1, a. 2.

20. *Summa theologiae*, I, q. 1, a. 5, obj. 2.

being created; and the creature is a kind of relation to God with newness of being (*nihil est aliud realiter quam relatio quaedam ad Deum cum novitate essendi*; "nothing but a relation of the creature to the Creator together with a beginning of existence").[21] The point is that both of these statements turn the customary Aristotelian philosophy of substance, accident, and relation on its head. Still another example of the twisting and breaking of Aristotle is Aquinas's account of transubstantiation. Though Aristotle certainly understood that a thing's accidents can change while its substance remains unchanged, he never imagined that a substance could change while its accidents remain in place. In both these cases, philosophy is being rather clearly used by the theologian and not adopted as an explanatory matrix. It is indeed *ancilla*, handmaiden, and not *domina*, ruler. Aquinas is not correlating revelation to philosophy, not allowing the questions posed by philosophy to determine the interpretation of the answers given by theology. Rather, he is allowing theology to remain the Queen of the sciences, even as he uses a secondary and subordinate science in her service. This confident, flexible, and assimilating approach to the increasingly dominant philosophy of his time indicates the proper use of a cultural form for evangelical purposes. I'll give Aquinas himself the last word on this score. When challenged by his intellectual opponents that he was diluting the wine of the Gospel with the water of Aristotle, Aquinas responded, "Wherefore those who use philosophical doctrines in sacred Scripture in such a way as to subject them to the service of faith, do not mix water with wine, but change water into wine." [22]

Doctrine of God

Many today—especially young people—are under the influence of the so-called 'new' atheists, led by Christopher Hitchens, Richard Dawkins, and Daniel Dennett. In my evangelical work, I encounter

---

21. Aquinas, *On the Power of God (Quaestiones Disputatae de Potentia Dei)*, translated by English Dominican Fathers (Westminster, MA: The Newman Press, 1952), q. 3, a. 3, *respondeo*. Hereafter *De Potentia*.

22. Aquinas, *Expositio super librum Boethii De Trinitate*, trans. Rose E. Brennan (St. Louis: Herder Books, 1946), part 1, q. 2, a. 3, ad 5.

the disciples of these gentlemen on a daily basis. There is, of course, little that is new in the argumentation presented by these figures: most of what they say is warmed over Feuerbach, Nietzsche, Freud, and Sartre. What is new is their nastiness and condescension toward religious believers. Their consistent claim is that belief in God is irrational, unnecessary, dangerous, and dehumanizing: in Hitchens's summary, "religion poisons everything."[23]

But I have found that, without exception, they don't know what serious religious believers mean when they use the word 'God.' The new atheists subscribe to what has been termed the 'Yeti theory' of God, by which God is a hidden being among many, one causal agent within the nexus of contingent things, whose existence is affirmed by some and denied by others. Accordingly, they call, time and again, for 'evidence' of this mysterious reality's existence, almost in the manner of a search for physical traces. In line with this assumption, Hitchens delighted in recounting the well-known story of the conversation between the astronomer Laplace and Napoleon. When the Emperor asked how God fit into the elaborate system proposed by the scientist, Laplace replied, "*Je n'ai pas besoin de cette hypothèse*" ("I do not need this hypothesis").[24] And Dawkins, operating out of the same presumption, characterizes the theist position as follows: "The God-Hypothesis suggests that the reality we inhabit also contains a supernatural agent who designed the universe and…maintains it and even intervenes in it with miracles."[25] Again, from the new atheist point of view, God is a being *in* the world, a cause among causes. This is precisely why Dawkins can compare God to "the Flying Spaghetti Monster,"[26] a fantastical imaginary being for which there is not a trace of evidence. In saying so, he is simply echoing his mentor Bertrand Russell, who opined that "nobody can prove that there is not between the Earth and Mars a china teapot revolving in an elliptical orbit, but nobody thinks this sufficiently likely to be taken into account in practice. I think the Christian God just as

23. Christopher Hitchens, *God is Not Great: How Religion Poisons Everything* (New York: Twelve/Hachette Book Group USA, 2007), 13.

24. Hitchens, *God is Not Great*, 66–67.

25. Richard Dawkins, *The God Delusion* (Boston: Houghton Mifflin Company, 2006), 58.

26. Dawkins, *The God Delusion*, 53.

unlikely."[27] This understanding of God also gives rise to the obsession with the so-called "god of the gaps," the cause inserted into the
lacunae in our present scientific understanding of things.[28] They
say that when the contemporary Dominican theologian Herbert
McCabe would debate with atheists, he would allow them to speak
first and lay out their position clearly. Then he would typically
respond, "I completely agree with you," for he sensed exactly what
I'm pointing out here: they were but knocking down an elaborately
constructed straw god.[29]

Thomas Aquinas proves remarkably helpful in clearing things up
in this regard. As is often observed, one of the most striking features
of Thomas's doctrine of God is his 'agnosticism.' In the question in
the first part of the *Summa theologiae* dealing with the divine simplicity,[30]
Thomas writes, "Because we cannot know what God is, but rather
what He is not, we have no means for considering how God is, but
rather how He is not."[31] Thomas enthusiastically employs the *via negativa* (the 'negative way') when speaking of God—namely, removing
from the concept of God all that smacks of finitude, creatureliness, or
contingency. Thus, God is not material, not temporal, not marked by
potentiality, incapable of change, and so on. But what he *is*, what it is
like not to be temporal or material or potential or changeable is not
really made clear—because it can't, at least to finite minds deriving
their raw material from the physical world. Even when Thomas speaks
of God in a more positive vein, designating him, for instance, as just
or good, he's not quite sure of what he is saying, since the *res signifi-
cata* and the *modus significandi* remain so distinct. His positive discourse

27. Bertrand Russell, "Letter to Mr. Major," in *Dear Bertrand Russell: A Selection of
his Correspondence with the General Public, 1950–1968* (Boston: Houghton Mifflin Company,
1969), 6. See also Russell, "Is There a God?," in *The Collected Papers of Bertrand Russell*,
vol. 11, *Last Philosophical Testament, 1943–68* (London: Routledge, 1997), 547–548.

28. Friedrich Nietzsche, *Thus Spoke Zarathustra*, trans. Adrian Del Caro (Cambridge: Cambridge University Press, 2006), 71.

29. McCabe expressed the ineffability of the true God in this way: "We do not
have even a rough idea of what God is …Whatever we are referring to when we use
the word 'God' it can no more be a god than it can be a model aeroplane or half-past
eleven." Herbert McCabe, *God Still Matters* (London: Continuum, 2005), 55.

30. *Summa theologiae*, I, q. 3.

31. *Summa theologiae*, I, Prologue, q. 3.

about God is thoroughly disciplined by the great principle of the Fourth Lateran Council, *Quia inter creatorem et creaturam non potest tanta similitudo notari, quin inter eos maior sit dissimilitudo notanda* ("For between Creator and creature no similitude can be expressed without implying a greater dissimilitude").[32] Thomas sums this up in his insistence that God, pace the atheists both old and new, is not a being, *ens summum* (highest being), but rather Being Itself, *ipsum esse subsistens* (subsistent being itself).[33] God cannot be defined; he is not an individual; and he cannot be placed in any genus, even the genus of existence. So much for orbiting teapots and flying spaghetti monsters.

Now if we press the question why this should be the case, why the God of Thomas Aquinas remains so elusive and mysterious, we are compelled to turn to the Bible, especially to the passages that refer to God as creator of all things. Precisely because God brings the whole of the finite order into being from nothing, God cannot possibly be an ingredient within the universe. He must be other in a way that transcends all the ordinary modes of otherness discernible within creation. Spatial difference; modal diversity; differences in grade, kind, degree, or species; variations in speed, temperature, density—none of these can begin to indicate the radicality of the otherness that obtains between God and the world. God is not simply other, in the manner of the planet Jupiter or the most distant nebula; instead, he is 'otherly other,' other by way of a qualitatively different kind of otherness. Nicholas of Cusa expressed the same idea strikingly when he said that God, while remaining *totaliter aliter* ('totally other'), is nonetheless the *non-Aliud* ('not-Other').[34] The paradoxical observation of Nicholas of Cusa calls very much to mind the formulation of another of my great Catholic University of America professors, Msgr. Robert Sokolowski, who

---

32. Heinrich Denzinger, *Enchiridion symbolorum definitionum et declarationum de rebus fidei et morum: Compendium of Creeds, Definitions, and Declarations on Matters of Faith and Morals*, 43rd ed., ed. Peter Hünermann (San Francisco: Ignatius Press, 2012), no. 806, pg. 269.

33. Aquinas, *Summa Contra Gentiles: Book Three, Providence, Part 1*, trans. Vernon J. Bourke (Notre Dame, IN: University of Notre Dame Press, 1975), III.19; *Summa theologiae*, I, q. 4, a. 2; q. 11, a. 4.

34. Nicholas of Cusa, *Nicholas of Cusa on God as Not-Other: A Translation and Appraisal of De Li Non Aliud*, trans. Jasper Hopkins (Minneapolis: The Arthur J. Banning Press, 1983), 20–22, 49–53.

maintains that God's transcendence is a noncompetitive and non-contrastive otherness.[35]

Of course, the scriptural *locus classicus* for this manner of speaking is the third chapter of Exodus, God's revelation to Moses from the burning bush: "I am who I am" (Ex 3:14). Moses was asking a commonsensical question—namely, of all the gods, which one are you? He was assuming, again in a manner congruent with his general culture, that the one speaking to him was a being, however exalted, among many. The answer/non-answer of the Lord implies that Moses's question was dysfunctional from the start, for God is not this rather than that, not here rather than there, not this one rather than that one; instead, his very nature is to be. In David Burrell's phrase, "to be God is to be to-be."[36] All of this means that God and the world are not competing for space on the same ontological grid, not placed together on a common field or against a shared background. And this in turn implies that, as the burning bush itself indicates, the proximity of God is not a threat to creation; on the contrary, it makes created things radiant and beautiful, without consuming them. As St. Irenaeus had it: *Gloria Dei homo vivens* (The glory of God is a human being fully alive)."[37]

And this is precisely why the correct characterization of God is so important in our dialogue with the atheists. Fundamental to their argument is that God is the enemy of human flourishing: "the no to God is the yes to man," as Feuerbach had it.[38] But Aquinas would hold that the divine causality does not negate or compromise human causality—just the contrary. He says, "The higher the cause, the more common and efficacious, and the more efficacious, the more profoundly it can penetrate into the effect."[39] Finite things

---

35. Robert Sokolowski, *The God of Faith and Reason: Foundations of Christian Theology* (Washington, DC: The Catholic University of America Press, 1995), 36.

36. David B. Burrell, *Aquinas: God and Action* (Notre Dame, IN: University of Notre Dame Press, 1979), 26.

37. St. Irenaeus of Lyons, *Against Heresies*, IV.20.7. In *Irenaeus on the Christian Faith: A Condensation of* Against Heresies, trans. and ed. James R. Payton, Jr. (Eugene, OR: Pickwick Publications, 2011), 116.

38. This paraphrase of Feuerbach comes from Walter Kasper, *The God of Jesus Christ* (New York: This Continuum Books, T&T Clark International, 2012), 29; see also Walter Kasper, *Der Gott Jesu Christi* (Mainz: Matthias-Grünewald-Verlag, 1982), 45.

39. Aquinas, *De Potentia*, q. 3, a. 7, no. 16.

necessarily remain, to some degree, repugnant to one another, for their integrity depends upon their capacity to resist the totalizing influence of a competing influence. But God, who is not one finite thing among others, who in fact is the highest possible type of cause, can enter into a creature completely and yet noncompetitively. Didn't the prophet Isaiah express this idea when he said, in regard to God, "Lord, you have accomplished all we have done" (Is 26:12)? And didn't Paul give voice to it when he declared, "It is no longer I who live but Christ who lives in me" (Gal 2:20)?

Conclusion

And all of this means, finally, that biblical religion constitutes the greatest humanism ever proposed—indeed, that ever can be proposed. Many of the Church Fathers summed up Christianity with the pithy phrase, *Deus fit homo ut homo fieret Deus* ("For he [God] was incarnate that we might be made god"), implying that the ordinary goal of the Christian life is deification, a term used by Aquinas. No humanism, ancient or modern, has ever proposed such an exalted consummation of human being and activity.

Therefore, in our evangelizing of the contemporary culture, we can and should turn with enthusiasm to the Common Doctor, who teaches us, in substantial ways, both what to say and how to say it. Congratulations to our graduates. May you embrace St. Thomas Aquinas as your spiritual father!

CHAPTER 4

JACOB'S LADDER

A Homily for the Ordination of Dominican Priests, 2019

Praised be Jesus Christ! May I say as I commence this homily that it is a particular joy for me to be with all of you today. This is the first ordination of priests at which I have presided as bishop, and given my long association with, and deep affection for, the Dominican Order, I couldn't be happier that the first priests I will ordain will be Dominicans.

Venerable Fulton Sheen said that every priest is a Jacob's ladder—that is to say, someone who connects heaven and earth.[1] With typical economy of expression, Thomas Aquinas asserts simply that the priest is a mediator, a bridge, between human beings and God.[2] In this, the priest participates in the very being of Jesus Christ, who is, in person, the bringing together of divinity and humanity. We recall the words of the Lord to Nathaniel in this context: "You will see greater things than this… Amen, amen, I say to you, you will see the sky opened and the angels of God ascending and descending upon the Son of Man" (Jn 1:50–55).

---

1. Fulton J. Sheen, *The Priest is Not His Own* (San Francisco: Ignatius Press, 2004), 31–35, esp. 31.

2. St. Thomas Aquinas, *Summa theologiae Tertia Pars 1–59*, trans. Fr. Laurence Shapcote (Lander, WY: The Aquinas Institute for the Study of Sacred Doctrine, 2012), q. 26, a. 1, ad. 1.

We can exaggerate the importance of either extreme of Jacob's ladder. If someone stands predominantly on the transcendent end, he might be a good monk, mystic, or pure intellectual, but he won't be a good priest, for he won't be sufficiently grounded in the lives of those he serves. And if someone stands predominantly at the immanent end, he might be a good psychologist, counselor, or political activist, but he won't be a good priest, for he will not draw his people upward to God. All your life long, brothers, you should make sure that your identity as Jacob's ladder is strong and clear. You must be able, so to speak, to travel down far enough to reach even the most 'lost of the lost'; and you must be able, at the same time, to reach up high enough to facilitate the journey to heaven. You have to have what Pope Francis famously calls the "smell of the sheep,"[3] and you have to be comfortable in the company of angels.

A passage from our second reading, often cited by Thomas Aquinas in his discussion of the priesthood, sums up everything I've been saying so far: "Every high priest is taken from among men and made their representative before God" (Heb 5:1).[4] The Pope is indeed the *Pontifex maximus* (the preeminent bridge builder), but every priest is a *pontifex*, for he makes of his own life a bridge between God and human beings.

Priest

Now, this mediating, Jacob's-ladder identity manifests itself in terms of three basic offices—namely, priest, prophet, and king. As priests, you will sanctify; as prophets, you will teach; and as kings, you will shepherd and govern. I should like to make a few simple observations regarding each of these three great tasks. To be holy is to be a friend of God, and therefore your work as sanctifier will be to foster and cultivate a friendship between God and the people that you serve. Your life will be about bringing people into intimacy with God, and this will happen primarily through the instrumentality of the

---

3. Pope Francis, *Chrism Mass: Homily of Pope Francis* (March 28, 2013).

4. St. Thomas Aquinas, *Summa theologiae Secunda Secundae 1–91*, trans. Fr. Laurence Shapcote (Lander, WY: The Aquinas Institute for the Study of Sacred Doctrine, 2012), II-II, q. 86, aa. 2, 4.

sacraments. These sacred signs give life in the spiritual order, and it is due to them that you will be called, quite rightly, 'father.' Priests are, preeminently, men of the sacraments. When I was going through my CPE (Clinical Pastoral Education) program many years ago, I was the sole Catholic in my group. My Protestant colleagues would often gently tease me that, while they were compelled to do counselling with the hospital patients they visited, I was able, in their words, "to hide behind the sacraments." I took their good-natured ribbing well enough, and I certainly have nothing against the use of psychological counseling within a pastoral context, but I cannot tell you how often during my thirty-three years of priesthood that I have been delighted to hide behind the sacraments! Long ago, I learned that these sacred signs and gestures, grounded in the life and ministry of Jesus himself, have far more power than any words of mine, no matter how clever or insightful.

Having said all of this, and having kept, I hope, the dangers of both Pelagianism and Donatism at bay, I feel obliged to add that a powerful help in the sanctification of your people will be your own personal holiness. Those you serve will be attracted to friendship with Christ when they see what that friendship looks like in your life. You know all the ordinary means to sanctity, and you don't need me to rehearse them for you, but allow me to mention one practice in particular. I have always told those about to be ordained to commit themselves to making a Holy Hour of prayer before the Blessed Sacrament every day of their lives until the day they die. I say the same to you now.

Prophet

So, you will be sanctifiers, but you will also be prophets, which is to say, men who speak the Word of God. I suppose this is an excellent example of carrying coals to Newcastle, but I will nevertheless urge this class of Dominican priests-to-be: Preach! Your holy father, St. Dominic, saw the need to preach against the Albigensian heresy; great Dominicans up and down the centuries have discerned the spiritual and intellectual needs of their time and have preached the Word accordingly. Our moment, brothers, is one specially in need of intelligent and passionate preaching. I am sure you are aware of the depressing statistics regarding the religiously unaffiliated in our country. In the 1970s, and even into the 1990s, approximately 6% of Americans would have claimed no religious affiliation. Today, that number has risen to 25%, and among the young, the figures are even more startling. Fully 40% of those under thirty now claim to be unreligious.[5]

Secularism, moral relativism, materialism—all rampant among younger people in the West—have contributed to the creation of what Charles Taylor calls "the buffered self,"[6] which means the self cut off from any contact with transcendence. But as St. Augustine told us long ago, the human heart is inescapably wired for God: "For Thou hast made us for Thyself and our hearts are restless till they rest in Thee."[7] Therefore, this widespread alienation from the Church and from God is no mere academic problem. It is, in fact, doing incalculable spiritual harm, especially to young people. And brothers, if you study the numerous surveys of the unaffiliated, you will learn that the principal reason they have left the Church is that they no longer believe in the teachings of Catholicism. We might be tempted to think that the moral failures of church leaders are the leading cause of disaffiliation—and they do indeed play a role—but by far the most significant cause is intellectual confusion and disagreement.

Well Dominicans, this is your moment! You have had the privilege these past many years to move among the masters— Chrysostom, Jerome, Augustine, Anselm, Bonaventure, Bellarmine, Newman, Chesterton, and Ratzinger. And you have been profoundly shaped by the geniuses of your own order: Dominic, Albert, Thomas Aquinas, Humbert of Romans, Catherine of Siena, Báñez, Cajetan, Lacordaire, and Congar. In accord with

---

5. Robert P. Jones, Daniel Cox, Betsy Cooper, and Rachel Lienesch, *Exodus: Why Americans are Leaving Religion—and Why They're Unlikely to Come Back* (Washington, DC: Public Religion Research Institute, 2016).

6. Charles Taylor, *A Secular Age* (Cambridge, MA: The Belknap Press of Harvard University Press, 2018), 37–42. See chapter eleven, "*Optatam Totius* and the Renewal of the Priesthood," 189–190, for more on Taylor's understanding of the buffered self.

7. St. Augustine, *Confessions*, 2nd ed., trans. F. J. Sheed (Indianapolis: Hackett Publishing Company, Inc., 2006), 3.

your great motto, *contemplata aliis trader* (to hand on the fruits of contemplation), unleash now what you have learned. Again, the pure intellectual might make this learning the object of his contemplation alone, but priests use it as part of their mediating ministry. Trust me when I tell you that the buffered self is starving for spiritual food. Give it out generously! Preach!

Keep in mind the perhaps overworked analogy proposed by Karl Barth that the preacher holds the Bible in one hand and the newspaper in the other.[8] The priestly preacher is always interested in affecting a correlation between the anxieties, expectations, and questions that arise from human experience, on the one hand, and the illumination that comes from the Bible on the other. A bad preacher offers answers to questions no one is asking. Therefore, be rooted in the culture of our time—both high and low. Understand the forces that are shaping the hearts of your listeners, for weal or for woe. At the same time, a bad preacher simply repeats and wallows in questions. The people of God do not want preachers who are permanently straddling the fence of ambivalence. They want answers that feed their souls. Provide them! And finally, remember a key insight of the bishops' statement on preaching, *Fulfilled in Your Hearing*: what the people want from homilies is to hear a man of faith preaching.[9] They want to hear how you have been transformed by the Gospel you proclaim.

King

So you will be priests, and you will be prophets. Finally, you will be kings. I realize that kingship is not something that we in the West find agreeable, but the category is basic to the Bible and to the great tradition. Aquinas says that, in his kingship, the priest participates in the monarchy of God, which is to say, God's benevolent governance

---

8. Karl Barth, "Interview with Freddy Klopfenstein (1966)," in *Barth in Conversation*, vol. 3, *1964–1968*, ed. Eberhard Busch, The Center for Barth Studies (Louisville, KY: Westminster John Knox Press, 2019), 161.

9. United States Conference of Catholic Bishops, *Fulfilled in Your Hearing: The Homily in the Sunday Assembly* (Washington, DC: United States Conference of Catholic Bishops, 1982), 15.

of the universe.[10] God, Aquinas argues, is like the head of a bustling household, ordering all of its activities toward one end. Or, he is like the general of an army on the march, directing all of its materiel and personnel to the accomplishment of its task.[11]

Therefore, the ordained king is the one who orders the charisms of the community he has been appointed to serve, directing all of the souls under his care toward the accomplishment of Christ's Kingdom. When Karol Wojtyła was Archbishop of Krakow, he said that whenever someone came to him with a problem or an opportunity, he would ask two questions. First, what does our faith tell us about this? Second, whom can we get to help us solve the problem or realize the opportunity?[12] In short, he was seeking to order, in light of the Scriptures, the charisms available in the community. That's what priestly kings do. A mistake that rookie priests often make is to try to do everything themselves. Full of energy, fresh ideas, and a good amount of naïveté, they assume the messianic role. Seasoned kings know that they will accomplish much more for the Kingdom by helping others under their care to find their own task and mission.

The great kings of Israel were, practically without exception, warriors. Their responsibility was to defend the Holy Nation and, when possible, to go on march, extending its borders outward. We are to read this as a spiritual symbol. Priestly kings defend their people from enemies both visible and invisible and, whenever they can, they go on the march, seeking to expand the influence of the Kingdom of God. Accordingly, good kings inspire their people to sanctify the realms of business, finance, entertainment, sports, education, law, and politics. Again, priestly kings are not expected to function as businessmen, financiers, entertainers, or politicians, but they are indeed expected to guide and inspire those Catholics in their charge who move in those arenas. That the majority of Catholics in

---

10. Aquinas, *Supplementum*, trans. Fr. Laurence Shapcote, Latin/English Edition of the Works of St. Thomas Aquinas 21 (Steubenville, OH: Emmaus Academic Press, 2017), q. 37, a. 1, ad. 3.

11. Aquinas, *De Veritate*, q. 5, a. 2, *respondeo*.

12. George Weigel's interview with Bishop Stanisław Smoleński (April 9, 1997), as cited in George Weigel, *Witness to Hope: The Biography of Pope John Paul II 1920–2005* (New York: Harper Perennial, 2001), 187–188.

our country basically track with the national consensus on most contested moral issues and present little distinctive profile in the wider culture is a sign of failure in kingly leadership.

I would like to make a final observation about spiritual kingship. A key feature of the ordering of the people of God toward the work of the Kingdom is stewardship over the goods of the Church. Sometimes, wrapping themselves in the mantle of 'spirituality,' priests will declare themselves above such matters as fundraising, building, maintenance, personnel, hiring and firing, and strategic planning. But these humble administrative tasks are unavoidably part of the kingly responsibility, and, like it or not, you will be immersed in them to one degree or another. By training and predilection, I am a prophet, a teacher. But when I became rector of Mundelein Seminary, I found myself up to my neck in the world of practical administration. At first I balked at this, but I remember distinctly when, after an entire day of administrative meetings, I returned to my room actually exhilarated, for I sensed that the decisions I had made that day would truly redound to the spiritual benefit of the community. I realize that this sounds like an oxymoron, but I experienced that day the joy of administration! I saw how truly it is an ingredient in the kingly mission that I had been given.

Everything I have been saying about spiritual kingship and shepherding is beautifully summed up in Paul's words of farewell to the elders of the Church of Ephesus, contained in our first reading: "Keep watch over yourselves and over the whole flock of which the Holy Spirit has appointed you overseers, in which you tend the Church of God.... I know that after my departure savage wolves will come among you … So be vigilant" (Acts 20:28–29, 31).

Conclusion

In conclusion, brothers, permit me to remind you of Pope Francis's warnings regarding clericalism. The late Cardinal Francis George, who was a spiritual mentor to me, once defined clericalism as the attitude that follows from the severing of the tie between Holy Orders and Baptism. He meant that the clericalist priest clings to prerogatives and perquisites, forgetting that the entire purpose of his priesthood is to serve the baptized, helping them to become saints.

Brothers, you will be bridges that others might climb on you to God. You will be priests so that your people might be sanctified; you will be prophets that your people might hear the saving truth; you will be kings that your people might walk the path of salvation.

How can I possibly go wrong by giving the last word to Jesus himself, taken from our Gospel for today? The very first priests were tempted by clericalism: "Then an argument broke out among them as to who should be regarded as the greatest. He said to them, 'The kings of the Gentiles lord it over them, and those in authority over them are addressed as 'Benefactors'; but among you it shall not be so. Rather, let the greatest among you be as the youngest, and the leader as the servant'" (Lk 22:24–26).

Love the people you serve. Sanctify them, teach them, shepherd them. Be a Jacob's ladder for them.

Part 2
RENEWING OUR **MINDS**

CHAPTER 5

HOW VON BALTHASAR CHANGED MY MIND

I distinctly remember the first time I became aware of the theology of Hans Urs von Balthasar. It was in April 1986, and I was at St. Meinrad Archabbey on retreat in preparation for my ordination to the priesthood. Through a mutual friend, I made the acquaintance of Fr. Guy Mansini, a monk of St. Meinrad and an inveterate professor and theological writer. In the course of a lively conversation in Fr. Guy's office, I remarked on the number of Karl Rahner's books that lined his shelves. Much to my surprise, he made a sort of grunt of disapproval and then said, "Yes, I cut my teeth theologically on Rahner, but I don't read him much anymore. Now I'm reading Balthasar, and you should too." That kind of curt dismissal of Rahner was by no means common in the mid-1980s. In the course of my seminary studies, Rahner was more or less *the* voice in contemporary Catholic theology, a figure of almost magisterial authority. I must confess that I did not immediately follow Mansini's advice, but his particular juxtaposition of Rahner and Balthasar stayed very clearly in my mind as an intriguing indication that something was perhaps beginning to shift.

My first real exposure to Balthasar's writings occurred in the summer of 1989, when I was a doctoral student at the Institut Catholique in Paris. One day I found myself rummaging around in the theology section of La Procure, the best Catholic bookshop in Paris. I saw a number of texts by Hans Küng, Edward Schillebeeckx,

Rahner, and Walter Kasper—the most popular authors of the time—but then I noticed that two entire shelves were devoted to the books of Hans Urs von Balthasar. I saw *Herrlichkeit* (*Glory of the Lord*) in its entirety, French translations of *Mysterium Paschale*, even some English versions of Balthasar's collections of articles and writings on prayer. It was the way that Balthasar dominated the theology section of this French bookstore that impressed me and reminded me of that conversation at St. Meinrad. I decided to buy the French version of *Mysterium Paschale*, more, I must admit, to work on my French than to understand Balthasar. For the next several days I took the book down to the banks of the Seine, just behind Notre Dame Cathedral, and read it, puzzled both by the French rendering of Balthasar's German and by the novelty of the theology. I realized even then that the method employed was radically other than the one to which I had become accustomed.

In the course of my three years in Paris, I participated in a number of doctoral seminars conducted by Fr. Michel Corbin, a Jesuit of the Centre Sèvres and a specialist in Hegel, Aquinas, and Anselm. Corbin usually structured his seminars as follows: the reading of texts by Aquinas on a given topic, followed by a study of texts by earlier figures such as Bernard, Anselm, or Augustine on the same subject, and finally a critical assessment of the thirteenth-century master in light of the predecessors. It soon became clear that what Corbin preferred in those earlier doctors was a scriptural density, unambiguous Christocentrism, and spiritual power that was at least relatively lacking in the more detached and philosophical Aquinas. At the close of the first seminar, I learned that Corbin had been a student of Henri de Lubac, one of the greatest advocates and allies of Balthasar, and as I plowed through more and more of Corbin's own writings, I found numerous references to Balthasar. A certain pattern and a certain style of theological thinking were becoming clearer to me.

When I returned from Paris to commence my teaching career at Mundelein Seminary, I resolved to undertake a formal and careful reading of this figure whose traces I had been following for several years. But given the press of my obligations—preparing a wide variety of courses, lectures, talks, and so on—I never managed to do it. Finally, I decided to compel myself. In the winter of 1994, I spoke to the academic dean and arranged to teach a course in the theology of Hans Urs von Balthasar the following fall. This rather rash move absolutely forced the issue, and I spent that winter, spring, and summer plowing through the Balthasarian corpus. That effort of working through literally thousands of pages of Balthasar's writings rather decisively changed my mind. Here I will explore this change in relation to three major issues: theological method, Christology, and theological anthropology.

Becoming Uneasy with Modern Experientialism

My theological formation, especially in the seminary, was largely modern in form and inspiration. By this I mean, above all, that experience was consistently constructed as the starting point and interpretive matrix for doctrine. As I suggested above, the contemporary theologian who had the greatest impact on my thinking was Karl Rahner. By the time I finished my four years in the seminary, I had read through most of Rahner's major texts, and I had composed my STL dissertation on Rahner's interpretation of the Christology of the Council of Chalcedon. Moreover, in my earliest years as a professor at the seminary, I had taken my own licentiate students through a careful reading of Rahner's early career masterpiece, *Hearers of the Word*. I had come to recognize and appreciate the standard Rahnerian method of commencing, in the modern mode, with theological anthropology, more precisely, with the human experience of standing in the "presence of Absolute Mystery."[1] In article after article, book after book, Rahner began with an analysis of the dynamic and self-transcending quality of every act of knowing and willing. By its very nature, Rahner argued again and again, the mind reaches out beyond any particular object to the infinite horizon of all that can in principle be known. Bernard Lonergan maintained, in a very similar vein, that the mind cannot be satisfied until it knows "everything about everything," until, in

---

1. Karl Rahner, *Foundations of Christian Faith: An Introduction to the Idea of Christianity*, trans. William V. Dych (New York: The Crossroad Publishing Company, 1978), 44–51, esp. 44.

short, it grasps Being itself.[2] And the will, Rahner said, has the same sort of restless and questing nature. Beyond any particular good that it desires or attains, the will wants the Good itself, all that can possibly be willed. Rahner called this natural capacity of the human spirit to transcend itself in the direction of the infinite "the supernatural existential,"[3] and he identified this dynamic as the foundational religious experience, the characteristic manner in which human beings stand in the presence of God.

Then, in regard to issue after issue—God's existence, human freedom, Jesus Christ, the nature of sin and salvation—Rahner interpreted doctrine in light of this fundamental religious experience. Thus, God is the "whence" of the self-transcending dynamism; Christ is the meeting point of the human tendency upward and the divine condescension in love and grace; sin is the refusal to respond positively to the lure of God; salvation is the restoration of this attitude of openness; sacraments are word-events that call out to the transcendental longing;[4] and so on. In short, he consistently brought doctrine before the bar of subjective experience for adjudication, explanation, and evaluation, hoping thereby to convince a skeptical audience that Christian claims enjoyed a basic coherence.

In this fundamental approach, Rahner showed himself to be a close ally of the contemporary Protestant thinker Paul Tillich, who also commenced the theological undertaking with an appeal to a basic and universal religious experience. Tillich argued that we are claimed by hundreds of concerns in the course of our lives, but that we can discern, under and through all of those particular interests, an abiding and unavoidable preoccupation, something that presses on us unconditionally. This he calls "ultimate concern."[5] It speaks not to some superficial dimension of the self but rather to the deepest roots of the ego, and its demands are absolute. This unconditioned

---

2. Bernard Lonergan, *Insight: A Study of Human Understanding*, ed. Robert Doran and Frederick Crowe, vol. 3, *Collected Works of Bernard Lonergan* (Toronto: University of Toronto Press, 1992), 666–667.

3. Rahner, "Eine Antwort," *Orientierung* 14 (1950): 141–145.

4. Rahner, *The Church and the Sacraments* (New York: Herder and Herder, 1963).

5. Paul Tillich, *Systematic Theology*, vol. 1 (Chicago: University of Chicago Press, 1967), 8–12, 211–213.

concern can manifest itself as the Good, which undergirds all of moral activity, or as the Beautiful, which governs every action of the artist, or as Justice, which animates the work of the lawyer and the judge, just as a few examples.[6] Having named and awakened this experience, Tillich proceeds to interpret doctrine, dogma, and practice in its light. God is "what ultimately concerns us," or "the unconditioned;"[7] creation is the rapport between conditioned beings and this infinite ground; revelation is the "shaking and turning"[8] of the self that occurs when the unconditioned breaks into ordinary experience; and Jesus is the definitive appearance of "the new being" under the conditions of estrangement.[9] The theological method that Tillich practiced and defended is that of correlation, which is to say, the coordination of the "questions" that well up from human experience to the "answers" that come from the biblical and theological tradition.[10] Tillich felt that, for too long, Christian thinkers have been proposing answers to questions that no one was asking. Although this correlational method seems to presume a balance between the questioning subject and the answering tradition, in point of fact, it favors the former. As any reader of the Platonic dialogues can attest, the one who poses the questions is always the one who determines the nature, flow, and finally the conclusion of the conversation. Thus, for Tillich, as for Rahner, religious experience is foundational and explanatory, the privileged criterion by which doctrine is assessed.

In this move, of course, both Rahner and Tillich were the disciples of Friedrich Schleiermacher. At the beginning of the nineteenth century, Schleiermacher endeavored to reconfigure theology in such a way as to make the faith acceptable to the "cultured despisers" of religion,[11] namely those Enlightenment-era rationalists who were gleefully predicting the imminent disappearance of Christianity. He

---

6. Tillich, *Systematic Theology*, vol. 1, 207–208.

7. Tillich, *Systematic Theology*, vol. 1, 8–12, 211–213.

8. Tillich, *Dogmatik* (Düsseldorf: Patmos Verlag, 1986), 96.

9. Tillich, *Systematic Theology*, vol. 2 (Chicago: University of Chicago Press, 1957), 118–138, et alia.

10. Tillich, *Systematic Theology*, vol. 1, 61–62.

11. Friedrich Schleiermacher, *On Religion: Speeches to Its Cultured Despisers*, trans. Richard Crouter (Cambridge: Cambridge University Press, 1988).

did so by rooting the faith not in doctrine (about which there was endless dispute), metaphysics, ethics, or in received tradition, but rather in personal, subjective experience. In his *On Religion: Speeches to Its Cultured Despisers*, Schleiermacher argued that all religious people, despite their differences in regard to dogma, cult, and ethical practice, have in common a "sensibility and taste for the infinite," a feel for Being considered as a totality.[12] It is this sensibility that makes them, properly speaking, religious. In his later, more systematic text, *Glaubenslehre* (*The Christian Faith*), Schleiermacher articulated this grounding religious sense as "the feeling of absolute dependence."[13] We are proximately dependent upon all sorts of things—from the air that we breathe, to the floor on which we stand, to the people to whom we speak—but we find ourselves ultimately and unavoidably dependent upon the power of Being itself or the Universe. The method used in the *Glaubenslehre* and a bit more indirectly in *On Religion* is precisely the one that we have seen already in Tillich and Rahner: the interpretation of dogma and practice in terms of this undergirding experience. Schleiermacher shows how hundreds of features of classical Christianity are expressive, in various ways, of this religious feeling. But one of the most notorious moves in the *Glaubenslehre* is the relegation of the doctrine of the Trinity to an appendix. Schleiermacher could find no correlation between this teaching, which every theologian from Origen and Augustine to Aquinas and Luther recognized as central, and the feeling of absolute dependence, and thus felt obliged to marginalize Trinitarian doctrine in his dogmatics.

To be sure, we can trace the Schleiermacher method back even further, to the work of both Martin Luther and René Descartes. As Jacques Maritain pointed out long ago, Luther and Descartes together launched the epistemological revolution that inaugurated modernity when they radically questioned the received tradition on the basis of a subjective experience deemed to be indubitable and foundational, in Descartes' case the *cogito ergo sum*, and in Luther's

---

12. Schleiermacher, "Explanations of the Second Speech," in *On Religion*, trans. Oman, 103.

13. Schleiermacher, *The Christian Faith*, vol. 1, trans. Terrence N. Tice, Catherine L. Kelsey, and Edwina Lawler (Louisville, KY: Westminster John Knox Press, 2016), §4.4, pg. 24; §5.1, pg. 27; §5.3, pg. 31; §8.2, pg. 52; §8.4, pg. 56.

case the feeling of being justified by grace through faith.[14] And whatever both Luther and Descartes kept from their respective intellectual traditions was reconfigured and reinterpreted in light of the grounding subjective sensibility. At the dawn of the modern period, in short, a crisis of doubt led to a turning inward in order to find justification, religious and intellectual. Both the prompt (a crisis of skepticism) and the method (subjective foundationalism) can be seen in the modern theologians whom I have sketched.

Lest I give the impression that all of this philosophical and theological reconfiguration remained at the level of academic abstraction, I want to consider the work of one of my own teachers at Mundelein Seminary, the influential practical theologian John Shea. Shea did his doctoral work on the writings of Langdon Gilkey, certainly Paul Tillich's most important American disciple. What Shea did, both in theory and practice, was to adapt the typically modern Schleiermacher/Tillich method to the discipline of theological reflection. In the course of my formation at the seminary, I took a variety of Shea's courses and also sat in on any number of his sessions of theological reflection. Invariably, he would commence these latter exercises in the Schleiermacher mode by encouraging the participants to recall a time when they felt 'forgiven,' felt 'God's presence in their lives,' or experienced sin and redemption. Then he would lead the group through a process of coordinating those experiences to symbolic and then doctrinal expression. He was, in short, popularizing and concretely practicing the method of correlation that Gilkey picked up from Tillich and that Tillich, at least implicitly, adapted from Schleiermacher.

This "experiential-expressivism" (to give it the moniker provided by George Lindbeck),[15] which I learned from Rahner, Tillich, Shea, and many others, seemed so self-evidently correct that it never occurred to me in those years of formation to question it. Its chief virtue was to have found a ground for Christian claims in an experience that could be immediately verified, and thus to make doctrinal

---

14. Jacques Maritain, *Three Reformers: Luther—Descartes—Rousseau* (New York: Charles Scribner's Sons, 1934), 15–17, 70, 168.

15. George Lindbeck, *The Nature of Doctrine* (Philadelphia, PA: The Westminster Press, 1984), 31.

assertions seem not so alien, not so abstract, not so incredible. It
would, I was convinced, make my teaching and my preaching relevant to life and thus convincing and efficacious.

Then I read Balthasar. Having been immersed for many years
in the modern theological thought world, I found the confrontation
with Balthasar wrenching, disconcerting, but ultimately bracing. As
I perused his texts, I kept waiting for the apologetic or explaining
move, the justification for the project on the basis of some self-val-
idating experience, but what I found instead was a stubborn command to look at the form of Christ. As I tried to get hold of Christian
doctrine, Balthasar kept telling me to relax and let Christian doctrine
get hold of me. I was so accustomed to doing 'epic' theology—con-
trolling revelation from the standpoint of some higher interpretive
vantage point—that the 'lyrical' version presented by Balthasar
was vertiginous. I wanted to draw revelation into experience, and
Balthasar, like Barth, was trying to extricate me from the musty confines of 'religious self-consciousness' and draw me into a new world.

It is not the case that Balthasar had no appreciation for the
standard modern method. In fact, he had great respect for his Jesuit
colleague Rahner, commenting that Rahner far surpassed him in
speculative capacity and acknowledging that Rahner's analysis of
religious psychology was largely right. But he added that theology
becomes really interesting precisely where Rahner tends to stop, at
the verge of revelation. Yes, we have a *capax Dei* (capacity for God), but
the *capax* should never become the measure of what *Deus* actually says.
In the *Theo-Drama*, Balthasar famously compared the human capacity for God to turbines poised at the foot of a great mountain, ready
to receive and transform the energy coming from the melting snows
above. But when those mighty waters arrive, von Balthasar implies,
they so overwhelm the turbines as to effectively render them useless.[16] So it goes with the *capax Dei* in relation to *Deus*. When asked the
difference between himself and Rahner, Balthasar responded simply,
"Rahner has chosen Kant, or if you will Fichte—the transcendental

---

16. Hans Urs von Balthasar, *Theo-Drama: Theological Dramatic Theology*, vol. 3,
Dramatis Personae: Persons in Christ, trans. Graham Harrison (San Francisco: Ignatius Press,
1978), 26.

approach. And I have chosen Goethe—as a Germanist."[17] Kant was, along with Descartes, the paradigmatically modern philosopher. His project was the effecting of a Copernican revolution in epistemology, according to which the world of experience is received and structured by the *a priori* structures of receptive consciousness. And this, according to Balthasar, provided the template for Rahner and his modern theological colleagues: measuring the data of revelation by the structures of religious self-consciousness.

But Goethe was playing an entirely different game. Over and against the regnant Enlightenment science of his time, marked by an aggressively analytical technique, he opted for a more contemplative way of knowing, one more respectful of the integrity of the object under study. Thus, Goethe said that the modern scientist would tear a plant out of the ground, severing its roots and extricating it from its natural environment, place it under bright lights, and take it apart, compelling it all the while to answer the scientist's questions. Such a method, he felt, would reveal certain data concerning the plant but would tell the investigator finally very little about the living organism. Goethe proposed that the authentic scientist ought to have the patience to sit next to the plant, observing it over long periods of time, watching how it interacts with its environment and changes with the seasons. He might draw it or chart its developments, but he must allow the plant to ask and answer, so to speak, its own questions.[18]

When he called for a 'kneeling' rather than a 'sitting' theology, it was this distinction between Goethe and Kant that Balthasar had in mind.[19] The rationalist theologian, sitting at a professor's desk, attempts to master the world of revelation according to familiar receptive categories; the contemplative theologian, kneeling in prayer, allows the Bible, the liturgy, the mystical tradition, and Christ himself to be master and to ask questions. Another telling Balthasar

17. Von Balthasar, "Geist und Feuer: Ein Gespräch mit Hans Urs von Balthasar," *Herder Korrespondenz* 30, no. 2 (1976): 76, as quoted in and translated by James K. Voiss, "Karl Rahner, Hans Urs von Balthasar, and the Question of Theological Aesthetics: Preliminary Considerations," *Louvain Studies* 29, nos. 1–2 (Spring-Summer 2004): 148.

18. Johann Wolfgang von Goethe, *The Metamorphosis of Plants* (Cambridge, MA: MIT Press, 2009).

19. Von Balthasar, *Explorations in Theology*, vol. 1, *The Word Made Flesh*, trans. A. V. Littledale and Alexander Dru (San Francisco: Ignatius Press, 1989), 206.

image, apposite here, is that of the windows at Chartres. Viewed from the outside, the Chartres stained glass is rather drab gray, but when seen from inside the church, it becomes radiant and spiritually eloquent. The project of much modern theology, Balthasar felt, was to draw skeptics into the cathedral of Christian truth by showing them the windows from the outside—that is, on their terms—but this finally had little or no compelling power. As Barth first pointed out, the 'cultured despisers' have not come streaming back to the faith on the basis of the theological experientialism that was meant to lure them. In point of fact, people will understand the truths of Christian revelation and find them beautiful only from within the Church— that is, from the standpoint of worship and contemplation.

So what does the Balthasarian method look like on the ground? It looks like an elaborate, detailed, and patient tour of the biblical universe and the forms that obtain therein. It is a display of the peculiar patterns that emerge from the content of revelation, those matrices of meaning and value out of which Abraham, Isaac, Jacob, Noah, Moses, David, Isaiah, Jeremiah, Ezekiel, Ruth, Peter, Paul, Mary Magdalene, and, above all, Jesus himself operate. If Tillich's and Rahner's biblical theologies are 'thin,' Balthasar's is 'thick.' If the approach of the moderns is largely apologetic, Balthasar's is liturgical and iconic. He does not so much justify the biblical world as show it, confident that it has its own convincing and transforming power. It is in this context that we can best understand Balthasar's option for the beautiful as a point of departure for the theological project.[20] Beautiful objects, faces, and lives resist being explained in terms alien to themselves, and they conceal themselves from those who would investigate them too aggressively. Instead, they provide their own interpretations, and they stop (aesthetic arrest), change, and commission those who come into their ambit. Far too long, Balthasar felt, the true, especially in its Cartesian and Kantian construal, had come to dominate the theological enterprise, much to the detriment of the very object to be studied. It was well past time for the reign of the beautiful. There is, to be sure, something risky in the Balthasarian method, a sense that, in following it, one is walking a tightrope over

---

20. Von Balthasar, *The Glory of the Lord: A Theological Aesthetics*, vol. 1, *Seeing the Form*, trans. Erasmo Leiva-Merikakis (San Francisco: Ignatius Press, 2009), 18.

an abyss. But one also has the impression that, in this very riskiness, it corresponds more correctly to the radical content of the Christian faith. If modern experientialism has made Christ more credible, it has also domesticated him; if Balthasar's aesthetic and iconic approach is more dangerous, it also honors a Christ worth believing in.

Who Is Jesus Christ?

The methodological shift that I have been describing emerges with special clarity around the question of Jesus Christ. In his three-volume *Systematic Theology*, Tillich developed a rich theological anthropology, a subtle and carefully articulated theology of God, and a detailed theology of the Spirit and the Church. But by far the smallest and thinnest of the major sections of the great dogmatics is the second, the part dealing with Christ. Jesus is so thoroughly 'positioned' by the anthropology and theology that Tillich lays out that he evanesces into more or less an abstraction, the "bearer of the New Being."[21] We find something very similar in Rahner's *Foundations of Christian Faith*. While Rahner's theological anthropology and the account of God are extremely rich and thorough, his Christology is thin and abstract. As I hinted above, the most remarkable thing about the Christologies of both Tillich and Rahner is how unbiblical they are. Jesus is presented not so much in scriptural terms as in the light of philosophical and psychological categories adapted from the contemporary culture. N. T. Wright has made the observation that much of the Christology of the last two hundred years—say, from Schleiermacher on—is basically Marcionite in form, which is to say, marked by a surprising indifference to the manner in which Jesus should be read against the background of the Old Testament.[22] Balthasar diagnosed the central difficulty with liberal Christology as a problem of logic. In the measure that Jesus is positioned and explained by a principle of reason or experience outside of himself, he is no longer functioning as the Logos. According to the Johannine

21. Paul Tillich, *Systematic Theology*, vol. 2 (Chicago: The University of Chicago Press, 1957), 177.

22. N. T. Wright, *Jesus and the Victory of God*, vol. 2 of *Christian Origins and the Question of God* (Minneapolis: Fortress Press, 1996), 25–27.

prologue, Jesus is the Word who was present with God from the beginning and through whom all finite things were made (Jn 1:1–3). And, according to the lyrical language of the first chapter of Colossians, Jesus is the power through which all things were made, in which they hold together, and toward which they tend (Col 1:15–20). He is, accordingly, not one word among many, not one *logos* alongside of competing *logoi*; he *is* the divine reason itself, and hence must be that which positions, explains, and grounds everything else. Balthasar was influenced strongly in this regard by Romano Guardini's reflections on the nature of authentic theology over and against various forms of 'scientific' theology that were emerging in the twentieth century. Following the Apostle Paul, Guardini held that the "spiritual man" is "judged by no man," and in fact judges all.[23] In a word, theologians cannot be positioned by a system of thought outside of what is given through the Holy Spirit, though they can draw those systems into the thought world opened up by the Spirit. In very recent years, Bruce Marshall has been making much the same point when he speaks of the narratives and doctrines dealing with Jesus as an "epistemic trump."[24] This means that in light of the Christian claim about Jesus as Logos, any system of thought—psychological, metaphysical, scientific, or historical—that finally contradicts the fundamental truths revealed in Jesus Christ must certainly be false. Again, this principle by no means precludes the use of systems of secular thought within the ambit of theology, but it insists that there can be no competition in regard to claims of ultimacy. In light of these clarifications, Balthasar identifies the logical difficulty with all forms of correlationalism and experientialism: they presume that the unmeasurable norm is itself capable of measurement. They assume that the *norma normans sed non normata* ('the norm of norms which cannot be normed') is in fact normed by a superior or at least coequal epistemic principle.

A key consequence of the liberal approach is an inability adequately to articulate and defend the divinity of Jesus. Indeed, if

23. Romano Guardini, *The Lord*, trans. Elinor Castendyk Briefs (Chicago: Henry Regnery Company, 1954), v.

24. Bruce D. Marshall, *Trinity and Truth*, Cambridge Studies in Christian Doctrine 3 (Cambridge, UK: Cambridge University Press, 2000), 44–47, 115–117.

Jesus is but the means by which a general religious consciousness is awakened (Schleiermacher), the bearer of the state of affairs that can obtain apart from him (Tillich), or the full expression of the dynamic tendency within the human spirit (Rahner), it is hard to account for his uniqueness or indispensability. He becomes, to use Kierkegaard's language, the teacher who can be left behind once his lesson has been learned, rather than being the savior whose presence and person remain a permanent point of reference.[25] Thus, central to Balthasar's Christology is an affirmation of the uniqueness of Jesus. Whereas the Buddha claimed to have found a way that benefited him and that would, he wagered, offer salvation to others, Jesus said, "I am the way." Whereas Confucius articulated a form of the moral life that would rightly order human affairs, Jesus said, "I am the life." Whereas Muhammad maintained that he had been given the final revelation of religious truth, Jesus said, "I am the truth" (Jn 14:6). Forgiving sinners, claiming authority over the Temple and interpretive sovereignty over the Torah, demanding that he himself be loved above all things, Jesus consistently spoke and acted in the person of God, and in doing so he compelled a decision in a way that none of the other religious founders did. We must either stand utterly with him or we should be against him, for, as C. S. Lewis emphasized, "Either he is God or he is a bad man" (*aut Deus aut homo malus*).[26] This is why Balthasar says that although there are superficial similarities between Jesus and other founders of religion, in point of fact, when we look closely at them, what emerges with increasing clarity is the difference between Jesus and the others.

Another major point of demarcation between the standard liberal Christology and Balthasar's is their differing accounts of the

---

25. Søren Kierkegaard, "The God as Teacher and Savior," in *Philosophical Fragments: Johannes Climacus*, trans. Howard V. Hong and Edna H. Hong (Princeton, NJ: Princeton University Press, 1985), 23–36.

26. C. S. Lewis, *Mere Christianity* (New York: Macmillian Publishing Co., Inc., 1952), "The Shocking Alternative," Bk. 2, Ch. 3, 56; Lewis, *God in the Dock: Essays on Theology and Ethics* (Grand Rapids, MI: William B. Eerdmans Publishing Company, 1970), 101; Lewis, "Letter to Owen Barfield" (August 1939), in *The Collected Letters of C.S. Lewis*, vol. 2, *Books, Broadcasts, and the War, 1931–1949*, ed. Walter Hooper (New York: HarperCollins Publishers, 2004), 269.

rejection of Jesus. For the modern theologian, skeptical nonbelievers are accorded a sort of pride of place. Their puzzlement over Jesus is seen as understandable, and the theological project is construed as an attempt to make belief in Christ credible to them and on their terms. But this, for Balthasar, is conceding far too much. On biblical terms, he argues, the rejection of Christ is not primarily an intellectual issue but rather a moral one. Those who do not understand Jesus properly are those who, for various reasons, have refused to submit to him, or to state it somewhat more accurately, have failed to fall in love with him. Thus, some have insisted on drawing him into their categories of explanation and expectation, but this is like trying to record an entire symphony on a few inches of tape. Others saw him as a threat or a rival and thus refused to surrender to him. Concomitantly, those who did 'get' him—John the beloved disciple, Mary Magdalene, Mary the Mother of God, Peter—were the ones who loved him and allowed him to be the criterion and measure of their lives. In making this methodological move, Balthasar seizes, as it were, the high ground and compels the despisers of Christ to make an account of their opposition, reversing thereby the standard approach of the Schleiermacherians.

Infinite and Finite Freedom

It has been said that the distinctively modern quality in Ignatius of Loyola's spirituality is his stress on freedom. In his famous *Suscipe* prayer, Ignatius employs the classical Augustinian triplet of memory, understanding, and will, inviting God to receive these essential faculties. But prior to the familiar three, he mentions freedom: "Take, O Lord, receive, all my liberty."[27] The puzzle, of course, is that Ignatius, having invoked and specified his freedom, invites God utterly to take it, to claim it as his own. Does this not involve the founder of the Jesuits in a contradiction? Well, only if liberty is constructed on modern terms as self-assertion and self-definition. Commencing with Duns Scotus and William of Ockham in the late Middle Ages, and coming to radical expression in Nietzsche and Sartre, the modern

---

27. St. Ignatius of Loyola, *The Spiritual Exercises of St. Ignatius*, trans. Anthony Mottola (New York: Image Books, 1964), 104.

conception of freedom privileges choice, the capacity of the subject to hover above affirmation and denial and to make, on the basis of no internal or external constraint, a sovereign decision.

Balthasar, a Jesuit by training and predilection, explains the coherence of Ignatius's prayer through an appeal to the Council of Chalcedon's rendering of the relationship between the divine and human natures in Christ. Following the instincts of the Chalcedonian Fathers, even as he improves to some degree on their overly abstract, somewhat static categories, Balthasar sees the natures in Jesus as a play of two freedoms, infinite and finite. In the person of Jesus, divine freedom and human freedom dovetail in an absolutely unique and noncompetitive manner, so that nothing of the human has to give way in the presence of the divine, and nothing of the divine has to be compromised to make way for the human. From this remarkable *Ineinander* (one in the other), one can read off, as it were, the quality of both authentic human liberty and true divine liberty. Balthasar holds that finite freedom finds itself precisely in relation to the infinite ground of being, which is God. When the finite subject emerges into self-consciousness and freedom, it realizes, immediately, that its liberty is co-involved with and called out by the horizon of Being itself. In other words, it knows its proper *telos* in the ultimate good, without which it would lose its orientation. To be sure, this realization has nothing to do with Ockhamist freedom of choice but everything to do with what Servais Pinckaers has called "freedom for excellence."[28] Such freedom is not choice so much as the disciplining of desire so as to make the achievement of the good first possible and then effortless. Thus someone gradually becomes free to play the piano through a long process of discipline and the ordering of the body and mind toward a very particular good. If, on the Ockhamist reading, the objective good is a threat to freedom, on the Chalcedonian reading, it is the very ground and matrix of freedom.

And from the relationship of the natures in Christ, we can interpret God's freedom as well. In both classical and modern philosophy there is a tendency to construe the divine freedom as supreme

---

28. Servais Pinckaers, OP, *Sources of Christian Ethics*, 3rd ed., trans. Sr. Mary Thomas Noble (Washington, DC: The Catholic University of America Press, 1995), 329.

arbitrariness, the Ockhamist subjectivity writ large. Thus, the Aristotelian prime mover is blithely indifferent to the world that is so profoundly shaped by its attraction to him, and the Calvinist double-predestinating God hovers with complete capriciousness over the ultimate choice of salvation or damnation. But there is nothing, thinks Balthasar, of this voluntarism in the biblical-Chalcedonian understanding of God's freedom. The God revealed in the Incarnation is not hovering arbitrarily over the world he has made; rather, his freedom is coincident with fidelity to his own being and hence to all things that participate in his act of "to-be."[29] And this is why God's freedom is fully expressed as love, willing the good of the other as other. What Balthasar sees in the Chalcedonian account of the noncompetitive interplay of the natures in Jesus is just this ecstatic quality of the divine freedom, God's capacity to let the humanity of Jesus be. Indeed, as Irenaeus pointed out long ago, "The glory of God is a human being fully alive."[30]

At the heart of Balthasar's deeply biblical anthropology is the conviction, therefore, that humans are most themselves precisely when they enter into a kind of loop of grace, accepting life from God (who wants nothing more than to give it) and promptly returning it as an act of love, thereby receiving more and more of it. It is into this ecstatic loop that Jesus invites the woman at the well, luring her out of her cramped and fearful self-regard. As he says, "If you knew the gift of God, and who is saying to you, 'Give me a drink,' you would have asked him and he would have given you living water … a spring of water welling up to eternal life" (Jn 4:10, 14). It is into that same circumincession of love that the father in Jesus' best-known parable entices both of his errant sons.

Theologizing in a Balthasarian Context

My confrontation with the Balthasarian thought world coincided with the commencement of my own career as a writer and speaker within

---

29. David B. Burrell, *Aquinas: God and Action* (Notre Dame, IN: University of Notre Dame Press, 1979), 26.

30. St. Irenaeus of Lyons, *Against Heresies*, IV.20.7. In *Irenaeus on the Christian Faith: A Condensation of* Against Heresies, trans. and ed. James R. Payton, Jr. (Eugene, OR: Pickwick Publications, 2011), 116.

the Church. Although I have drawn from a wide variety of sources in my work, Balthasar has remained perhaps my most significant influence among contemporary theologians. In a number of articles composed just after I returned from studies in Paris, I began to complain about the 'beige' quality of the Catholicism that I experienced in the years when I was coming of age. By this I meant a Catholicism drained of its unique and distinctive coloration, designed to be inoffensive, inclusive, and attuned to the secular culture.[31] This was evident, I argued, not only in the theological style of the postconciliar Church, but also in its preaching, its pastoral practice, and its art and architecture. The edgy, challenging, and countercultural Church of Jesus Christ was in danger of becoming a vague echo of the secular world, one 'spirituality' among many. Balthasar's critique of modernity, which I sketched above, allowed me to articulate with greater theological precision not only my unease with the postconciliar scene, but also a vision of a richer, more colorful Catholicism. Much of this came to expression in my book *The Strangest Way: Walking the Christian Path*.[32] To a generation grown accustomed to a toothless, harmless Christianity, I wanted to present the way of Jesus Christ as unsettling, unnerving, and unfamiliar. I began with the story of a gathering of monks—Catholic and Buddhist—at the Trappist Monastery of Gethsemani in Kentucky some years ago. They had come together for fellowship and interreligious dialogue, and for the first couple of days the conversations had unfolded in the accustomed benign manner. But then, one of the Buddhist participants rose to make an observation. He said that throughout the conference he had been offended by the ubiquitous presence of depictions of the suffering Christ, nailed to his cross. His own religion, he argued, was meant to be a path that conduced away from suffering, and yet in this place of Christian prayer and recollection, he was forced constantly to face the image of crucifixion. How, he wondered, could the Christians there explain this to him and his Buddhist colleagues? Those

---

31. Robert Barron, *Bridging the Great Divide: Musings of a Post-Liberal, Post-Conservative Evangelical Catholic* (Lanham, MD/Oxford: Rowman & Littlefield Publishers, Inc., 2004), 11–21; *Exploring Catholic Theology: Essays on God, Liturgy, and Evangelization* (Grand Rapids, MI: Baker Academic, 2015), 204–207.

32. Barron, *The Strangest Way: Walking the Christian Path* (Maryknoll, NY: Orbis Books, 2002), 9–10.

who were in attendance witnessed that this question—blunt, direct, ecumenically incorrect—changed the tenor of the meeting much for the better. The Christians were compelled to grasp the nettle of the gospel: the strange and disturbing Christ, the one who, as Paul said, was a stumbling block to the Jews and a scandal to the Greeks (1 Cor 1:23). They were forced, furthermore, to explain how the very peculiarity and scandal of Christ crucified *was* the point. In the course of my book, I tried, in the Balthasarian spirit, to bring into sharp relief this very strangeness of Jesus.

I also attempted to lay out a new sort of theological method. Over and against the regnant experientialism, I proposed the model of learning to play a game. To learn basketball, one has to play it, and in order to play it, one must surrender to its rhythms, rules, practices, and basic moves. The person who continues to stand on the sideline, analyzing the game in terms of its analogous relation to similar games or in the light of the generic experience of playing 'sports,' will never know it. The learner must trust those who have fallen in love with basketball and who have played it with an abandon made possible by certain definite rules that circumscribe and direct their movement. This, I suggest, is similar to the way that one learns the practices and doctrines of Christianity: through apprenticeship, obedience, and embodied imitation. One does Christian things and thereby learns the rules of the game; one plays the game and discovers in one's bones how beautiful it is. The "experiential-expressivism" that was all the rage after the Second Vatican Council in Catholic circles prevented, I argued, just this sort of participation.[33] It allowed people to continue playing a game that they already knew in the secular world, and to give Christian names to its rules and practices. My more Goethean approach grew up out of the rich soil of Balthasar's thought.

In my book *The Priority of Christ: Toward a Postliberal Catholicism*, I explored the implications of a consistent Christocentrism, especially in regard to ethics, epistemology, and the doctrine of God.[34] In the epistemology section, for instance, I squinted through a Balthasarian

---

33. George Lindbeck, *The Nature of Doctrine* (Philadelphia, PA: The Westminster Press, 1984), 31.

34. Barron, *The Priority of Christ: Toward a Postliberal Catholicism* (Grand Rapids, MI: Brazos Press, 2007), 145–152.

lens at Thomas Aquinas's understanding of faith and reason. Thomas, I argued, did not conceive of philosophy as either a foundation or necessary propaedeutic for theology; instead, he saw it as a tool that the theologian can use in his pedagogical task of bringing Christian doctrine to the light of understanding. Theology, in a word, is neither positioned nor conditioned by natural philosophy. Instead, the science of the Logos can utilize the *logos* of philosophy as an *ancilla* (handmaid) in its work of exposition. In point of fact, I maintain, neo-scholasticism, which held to a much more foundationalist understanding of the relationship between philosophy and theology, was conditioned much more by modernity than by Aquinas's own intentions. Here I very much join forces with the Balthasar who, in his youth, rebelled against the rationalism of neoscholastic Thomism, and who tried, under de Lubac's tutelage, to recover the scriptural and patristic Aquinas. In the ethics section of *The Priority of Christ*, I criticize both deontologism and consequentialism as modernisms and opt for an ethics that takes its point of orientation from the saints—that is, from those who are concretely displaying the Christian form of life.[35] Moral truth cannot, I argued, be arrived at abstractly through deduction from first principles, but rather only through looking at the form of Christ as it is on dramatic display in his faithful followers. In this, quite obviously, I was massively influenced by Balthasar.

In practically everything I have written, the theme of God's noncompetitive transcendence emerges. I have come to appreciate this peculiar mode of divine otherness as a sort of master idea of Christianity. In its light, we can come to understand more clearly how God can be universally provident over creation and still allow for the integrity of secondary cause; how God's grace is not repugnant to human freedom but rather its ground; how surrender to God is tantamount to human flourishing; how both heteronomy and autonomy are gathered and overcome in theonomy; and how love (willing the good of the other as other) is the fundamental truth of things. All of these themes, which I have tried in a minor way to develop in my own work, I learned implicitly from Balthasar's reading of the noncompetitive play of infinite and finite freedom within the person of Jesus.

---

35. Barron, *The Priority of Christ*, 259–273 (for the criticisms); 281–340 (for my positive proposals).

Conclusion

Although I draw back from Hans Urs von Balthasar in certain ways
(a subject, perhaps, for another essay), I remain deeply indebted and
grateful to him. The boldness and beauty of his theologizing affected
in me a sort of *metanoia*, a shift in consciousness and attitude, an
entirely new way of looking at the world. In many of the Eastern
icons depicting the Last Supper, the Apostle John is presented in a
peculiar pose. As he rests his head on the breast of Jesus, he twists
his face so as to face outward, toward the viewer. He has positioned
himself so as to see the world from the standpoint of Christ, through
the eyes of the Lord. Balthasar, who was so personally devoted to
St. John, attempted to theologize from that very distinctive point of
vantage. If I may shift metaphors: as I was about to race my theological car down the Schleiermacher Autobahn, Balthasar taught me
not only to stop and change direction, but also to set out down an
entirely different road.

CHAPTER 6

WHY THE DIVINE SIMPLICITY MATTERS

I find the debate in contemporary philosophy of religion concerning the divine simplicity to be not only compelling as sheer intellectual exercise but also of supreme significance in regard to both the dialogue with nonbelievers and to the ecumenical conversation among Christians. In the course of this brief presentation, I will attempt to lay out the doctrine of God's simplicity, especially as it has been articulated by Thomas Aquinas, to respond to some of the principal objections that have been raised in recent years, and finally to demonstrate how this teaching has a significant bearing on the doctrine of the Incarnation. Finally, I will try to show that the doctrine of the divine simplicity helps us to avoid many of the dilemmas and puzzlements bequeathed to us by the sixteenth-century Reformers.

What is Meant by Saying that God is Simple?

To say that God is simple is to say that in him there is no distinction between his essence and his existence, between what he is (*quidditas*) and that he is.[1] For Thomas Aquinas, this divine simplicity follows clearly from God's status as the uncaused cause of the being of the

---

1. St. Thomas Aquinas, *Summa theologiae*, I, q. 3, a. 4; Aquinas, *On Being and Essence*, 2nd ed., trans. Armand Maurer (Toronto: Pontifical Institute for Mediaeval Studies, 1968), 5.2, pg. 60.

created world.[2] According to Thomas's metaphysical program, a thing's existence is a function either of its own essence or of the influence of an extrinsic cause: either it explains itself or it has to be explained through appeal to some agent beyond itself.[3] Now everything in our immediate experience is marked by a real distinction between essence and existence, for we can contemplate their natures apart from their acts of existence. In regard to all such things, therefore, we are logically compelled to seek a cause of their being.[4] Precisely because there cannot be an infinite regress of caused causes, in a series subordinated *per se* and not merely *per accidens*, there must exist, finally, a reality whose existence is a function, not of an extrinsic agency, but of its own essence or nature. And this simple reality, whose very *quidditas* is to be, and who grounds the to-be of every creature, is what the great tradition has meant by the word "God."[5]

Another way to explicate this doctrine is through appeal to the distinction between act and potency. For Thomas, the first reality— whether construed as unmoved mover, uncaused cause, or necessary being—must be characterized as *actus purus* (pure energy or actuality).[6] But essence functions as a principle of potency, since it delimits the *actus essendi*, somewhat in the manner that matter sets a limit to form. Thus my humanity determines that I am a very particular type of being, relating to my existence as potency to act. Therefore, in the *actus purus* of God, there can be no principle that delimits the divine act of to-be, or to state the same thing, there can be no distinction between essence and existence in God. As David Burrell put it, "to be God is to be to-be."[7] In regard to any

---

2. *Summa theologiae*, I, q. 2, a. 3; q. 3, a. 7, *corpus*.

3. Aquinas, *On Being and Essence*, 2.3, pp. 35–36; 4.7, pg. 56.

4. *Summa theologiae*, I, q. 2, a. 3.

5. Aquinas, *On Being and Essence*, 5.7, pg. 57; Aquinas, *In Librum de Causis*, ed. H. D. Saffrey (Fribourg: Société Philosophique, 1954), Prop. 6, pp. 42–48; *Summa theologiae*, I, q. 44, a. 1; q. 13, a. 11; Aquinas, *Treatise on the Separate Substances*, trans. Francis J. Lescoe (Carthagena, OH: The Messenger Press, 1963), no. 42, pg. 79.

6. Aquinas, *Summa Contra Gentiles: Book One, God*, trans. Anton C. Pegis (New York: Hanover House, 1955), I.16; *Summa theologiae*, I, q. 3, a. 2; q. 4, aa. 1–2; q. 12, a. 1; q. 14, aa. 1–2.

7. David B. Burrell, *Aquinas: God and Action* (Notre Dame, IN: University of Notre Dame Press, 1979), 26.

creature—from an archangel to a stone—no such formula could possibly be applied.

A third way to illuminate this teaching is through the principle of the one and the many. In the medieval metaphysical schema, any reality that is complex, which is to say, composed of parts, would have to be reduced to a more basic cause that brought the parts together. This is particularly clear in regard to matter and form. By an altogether correct intuition, we are led to wonder precisely why matter is found in a given configuration, at a particular speed, here rather than there, according to this modality rather than that. In a word, the distinction between form and matter compels us to search for the cause that brought them together. The same principle holds regarding essence and existence. If the two are distinct—as indeed they are in every creature—then we must seek for the cause that brought them together.[8] Therefore, if essence and existence were not identical in God, then we would have to search out the extrinsic cause of the divine being. But this is repugnant to the claim that God is the uncaused cause of finite existence.

In light of these clarifications, we can understand why, for Thomas Aquinas, God cannot be, strictly speaking, defined, for as the word itself indicates, any definition involves the setting of a limit, and all limitation is a type of potency. This is also why it would be incorrect to say that God belongs to any genus, even that most generic of genera—namely, being. Accordingly, God is not, for Thomas, 'a' being, one thing among many, however ontologically impressive. It is invalid, he says, to refer to God as an 'individual.' For this reason, Thomas uses the expression *ipsum esse subsistens* (the subsistent act of to-be itself) to describe God.[9]

As my own manner of expression is suggesting, I believe that the divine simplicity is best read under the rubric of the *via negativa*—that is to say, the removal from the idea of God of any and all creaturely imperfection. In service of defending the divine transcendence and sovereignty, the doctrine holds off any temptation to describe God in categorical terms. As Thomas himself said, "Because we cannot

---

8. Aquinas, *Summa Contra Gentiles: Book Two: Creation*, trans. James F. Anderson (Notre Dame, IN: University of Notre Dame Press, 1956), 2.43.8.

9. *Summa theologiae*, I, q. 4, a. 2; q. 11, a. 4.

know what God is, but rather what He is not, we have no means for considering how God is, but rather how He is not."[10]

The Objections

Before considering some of the objections to this doctrine that have arisen in recent years, I feel constrained to point out that the position Thomas defends is by no means peculiar to him. Rather, he summarizes and gives pointed expression to a tradition that stretches back to the Church Fathers and comes up through the High Middle Ages. Augustine, Ambrose, Anselm, and Bonaventure all defend the divine simplicity, and, in point of fact, as D. Stephen Long has demonstrated, none of the Reformers essentially quarreled with the idea.[11] Nevertheless, as Thomas himself insisted, "The proof from authority is the weakest form of proof;"[12] so let us consider the rather strenuous exception that a number of serious critics, including William Lane Craig, have taken to this classical idea.

Objection 1: Is not the doctrine of divine simplicity unbiblical?

A first objection, voiced by a number of critics especially in the Protestant world, is that the doctrine of the divine simplicity is unbiblical. Drawing it seems far more on pagan philosophical sources than on the scriptural witness, Thomas is said to have presented a deeply distorted and hopelessly abstract notion of God, more akin to a Buddhist abyss or a Hindu absolute than to the living, personal, and very particular God of the Bible. Here is how the Catholic scholar Eleonore Stump summed up the problem: "Nothing that is not an *id quod est* could be a person or enter into personal relationship with human persons. As far as that goes, nothing that is not an *id quod est* can act at all."[13]

---

10. *Summa theologiae*, I, q. 3, *proem*.

11. D. Stephen Long, *The Perfectly Simple Triune God: Aquinas and His Legacy* (Minneapolis: Fortress Press, 2016), 22.

12. *Summa theologiae*, I, q. 1, a. 8, obj. 2.

13. Eleonore Stump, "God's Simplicity," in *The Oxford Handbook of Aquinas*, ed. Brian Davies and Eleonore Stump (Oxford: Oxford University Press, 2012), 139.

Before getting to a pointed response to this, it might be illuminating to consider something that is often overlooked—namely, Thomas's rather intense relationship to the Bible. As a young man at the University of Naples, he was beguiled by the street preaching of the Dominicans, an order devoted to a back-to-basics evangelicalism. When Thomas assumed his role as *magister* at the University of Paris, one of his first responsibilities was preaching.[14] Attendant immediately upon this was the obligation to engage in biblical commentary, which he would ultimately pursue throughout his life.[15] In the course of his career, Thomas produced a substantial number of such commentaries, including a late-career masterpiece on the Gospel of John.[16] Moreover, during his time at Orvieto, he assembled the so-called *Catena Aurea*, a compilation of patristic observations on the Gospels.[17] Indeed, one of the titles he bore was *magister sacrae paginae* ('Master of the Sacred Page'). As any serious commentator on the Scriptures realizes, a close reading of the Bible leads, naturally enough, to questions, conundrums, and puzzles. Hence, a *magister sacrae paginae* would become, inevitably, preoccupied with what the medievals called *quaestiones disputatae* (disputed questions), and indeed Thomas entertained such questions throughout his public career.[18] Finally, eager to present these theological musings in an organized, systematic manner, Thomas produced summaries (*summae*) of his thought.[19] Far too often, even careful students of Thomas read only the *summae* and overlook the rootedness of these texts in biblical commentary and preaching, and this produces a deeply distorted understanding of him as a pure philosopher, a detached rationalist. Indeed, the master was composing the *Summa theologiae*, including the great texts on the divine simplicity, at the same time that he was writing commentaries on John, Isaiah, and the Apostle Paul. I think

---

14. Jean-Pierre Torrell, *Saint Thomas Aquinas*, vol. 1, *The Person and His Work*, trans. Robert Royal (Washington, DC: The Catholic University of America Press, 2005), 36–39.

15. Torrell, *The Person and His Work*, 55.

16. Torrell, *The Person and His Work*, 198–201.

17. Torrell, *The Person and His Work*, 136–141.

18. Torrell, *The Person and His Work*, 59–63.

19. Torrell, *The Person and His Work*, 145–148.

that, at the very least, it should give the critics pause to consider that the subtlest mind of the Middle Ages quite evidently did not see the slightest contradiction between the God of the Bible and the simple God articulated through more philosophical categories.

The clearest conceptual link between the God of the Scriptures and the simple God is the notion of creation, which runs throughout the sacred writings. For Thomas, the claim that God makes the world *ex nihilo* is functionally equivalent to the assertion that God is the unique reality in which essence and existence coincide, for anything that is marked by a distinction between *quidditas* and the *actus essendi* would require, ultimately, the sustaining influence of the one whose very essence is to be.[20] To put it in more straightforwardly biblical terms, creatures depend upon the Creator. To claim, as the Bible does, that God is the Creator of the heavens and the earth, a reality qualitatively other than anything in the universe, is tantamount to affirming that God's essence is not other than God's existence.

What becomes apparent upon even the most cursory reading of Thomas's texts on the matter is that the identity of essence and existence in God is in fact signaled by one of the most famous and influential of all biblical verses. To give just one example from his oeuvre, in article eleven of question thirteen of the first part of the *Summa theologiae*, Thomas wonders whether *Qui est* (the one who is) is the "most proper name of God." In the *sed contra* of that article, he cites the third chapter of Exodus: "It is written that when Moses asked, 'If they should say to me, What is his name? what shall I say to them?' The Lord answered him, 'Thus shall you say to them, HE WHO IS has sent me to you.' Therefore, this name HE WHO IS (*Qui est*) most properly belongs to God (*maxime proprium nomen Dei.*)."[21] In the *respondeo* of that article, we discover this elaboration: "Since the existence of God is His essence itself, which can be said of no other, it is clear that among other names this one specifically denominates God."[22] The great twentieth-century Thomist Etienne Gilson went so far as to characterize Thomas's doctrine of

---

20. *Summa theologiae*, I, q. 45, a. 1.

21. *Summa theologiae*, I, q. 13, a. 11, *sed contra*.

22. *Summa theologiae*, I, q. 13, a. 11, *respondeo*.

God in terms of the Exodus,[23] such that it could be called a 'metaphysics of Exodus.'

Of course, this biblical critique of Thomas's teaching on God becomes more pointed. How could a God who is not an individual, not a definite existent, not a person in possession of attributes other than existence itself, possibly be the God who speaks to his people, enters into covenant with them, becomes aroused in anger at their sin, and loves them abidingly? Doesn't the Bible speak of God as good and righteous, as intelligent and compassionate, as provident and merciful? Then how could Thomas possibly assert that all we can know of God is what he is not? How could a *magister sacrae paginae* set before us a vague entity that cannot be defined and that seems to possess only that thinnest of qualities—namely, existence itself? Here we have to be careful lest we construe Thomas's *via negativa* as sheer apophaticism. We must indeed remove from our conception of God anything that smacks of creaturely imperfection or finitude, but by the same token, we must affirm of God anything that is good and perfect within the realm of creatures. Thus, under the rubric of the negative way, we must say that the simple God is immutable (since he cannot be reduced from potency to act),[24] eternal (since he cannot be circumscribed temporally),[25] and immaterial (since he is not susceptible to formal change).[26] On the other hand, under the rubric of the *via positiva*, we must also say that he is intelligent,[27] loving,[28] providential,[29] personal, powerful,[30] etc. *Ipsum esse* is not a thin abstraction—just the contrary. He (and I use the personal pronoun here on purpose) is unlimited to-be, that is to say, fully actual, entirely realized existence. Hence, it is altogether correct to say that the simple

---

23. Cf. Ex 3:14. Etienne Gilson, *The Christian Philosophy of St. Thomas Aquinas*, trans. L. K. Shook (New York: Random House, 1956), 84–95.

24. *Summa theologiae*, I, q. 9.

25. *Summa theologiae*, I, q. 10.

26. *Summa theologiae*, I, q. 3, aa. 1–2.

27. *Summa theologiae*, I, q. 14.

28. *Summa theologiae*, I, qq. 20 and 37.

29. *Summa theologiae*, I, q. 22.

30. *Summa theologiae*, I, q. 25.

God is in absolute possession of any and all ontological perfection.[31] To affirm, therefore, that God is not a being or an individual is by no means to imply that he is less than personal.

Objection 2: Is not the simple God impersonal, abstract, and incapable of action?

A second principal criticism of the doctrine of the divine simplicity comes from Alvin Plantinga and his school, marked by an analytical philosophical approach to these matters. Plantinga correctly points out that an implication of the classical teaching is that God, precisely as simple, is identical to his 'properties.' Thus it is not the case that God is a subject that has certain qualities; rather, God is his own goodness, his own justice, and his own power. But this seems to involve, the Plantinga school argues, the identification of God's manner of being with the manner of being of a property, which is to say, impersonal, abstract, and incapable of engaging in action: "No property could have created the world; no property could be omniscient, or indeed, know anything at all. If God is a property, then he isn't a person but a mere abstract object."[32] But this critique is born of a confusion. In creatures, we find a distinction between substance and accident or subject and properties, and in this sort of metaphysical composite, the latter does indeed have a mitigated mode of existence vis-à-vis the former. It would be silly to say, for instance, that 'My power is acting' or that 'My justice is offended.' But it is precisely this sort of distinction that does not obtain within the simple God. Therefore, instead of saying that God is a property or set of properties, one should say that God has no properties, that God is all substance, if you will.

A related criticism is that, given the simplicity of the divine being, all 'properties' of God are in fact identical. Thus, his intelligence is his power, which is his mercy, which is his justice, and so on. But this just seems, on the face of it, contradictory, for those attributes are quite obviously distinguishable one from another.

---

31. *Summa theologiae*, I, q. 4.

32. Alvin Plantinga, *Does God Have a Nature?* The Aquinas Lecture Series (Milwaukee, WI: Marquette University Press, 1980), 47.

Well, they are indeed distinct in creatures—that is to say, in finite substances that have properties—but God is not a creature, not a supreme being among many. What appear as separable qualities in finite things cohere in God, just as a prism breaks the sheer white light into an array of colors. To illustrate this principle with just a few examples, consider the knowledge, will, love, and power of God. For Thomas Aquinas, God's knowledge is not passive and derivative as ours often is; rather, it is always creative. Citing Augustine, Thomas demonstrates that God doesn't know things because they are; they are because he knows them.[33] And this is but a philosophically refined expression of the biblical idea of the Divine Word as productive of what it enunciates: "Yet just as from the heavens the rain and the snow come down and do not return there till they have watered the earth…so shall my word be that goes forth from my mouth. It shall not return to me empty" (Is 55:10–11). Thus, knowledge and power are identical in him.[34] Moreover, to know the good as good is precisely what it means to will, and since God knows himself completely as the supreme good, will and knowledge coincide in him.[35] Finally, to love is either to will the absent good or to savor the good that one possesses.[36] Since God is always, by his knowledge and will, in possession of his own good, he is, by the same token, marked by the sheerest love. Hence, knowledge, will, power, and love coincide in him, or to state it differently, all are different ways of squinting at the simple divine act of *to-be*.

Objection 3: Would not divine simplicity eliminate divine freedom?

A third major objection also comes from the Plantinga analytical school. The charge is that the doctrine of the divine simplicity locks God into a sort of necessitarianism, whereby every move, thought, and action on his part would be determined and his freedom

---

33. *Summa theologiae*, I, q. 14, a. 8, *sed contra*.

34. *Summa theologiae*, I, q. 25, a. 1, ad. 4.

35. *Summa theologiae*, I, q. 6, a. 2; q. 19, a. 1; Aquinas, *Summa Contra Gentiles: Book One*, I.41; Aquinas, *Summa Contra Gentiles: Book Three, Providence, Part 1*, trans. Vernon J. Bourke (Notre Dame, IN: University of Notre Dame Press, 1975), III.19.

36. *Summa theologiae*, I, q. 20.

effectively eliminated.[37] If God has no accidental properties, it seems impossible to imagine that God could have created a world different than the one he has in fact created, or indeed that God might have chosen not to create at all. Using (as is their wont) a possible worlds schema, the followers of Plantinga argue that if God is truly free, we must be able to imagine a variety of scenarios in which God remains God but in which God has different relationships to creation and in which he performed a different set of actions.[38] But if we can imagine this, we must assert that, along with certain essential features (which would obtain in all the different worlds), God must have accidental qualities that obtain in only a given world. But this militates against divine simplicity.

By way of an initial response to this objection, I would note that, from the beginning to the end of his career, Thomas maintained both that God is simple and that there is a distinction between things that obtain necessarily within God (such as the Trinitarian relations) and things that are the result of God's free choice.[39] Unlike Alvin Plantinga, Thomas saw absolutely no contradiction in the matter. The explanation for this hinges upon the difference between the world's relationship to God, which involves causal dependency, and God's relationship to the world, which involves no such dependency. In Thomas's admittedly ambiguous formulation, the former is a "real" relationship, while the latter is not.[40] Creatures are utterly different depending upon how God relates to them, whereas God is utterly the same whether creatures are related to him or not. As Robert Sokolowski specified this unique state of affairs, "After creation, there are more beings, but no more perfection of Being."[41] Hence, we can indeed imagine an array of possible worlds, even the scenario in which God didn't create at all, but in any and all such worlds, God's simple nature would remain unaffected.

---

37. Plantinga, *Does God Have a Nature?* 32–33.

38. Plantinga, *Does God Have a Nature?* 35–37, 41–44.

39. *Summa theologiae*, I, q. 32, a. 1, ad. 3; Aquinas, *Summa Contra Gentiles: Book Two*, II.23.

40. *Summa theologiae*, I, q. 28, a. 1.

41. Robert Sokolowski, *The God of Faith and Reason: Foundations of Christian Theology* (Washington, DC: The Catholic University of America Press, 1995), 42.

Some Implications for the Doctrine of the Incarnation

I would like, by way of conclusion, to make a connection between the doctrine of the divine simplicity and that most characteristic of all Christian doctrines—namely, the Incarnation. The Chalcedonian claim that two natures, divine and human, come together in the person of Christ, "without confusion or change, without division or separation"[42] is predicated upon the assumption that the 'to-be' of God is qualitatively different than the 'to-be' of a creature. Finite natures always exist in an ontologically competitive manner: what is distinctive to one nature militates necessarily against what is distinctive to another nature. Hence we could speak of one creaturely nature becoming another only through some process of destruction or assimilation, the wildebeest becoming the flesh of the lion or a podium becoming a pile of ash. But in Jesus, God becomes human without ceasing to be God or compromising the integrity of the created nature he assumes. This means that God is transcendent but precisely in a noncompetitive manner. He is indeed other, even *totaliter aliter*, but by a noncontrastive otherness, for he is not competing for space, so to speak, on the same ontological ground as creatures.[43] The best way to express this unique form of transcendence is to speak of God not as a being but rather as the sheer act of 'to-be' itself. *Ipsum esse* is obviously other than anything in the realm of beings, but at the same time, he is the most intimate ground of whatever exists in the finite arena. If God were simply one being among many, the supreme instance of the genus being, it is difficult indeed to imagine how his nature could come together noncompetitively with a created nature.

Extrapolating from this insight, Catholic theology sees many of the conundrums and dilemmas posed by the sixteenth-century Reformers to be false problems. The desperate zero-sum game that Luther and his disciples saw as obtaining between faith and works, or between divine glory and human achievement, or between grace

---

42. Heinrich Denzinger, *Enchiridion symbolorum definitionum et declarationum de rebus fidei et morum: Compendium of Creeds, Definitions, and Declarations on Matters of Faith and Morals,* ed. Peter Hünermann, 43rd ed. (San Francisco: Ignatius Press, 2012), no. 302, pg. 109.

43. For more on this point, see chapter three, "Thomas Aquinas and the New Evangelization," 51–53.

and the cooperation with grace is born of a misconstrual of God as competitive with his creation. I won't explore here the roots of that misconception in the abandonment of an analogical understanding of being, but suffice it to say that, from a Catholic perspective, the best way to avoid these false dilemmas and to embrace with enthusiasm the Irenaean motto *Gloria Dei homo vivens* ("The glory of God is a human being fully alive")[44] is to return to an understanding of God as the simple act of to-be itself.

---

44. St. Irenaeus of Lyons, *Against Heresies*, IV.20.7. In *Irenaeus on the Christian Faith: A Condensation of* Against Heresies, trans. and ed. James R. Payton, Jr. (Eugene, OR: Pickwick Publications, 2011), 116.

CHAPTER 7

THE ONE WHO IS, THE ONE WHO GIVES

Derrida, Aquinas, and the Dilemma of the Divine Generosity

It is a favorite technique of those trained in the Derridean decon-structionist method to find a loose thread—an anomaly, a contradiction, an unresolved tension—in even the most venerable philosophical weave and then to pull on it until the fabric comes undone. A prime example of this is the way a number of postmodern thinkers, including Jacques Derrida himself, tugged on the thread of the *aporia* (or dilemma) of the gift in order to problematize central claims of the religious traditions.[1] I would like to turn the tables on the postmodern philosophers by using their own method, pulling the loose thread of their very critique of the *aporia* of the gift. For it is my contention that their analysis of the anomalies within the idea of giftedness can actually serve to clarify what stands distinctively at the heart of the Christian spiritual and philosophical tradition. I will use the texts of St. Thomas Aquinas to make my argument.

---

1. See Jacques Derrida, *Given Time*, vol. 1, *Counterfeit Money*, trans. Peggy Knauf (Chicago/London: The University of Chicago Press, 1992). Also Derrida, *Aporias*, trans. Thomas Dutoit (Stanford University Press, 1993).

The *Aporia* of the Gift

The postmodern preoccupation with the theme of the gift finds its roots in the sociological work of the French thinker Marcel Mauss. In his studies of primal peoples, Mauss uncovered the dynamics of an economy of exchange, whereby the giving of a gift by one tribal chief would prompt in his rival an answering gift, lest the latter be shamed by the former.[2] Émile Benveniste engaged in similar research, which revealed that, in some cultures, one act of hospitality would awaken in the one who received it an act of even more extravagant hospitality, which would in turn compel the original giver to give even more generously, until the two communities essentially ruined one another through a kind of mutual shaming. This is why Benveniste could playfully suggest an etymological link between "hospitality" and the Latin word *hostis* ("enemy").[3]

In texts such as *Given Time* and *Aporias*, Derrida elaborates upon this phenomenon in a more strictly philosophical vein. It appears, he says, that the first condition of the authentic gift is that it is offered without consideration of compensation. Were strings attached to a present that I have made, one would be hard-pressed to refer to it as a true gift. Indeed, were I to receive such a present, I would not feel gratified and grateful, but manipulated. Even a gift as seemingly uncomplicated as a birthday present from a relative carries with it the at least implicit obligation of writing a thank-you note as compensation. Anyone who has ever had the exquisitely awkward experience of confronting a person who plaintively and resentfully observes 'I hope you received the gift I gave you' feels the force of this demand. The second fundamental condition for the possibility of a gift is presence—that is to say, the appearance of the gift *qua* gift. If some boon appeared simply out of the blue, with no indication as to its provenance, one might consider it luck or good fortune, but one would hardly call it a gift, except in the most blandly metaphorical sense.

Derrida argues that, once we acknowledge these two indispensable conditions, it is difficult to see how a true gift is even possible, for

---

2. Marcel Mauss, *The Gift: Expanded Edition*, trans. Jane I. Guyer (Chicago: Hau Books, 2016), 55–75, 85–87, 113–117, 120, 121–130, 144.

3. Émile Benveniste, *Dictionary of Indo-European Concepts and Society*, trans. Elizabeth Palmer (Chicago: Hau Books, 2016), 46–47, 61, 66–67, 70–71.

the moment something appears *qua* gift, it would seem, necessarily, to awaken in the recipient the need to reciprocate. Precisely as a present, a gift can never be free, and in order to be free, it cannot be present. On this score, Derrida rejoices in the delicious link between the English 'gift' and the German '*Gift*,' designating poison; the need for a response or reciprocation poisons the waters, so to speak, of the pure gift. Finally, any gift is noxious for both giver and receiver, since it locks both into a mutually destructive economy of exchange.

Now, the full exploration of this motif in the postmoderns would take us way too far afield, but for our purposes, it might be worthwhile to note some troubling implications for the classical Christian tradition, for which the notions of gift and grace are obviously so crucial. It is elemental for Christian philosophy and theology, and perhaps from the Derridean perspective most problematical, that worship is an act of thanksgiving, an obligation to return to God what God has given. That Derrida himself was aware that the *aporia* of the gift poses problems for Christianity in particular is made manifest in his insistence that the only kind of messianism that is viable is a messianism without a Messiah—that is to say, an expectation of a divine gift that never really arrives. His famous characterization of deconstruction as the attitude of *"viens, oui, oui!"* is conditioned by the assurance that the definitive Other, the final answer to our longing, never actually comes.[4]

God as Giver of Gifts

Far from undermining central claims of Christianity, the Derridean dilemma provides, in fact, a route of access to understanding central Christian mysteries more fully. It serves, if you will, as the grit in the oyster around which the pearl forms—and Thomas Aquinas helps us to appreciate this. Indeed, the term 'gift' (*donum*) and its variants appear 1756 times in the writings of Aquinas.[5] As we shall see anon,

---

4. Jacques Derrida, *Parages* (Paris: Galilée, 1986), 116. Cited in John D. Caputo, *The Prayers and Tears of Jacques Derrida: Religion without Religion* (Bloomington: Indiana University Press, 1997), 100. English translation (with same title) edited by John P. Leavey (Stanford University Press, 2011).

5. Determined using Index Thomisticus search engine found at http://www.corpusthomisticum.org/it/index.age.

the word turns up with special frequency in regard to the Holy Spirit, but another particularly prominent context for its usage is Aquinas's discussion of creation, wherein God is typically characterized as the one who *dat esse* (gives being). What I shall endeavor to show first is that, granted the Derridean prerequisites of presence and utter gratuitousness, the truest gift possible is that which comes from God in the act of creation.

Though these issues are broached frequently in Aquinas's writing, perhaps the clearest and most succinct presentation is found in a text from the very beginning of the master's career, composed in the early 1250s—namely, the *De ente et essentia* (*On Being and Essence*). The young Aquinas uses the distinction between essence and existence to clarify both the nature of God and the unique relationship that obtains between the infinite God and finite things. In chapter four of the *De ente et essentia*, Aquinas proves the reality of the distinction between the two principles through a sort of thought experiment. It is altogether possible, he says, to consider a *quidditas* apart from the actual existence of the essence under consideration.[6] One can think, he suggests, of the nature of a phoenix, even though no such animal exists.[7] Putting the matter in an even broader context, we can notice the demarcation in the very fact that nothing in our immediate experience has to exist, that nothing in the world, in a word, possesses a nature that requires actual existence.

Now, in regard to those things in which this real metaphysical distinction obtains, we must look for an extrinsic cause, or to state the matter a bit differently, for an agent that effected the juxtaposition of essence and existence, some cause that actualized this particular potentiality toward being. Following a logical rhythm familiar from many of his later writings, the young Aquinas argues that this extrinsic cause is either self-explanatory or itself derived from a cause extrinsic to its nature.[8] Because a series of caused causes, subordinated *per se*, cannot proceed infinitely, we must arrive finally at some reality whose nature is *to be*, in whom essence and existence coincide,

---

6. St. Thomas Aquinas, *On Being and Essence*, trans. Armand Maurer, 2nd ed. (Toronto: Pontifical Institute for Medieval Studies, 1968), 4.3, pg. 53.

7. Aquinas, *On Being and Essence*, 4.6, pg. 55.

8. Aquinas, *On Being and Essence*, 4.7, pg. 56.

and who is, therefore, responsible for the being of any and all things in whom essence and existence are distinct. This unconditioned reality, Aquinas continues, can only be characterized as *actus purus* ("pure actuality").[9] By definition, this being cannot be limited by either an extrinsic cause or intrinsic principle.[10] Anything marked by the play between essence and existence could be further actualized, rendered more perfect, but the reality in whom essence and existence coincide could not possibly be 'improved' in any way or more fully realized. Nothing could add to its being; it could benefit from no ontological gift. It is this utterly distinctive and strange source of finite existence that thoughtful people call God.

What does this analysis tell us about the creaturely mode of existence? Here I would like to turn to the great texts on creation in both the *Summa theologiae* and the disputed question *De Potentia* (*On the Power of God*). From the essence/*esse* distinction, Aquinas draws the logical conclusion that the coming-to-be of finite things must be continual and *ex nihilo*.[11] Since nothing in the nature of a creature requires it to be, its ongoing existence must be the result of the continual influence of the one in whom essence and existence come together. Moreover, since the entirety of the creature's being is dependent, the creative act by which it is sustained must be distinguished from all forms of making, or fashioning from something.[12] God does not shape anything preexistent to form a creature.[13] Similarly, creation is not a type of motion, since it involves no transition from potency to act; nor is it a temporal act, since time is the measure of motion. In the *De Potentia*, Aquinas gives this rather apophatic description of creation: *nihil est aliud realiter quam relatio quaedam ad Deum cum novitate essendi* ("nothing but a relation of the creature to the

---

9. Aquinas, *Summa theologiae*, I, q. 9, a. 1.

10. Aquinas, *On Being and Essence*, 4.6–4.7, pp. 55–57.

11. Aquinas, *On the Power of God (Quaestiones Disputatae de Potentia Dei)*, trans. English Dominican Fathers (Westminster, MA: The Newman Press, 1952), q. 3, a. 3, ad. 6. Hereafter *De Potentia*.

12. *Summa theologiae*, I, q. 19, a. 4; q. 46, a. 1.

13. Aquinas, *De Potentia*, q. 3, a. 1, ad. 12; q. 3, a. 4, *respondeo*; *Summa Contra Gentiles*, II.16; *Summa theologiae*, I, q. 45, a. 1.

Creator together with a beginning of existence").[14] He is using the familiar Aristotelian category of relation, but, as is his wont, he is giving it a radically transformed meaning. On the standard reading, a relation obtains between two beings, but in regard to creation this cannot be the case, since there is literally nothing independent of the act of creation by which God establishes the relationship. As Aquinas says, "God at the same time gives being and produces that which receives being."[15]

From this exposition, we must conclude that every creature is a sheer and unadulterated gift, for there is, quite literally, nothing in the *to-be* of a creature that has not been given by another. The same could not be said of finite things within a standard Aristotelian or Platonic context. Aquinas, we might argue, has given careful metaphysical expression to Paul's observation: "What do you have that you have not received?" (1 Cor 4:7). In the second place, we must conclude that the source of creaturely being has absolutely no need of creation. The entire universe, even in principle, would add nothing to God's perfection, for any such addition would be repugnant to God's unconditioned mode of existence. As Robert Sokolowski, one of the most trenchant analysts of the metaphysics of creation, put it, "God plus the world is not greater than God alone,"[16] and "After creation, there are more beings, but no more perfection of *esse* (being)."[17] We might usefully contrast this account with the theologies emerging from the Greek and Roman myths, according to which the gods are co-implicated with the world in a range of shared obligations and needs, as well as with Hegelianism and its many offshoots, which call for a rapport of mutual dependency between God and creation.

The classical philosophical accounts, the mythic presentations, and the Hegelian construal of the God-world relationship would, accordingly, all be susceptible to the Derridean critique of the gift, but Thomas Aquinas's account is not. Aquinas's explanation allows

---

14. Aquinas, *De Potentia*, q. 3, a. 3, *respondeo*.

15. Aquinas, *De Potentia*, q. 3, a. 1, ad. 17.

16. Robert Sokolowski, *The God of Faith and Reason: Foundations of Christian Theology* (Washington, DC: The Catholic University of America Press, 1995), 8.

17. Sokolowski, *The God of Faith and Reason*, 42.

for both conditions of giftedness—namely, receiving a gift without necessary compensation and presence of the gift *qua* gift—to be realized simultaneously. Once we have grasped the truth of the essence /existence distinction in creatures, we understand that their being is not their own, that they indeed present themselves, they show up in the world, in gift form. This metaphysical truth is beautifully honored in the German expression for "there is," namely, *es gibt* (it gives). Thus the criterion of presence is met. More to it, the one who ultimately gives the gift, the one who by his nature simply is, cannot even in principle benefit from what he offers. And thus the criterion of sheer liberality is met.

A beautiful text from question 44, article 4, of the first part of the *Summa theologiae* catches so many aspects of this uniquely generous rapport between the one who is and those things that are. Under the aegis of considering whether God is the final cause of all creatures, Aquinas speaks of the manner in which creaturely agents act: "Some things, however, are both agent and patient at the same time: these are imperfect agents, and to these it belongs to intend, even while acting, the acquisition of something. But it does not belong to the First Agent, Who is agent only, to act for the acquisition of some end."[18] Created actors, in other words, even as they influence others, are themselves influenced; even as they give to others, they themselves receive. But this type of mutuality cannot obtain in regard to God. As the first objection to this article states, "It would seem that God is not the final cause of all things. For to act for an end seems to imply need of the end. But God needs nothing. Therefore it does not become him to act for an end."[19] Aquinas's typically pithy response seems to anticipate the concerns of Marcel Mauss and Jacques Derrida by seven centuries: "To act from need belongs only to an imperfect agent, which by its nature is both agent and patient. But this does not belong to God, and therefore He alone is the most perfectly liberal giver (*et ideo ipse solus est maxime liberalis*), because He does not act for His own profit, but only for His own goodness."[20]

---

18. *Summa theologiae*, I, q. 44, a. 4, *corpus*.

19. *Summa theologiae*, I, q. 44, a. 4, obj. 1.

20. *Summa theologiae*, I, q. 44, a. 4, ad. 1.

God's Highest Name

The upshot of the foregoing discussion is that God's capacity truly
to give is predicated upon God's absolutely unique manner of existence, giving following from being. And this clarification brings to
mind a debate that was of keen importance to the medievals and
that has been resurrected in our time by a former student of Jacques
Derrida, Jean-Luc Marion, who is one of the world's most prominent Catholic philosophers. Marion, who has wrestled for decades
with the *aporias* and possibilities of the idea of giftedness, argued
in his seminal text *Dieu sans l'etre* (*God Without Being*) that goodness is
God's highest or most proper name,[21] and that the title "being" or
"the one who is" carries with it the danger of idolatry.[22] Showing
why he is wrong about this will help us refine our answer to Derrida's
original challenge.

Marion argues that the name "existence" or "being" falls so
neatly into our cognitive categories that when we ascribe it to God,
we run the severe risk of reducing God to the level of comprehensi-
ble things. Hence the application of the concept of *esse* to God, even
when pushed and expanded in the direction of total transcendence,
tends to foster in the mind of the philosopher a kind of intellectual complacency, a sense of having corralled and understood God.
Calling explicitly into question the tradition, running from Thomas
Aquinas to Etienne Gilson, that defends the thesis that *qui est* is
God's highest name, Marion sides with Aquinas's Franciscan counterpart, St. Bonaventure, who famously argued in *The Soul's Journey
into God* that, though being is God's highest Old Testament name,
goodness or love is a higher name still, since it designates the play
of the Trinitarian persons.[23] Bonaventure (and Marion) adopts the
Platonic/Dionysian view that the good, that which gives, is "beyond
the beings"—that is to say, metaphysically antecedent to the gift of
existence itself. And this transcendence of even the most abstract

---

21. Jean-Luc Marion, *God Without Being*, trans. Thomas A. Carlson (Chicago:
The University of Chicago Press, 1991), 73–83.

22. Marion, *God Without Being*, 33–49.

23. Bonaventure, *The Soul's Journey into God*, in *Bonaventure: The Soul's Journey into
God, the Tree of Life, and the Life of St. Francis*, trans. Ewert Cousins (Mahwah, NJ: Paulist
Press, 1978), 5.2, pp. 94–95; 6.1–2, pp. 102–104.

category of the mind implies that the language of goodness, applied to God, is less susceptible to idolatrous misuse and can serve as a properly iconic manner of naming the divine reality.

A careful consideration of Aquinas's texts on this matter of the divine naming sheds quite a bit of light on the general problem that we have been examining in this paper. First, no one can possibly doubt that Aquinas had a thoroughgoing knowledge of the Dionysian tradition, which he first took in as a young apprentice to Albertus Magnus and which he continued to integrate into his own work throughout his career. Pere Chenu is certainly correct in asserting that Dionysius's *exitus-reditus* program provides the chief structuring element in Thomas's mature theological program.[24] The Dionysian influence is especially clear in Aquinas's treatment of God's nature, creation, and theological language. And thus it is of considerable interest to note that Aquinas consciously and repeatedly departs from the Dionysian heritage on the key question of God's highest name. His reasons must have been serious ones.

There are two principal passages from the *Summa theologiae* worth examining in this regard. The first is ST I, q. 5, a. 2, which considers whether good is prior in idea to being—the familiar Dionysian proposal. In his crisp response, Aquinas argues that what is prior in idea is what is first conceived by the intellect. But the first thing that the intellect can possibly conceive is being, since actuality is the objective correlate of any and all acts of knowledge. "Hence, being is the proper object of the intellect, and is primarily intelligible; as sound is what is primarily audible."[25] But what of the explicit Dionysian priority given to the good? Aquinas answers this objection by a subtle but crucial elision of terms in an Aristotelian direction.[26] For the Stagyrite, and Aquinas follows him here, goodness always has the nature of an end—that is to say, as something desirable. As such, it has a sort of causal primacy over being, since even prime matter is moved to form by its attraction to an end. However, precisely as an end, the good must be equivalent to some perfection of being, since actuality is what

---

24. Marie-Dominique Chenu, *Toward Understanding St. Thomas*, trans. A.–M. Landry and D. Hughes (Chicago: Henry Regnery Company, 1963), 304–307.

25. *Summa theologiae*, I, q. 5, a. 2, *corpus*.

26. *Summa theologiae*, I, q. 5, a. 2, ad. 1.

any agent seeks. Hence, being reasserts itself in the prime position.[27] This Aristotelian transposition allows Aquinas to recover the Dionysian assertion that the good is diffusive of itself, not so much in terms of efficient causality, but final causality. What permits God to give so dramatically and over such a universal range is, once again, the properly unconditioned quality of his manner of being.

The second principal text to examine is ST I, q. 13, a. 11, in which Aquinas explicitly asks, "Whether this name, He Who Is, is the most proper name of God." The second objection cuts to the issue raised from Pseudo-Dionysius to Jean-Luc Marion: "'The name of good excellently manifests all the processions of God' (Dionysius, *Div. Nom.* iii). 'Good,' however, especially belongs to God as the universal principle of all things. Therefore, this name good is supremely proper to God, and not this name He Who Is."[28] The objector is referring, of course, not simply to the procession of finite things from God in creation but of the more primordial processions that obtain within the Trinity. Thus, he implicitly gives voice to the Bonaventurian objection that being, however sacred a name, is an Old Testament designation, superseded by the New Testament name of goodness or love.

Before turning to Aquinas's answer to this particular argument, let us look at the substance of his *respondeo*. Since, he argues, the name being designates not any particular mode of existence but existence itself, and since God is uniquely to be categorized as *ipsum esse*, this term is maximally appropriate to God. His second argument hinges on the universality of the name He Who Is. "For all other names are either less universal, or, if convertible with it, add something above it at least in idea; hence in a certain way they inform and determine it."[29] Once again, following his Aristotelian instinct, Aquinas says that the name 'good' is simply convertible with the name 'being,' since the desirable and the actual coincide. Moreover, in the measure that goodness designates causality, it modifies or specifies the idea of being, occupying, therefore, a less universal place in the conceptual hierarchy.

And this is precisely the approach he takes in responding to the Dionysian second objector. The name 'good,' Aquinas insists,

---

27. *Summa theologiae*, I, q. 5, a. 2, ad. 1.

28. *Summa theologiae*, I, q. 13, a. 11, obj. 2.

29. *Summa theologiae*, I, q. 13, a. 11, *respondeo*.

is indeed the principal name of God insofar as he is a cause (*bonum diffisivum sui* [the good is diffusive of itself]), but it does not designate the divine being in itself, for "existence considered absolutely comes before the idea of a cause."[30] This sentence is perhaps the best one-line summary of my argument. In line with the adage *nemo dat quod non habet* ("no one can give what he does not have"), Thomas maintains that whatever truth is conveyed by the name 'good' is necessarily subordinate to and conditioned by the truth conveyed by the name *esse*. Or to transpose this discussion from the linguistic to the metaphysical dimension, it is only because God exists in such a distinctive manner that he is able to give in such an utterly generous and gratuitous way.

The Holy Spirit as *Donum*

To this point, we have been following Aquinas's teaching regarding God as such in relation to the created realm. I would now like to move into even deeper waters, searching out the play between being and gift that can be found within the Trinitarian relations. One of the deftest moves that Aquinas makes is to show that the simplicity of the divine nature and the plurality of the divine persons are not only not mutually repugnant but in point of fact mutually implicative. We might characterize the logical moves as follows. Because God is simple, God must be perfect, since simplicity implies pure actuality.[31] But if God is perfect, he must be in possession of every ontological perfection, including intelligence.[32] And if God is intelligent and his intelligence unlimited, then he must be able to form an *imago* of himself, an interior Word. Further, through his intelligence, he must grasp the interior Word as supremely good and hence must love it, since will is a consequence of understanding the good as good. Therefore, the very simplicity of God implies a relationship between Father (the generator of the interior Word), the Son (the interior Word), and the Holy Spirit (the love that obtains between Father and Son).[33]

---

30. *Summa theologiae,* I, q. 13, a. 11, ad. 2.

31. *Summa theologiae,* I, q. 4, a. 1.

32. *Summa theologiae,* I, q. 4, a. 2.

33. *Summa theologiae,* I, qq. 31–38.

Though 'love' indeed is a principal name of the Spirit, the other great name for the third person of the Trinity is *donum* (gift), and this brings us back to our central theme. Aquinas explores the ramifications and implications of this mode of nomination in ST I, q. 38, a. 2, in which he asks "Whether 'gift' is the proper name of the Holy Spirit."[34] In his *respondeo*, Aquinas cites Aristotle to the effect that "a gift is properly an unreturnable giving" (*donum proprie est datio irredibilis*) and hence carries with it the sense of gratuitous donation.[35] However, the *ratio* or intelligible form of gratuitous donation is love, since we give a gift only "forasmuch as we wish him well."[36] Therefore, it follows that love "has the nature of a first gift, through which all free gifts are given."[37] And this is why St. Augustine can say, "Many gifts, which are proper to each one, are divided in common among all the members of Christ by the Gift which is the Holy Spirit."[38] The Holy Spirit is the metaphysical matrix of both the act of creation and the gracing that enables human beings to participate in the divine life. But what I want to make clear is that the condition for the possibility of this kind of donation, even within the inner life of the Trinity, is the simplicity shared by the Father and the Son. Were the Father to benefit in any sense from the Son or the Son from the Father, then the love that they share would not be absolute; it would in fact be marked by a kind of Derridean economy of exchange. Therefore, in singling out the proper name of the Holy Spirit, Aquinas has uncovered the ultimate solution for the *aporia* of the gift.

The Indwelling of the Holy Spirit

After this rather heady exploration of the nature of God, the act of creation, and the Trinitarian relations, let us return, in this final section, to the ground and the very concrete observations of the

---

34. *Summa theologiae,* I, q. 38.

35. *Summa theologiae,* I, q. 38, a. 2, *respondeo.*

36. *Summa theologiae,* I, q. 38, a. 2, *respondeo.* (slightly different translation)

37. *Summa theologiae,* I, q. 38, a. 2, *respondeo.*

38. St. Augustine, *The Trinity,* trans. Stephen McKenna, The Fathers of the Church Series: A New Translation 45 (Washington, DC: The Catholic University of America Press, 2002), XV.19.34, pg. 500. See *Summa theologiae,* I, q. 38, a. 2.

postmoderns regarding the impossibility of interpersonal gift-giving. I believe that the observations made by Derrida and his colleagues are, in point of fact, quite right: it is virtually impossible, within a purely natural framework, to offer a true gift, especially when we take our fallen condition into account. Most realistic political philosophers and ethicists—Aristotle, Augustine, Hobbes, Machiavelli, Adam Smith, John Rawls—take for granted the elements of self-interest that inevitably mark every type of human interaction at the natural level. A society, great or small, based on authentic gift-giving is correctly viewed as utopian.

But what makes all the difference is the peculiar Christian claim that the divine manner of being and action, which we have been exploring, can, through grace, become our manner of being and action. Those who are, naturally speaking, utterly incapable of escaping the economy of exchange, can become sons and daughters of the God whose very nature is disinterested love. And this brings us to a consideration of the divine missions and the indwelling of the one whose proper name is *donum* (gift).

Aquinas treats of the divine sendings in ST I, q. 43. To be sure, all three persons of the Trinity are in any and all creatures through "essence, presence, and power,"[39] in the measure that God the creator sustains them in being. However, particular divine persons are said to be sent inasmuch as they commence to exist in rational creatures in a new way, dwelling in them "as in his own Temple."[40] Specifically, the Son is "sent" in the sense that he becomes the object of a rational creature's intellect and the Spirit in the sense that he becomes the object of that creature's will.[41] Possessed by the Holy Spirit, the human will becomes radically ordered to the love that the Spirit is, or to state the same thing in other words, it receives the theological virtue of charity. In ST I-II, q. 62, a. 3, we find this extraordinary description of this greatest of the theological virtues: "A certain spiritual union whereby the will is, so to speak, transformed into that end"—that is to say, into the Holy Spirit himself.[42] Throughout his

---

39. *Summa theologiae,* I, q. 8, a. 3.
40. *Summa theologiae,* I, q. 43, a. 3, *respondeo.*
41. *Summa theologiae,* I, q. 43, aa. 5, 7.
42. *Summa theologiae,* I-II, q. 63, a. 3.

treatment of the divine missions and the theological virtues, Thomas occasionally references the text of 2 Peter, according to which we become "participants of the divine nature" (2 Pt 1:4).[43] This discussion segues neatly into the description of charity in the *Secunda Secundae* as a type of friendship with God. Following Aristotle's famous description, Aquinas argues that friendship is indeed a relationship in which each partner wills the good of the other, distinguishing it from relationships of utility.[44] But the Angelic Doctor moves beyond Aristotle and says that real mutuality and communication must obtain in an authentic friendship: *Talis autem mutua benevolentia fundatur super aliqua communicatione* ("For such well-wishing is founded on some kind of communication").[45] This ecstatic communication occurs when God wills our happiness, and we will the glory of God, which redounds, in turn, to our greater happiness. Possessed by the Holy Spirit, we can love with the very love with which God loves; therefore, we can give gifts as generously as God does. How do we resolve the *aporia* of the gift? We can do so only through recourse to God and those whom God deigns to make saints.

So there we have the abstract description of the central dynamic, but what does this transformed life look like? How does the solution to the *aporia* of the gift show up in the world? Here we have to turn to the moral teaching of Jesus, which can indeed be construed as a series of commands, but commands given, not to the natural person, but to the one who has been supernaturalized, the one to whom Jesus can reasonably say, "Be perfect, just as your heavenly Father is perfect" (Mt 5:48). The new life that Jesus urges—indeed that he makes possible—is one of absolutely radical gift-giving. "You have heard that it was said, 'You shall love your neighbor and hate your enemy.' But I say to you, love your enemies and pray for those who persecute you" (Mt 5:43–44). In the ordinary dispensation, one loves those to whom he is already connected and therefore from whom he can expect some sort of compensation, emotional or otherwise; but in the new dispensation, love must be given precisely to those who

---

43. *Summa theologiae,* I, q. 13, a. 9, obj. 1; *Summa theologiae,* I-II, q. 62, a. 1, *respondeo* (sc).

44. *Summa theologiae,* II-II, q. 23, a. 1.

45. *Summa theologiae,* II-II, q. 23, a. 1, *respondeo*.

will not return the favor. Jesus makes the principle eminently clear: "For if you love those who love you, what recompense do you have?" (Mt 5:46a).

In Jesus' Sermon on the Plain recounted in the Gospel of Luke, we find something similar: "For if you love those who love you, what credit is that to you? … If you do good to those who do good to you, what credit is that to you? Even sinners do the same. If you lend to those from whom you expect repayment, what credit is that to you? Even sinners lend to sinners, and get back the same amount. But rather, love your enemies and do good to them, and lend expecting nothing back" (Lk 6:32–35a). In doing so, you will indeed be like your heavenly Father, "who makes his sun rise on the bad and the good" (Mt 5:45). And to give just one more example of the principle, we have this from the fourteenth chapter of Luke: "Then he said to the host who had invited him, 'When you give a lunch or a dinner, do not invite your friends or your brothers or your relatives or your wealthy neighbors, in case they may invite you back and you have repayment. But when you hold a banquet, invite the poor, the crippled, the lame, the blind; blessed indeed will you be because of their inability to repay you" (Lk 14:12–14a). This is the undoing of the *hostis* / hospitality problem raised by Benveniste[46] and the dissolving of the *Gift* / gift dilemma presented by Derrida.[47] What cuts the Gordian knot is nothing other than the grace—the gift-giving capacity—of the one who cannot even in principle be repaid.

Conclusion

In a way, the dilemma of the gift is a particularly eloquent way of expressing the spiritual struggle at the heart of every person in our finite, fallen, and conflictual world. On the one hand, we want to give, for giving is the nature of God, and, consciously or not, we are all striving for union with God. But on the other hand, we cannot give, for we are, as Derrida and company have correctly intuited,

---

46. Émile Benveniste, *Dictionary of Indo-European Concepts and Society*, trans. Elizabeth Palmer (Chicago: Hau Books, 2016), 46–47, 61, 66–67, 70–71.

47. Jacques Derrida, *Dissemination*, trans. Barbara Johnson (London/New York: Continuum, 1981), 180.

caught in the grip of the economic exchange. What becomes clear is that the *aporia* of the gift is not merely an intellectual conundrum, but a spiritual predicament.

Aquinas's technical descriptions of God, creation, and the indwelling of the Holy Spirit clarify the mind to be sure; but they also, and more importantly, liberate the captive soul. What the postmodern thinkers considered an obstacle to religious belief in point of fact functions as a particularly radiant light to illuminate the Christian mystery.

CHAPTER 8

JOHN HENRY NEWMAN AND THE NEW EVANGELIZATION

I am particularly delighted, as the entire Church celebrates the recent canonization of John Henry Newman, to write about what is arguably the central theme of his writing and pastoral work— namely, the psychological, intellectual, and spiritual dynamics of assenting to the proposals of the Christian faith. Though he was, doubtless, one of the most intelligent men of the nineteenth century, Newman was not a 'pure' intellectual—that is to say, someone primarily interested in ideas for their own sake. Indeed, he frequently denied that he was a theologian, and this was not false modesty.[1] He was, rather, a controversialist, an apologist, preoccupied with the role that ideas play in the process of conversion. Given this practical commitment, he was deeply interested in knowing what moves a person to say, in regard to a religious proposition, "I accept that. I assent to it."[2]

---

1. John Henry Newman, "Letter to W. G. Ward (February 18, 1866)," in *The Letters and Diaries of John Henry Newman*, vol. 22, ed. Charles Stephen Dessain (London: Thomas Nelson and Sons Ltd., 1972), 157; John Henry Newman, "Letter to Miss M. R. Giberne (February 10, 1869)," in *The Letters and Diaries of John Henry Newman*, vol. 24, ed. Charles Stephen Dessain and Thomas Gornall (Oxford: Clarendon Press, 1973), 212–213; John Henry Newman, "Letter to Sir John Simeon (March 24, 1870)," in *The Letters and Diaries of John Henry Newman*, vol. 25, ed. Charles Stephen Dessain and Thomas Gornall (Oxford: Clarendon Press, 1973), 66.

2. John Henry Newman, *Apologia Pro Vita Sua*, ed. Martin Svaglic (Oxford: Clarendon Press, 1967), 4.

And this makes him, I would contend, massively relevant to the pastoral concerns of the present day. For the past twenty years or so, I have been pointing out that the number of the 'nones' or the religiously unaffiliated has been climbing precipitously. Throughout the Western countries, once solidly Christian, religion in general and Christianity in particular are in sharp decline. One might argue that what Newman saw commencing in the nineteenth century has come now, sadly, to fruition. And so, as Vatican II implied and as the last four Popes have explicitly urged, a new evangelization of formerly Christian lands is urgently needed.

Therefore, a rediscovery of what Newman recommended one hundred and fifty years ago might prove helpful in the concrete work of teaching, preaching, and evangelizing today. I should like to be clear about something at the outset: I do not think that Newman's apologetics (or what we might call today his 'fundamental theology') is uniquely important or exclusive of other approaches. As we shall see, he proposed what would strike most people today as a rather dark apologetic, grounded in a keen sense of our sin and helplessness. Might other avenues, both classical and contemporary, be useful? Well, of course. However, I do believe that Newman's apologetic path—intelligent, spiritually honest, psychologically astute, and biblically grounded—will prove efficacious in our work of evangelizing the unaffiliated.

Real and Notional Assent

For our purposes, I am going to concentrate on Newman's late-career masterpiece, *The Grammar of Assent*. Much supplementary material can be found, of course, in the marvelous *University Sermons* and in any number of Newman's other works, but the most thorough statement of his position on evangelization and the assent to religious propositions is in *The Grammar*. I would like, first, to make a general observation about this book. A wonderfully dense and seminal text, *The Grammar of Assent* has been examined from myriad points of view, and commentators have, quite rightly, seen links between Newman's arguments and American pragmatism, Husserlian phenomenology, and postmodernism. It has been correctly interpreted as a pivotal text in the history of religious epistemology. However, what almost every commentator has tended to overlook are the roughly seventy-five pages at the very end of the text, which provide, in fact, the hermeneutical key to the entire book. Analysts have focused almost exclusively on the great sections dealing with notional and real assent, the difference between formal and informal inference, and the nature of the illative sense, but they have neglected to notice how all of that is but a propaedeutic to what Newman is attempting in those final pages—namely, a vigorous apologetic for the Catholic faith. The lengthy and sometimes frankly tortuous journey through the first three quarters of the *Grammar* is intended to make us more effective evangelizers.

To make this clear, I would like to focus first on the famous distinction that Newman draws between real and notional assent. He states the point of demarcation bluntly enough: "In its notional assents...the mind contemplates its own creations instead of things; in real, it is directed towards things, represented by the impressions which they have left on the imagination."[3] Though Newman harbors no hostility toward notions or pure ideas, he realizes that they are contrivances of the mind, artificial constructs designed to help us understand universal qualities of being, and hence they tend, he thinks, to put us at a certain remove from concrete things. As others have pointed out, we see here how firmly Newman stands in the empirical tradition associated with Hume and Locke and stretching back to Duns Scotus and his insistence that real cognition terminates, not in abstractions, but in the form of particularity, *haecceitas* ("thisness").[4] But Newman's principal point in making this distinction is to stress that real assent has greater power than notional assent to move persons to action and engagement.

He provides the helpful example of opposition to slavery. While at the notional level many had long held slavery to be a moral offense, it required "organized agitation, with tracts and speeches innumerable, so to affect the imagination of men as to make their

---

3. John Henry Newman, *An Essay in Aid of a Grammar of Assent*, ed. I. T. Ker (Oxford: Clarendon Press, 1985), 55.

4. Duns Scotus, "Six Questions on Individuation from His *Ordinatio* II. d. 3, part 1, qq. 1–6," in *Five Texts on the Mediaeval Problem of Universals*, trans. and ed. Paul V. Spade (Indianapolis: Hackett Publishing Company, Inc., 1994), d. 3, p. 1, q. 2, n. 52 (pg. 69); II, d. 3, p. 1, q. 1, n. 34 (pp. 64–65); II, d. 3, p. 1, q. 1, n. 8 (pg. 59).

acknowledgement of that iniquitousness operative."[5] Many have
remarked something strikingly similar in the American context.
Though many in the United States in the mid-nineteenth century
would have held to the moral conviction that slavery is objection-
able, the novel *Uncle Tom's Cabin* was in fact what roused them to
indignation and action.[6] This Newmanian principle is illustrated by
a famous (although perhaps apocryphal) anecdote that President
Lincoln, upon receiving Harriett Beecher Stowe, the author of *Uncle
Tom's Cabin*, at the White House during the Civil War, reportedly
called her "the little woman who made the great war."[7] Here is Newman's own pithy account of this practical power of real assent: "…
the imagination has the means, which pure intellect has not, of stim-
ulating those powers of mind from which action proceeds,"[8] and "…
we shall not…be very wrong in pronouncing that acts of Notional
Assent and of inference do not affect our conduct, and acts of Belief,
that is, of Real Assent, do…affect it."[9]

In one of the most celebrated passages of *The Grammar of
Assent*, Newman makes the explicit connection between real assent
and religious conversion: "This is why science has so little of a religious tendency; deductions have no power of persuasion. The heart
is commonly reached, not through reason, but through the imagination, by means of direct impressions, by the testimony of facts and
events, by history, by description. Persons influence us, voices melt
us, looks subdue us, deeds inflame us. Many a man will live and die
upon a dogma; no man will be a martyr for a conclusion."[10] I do
realize how extreme, even frankly anti-intellectual, this can sound,
but recall that Newman says "the heart is commonly reached" in this
manner.[11] And as we will see anon, he firmly holds that inference

---

5. Newman, *Grammar of Assent*, 56.

6. Harriet Beecher Stowe, *Uncle Tom's Cabin* (Oxford: Oxford University Press,
1998).

7. Amanda Claybaugh, "Introduction," in Harriet Beecher Stowe, *Uncle Tom's
Cabin* (New York: Barnes and Noble Classics, 2003), xviii.

8. Newman, *Grammar of Assent*, 63.

9. *Grammar of Assent*, 64.

10. *Grammar of Assent*, 66.

11. *Grammar of Assent*, 65.

and notional assent do indeed typically play a role in moving the mind to assent. But still there is no question that, when we have quit the halls of academe and have moved into the arena of evangelical engagement, Newman favors the real over the notional.

Having made (and perhaps overdrawn) this famous distinction, Newman turns to an explicit consideration of the act of believing in God. In chapter five of the *Grammar*, he first lays out, with admirable precision, the predicates that are proper to the God of the Christian faith: "A God who is numerically One, who is Personal, the Author, Sustainer, and Finisher of all things, the life of Law and Order, the Moral Governor, One who is Supreme and Sole; like Himself, unlike all things besides Himself, which are but His creatures...the Truth itself, Wisdom, Love, Justice, Holiness; One who is All-powerful, All-knowing, Omnipresent, Incomprehensible."[12] These predications, he admits, are the objects of notional assent, since they are discovered through formal inference and can be laid out in a coherent theological program—for instance, in the first twelve questions of Aquinas's *Summa theologiae*. Newman, to be sure, is not denying that this sort of predication and the ratiocination that stands behind it are useful, but he does question whether they would ever move people to action, stirring their hearts to conversion. And given that immateriality is one of the predicates associated with God, he wonders whether there could ever be grounds for giving real assent to the proposition that God exists: "Can I enter with a personal knowledge into the circle of truths which make up that great thought?"[13]

Answering this question proves to be one of the principal pivots upon which *The Grammar of Assent* turns. Newman argues that there is a "real" path to God and that it comes through the deep sense of moral obligation grounded in the conscience.[14] Because he will place so much weight on this idea, Newman spends a good deal of time clarifying precisely what he means when he refers to this phenomenon. He recognizes, in the first place, that amid the many other acts that make up our sensual and interior lives (e.g., memory, reasoning, imagination, a sense of the beautiful), there is also a faculty by which,

12. *Grammar of Assent*, 70–71.

13. *Grammar of Assent*, 71.

14. *Grammar of Assent*, 72–76.

upon the performance of properly moral acts, we feel approbation
or blame, a specific type of pleasure or pain with its own distinctive
texture. This faculty is the conscience.[15] Its nature, Newman says, is
twofold, including a moral sense and a sense of duty—that is to say,
"a judgment of the reason and a magisterial dictate."[16] In a word,
conscience both judges whether acts are right or wrong and rewards
or punishes the moral actor accordingly.

What makes this moral intuition different from, say, an aesthetic sensibility? Newman says that a perception of beauty or ugli-
ness bears no relation to a person external to the perceiver, but only
to the objects under consideration. Relying on his taste, the aesthete
declares something beautiful or not, but he feels no approbation or
shame for having made such a declaration. But with conscience it is
otherwise.[17] The moral actor does not simply assess right and wrong
behaviors objectively and dispassionately; rather, guided by conscience, he "reaches forward to something beyond self, and dimly
discerns a sanction higher than self for his decisions."[18] And hence
we speak, as we never would in regard to our aesthetic sense, of
the "voice" of our conscience, indeed a voice "imperative and constraining, like no other dictate in the whole of experience," a voice
unquestionably not our own.[19]

May I observe that this Newmanian insistence, present in many
of his writings, gives the lie to anyone (whose number today is, sadly,
legion) who would simply equate conscience with subjective willful-
ness, with doing whatever one thinks is right. In point of fact, conscience links us to someone radically other than the self, someone
reigning sovereignly over the self. If a painter produced an aestheti-
cally defective work of art, he might be mortified, but he would not
feel guilty. He might sense that he has violated some principle of
good art, but he would not feel ashamed, as though he had let someone down. But this is precisely how one feels upon performing an
immoral act. And therefore, "If, as is the case, we feel responsibility,

15. *Grammar of Assent*, 72.

16. *Grammar of Assent*, 73.

17. *Grammar of Assent*, 75, 252.

18. *Grammar of Assent*, 74.

19. *Grammar of Assent*, 75.

are ashamed, are frightened, at transgressing the voice of conscience, this implies that there is One to whom we are responsible, before whom we are ashamed, whose claims upon us we fear."[20] In still another justly celebrated passage of the *Grammar*, Newman poetically describes the feeling-tone of the conscience, emphasizing its inescapably interpersonal implication: "If, on doing wrong, we feel the same tearful, broken-hearted sorrow which overwhelms us on hurting a mother; if, on doing right, we enjoy the same sunny serenity of mind, the same soothing, satisfactory delight which follows on our receiving praise from a father, we certainly have within us the image of some person, to whom our love and veneration look..."[21] This visceral sense, this intense and deeply personal contact with a transcendent Other, is the ground for real assent in matters of religion, and therefore, as we shall see, the optimal starting point for any effective apologetic.

But why should Newman be so confident that the person with whom the conscience puts us in contact is the God described by classical Christianity? We must recall, he says, that the Person so met is "a Supreme Governor," since he makes laws, "a Judge, holy, just, powerful," since he passes sentence, "all-seeing," since he looks into the private recesses of the heart.[22] In short, conscience puts us really and experientially in contact with God, thickly described; whereas the classical cosmological arguments, with which Newman seems to have very little patience, only relate us notionally to the very thin abstraction of a prime cause.

Assent in Relation to Formal and Informal Inference

Having explored, however briefly, Newman's seminal distinction between real and notional assent, let us turn now to a consideration of his treatment of formal and informal inference. At the heart of this densely epistemological section of the *Grammar* is a disagreement with John Locke. Mind you, Newman demonstrated, throughout his career, a profound respect for Locke, often invoking him as a model

---

20. *Grammar of Assent*, 76.

21. Ibid.

22. Ibid.

of philosophizing, and certainly, as we saw, Locke's more empirical turn of mind was amenable to Newman's. But in many ways, the pivot on which the entire *Grammar of Assent* turns is Newman's dissociation of what Locke took to be properly associated—namely, assent and inference. For the great English empiricist, the quality of assent ought to be correlated tightly to the quality of inferential support that can be mustered for it. Thus, "it is not only illogical, but immoral, to 'carry our *assent above* the *evidence* that a proposition is true,' to have 'a surplusage of *assurance beyond* the degrees of that evidence.'"[23]

Newman takes this apparently commonsensical analysis as a sign of angelism on Locke's part, in the measure that it is predicated on the assumption that we reason and draw conclusions in a manner other than we actually do. Perhaps in a higher world, Locke's strict linkage between inference and assent might obtain, but here below, Newman argues, we frequently, indeed typically, give unconditioned assent to propositions for which there is far less than unconditioned inferential support.[24] He endeavors to show this through appeal to a wide range of cognitive acts. For example, the "furniture of the mind,"[25] which is to say, that whole range of basic assumptions about the nature of physical reality, is blithely and implicitly assented to, though we hardly ever aver to the reasons for this acquiescence. Also, sometimes we cease to assent to a claim, though the inferential ground for it remains fundamentally unchallenged and intact. This could be due to prejudice, the shock of the new, external pressure, or new experiences. Still other times we come, for a variety of reasons, to accept a truth claim that we had previously rejected, though no one has proffered anything like a compelling argument for it. The upshot is that inference and assent, though always to a degree tethered to one another, are by no means identical. The principal difference between them (and this is the insight that came to Newman in 1866, prompting the undertaking of *The Grammar of Assent*) is that inference is always conditional, but assent is unconditional.[26] Hence, "Locke's theory of the duty of assenting more or less according to

---

23. *Grammar of Assent*, 108.

24. *Grammar of Assent*, 120.

25. *Grammar of Assent*, 110.

26. *Grammar of Assent*, 114.

degrees of evidence is invalidated by the testimony of high and low, young and old, ancient and modern, as continually given in their ordinary sayings and doings."[27]

Once again, I realize that some of Newman's rhetoric can give the impression that he is indifferent to inference or even more than slightly anti-intellectual. Nothing, of course, could be further from the truth. Newman reverences inferential ratiocination, but he's convinced that it is inadequate in itself (though usually necessary) to bring the mind to assent. And the reason for this is that formal inference, expressible in terms of the classical Aristotelian syllogism, never reaches fully to particulars. Consider, Newman suggests, the following syllogism: All men have their price; Fabricius is a man; therefore, Fabricius has his price.[28] It is certainly in valid logical form, but does it deliver the truth? Only, Newman says, to the degree that the abstraction "man" adequately describes the utterly unique individual Fabricius.[29] Perhaps Fabricius is the only man who doesn't have a price. One might recall here the delicious scene from *A Man for All Seasons* in which the corrupt Cromwell insinuates to Norfolk that Thomas More, when he was chancellor, took bribes. The Duke explodes: "Dammit, he's the only judge since Cato who *didn't* take bribes." Here is Newman's gorgeously crafted summary of the limits of syllogistic reasoning: "Thus it is that the logician…turns rivers, full, winding, and beautiful into navigable canals."[30] Abstractions are always deeply attractive to the inquiring intellect, but they carry with them the deep shadow of never being able to reach to the messy but eloquent particularity of things: "Words, which denote things, have innumerable implications; but in inferential exercises, it is the very triumph of that clearness and hardness of head, which is the characteristic talent for the art, to have stripped them of all these connatural senses, to have drained them of that depth and breadth of associations which constitute their poetry, their rhetoric, and their historical life…"[31]

---

27. *Grammar of Assent*, 116.

28. *Grammar of Assent*, 181.

29. *Grammar of Assent*, 182.

30. *Grammar of Assent*, 174.

31. Ibid.

Precisely because they commence with abstractions, syllogisms end with abstractions, and this means that they indeed indicate the direction in which the truth lies, but they can never, by themselves, deliver the truth in its fullness. "They may approximate to a proof, but they only reach the probable, because they cannot reach to the particular."[32] Using language that his Oxford predecessor Duns Scotus would have heartily approved, Newman says, "Let units come first and (so-called) universals second; let universals minister to units, not units be sacrificed to universals."[33] And therefore, in summary, Newman can say of the syllogism, "Its chain of conclusions hangs loose at both ends…it comes short both of first principles and of concrete issues."[34]

Now we would be derelict indeed if we drew from these considerations the conclusion that the epistemic project is doomed to failure or at least to frustration. For Newman feels that formal inference—which, again, is indispensable in moving the mind toward assent—is supplemented by what he calls "informal inference."[35] Naming and defending the legitimacy of this mode of inferential argument is, perhaps, the gravamen of the entire argument of the *Grammar*. What does Newman mean by informal inference? He provides a sinuously beautiful description at the very commencement of his consideration: "It is the cumulation of probabilities, independent of each other, arising out of the nature and circumstances of the particular case which is under review; probabilities too fine to avail separately, too subtle and circuitous to be convertible into syllogisms, too numerous and various for such conversion, even were they convertible."[36] Newman demonstrates here, as he often does, his indebtedness to Bishop Butler, who argued for the crucial role played by probability in the determination of truth and action;[37] he also shows

---

32. *Grammar of Assent*, 181.

33. *Grammar of Assent*, 182.

34. *Grammar of Assent*, 185.

35. *Grammar of Assent*, 187–213.

36. *Grammar of Assent*, 187.

37. Jane Garnett, "Joseph Butler," in *Oxford Handbook of John Henry Newman*, ed. Frederick D. Aquino and Benjamin J. King, 135–153 (Oxford: Oxford University Press, 2018).

an affinity to the American pragmatists Charles Sanders Peirce and, to a lesser degree, William James, both younger contemporaries. All of these thinkers would concur that we rarely if ever settle a matter on the basis of clinching and utterly convincing formal argumentation. Much more commonly, we come to our real beliefs through the process—grounded in and guided by informal inference—of assessing probable arguments, hunches, and experiences that point in the same direction. And often, even typically, this undertaking is as much unconscious as conscious: "so is the mind unequal to a complete analysis of the motives which carry it on to a particular conclusion."[38] In accord with this insight, Newman recommended to judges and administrators that they should make their judgments firmly and announce them confidently but should refrain from giving the reasons that led them to these determinations, for their ability to articulate the grounds for a decision will always be limited.[39]

The famous example of this implicit and informal intellection that Newman provides is coming to the absolutely certain conviction that Great Britain is an island. Only insane people would seriously doubt it; mentally sound people universally and unhesitatingly assent to the truth of the proposition; and yet, *pace* Locke, nothing like airtight inferential support for the claim is available.[40] There is no Aristotelian syllogism that could ever render the indubitable conclusion that Great Britain is surrounded on all sides by water, and yet, assent to the claim is absolute. In point of fact, this intellectual acquiescence is produced by a complex process of informal inference: "We have been so taught in our childhood, and it is so on all the maps; next, we have never heard it contradicted or questioned; on the contrary, every one whom we have heard speak on the subject of Great Britain, every book we have read, invariably took it for granted; our whole national history, the routine transactions and current events of the country, our social and commercial system…imply it one way or another…"[41] Mind you, none of this would rise to the level of requisite Lockean inferential support; and yet it gives rise

---

38. *Grammar of Assent*, 190.

39. *Grammar of Assent*, 212.

40. *Grammar of Assent*, 191–192.

41. *Grammar of Assent*, 191.

to unconditioned assent. In line with many of his nineteenth-century intellectual colleagues, Newman does not hesitate to say that the same indirect and informal process obtains even in the so-called hard sciences: "Here, as in Astronomy, is the same absence of demonstration of the thesis, the same cumulating and converging indications of it, the same indirectness of proof."[42] This example was taken from the research, fascinating to many scientists in the nineteenth century, that the position of stars and other heavenly bodies could be determined only imperfectly, through assessment of statistical probabilities. And the principle of epistemic indeterminacy has only been further confirmed in our time in the context of quantum mechanics.

Having laid out the difference between formal and informal inference, Newman wonders whether there is a faculty or sense by which the various arguments, both formal and informal, are assessed and that, therefore, produces the psychological state of certainty.[43] He determines that there is, and he characterizes it as follows: "This power of judging and concluding, in its perfection, I call the Illative Sense."[44] To shed light on its nature and function, Newman makes a comparison to the moral sensibility that Aristotle termed *phronesis* or right judgment, often rendered, in the Latin context, as the moral virtue of prudence.[45] One might know the relevant principles that govern a moral action, but if that person lacks prudence or sound judgment, he will not know how to apply them to the particular situation.[46] And, as Aquinas consistently indicates, prudence is a type of knowledge born of experience rather than through purely rational moves.[47] Newman also makes a comparison with our artistic sense. Again, one might grasp the great principles and rules that govern the art of painting, but unless he has some innate and developed aesthetic know-how, he will not be able to judge the quality of particular

42. *Grammar of Assent*, 207.

43. *Grammar of Assent*, 222–223.

44. *Grammar of Assent*, 228.

45. Ibid.

46. *Grammar of Assent*, 228–229.

47. St. Thomas Aquinas, *Summa theologiae Secunda Secundae 1-91*, trans. Fr. Laurence Shapcote (Lander, WY: The Aquinas Institute for the Study of Sacred Doctrine, 2012), II-II, qq. 47–51.

paintings. So why, Newman wonders, should "ratiocination be an exception to a general law which attaches to the intellectual exercises of the mind?"[48] The epistemic correlate of *phronesis* in the moral order and the artistic intuition in the aesthetic order, the illative sense is the faculty that carries (*ferre, latus*) the mind from the deliverances of formal and informal inference to actual assent.[49]

Application to Apologetics and Evangelization

Once again, one might be forgiven for overlooking the final section of Newman's masterpiece, since what has gone before is so densely textured and so filled with rich insight. But just as the most important figure in a liturgical procession comes last, so the most significant part of this book comes at the end. Everything that Newman has said about real and notional assent, formal and informal inference, and the illative sense is meant, finally, to shed light on the project of making an apologetic for the Catholic faith.

Relying on the classically Catholic idea that grace supposes and perfects nature, Newman turns, first, to a consideration of what he terms 'natural religion.' His strategy is fundamentally Pauline, in the measure that he imitates the Apostle's *apologia* on the Areopagus in Athens: "the Unknown God...[whom] you unknowingly worship, I proclaim to you" (Acts 17:23). By 'natural religion' he means the form of religiosity that follows from the vivid experience of God given in conscience and hence present, at least in principle, universally.[50] Though some knowledge of God can indeed be given through history and nature, Newman holds that the surest and most complete sense of the divine, and one likely to lead to action, is delivered to us, as we saw, through the conscience.[51]

Though it suggests a number of things regarding the nature of God, conscience primarily presents God under his attribute of just judge. And though it certainly runs counter to most approaches used today, Newman insists, "we learn from its Information to conceive of

48. *Grammar of Assent*, 231.

49. *Grammar of Assent*, 232–234.

50. *Grammar of Assent*, 251.

51. Ibid.

the Almighty, primarily, not as a God of Wisdom, of Knowledge, of Power, of Benevolence, but as a God of Judgment and Justice."[52] And we must face the rather awful fact that, since most of our actions are wicked rather than virtuous, "it follows that the aspect under which Almighty God is presented to us by Nature is One who is angry with us and threatens evil."[53] In a word, conscience reveals to us the exceptionally good news that God exists and at the same time the rather exceptionally bad news that God is not happy with us. In one of the more memorable lines from the *Grammar*, Newman observes that, in its natural form, religion "has almost invariably worn its dark side outwards."[54] An obvious implication of the conviction of alienation from God—and this can be seen in almost all religions worldwide—is the institution of the priesthood and the practice of sacrifice. Nearly all religions involve acts of propitiation offered to an offended divinity or divinities and therefore give rise to a caste of sacred persons whose primary obligation is to preside over these acts. In its more refined expressions, natural religion tends to gravitate toward the idea of atonement or ritual satisfaction.

What does the experience of God given in conscience tell us about the Creator's relationship to nature? Whereas the overwhelming majority of Christian apologists across the centuries use some form of the cosmological argument to indicate God's necessary connection to the natural world, Newman does no such thing. He takes the existence of God as a given, but what he notices is not so much God's presence in the movements and dynamics of nature, but rather his distance: "what strikes the mind so forcibly and so painfully is his absence (if I may so speak) from his own world."[55] Though probably counterintuitive to many apologists, I wonder whether this approach might actually find a good deal of traction today, for what impresses many young people is how distant God seems from the affairs of the world. That they complain of this, or at least feel the pain of it, is a sign that they don't exactly disbelieve in God; rather, they are keenly aware that God ought to be present but is not. Perhaps the task of

---

52. *Grammar of Assent*, 252.

53. Ibid.

54. *Grammar of Assent*, 252–253.

55. *Grammar of Assent*, 255–256.

the apologist today is to show that this is not so much God's doing as ours, or in other words, to show that the explanation of the absence of God is not so much scientific or metaphysical but rather moral. Here is how Newman puts it, succinctly, even a tad waspishly: "I see only a choice of alternatives in explanation of so critical a fact: either there is no Creator or He has disowned his creatures."[56] Conscience infallibly dictates which of the two is correct. Another universal feature of natural religion, Newman holds, is prayer.[57] Whether it is the dancing of the priests of Ba'al or the whirling of Dervishes, prayer expresses the human longing that the alienation with God might be overcome. And immediately consequent upon prayer is the expectation of a response from God, some revelation of the divine will and healing purpose: "Accordingly, it is another alleviation of the darkness and distress which weigh upon the religions of the world, that in one way or other such religions are founded on some idea of express revelation, coming from the unseen agents whose anger they deprecate."[58] So, in sum, the 'natural' religious person knows that God exists, that she is alienated from God, that she longs for reunion, but that she is incapable of affecting that reconciliation on her own.

Having clarified these basics, born of real assent, Newman lays his apologetic cards on the table. He is extremely wary of the apologist who would seek to provide a 'scientific' and objective argument, designed to be convincing to any prospective conversation partner.[59] Rather, he would prefer to follow informal inference and the illative sense: "For me, it is more congenial to my own judgment to attempt to prove Christianity in the same informal way in which I can prove for certain that I have been born into this world and will die out of it"—namely, through the accumulation of probabilities.[60] And so, he commences with those already imbued with a keen sense of natural religion, those who have ears to hear. To those insufficiently attentive to the instincts of natural religiosity, Newman really has nothing to say. What he shall attempt is

---

56. *Grammar of Assent*, 256.
57. *Grammar of Assent*, 260.
58. Ibid.
59. *Grammar of Assent*, 264.
60. *Grammar of Assent*, 264.

a pulling together of a variety of strands, proceeding from conscience and tending in the direction of Christianity.

His initial move is a negative one—namely, to state that any religion that is predicated upon obvious immorality and hence repugnant to conscience is, ipso facto, not a true religion.[61] Therefore, for instance, the mythological religions of ancient Greece and Rome, which lionized divinities who were engaged in patently immoral behavior, are certainly not authentic. In the manner of Augustine, Newman does not hesitate to affirm: "Jupiter and Neptune, as represented in classical mythology, are evil spirits and nothing can make them otherwise."[62] More positively, a religion that inculcates in its adepts the expectation of a saving revelation is likely to be true. Newman thinks that the ready conversion of Dionysius and Damaris on the Areopagus is an example of this principle in action. Though Paul gave very little of substance in his famous sermon reported in Acts 17, and though he performed no miracle, these two Greeks converted, precisely because Paul spoke of a revelation given in answer to their expectation.[63] In this context, Newman once again engages in polemics against Paley, and indeed against anyone who would attempt a detached, rationalistic form of apologetics: "I say plainly I do not want to be converted by a smart syllogism; if I am asked to convert others by it, I say plainly I do not care to overcome their reason without touching their hearts. I wish to deal, not with controversialists, but with inquirers."[64]

But can we make an even more specific case that Christianity is the one true religion? Newman says that it alone "has a definite message to all mankind."[65] Though one might quarrel with him on this score, he argues that Islam is tied inextricably to the culture that produced it and does not carry a properly *saving* message, and the various Eastern religions claim no definite communication from a personal God. "Christianity, on the other hand, is in its idea an announcement, a preaching; it is the depository of truths beyond

---

61. *Grammar of Assent*, 270.

62. Ibid.

63. *Grammar of Assent*, 272.

64. *Grammar of Assent*, 273.

65. *Grammar of Assent*, 277.

human discovery, momentous, practical, maintained one and the same in substance in every age from its first, and addressed to all mankind."[66] These observations put me in mind of N. T. Wright's assertion that Christianity is not trading in "timeless spiritual truths," but rather in the telling of a great story, the setting forth of a drama and our precise position within it, a drama, furthermore, in which every single person is meant to play a role.[67]

And this segues neatly into Newman's next section on the Mosaic anticipation of Christianity. There is, he asserts, no other people in the history of humanity who have more consistently and reliably conveyed the fundamental truths about God than the Jews.[68] What the Romans are to the law and the Greeks to abstract thought, the Jews are to correct religion. They taught not only monotheism and the doctrine of providence, but they cultivated that profound longing for deliverance and anticipation of revelation, which are central to a fully-evolved natural religion. And the biblical Jews specified this expectation further, holding that "a great Personage was to be born of their stock, and to conquer the whole world and to become the instrument of extraordinary blessings to it; moreover that he would make his appearance at a fixed date."[69] Though this sort of appeal to explicit prophecy was largely repudiated in the twentieth century, I believe it can and should be revived under a Wright-style rubric: ancient Israel did indeed anticipate a Messiah who would gather the tribes, cleanse the Temple in Jerusalem, deal with the enemies of the nation, and finally rule as Lord of the world.[70] All of this was taken for granted in the preaching of the first evangelists. Finally, from this lion of Judah there came forth a Church whose purpose indeed has been the domination of the world, spiritually speaking: "a Catholic Church, which aimed at the benefit of all nations by the spiritual conquest of all."[71] And this victory came not through military effort

---

66. Ibid.

67. N. T. Wright, *The New Testament and the People of God*, vol. 1 of *Christian Origins and the Question of God* (Minneapolis: Fortress Press, 1992), 40–41.

68. *Grammar of Assent*, 278–279.

69. *Grammar of Assent*, 284.

70. Wright, *The New Testament and the People of God*, 280, 300.

71. *Grammar of Assent*, 286.

or political manipulation but through the proclamation of the Word, something scarcely imaginable in purely human terms. That all of this congruence and logical sequence happened by sheer coincidence or historical accident strikes Newman as absurd.

What he has been doing throughout this closing section of the *Grammar* is exercising his illative sense, drawing together the various probable arguments, indications, hunches, and connections that all point in the direction of the truth of Christianity, and he has rested the entire exercise on the real assent to God's existence that flows from conscience and tends to give rise to action. In a word, he has finally been constructing the edifice of a convincing apologetic on the foundation that he had so painstakingly constructed in the first three hundred pages of the text. The entire *Grammar of Assent* closes with a magnificent evocation of the image of Christ. Whereas Caesar and Alexander the Great endure for the most part as names in books read by school children or specialist historians, Jesus is a vivid and powerful presence, lively in the imaginations of those who revere him. "Here is one then who is not a mere name, who is *not* a mere fiction, but a reality. He is dead and gone, but still he lives— lives as a living, energetic thought of successive generations, as the awful motive-power of a thousand great events."[72] Though notional assent is indeed given to creedal and theological claims about him, Jesus is the object of very real assent up and down the ages, awaking devotion and conducing to action.

Then, beautifully and aptly, Newman closes with the words of the Savior himself: "I am the Good Shepherd, and I know Mine and Mine know Me. My sheep hear my voice and I know them and they follow Me."[73] No bloodless abstractions or merely syllogistic demonstrations call forth faith, but rather a colorfully imagined Christ, fulfillment of the longing of Israel, personal revelation corresponding to the ache of the alienated soul, whose voice calls out to those who have ears to hear.

---

72. *Grammar of Assent*, 315.

73. *Grammar of Assent*, 316.

CHAPTER 9

GASTON FESSARD AND THE INTELLECTUAL FORMATION OF POPE FRANCIS

Those searching out the principal intellectual sources for Pope Francis's thinking and pastoral activity would probably look first to Romano Guardini, the theologian and philosopher around whom Jorge Mario Bergoglio's doctoral research centered. However, when Massimo Borghesi posed the question to Pope Francis himself, the answer came back unambiguously: "the [one] who had a big influence on me was Gaston Fessard. I've read *La Dialectique des 'Exercices Spirituels' de Saint Ignace de Loyola (Dialectic of the Spiritual Exercises of St. Ignatius of Loyola)*, and other things by him, several times. That work gave me so many elements that later became mixed in [to my thinking]."[1] That typically breezy statement indicates the fact that, though nothing approaching a systematic treatment of Fessard can be found in Francis's writings, nevertheless the Fessardian influence is everywhere in the Pope's manner of thought and speech.

Though crucial in the intellectual formation of Pope Francis, Gaston Fessard is not well known in the United States, even, I daresay, in academic circles. Many of his colleagues and intellectual peers are still widely-read: Henri de Lubac, Jean Daniélou, Teilhard de Chardin, Hans Urs von Balthasar, and Guardini, among others. But Fessard has

---

1. Massimo Borghesi, *The Mind of Pope Francis: Jorge Mario Bergoglio's Intellectual Journey* (Collegeville, MN: Liturgical Press, 2018), 6.

been largely forgotten. We might proffer a number of explanations for
this: the density of his style; his preoccupation with ideologies, namely
Nazism and communism, that are no longer at the forefront of our
concern; and his somewhat dated Hegelianism. But Pope Francis's
emergence provides a rich opportunity to rediscover and reappropri-
ate this exceptionally interesting and important figure. I will confess
that, despite my own theological formation in the Parisian context,
I knew next to nothing of Fessard when I was approached to prepare this paper. I have immensely enjoyed diving into his thought and
exploring the links between this great theoretician and Pope Francis.

A Biographical Sketch

Because Gaston Fessard is not a household name, I thought it would
be useful, as we get underway, to provide at least a sketch of his biography and principal themes. Fessard was born in 1897 and joined the
Society of Jesus at the tender age of sixteen in 1913. Like so many
of his generation, he was profoundly marked by the cataclysm of
the First World War, in which he actively participated as a soldier
between 1917 and 1918. He received a classical formation in philosophy, especially in the Thomistic mode, but as a young Jesuit, he
became interested in German idealism, especially Fichte and Schelling. While he was in Germany in 1926, he bought a copy of Hegel's
Phänomenologie des Geistes (*The Phenomenology of Spirit*) from a sidewalk
bouquinist, and it's fair to say that the encounter with the great German philosopher would decisively influence his life.[2]

During the 1930s, very much under the influence of Hegel's dialectical method, Fessard commenced his massive commentary on the
Spiritual Exercises of St. Ignatius.[3] This, his *chef d'oeuvre*, would appear
eventually in three volumes, the last of which was published posthu-
mously in 1984.[4] Between 1934 and 1938, Fessard participated in the

---

2. For example, see Gaston Fessard, *Hegel, le christianisme et l'histoire: textes et documents inédits présentés par Michel Sales* (Paris: Presses universitaires de France, 1990).

3. Borghesi, *The Mind of Pope Francis*, 25.

4. Fessard, *La dialectique des Exercices Spirituels de Saint Ignace de Loyola* (Paris: Édi-
tions Aubier-Montaigne, 1956); Vol. 2: *Fondement-Péché-Orthodoxie* (Paris: Éditions Aubier-
Montaigne, 1966). Vol 3: *Symbolisme et historicité*. Paris/Namur: Éditions Lethielleux
/Culture et Vérité, 1984.

famous seminars on Hegel offered by the Russian-born French phi-losopher Alexandre Kojève.[5] These lectures were followed by most of the leading French intellectuals of the mid-twentieth century, includ-ing Jacques Lacan, Georges Bataille, Jean-Paul Sartre, Maurice Mer-leau-Ponty, and Raymond Aron. At the end of the lecture series, Fessard, who had become a friend of Kojève, intervened to contest the master's atheistic interpretation of Hegel. So impressed was he by the younger man's intellectual acumen, Kojève commented that, if he so desired, Fessard could become the greatest Marx specialist writing in French.[6] Like Lacan, Fessard benefitted especially from Kojève's recuperation of Hegel's treatment of the master-slave dynamic.[7] The amplification of this idea, following a prompt from St. Paul in Galatians 3:28, would become eventually the central thematic template of Fessard's thought.[8]

In 1937, Fessard published a text entitled *La main tendue: Le dialogue catholique-communiste est-il possible?*, which proposed a strenuous argu-ment against those Catholics who were encouraging a rapprochement with communism.[9] I will return to this theme in some detail later in this paper, but suffice it to say for the moment that Fessard felt that communism amounted not simply to a social theory but to a rival and entirely secular religion. To balance his opposition to communism, Fessard turned in the late thirties and early forties to an equally vigor-ous attack on Nazism. In 1941, he published *France, prends garde de perdre ton âme*, and in 1945, he summed up his opposition to both forms of totalitarianism in *France, prends garde de perdre ta liberte*.[10] Throughout the fifties and turbulent sixties, Fessard continued to comment on Hegel, Marx, and Kierkegaard, and to engage the question of Catholic

---

5. Borghesi, *The Mind of Pope Francis*, 25.

6. Alexandre Kojève, "Communisme et christianisme," *Critique* 3–4 (1946): 308. As cited in Hugh Gillis, "Gaston Fessard and the Nature of Authority," *Interpretation* 16, no. 3 (1989): 447.

7. Borghesi, *The Mind of Pope Francis*, 25; Gaston Fessard, *De l'actualité historique*, vol. 1, *À la recherché d'une méthode* (Paris: Desclée de Brouwer, 1960), 53, 229–233.

8. Fessard, *De l'actualité historique*, vol. 1, 111–112, 231.

9. Fessard, *La main tendue? Le dialogue catholique-communiste est-il possible?* (Paris: Édi-tions Bernard Grasset, 1937).

10. Fessard, *France, prends garde de perdre ton âme*, Cahiers du témoignage chrétien 1 (St. Etienne: St. Etienne, 1941); Fessard, *France, prends garde de perdre ta liberté* (Paris: Éditions du Témoignage chrétien, 1946).

'progressivism,' which he took to be an updated but still dysfunctional attempt to reconcile Catholicism and Marxist social theory.

He undertook a major study of his friend and colleague Raymond Aron in the 1970s, but this book was published only after Fessard's death.[11] The last text that he prepared was *Eglise de France, prends garde de perdre la foi*, in which he once again discussed the issue of communism, proving that the engagement with this enormously influential philosophy was, along with the study of Hegel, the golden thread of his intellectual life.[12] Gaston Fessard died on Sunday morning June 18, 1978, while working at his desk at Ponte Vecchio in Corsica.

Philosophy of History

In order to grasp the thought of Fessard, we must explore the conceptual apparatus that he conceived early in his career and that he used, fairly consistently, throughout his writings on a variety of subjects. From Hegel's meditations on the relationship between pure spirit and absolute spirit, Fessard derived a fundamentally dialectical understanding of the movement of history. He furthermore took in Hegel's notion of the master/slave relationship as key to the process by which Spirit comes to self-possession; but, as I suggested above, he amplified this through the influence of St. Paul's great text from his letter to the Galatians: "There is neither Jew nor Greek, neither slave nor free, neither male nor female, for all are one in Christ Jesus" (Gal 3:28). Jesus breaks down the walls that separate these three elemental pairs, and hence he is the resolution of the principal dialectical tensions that govern history.

Therefore, along with the master/slave dialectic, there is the male/female tension and, most importantly, the play between Jew and Greek. And these three correspond to the basic dimensions of history—namely, the natural relationship in male and female, the human relationship of master and slave, and the supernatural relationship between Jew and pagan.[13] The last of the three controls and

---

11. Fessard, *La philosophie historique de Raymond Aron* (Paris: Julliard, 1980).

12. Fessard, *Eglise de France prends garde de perdre la foi!* (Paris: Éditions Julliard, 1979).

13. Fessard, *De l'actualité historique*, vol. 1, 45–49, 52, 95–119, 229–233, esp. 233.

orders the first two, so that everything depends upon the navigation of one's relationship to the supernatural.

At the physical, instinctive, and biological level, the dialectic between men and women holds sway. Following Hegelian prompts, Fessard appreciates that a man comes to self-possession precisely in relationship to a woman, and the inverse is true as well. And the mutual surrender and self-discovery of each finds concrete expression in the child that results from their union.[14] This dialectical play becomes dysfunctional when it devolves, as it frequently does, into forms of domination, violence, and subjugation. The relationship ought to tend in the direction of love and mutual self-gift, but this will happen only when it is placed consciously in relation to the call of God.

The second tension—the one massively studied by Hegel and so many of his disciples, especially Marx—is the master/slave rapport. Fessard learned the basic dynamics of this relationship from Kojève's lectures. In short, the master emerges through a willingness to risk his life and safety in the context of a dangerous world, and this act of courage enables him to subjugate others for his own purposes. Hence the slave emerges, accepting domination as a means of avoiding violent death.[15] However, the slave comes to self-possession through labor on behalf of the master, which gives him (the slave) a mastery over nature. And this in turn provides a sort of leverage vis-à-vis the one who dominates and brings about a reversal—the master coming to depend upon the achievement of the slave.[16] According to Hegel, much of human society and civilization is conditioned by this dialectical dynamic,[17] and it is not difficult to see the ample use that Marx would make of it in his analysis of the play between the proletariat and the bourgeoisie in a capitalist political economy.[18] Fessard borrowed from Hegel the idea that, ultimately, the master/slave relationship should evolve, by slow steps, to become the friendship of citizens within the State,[19] but once more, he appreciated that this evolution would be complete only

---

14. *De l'actualité historique*, vol. 1, 51, 163–174, 181, 183–184.

15. *De l'actualité historique*, vol. 1, 142–144.

16. *De l'actualité historique*, vol. 1, 145–146.

17. *De l'actualité historique*, vol. 1, 148–149.

18. *De l'actualité historique*, vol. 1, 130–138, 147, 149.

19. *De l'actualité historique*, vol. 1, 162.

when something like supernaturally-inspired love comes to obtain in place of domination and subjugation.[20]

The play between Jew and Greek is the dialectic that most fascinated Fessard and that he appreciated as most important in the work of discerning the movement of history.[21] In using this pair of terms, Fessard is speaking of the supernatural order, which is to say, the relationship to God, whether we understand that as pertaining to the individual or to the society.[22] Fessard held that this dialectic plays itself out in a fourfold way, corresponding to the attitudes of Jews and Greeks prior to Christ and after Christ. Before Jesus, the two options are the *Juif élu* (the elected Jew) and the *païen idolâtre* (the idolatrous pagan); after Jesus, the two options are the *Juif incrédule* (the unbelieving Jew) and the *païen converti* (the converted pagan).[23] To examine all of the permutations and combinations of these relationships would take us too far afield. So I will focus, as Fessard usually does, on the first pair.

The elected Jew is in right relation to the true God, but in a restricted and tribal manner; whereas the idolatrous pagan is in a positive relation to philosophy and beauty, but out of step with the true God. Christ, who is a Jew and a son of the Mosaic Law, as well as the Incarnation of the Logos, represents, accordingly, the overcoming of the split between Jew and Greek.[24] In him, as Paul points out in Romans 9–11, Israel finds the deepest meaning of its election, and Greeks find themselves properly and fully ordered to the Logos that they had always been seeking through their philosophy and mythology.[25] Ultimately, love is the resolution, for Christ, as Paul teaches, breaks down the wall of hatred that separates Jew from gentile (Eph 2:14).[26]

What remains key for Fessard—and here he differs from Hegel, who operates within a somewhat determinist framework—is that

---

20. *De l'actualité historique*, vol. 1, 173–175.

21. *De l'actualité historique*, vol. 1, 104–112, 217–221; Gaston Fessard, *De l'actualité historique*, vol. 2, *Progressisme chrétien et apostolat ouvrier* (Paris: Desclée de Brouwer, 1960), 49–71.

22. *De l'actualité historique*, vol. 1, 95–97.

23. *De l'actualité historique*, vol. 2, 55.

24. *De l'actualité historique*, vol. 1, 107.

25. *De l'actualité historique*, vol. 1, 104–106.

26. *De l'actualité historique*, vol. 1, 104–105.

the resolution of the various dialectical tensions always happens through freedom.[27] A person faces the option between truth and falsity, between being and nonbeing, ultimately between accepting or rejecting God's will, and upon the choice of the individual agents, everything depends. Here the influence of the Ignatian exercises, which we will examine in greater detail anon, is once again obvious.[28]

Critique of Totalitarianisms

As we saw, Fessard remained, throughout his writing career, preoccupied with the rival totalitarianisms that bedeviled the twentieth century—namely, National Socialism and communism.[29] He lived through a time when a considerable number of European Christians seemed to be making peace with Nazism, especially in the context of Vichy France. And from the thirties through the seventies, he wrestled with Catholics who felt that it was possible, even desirable, to make common cause with communism. Fessard saw both totalizing systems as pseudo-religions, borrowing many elements from Christianity but distorting them. His great 'no' to both the extreme right and the extreme left made him suspect to many in the French intellectual and religious establishment and, I would venture to say, helps to explain why he is not widely read today.

It is first important to point out that Fessard saw both totalitarianisms as a reaction to the excessive individualism promoted by Enlightenment rationalism.[30] The political movements that grew up out of the Enlightenment—in both Europe and America—were conditioned by an almost exclusive interest in the rights and privileges of the individual. Jefferson's rather vague appeal to the 'pursuit of happiness' on the part of each individual witnesses to the breakdown of any thick sense of the common good. The extremism of liberal democracy gave rise to an excessive reaction in the twentieth century in favor of the collective and the general—one putting a stress on race and the other on class.

---

27. *De l'actualité historique*, vol. 1, 42.

28. *De l'actualité historique*, vol. 1, 45.

29. *De l'actualité historique*, vol. 1, 125–149.

30. *De l'actualité historique*, vol. 1, 25, 81.

One is reminded of the speculation of Fessard's contemporary Paul Tillich, who spoke of the oscillation between individualization and participation that tends to mark every society. The Nazism against which Tillich fought so strenuously represented excessive "participation" (*ein Volk, ein Reich, ein Fuhrer,* one People, one Reich, one Leader), whereas the liberal democracies represented excessive "individualization."[31] Very much in the manner of Fessard, Tillich held that such a tension is resolvable, not through cultural or political evolution, but only through the grace of God, who stands beyond the one and the many.[32] One is put in mind as well of Hannah Arendt, who said that the "atomization" of society through modern liberalism excited a counterreaction in the direction of a mobilization of the masses through a common cause.[33] It seemed impossible to build a real society on the basis of such abstract ideas as liberty and equality and the universality of rights. Some sort of grounded solidarity was required, and the totalitarianisms provided it, however dysfunctionally. The problem was that they did so through a form of idolatry—that is to say, a substitute religion or a "political religion" in Raymond Aron's language.[34] And this is precisely why both Nazism and communism stood so resolutely against Christianity, unlike the liberal democracies that at least tolerated it.

The basic form of their idolatry, Fessard argued, was the placing of man and his temporal good as the supreme value. In communism, this meant the triumph of the proletariat; in the case of

---

31. Paul Tillich, *Against the Third Reich: Paul Tillich's Wartime Radio Broadcasts into Nazi Germany*, trans. Matthew Lon Weaver (Louisville, KY: Westminster John Knox Press, 1998); Paul Tillich, *Systematic Theology*, vol. 1 (Chicago: Chicago University Press, 1951), 174–178.

32. Paul Tillich, *Systematic Theology*, vol. 3 (Chicago: The University of Chicago Press, 1963), 420–422.

33. Hannah Arendt, *The Origins of Totalitarianism* (New York: Schocken Books, 1996), 341–384.

34. Raymond Aron, "Bureaucratie et fantisme," *La France Libre* III, no. 13 (1941): 49–59. Cited in Dietmar Herz, "The Concept of 'Political Religion' in the Thought of Eric Voegelin," in *Totalitarianism and Political Religions*, vol. 3, *Concepts for the Comparison of Dictatorships—Theory & History of Interpretation*s, ed. Hans Meier, trans. Jodi Bruhn, 158–175 (London: Routledge, 2008), 159n32.

Nazism, it meant the dominance of the master race. In his more specific criticisms, Fessard took advantage of his tripartite hermeneutic. Most famously, he analyzed both Nazism and communism in terms of the master/slave dynamic. Within capitalism, the proletariat plays the role of the slave, but in the great reversal of the revolution, the proletariat overthrows the capitalist and establishes not a new master/slave relationship but rather the end of private property and the oppressive system that protects it. Hence, the "classless" society proposed by Marx is, Fessard concluded, the universalization of the attitude of the slave. By the same token, Nazism employs the master race of Aryans to eliminate the subordinate slave races and hence to establish a raceless society, or if you will, a society made up entirely of masters. In point of fact, these immanentist and idolatrous systems can never resolve the tension between master and slave, except through the greatest and most brutal violence—as became startlingly clear in the twentieth century. It is, as St. Paul saw so clearly, only in Christ that the tension between master and slave is resolved, only through a breaking down of the wall of hatred (Gal 3:28; Col 3:11).

We find a similar one-sidedness in regard to the male/female dichotomy. Fessard's analysis depends upon an analogy he makes between masculinity and the State, and femininity and the society. In Nazism, the State is absolutized to such a degree that the mediating institutions of the society are effectively abolished. In communism, which involves the complete withering away of the State, the society—the arena of family, work, and community—is hyper-emphasized. Hence the former is all male and the latter all female. Here is Fessard's summary: "On one side, the Master Race reveals itself through its interdiction of all sexual commerce with the slave nations, as a man without a woman; on the other side, the classless society is as a woman without a man, due to its exclusion of the power of the State."[35] Once more, it is only in the mutual surrender to the will and purposes of God that men and women—as well as the masculine and feminine dimensions of public life—find their equilibrium.

Finally, Fessard analyzes the two totalitarianisms under the rubric of Jew and Greek. Both Nazism and communism represent

---

35. *De l'actualité historique*, vol. 1, 82 and surrounding pages.

a secularized and hence idolatrous messianism. On the one hand, Nazism corresponds to paganism in its desire to conquer the world through reliance upon its own powers, much in the manner of the Roman Empire. It is a messianism of the master race. Communism, on the other hand, corresponds to Judaism in its stress upon the categories of fall, redemption, and messianic intervention, but the messianism in this case is one of class, the proletariat taking the role of the suffering servant. In point of fact, communism and Nazism combine the negative poles of the Jew/Pagan split—namely, the unbelieving Jew and the unconverted pagan; whereas the Church, according to the Pauline dictum, combines the positive poles of elected Jew and converted pagan.[36]

Now since Nazism faded from the scene in 1945, but communism continued to assert itself in Europe to the end of Fessard's days, the Jesuit spent a considerable amount of time and effort unpacking the dynamics of communism as a false religion. The most fundamental difference between right-wing and left-wing interpretations of Hegel is that the former appreciates the chief protagonist of history as the divine spirit, which comes to itself through the vagaries and conflicts of history, while the latter sees the principal subject as the proletariat, which gradually comes to consciousness through the struggle against various forms of oppression. On the left-wing or Marxist reading, the proletariat functions as the messianic culmination of the process of history and hence as the means by which the definitive revolution is fostered and the era of pure communism ushered in. In one sense, the proletariat is the Son or the suffering servant, who bears the sins of the people; and in another sense, it is the Spirit whose mission is to transform the world.

This inversion or transposition of Christian themes can be seen throughout the Marxist enterprise. In this system, salvation comes not through the right rapport between human beings and God but rather through the right rapport between humanity and nature. Fessard insists: "For the disciples of Marx, the essential unity of man and nature…plays exactly the same role that the unity of God and

---

36. Fessard, *De l'actualité historique*, vol. 1, 37.

man does for Christians."[37] Further, for Marx, the original sin is no longer disobedience to God but rather the establishment of private property, which leads to a variety of alienations; salvation happens through the fomenting of class war. Fessard argued throughout his career that Marxism is predicated upon a fundamental contradiction—namely, that the clash of master and slave will end with the supremacy of the proletariat, even though history gives absolutely no warrant for this confidence. But his more basic difficulty is that the entire project involves the rejection of God and hence the establishment of what amounts to a false religion.[38]

Some of Fessard's interlocutors, following a more or less Leninist line, argued that atheism is the core supposition of the Marxist program. Others, more influenced by the writings of the early Marx, held that atheism functions as a corollary to the economic critique. In a word, they opined, people engage in the neurotic self-alienation described by Ludwig Feuerbach,[39] precisely because they are suffering from a more basic alienation from nature and from their own best selves, this latter estrangement produced by the system of private property. But in any case, Fessard maintained, atheism is at the very least close to the center of Marxism. When he turned his attention to the so-called 'progressive' Catholics of the sixties and seventies, Fessard complained bitterly that they supposed that one could do Marxist economics without adopting atheism.[40] Such an interpretive move, on his reading, was just naïve. And he particularly charged the progressives with abandoning the social teaching of the Catholic Church, which teaches the complementarity of social classes and that proposes, in fact, a far more convincing account of history than Marxism.

---

37. Ana Petrache, *Gaston Fessard, un chrétien de rite dialectique?* (Paris: Les Éditions du Cerf, 2017), 157. Incidentally, Fessard was one of the first European scholars to do extensive research into Marx's early texts, especially the *Economic and Philosophical Manuscripts of 1844*, in which the young revolutionary explores the deep alienation from nature that occurs through capitalism.

38. See Gaston Fessard, "Le christianisme des chrétiens progressistes," *Études* 260 (January 1949): 65–93.

39. Ludwig Feuerbach, *The Essence of Christianity*, trans. George Eliot (New York: Harper & Row, Publishers, 1957), 33.

40. Petrache, *Gaston Fessard,* 171.

The Link to Ignatius

The turn to the Church's social doctrine and to its spiritual reading of history allows us to explore Fessard's intense relationship with
the *Spiritual Exercises* of St. Ignatius. As a Jesuit, he had followed
the *Exercises* on retreat and had used them to guide others, and as
an academic, he had made the formal study of the *Exercises* one of
his principal preoccupations. At the heart of Ignatius's classic text,
on Fessard's reading, is the play between two freedoms, divine and
human. It is most important, he argues, that in the famous *Suscipe*
prayer, Ignatius invites God to take not only his "memory, understanding, and will," the well-known Augustinian triplet, but also his
"liberty."[41] This addition makes the text peculiarly modern. And it
provides the hermeneutical key to reading the entire project.

Unlike Hegel and Marx, who saw history as the unfolding of
largely abstract forces, Ignatius saw it as a function of the playing out
of two liberties, God's free offer of grace and our equally free acceptance or rejection of that offer. The novelty of Fessard was to take
the Ignatian analysis of the individual's relation to grace and apply
it to the social and political arena. The same sort of discernment of
spirits that takes place in the former setting ought to obtain in the
latter as well. We can remark upon the similarity to Balthasar here.
The great Swiss theologian, like Fessard, was thoroughly trained in
the Ignatian tradition, and he opposed what he called "epic" theology to "lyrical" theology, the former marked by abstraction and the
latter by concrete engagement of freedoms. The *Theodramatik* (*Theo-
Drama*), the second panel of Balthasar's great theological triptych,
is entirely predicated upon the play between infinite and finite freedom, precisely in the manner of our theologian.[42]

The "Principle and Foundation," in which St. Ignatius outlines
the *raison d'etre* of the human being, is central to discerning the divine
will, at either the personal or social level: "Man is created to praise,
reverence, and serve God our Lord, and by this means to save his

---

41. St. Ignatius of Loyola, *The Spiritual Exercises of St. Ignatius*, trans. Anthony
Mottola (New York: Image Books, 1964), 104.

42. Hans Urs von Balthasar, *Theo-Drama, Theological Dramatic Theory*, vol. 2, *Dramatis Personae: Man in God*, trans. Graham Harrison (San Francisco: Ignatius Press, 1990),
189–284.

soul."[43] Therefore, the drawing of all people together in the common praise of God, forming thereby one mystical body, is the goal that ought to lure any and all decisions in the social order. As Fessard writes, "This unity of all men destined to form one body, that of the New Man, at the end of history: that is what grounds the jurisdiction of the Church of all the temporal order and obliges us to have a social doctrine."[44] In a word, the fundamental decisions that we make in regard to God will govern the decisions that we make at the political, familial, and social levels. Discerning the difference between a choice born of our attachments and one born of our acquiescence to the divine will is the heart of the matter. Another condition for the possibility of correct discernment is the right ordering of temporal and spiritual goods, the former always subordinate to the latter. For Fessard, as for Ignatius, everything in the created or social order exists, finally, for the sake of salvation. Accordingly, if a society consistently ignores the demands of God and prioritizes wealth, power, and privilege, it will, in short compass, devolve into chaos and corruption.

Here an important distinction between Hegel and Ignatius is clear. Like the Jesuit founder, Hegel was interested in discerning the 'will' of God in history, but for the philosopher this was a matter of looking backward to see how Spirit actually had evolved through the conflicts of time. Ignatius always looked forward, to determine how God is calling the individual and the society toward the *magis* (the ever greater) praise of God.

As in the personal order, so in the social order, a kind of spiritual direction is required. Certainly, 'clerics' of liberalism and of the great totalitarianisms were (and are) thick on the ground; their ideological texts are widely available and carefully studied; and their perspectives are on general offer in the popular culture. The Church's task, according to Fessard, is to provide authentic spiritual direction to those engaged in the political and economic life of a given society

---

43. St. Ignatius of Loyola, *The Spiritual Exercises*, 47.

44. Gaston Fessard, "Le christianisme des chrétiens progressistes," *Études* 260 (January 1949): 77, as cited in: Petrache, *Gaston Fessard*, 244. "Cette unite de tous les hommes destines à former un seul corps, celui de l'Homme nouveau, à la fin de l'histoire, voilà qui fonde la juridiction de l'Église sur tout le temporel et l'oblige à avoir une doctrine sociale."

and to help them discern the relevant spirits. To be sure, this intervention on the part of the Church will not always be welcome, but it provides the leavening that a society needs in order to realize its potential, even at the natural level.

Fessard and Francis

Though Pope Francis has never laid out in a systematic way precisely how Gaston Fessard has influenced his own thinking and practice, I believe that, once we have grasped some of the French Jesuit's basic positions, it is easy enough to see multiple connections. I might draw attention first to Jorge Mario Bergoglio's consistent anti-communism. Though he is customarily seen, at least in the West, as a man of the political left, it is clear that Bergoglio/Pope Francis has steadily resisted the temptation to embrace a straightforwardly Marxist position or approach to economics. To Antonio Tornelli he said, unambiguously enough, and deftly summing up hundreds of pages of Fessardian analysis, "Marxism is a false ideology."[45]

Indeed, when the Marxist option of Latin American liberation theology was clearly on the table, Bergoglio consciously moved in another direction, embracing what he termed *la teologia del pueblo* (theology of the people). Uneasy with a Marxist reading of the people in purely economic terms, Bergoglio read *el pueblo* culturally and religiously, taking their concrete practices and aspirations as starting points. He also disliked the elitism and condescension of European-trained academics instructing the people of Latin America, and furthermore saw the danger in embracing the idea that class warfare is inevitable. This *teologia del pueblo* approach came to rich expression in the documents of the Puebla Conference of 1979, which emphasized the evangelization of the culture and the valorization of popular religiosity, over and against standard-issue themes of liberation theology. Bergoglio has remained, over the past four decades, a fervent advocate of the teaching of Puebla. Very much in the spirit of Fessard, he has fretted that liberation theology tends to reduce

---

45. Andrea Tornielli and Giacomo Galeazzi, "In Francis's Own Words," in *This Economy Kills: Pope Francis on Capitalism and Social Justice*, trans. Demetrio S. Yocum (Collegeville, MN: Order of St. Benedict, 2015), 151.

the question of salvation to a this-worldly matter. And this unease can be seen clearly in his resistance to the dominant understanding of the mission of the Jesuits in the period after the Council, when the Order shifted its purpose from "the defense and propagation of the faith" to "the promotion of justice" during the 32nd General Congregation.[46]

That said, there is no question that Bergoglio/Francis is also a sharp critic of an unfettered capitalism that would make an idol of wealth and would foster, very much along master/slave lines, an "economy of exclusion."[47] This citation from *Evangelii Gaudium* is representative of many similar comments that Pope Francis has made around the world: "The worship of the ancient golden calf has returned in a new and ruthless guise in the idolatry of money and the dictatorship of an impersonal economy."[48] The Fessardian element is clearly visible in the use of the term 'idolatry.' Pope Francis is not launching here so much an economic or sociological critique as a spiritual one, using the Principle and Foundation of Ignatius's *Exercises* in order to expose a phony religiosity. That same criterion of the right relationship between spiritual and material goods is neatly employed in another passage from *Evangelii Gaudium* critical of a capitalism free of moral constraint: "Behind this attitude lurks a rejection of ethics and a rejection of God. Ethics has come to be viewed with a certain scornful derision. It is seen as counterproductive, too human, because it makes money and power relative."[49] What the good Jesuit director knows, of course, is that money and power are among the worldly values that must indeed be relativized in relation to the goods of the soul.

It would be useful at this point to cast a glance toward a philosophical friend of Jorge Mario Bergoglio who played a role in drawing the future Pope's attention toward Gaston Fessard—namely, the Uruguayan *tomista silvestre*, Alberto Methol Ferré. A consistent theme

---

46. *Jesuit Life & Mission Today: The Decrees of the 31st-35th General Congregations of the Society of Jesus*, ed. John W. Padberg, Jesuit Primary Sources in English Translation 25 (Saint Louis, MO: The Institute of Jesuit Sources, 2009), no. 2–3, pg. 298; no. 18, pg. 301; no. 28, pg. 305; no. 41, pg. 308.

47. Pope Francis, Apostolic Exhortation *Evangelii Gaudium* (November 24, 2013), §53.

48. Francis, *Evangelii Gaudium*, §55.

49. Francis, *Evangelii Gaudium*, §57.

in Ferré's writing is that the 'messianic atheism' (*ateismo messianico*) of Marxism, prompted in large part by the individualism of the liberal democracies, has been succeeded by a "libertine" atheism (*ateismo libertino*).[50] Very much in line with Fessard, Methol Ferré saw Marxism as involving the transposition of Christian messianism into a purely economic key, whereby the proletariat plays the role of Christ, and God has been shunted from the stage entirely. A devotee of G. K. Chesterton and the social teaching of the Church, Methol Ferré would obviously find these moves unacceptable, but he was equally unhappy with the pleasure-driven individualism that seemed the triumphant successor of Marxism. Though belief in God was not formally prescribed in the West, the dominant attitude in that cultural framework is often, if I might borrow the terminology of John Paul II, a "practical atheism," the living of one's life as though God does not exist.[51] This sort of reading, born of an Ignatian discernment of spirits at the cultural and economic level, undergirds many of Pope Francis's statements regarding excessive individualism, materialism, and "an economy that kills."[52] It is not the market itself that Francis excoriates, but a godless market, one turned in on itself, no longer governed by moral and spiritual laws. And this brings him close indeed to John Paul's criticism of a capitalism "not circumscribed within a strong juridical framework which places it at the service of human freedom in its totality and which sees it as a particular aspect of that freedom, the core of which is ethical and religious."[53]

Another Fessardian theme, mediated to Francis through Methol Ferré, is that of the danger of a detached and ahistorical religiosity. Animated by the Ignatian command to 'find God in all things' and by his generally incarnational approach to spirituality, Fessard saw the movement of grace within the political and economic realms. This attitude inspired Methol Ferré to be suspicious of certain evangelical

---

50. Alberto Methol Ferré, "Grandes orientaciones pastorales de Pablo VI para América Latina" (Buenos Aires, October 10–11, 2000), in *Pablo VI y America Latina: Jornadas de studio* (Rome: Istituto Paolo VI–Studium, 2002), 28.

51. Pope John Paul II, Encyclical Letter *Fides et Ratio* (September 14, 1998), §§46–47.

52. Pope Francis, Apostolic Exhortation *Evangelii Gaudium* (November 24, 2013), §53.

53. Pope John Paul II, Encyclical Letter *Centesimus Annus* (May 1, 1991), §42.

churches that had become influential in Latin America. Here is the Uruguayan's rather frank assessment: "The world of the protestant sects within an evangelical matrix is an ahistorical place, in which grace is punctual, personal, interrupting mechanically and with an absolute verticality. This is why the adherents of the sects don't normally have an historical consciousness and don't feel the necessity to have one; they don't require an historical reading of the signs of the times and thus don't cultivate one. The sects are a world without history."[54] And here is Pope Francis variation on the same theme: "The other harmful ideological error is found in those who find suspect the social engagement of others, seeing it as superficial, worldly, secularist, materialist, populist, or communist....We cannot uphold an ideal of holiness that would ignore injustice in a world where some revel, spend with abandon and live only for the latest consumer goods."[55] Both are riffing on motifs central to Gaston Fessard.

A final Franciscan theme that I would identify as Fessardian is the deep respect for freedom even as the Church goes about its work of evangelization. Pope Francis would heartily agree with St. John Paul II that, at its best, the Church never imposes, only proposes.[56] Again and again, Papa Bergoglio rails (and that *is* the appropriate word) against "proselytism," by which he seems to mean an aggressive, overbearing, hyper-rationalistic manner of spreading the faith. The fundamental problem with this approach is that it does not honor the freedom of the one to be addressed. The true evangelist, Pope Francis implies, imitates the divine master who, in freedom, awakens an answering freedom, who proposes a path but never compels obedience. If divine providence were an imposition, then nothing like human discernment of spirits would be required, at either the personal or political level. As with the woman at the well, or with the man born blind, or with Zacchaeus, the Lord invites and engages errant freedom—and delights in the free response he elicits.

---

54. Alberto Methol Ferré and Alver Metalli, *El Papa y el Filósofo* (Buenos Aires: Editorial Biblos, 2013), 132.

55. Pope Francis, Apostolic Exhortation *Gaudete et Exsultate* (March 19, 2018), §101.

56. Pope John Paul II, Encyclical Letter *Redemptoris Missio* (December 7, 1990), §39.

Conclusion

There is much more that can and should be said, but allow me to draw this already too-lengthy paper to a conclusion. What became especially clear to me in researching this presentation is that Papa Bergoglio found in Gaston Fessard a kindred spirit precisely in the measure that he found him to be a true son of St. Ignatius. Having learned the discernment of spirits as a young man and having made the study of the *Exercises* his principal pursuit, Fessard read the signs of his own times with extraordinary perceptiveness, always alert to the ways God was engaging human freedom as well as the manner in which sinners tend to abuse that freedom. This double focus seems equally at play in the mind of Jorge Mario Bergoglio, making him one of the most insightful readers of the present moment.

Part 3
RENEWING OUR **CHURCH**

CHAPTER 10

EXAMINING THE SEXUAL ABUSE SCANDAL WITH BIBLICAL EYES

The Catholic Church, especially in the West, has been passing through one of the very worst crises in its history. The clergy sex abuse scandal has compromised the work of the Church in almost every way.[1] It has adversely affected teaching, preaching, evangelization, and the recruitment of priests and religious; it has cost many billions of dollars, which could otherwise have supported the Church's mission; it has almost completely undermined the credibility of the Church's ministers; and of course, most terribly, it has deeply wounded many thousands of the most innocent, those the Church is specially charged to protect. Given the gravity of this crime, it is just that the Church should suffer.

Those who reverence the Bible as the Word of God will not be surprised to discover that the Scriptures have a good deal to say about this crisis. I believe that any approach to solving it—psychological, legal, or institutional—must be grounded, finally, in the wisdom of God's revealed Word; otherwise, it will be a chase after wind.

I would suggest that we begin at the beginning, with the account of creation in the book of Genesis. In almost all of the other accounts of creation from the ancient world, order comes to the universe through some primordial act of violence, typically the victorious struggle of one god against another. Very often the elements of the world are made up of the severed body parts of the conquered deity.

---

1. Some of the content in this chapter also appears in my book *Letter to a Suffering Church: A Bishop Speaks on the Sexual Abuse Crisis* (Park Ridge, IL: Word on Fire, 2019).

But there is none of this in the biblical story, according to which God brings the universe into being through a nonviolent act of speech: "Let there be light...let the water teem with an abundance of living creatures," and so on. God faces down no rival as he makes the world but rather shares the bounty of his being through love.

The Church Fathers exulted in seeing the orderly coming forth of all things from the Creator as a kind of cosmic liturgical procession, each thing finding its place in the chorus of nature. On this reading, the human being, precisely as the last of creatures, took up the privileged place at the end of the procession, much as the priest or bishop would. This is because the role of the human being is to praise the Creator on behalf of all creation, giving prayerful voice to the sun, moon, earth, animals, and insects. The Fathers, accordingly, consistently read Adam as the high priest of creation, walking in easy fellowship with the Lord, communing with him 'mouth to mouth,' which is the root meaning of *adoratio*, and they interpreted the Garden of Eden as a kind of primordial temple. Adam was priest, and he was also prophet, philosopher, and scientist, since he named the animals in the presence of the Lord, literally cataloguing them, describing them *kata logon*, according to the intelligibility placed in them by their creator. Finally, Adam is construed as king, which is to say the one whose task is to protect and to foster the life in the garden and eventually to go on the march, turning the whole world into a place where God is praised and God's order is concretely realized. In exercising these offices, the human being is meant to show forth his identity as one made distinctively in the image and likeness of God, as one functioning as a sort of viceroy on behalf of the Creator.

The first command that God gives to his human creatures, "Be fertile and multiply" (Gn 1:28), is a summons to fulfill their priestly, prophetic, and kingly missions precisely through sexual love and reproduction. It is of supreme significance that this primal command is repeated at key moments in salvation history. As he brings the remnant of God's good order forth from the Ark after the flood waters had receded, Noah is told, "Be fertile, then, and multiply" (Gn 9:7). When he enters into covenant with Yahweh, Abraham is informed that he will be the father of many nations (Gn 17:4). When the Israelites flood into the Promised Land, they are called to produce life abundantly. It is absolutely no accident that the privileged sign of covenantal belonging for ancient Israel is a mark on the male reproductive organ (Gn 17:11–14). God's designs for the human race—and through the human race for the whole of the cosmos—are deeply tied to sexuality, and this means that sexual love, children, and family are paramount vehicles by which a compassionate, nonviolent stewardship of creation finds expression.

In light of these clarifications, it should not be the least surprising that, on the biblical reading, one of the principal marks of human dysfunction is sexual misconduct. The authors of Sacred Scripture know all about pride, ambition, envy, violence, and avarice, but they recognize something of a *corruptio optimi pessima* ("corruption of the best is the worst") quality in regard to sexual corruption. And they analyze it frequently and with a remarkable psychological and spiritual perceptiveness. In the course of this brief presentation, I can hardly do justice to the full richness of the scriptural treatment; therefore, I will focus on only a handful of particularly illuminating narratives.

Abraham, Lot, and the Angelic Visitors

I should first like to consider the strange but richly illuminating story from the eighteenth and nineteenth chapters of the book of Genesis, which treats of an angelic visit to the patriarch Abraham and its troubling aftermath. We are told that the Lord deigned to appear to Abraham through the mediation of three men/angels. After the patriarch received and served them, the visitors predicted that, despite their advanced years, Abraham and Sarah would, a year hence, have a son. Overhearing the conversation, Sarah laughs at the absurdity of the suggestion that she and her husband could still experience "sexual pleasure," but the Lord reproached Abraham, "Why did Sarah laugh and say, 'Shall I really bear a child, old as I am?' Is anything too marvelous for the Lord to do?" (Gn 18:13–14). What is marvelous, of course, is not simply that an elderly woman would bear a son but that the promise made to Abraham—that he would become the father of a great nation—was, against all odds, about to come true. God's lordship, faithful human cooperation, the fulfillment of the covenant, reproduction, laughter, and even sexual pleasure are all, in the typically Israelite manner, folded in together.

And this is why it is extremely instructive to examine the stories of sexual perversion and misconduct that immediately follow this one, for they demonstrate the negation of God's plan for human sexuality. At the beginning of the nineteenth chapter of Genesis, we hear that the angels who had visited Abraham have made their way to the city of Sodom, the home of Abraham's nephew Lot. After enjoying a meal in Lot's home, the angels find themselves hemmed in by a startlingly aggressive and lustful band of men, indeed, we are told, *all* of the men, both young and old, of the town. Without the slightest hesitation or shame, they announce their intentions: "Where are the men who came to your house tonight? Bring them out to us that we may have sexual relations with them" (Gn 19:5). The gang rape being proposed—violent, impersonal, self-interested, and infertile—is the precise opposite of what God intends for human sexuality. In the feral men of Sodom, the *imago Dei* has been almost completely occluded.

The narrative becomes, if anything, more disturbing as we consider the reaction of Lot. The nephew of Abraham begins promisingly enough: "I beg you, my brothers, do not do this wicked thing," but then he proposes an appalling solution, "I have two daughters who have never had sexual relations with men. Let me bring them out to you, and you may do to them as you please" (Gn 19:7–8). In order to stave off a brutal sexual assault, he presents his own virgin daughters for a violent gang rape. Could we imagine a more thoroughgoing undermining of the Creator's intention regarding sex? The men of Sodom, simmering with rage, are having none of it, and they press Lot against the door of his home. At this point, the angels intervene, pulling Lot inside and striking the men of the mob blind. The dramatic punishment should not be read simply as an intriguing twist in the narrative, but rather as the symbolic communication of a spiritual dynamic. Having devolved morally to the level of pack animals, the men of Sodom have become blind to any of the deeper dimensions of sexuality and human community. In response to the polymorphous dysfunction of the city, God, we are told, rained fire and brimstone upon Sodom (Gn 19:24). We must never interpret divine punishment in the Bible as capricious or arbitrary, the result of an emotional affront; rather, we should read it as a sort of spiritual physics, God allowing the natural consequences of sin to obtain.

Following the destruction of Sodom and Gomorrah, Lot and his daughters, we are told, flee to the surrounding hill country, where they take up residence in a cave (Gn 19:15–17, 30). Commenting on the annihilation of their city, Lot's older daughter suggests to the younger that since all the men have been wiped out, they should couple with their father and so bring forth children. Accordingly, on successive nights, they get their father drunk and sleep with him and both girls become, through these incestuous relations, pregnant (Gn 19:31–36). They give rise, thereby, to the Moabites and the Ammonites, two tribes that would come, in time, to be at odds with Israel (Gn 19:37–38).

Can anyone miss the connection between the shocking psychological and sexual abuse to which these girls were subjected— their own father offering them to a violent mob—and their subsequent abuse of Lot? Haven't we seen over and again in our time the sadly familiar dynamic of sexual abuse begetting sexual abuse, the sin passed on like a contagion from generation to generation? That this perversion of sexuality took place in a cave, the dwelling place of animals and primitives, is still another indication that the *imago Dei* has been rather thoroughly effaced. And that the disordered unions are the *fons et origo* of two peoples antagonistic to Israel is a further sign that what transpired between Lot and his daughters stands completely athwart God's salvific purpose.

Eli and His Sons

The narrative of Eli and his sons is an eerily accurate anticipation of many of the features of the clergy sex abuse scandal, and thus it behooves us to attend to it with some care. The first glimpse we get of Eli, high priest of Shiloh, is not edifying. Demonstrating not an ounce of pastoral sensitivity, Eli upbraids the distraught Hannah, who had been praying aloud in the sacred place, begging God for a child: "How long will you make a drunken show of yourself? Sober up from your wine!" (1 Sm 1:14). Then we hear of Eli's sons, Hophni and Phineas, who are priests like their father, but wicked, having regard neither for God nor for the people. We are told that they took the best meat from the sacrifices piously offered by the supplicants at Shiloh and that they were sexually abusing the women who worked

at the entry of the meeting tent (1 Sm 2:12–15, 22). The victims of
their abuse brought complaints to Eli, and the high priest responded
with strong enough words, remonstrating with his sons: "Why are
you doing such things? I hear from everyone that your behavior is
depraved. Stop this, my sons! The report that I hear the LORD's
people spreading is not good. If someone sins against another, anyone can intercede for the sinner with the LORD; but if anyone sins
against the LORD, who can intercede for the sinner?" (1 Sm 2:24–
25). But Hophni and Phineas disregarded their father's warning and
continued on their path of corruption, and Eli apparently took no
further action against his sons.

It is against this background that we must read the famous and
poignant story of the Lord's call to Samuel, the son whom Hannah
had sought from the Lord and whom she had given to the Lord for
service in the Temple. We are told that, at this time, "the word of
the LORD was scarce and vision infrequent" (1 Sm 3:1). One might
be permitted to wonder whether this was a function of the Lord's
refusal to speak or rather of the blindness and corruption of the spiritual leadership of the nation. During the night, God calls to Samuel,
but neither the boy nor his spiritual father understand the nature of
the summons. Only after several false starts does Eli give the proper
instruction: "If you are called, reply, 'Speak, LORD, for your servant
is listening'" (1 Sm 3:9). Since the version of this narrative that is
found in the lectionary ends at this point, most Catholics don't know
the devastating words that the Lord finally speaks to young Samuel:
"I am about to do something in Israel that will cause the ears of
everyone who hears it to ring. On that day, I will carry out against
Eli everything I have said about his house, beginning to end" (1 Sm
3:11–12). And God specifies precisely why he will exact such a severe
punishment: "I announce to him that I am condemning his family
once and for all, because of this crime: though he knew his sons were
blaspheming God, he did not reprove them" (1 Sm 3:13). In short, it
was not the crimes of Hophni and Phineas that particularly aroused
the divine ire, but rather Eli's refusal to act when he was made aware
of them.

Just after this unnerving revelation, the Philistines engaged
Israel in battle, and the result was an unmitigated disaster. After four
thousand Israelites were slain in a preliminary skirmish, the army

regrouped and resolved to bring the Ark of the Covenant itself into battle. Despite the presence of this talisman of the God who had brought Israel out of Egypt, the Philistines won a decisive victory, killing 30,000 Israelites, including Hophni and Phineas, and carrying away the Ark as booty (1 Sm 4:11). When news of the catastrophe reached Eli, the old priest was sitting by the gate of Shiloh. So overwhelmed was he that he fell over backward and broke his neck, thus bringing, as the Lord had predicted, his entire family to an end (1 Sm 4:18).

Now does any of this story strike you as familiar? We hear of priests abusing their people both financially and sexually; complaints are brought to their superior, who uses strong words and promises decisive action but does nothing to stop the abuse. And the result of this double failure is a disaster and deep shame for the entire people, as they are delivered into the hands of their enemies. I would suggest that the story of Eli and his sons is an almost perfect biblical icon of the clerical sex abuse scandal that has unfolded over the past fifty years. At the height of the troubles in the early 2000s, many Catholics in America were dismayed at the frank anti-Catholicism on display in many of the newspapers, journals, and television stations that covered the scandal. Those with a biblical frame of reference shouldn't have been surprised: the new Israel of the Church had been handed over to its enemies, precisely for the sake of purification.

David and Bathsheba

The endlessly fascinating and psychologically complex tale of David and Bathsheba, recounted in the eleventh and twelfth chapters of 2 Samuel, has beguiled artists, poets, and spiritual writers across the centuries. It is one of the most sensitive and subtle narratives that has come down to us from the ancient world, and it sheds a good deal of light on our subject in this chapter.

The commencement of the story is worth close attention: "At the turn of the year, the time when kings go to war… David himself remained in Jerusalem" (2 Sm 11:1). David was the greatest of Israel's campaigners, never shrinking from a fight, always at the head of the army, willing to undertake even the most dangerous missions. So why is he lingering at home, precisely at the time of year when kings typically sally forth? As we saw, the kingly task, rooted in Adam's mission, is to protect the Garden, to govern it well, and to extend its boundaries outwards. When kings refuse to undertake these tasks—whether out of cowardice, weakness, boredom, or distraction—trouble comes to Israel. Vacillating or indifferent kingship permits the serpent and his allies to hold sway. A clue to David's reticence is provided in the next verse, "One evening David rose from his bed and strolled about on the roof of the king's house" (2 Sm 11:2). To be sure, people in Mediterranean cultures typically take a siesta after the midday meal, but it is significant that the King rose *in the evening*, implying that he had been in bed quite some time. What the biblical author sketches here, in characteristically laconic manner, is a portrait of a king gone to seed, a military leader grown a bit indulgent and indifferent. When he was in his spiritual prime, David invariably inquired of God what he should do, even in regard to minor matters; but throughout the Bathsheba narrative, he never asks God for direction. Rather, David does the directing. From his Godlike point of vantage on the rooftop of his palace, David can see in every direction, and he can order things according to his whim. It is precisely from this perspective that he spies the beautiful Bathsheba, and through a series of quick and staccato commands, takes her to himself. It is doubtful that the biblical author is unaware of Bathsheba's own cooperation with the affair—does she just happen to be bathing within easy eyeshot of the king?—but he is especially interested in the king's deft but wicked use of his power to manipulate another.

In the wake of Bathsheba's pregnancy, David attempts, using every means at his disposal, to cover up his sin, cruelly playing with the upright Uriah who though an outsider, nevertheless proves more faithful to Israel's laws than does Israel's king. Finally, of course, David arranges things so as to bring about Uriah's death, stooping so low as to compel the man himself to carry his own order of execution to Joab, the commander in the field. The murder of Uriah allowed David to take Bathsheba as his wife and definitively to cover up his sin, but we are told, "in the sight of the LORD what David had done was evil" (2 Sm 11:27). Again and again, the Scriptures insist that any human power is grounded in and derived from a more fundamental divine sovereignty. Thomas Aquinas's insistence that the positive law nests in the natural law, which in turn nests in the eternal law, is but a specification of the biblical rule.[2] No matter how much rangy authority a human being has, he does not escape the moral oversight and sanction of God. This is the sense of Jesus' reminder to Pilate, the representative of the most powerful political institution of his time: "You would have no power over me if it had not been given to you from above" (Jn 19:11). In his laziness, self-indulgence, manipulation, and cruelty, David stands in the tradition of the sinful Adam whose bad kingship led to a compromising of the integrity of the garden.

Something like the law of karma typically obtains in the narratives of the Deuteronomistic history, and we see it in the court prophet Nathan's famous confrontation with the king. Nathan tells a parable about a rich man with many lambs who took the sole ewe of a poor man (2 Sm 12:1–4). When David responds indignantly, "As the LORD lives, the man who has done this deserves death!" (2 Sm 12:5), Nathan famously confronts the great ruler: "You are the man!" (2 Sm 12:7). As a consequence of David's actions, Nathan tells him that "the sword shall never depart from your house" (2 Sm 12:10). From the death of the child conceived with Bathsheba (2 Sm 12:18), through the rape of Tamar (2 Sm 13:1–22), the murder of Amnon (2 Sm 13:28–29), the rebellion of Absalom and his subsequent death in battle (2 Sm 15:1–18:17), to the disastrous census-taking that resulted in the deaths of seventy-thousand Israelites (2 Sm 24:1–15), the prophecy of Nathan is relentlessly fulfilled. Though the Lord pardoned David for his sin against Uriah, there isn't an ounce of 'cheap grace' in this narrative. Rather, David's sexual sin, and the violence and manipulation that attend it, result in horrific suffering for his family across several generations. In the wake of the scandals of our time, can anyone think that sexual abuse is relatively harmless, that its victims will 'get over it' promptly enough? Isn't it in fact the case that the sword continues to swing and to cut, producing ever more victims?

Amnon, Tamar, and Absalom

In the chapter that immediately follows the account of David and Bathsheba, we find the tragic story of Tamar, her brother Absalom,

---

2. St. Thomas Aquinas, *Summa theologiae*, I-II, q. 91.

and her half-brother Amnon. These three children of David find
themselves implicated in a nasty net of intrigue, violence, retribu-
tion, and above all, uncontrolled and self-serving sexual desire. We
are told that Amnon "loved" his beautiful half-sister, but the Bible's
description of his inner state reveals that he is, in fact, sexually
obsessed with her: "He was in such anguish over his sister Tamar that
he became sick; she was a virgin, and Amnon thought it impossible
to do anything to her" (2 Sm 13:2). What becomes eminently clear is
that his approach to her is predatory and aggressive, not unlike that
of his father in regard to Bathsheba. One of St. Augustine's pithiest
definitions of sin is the *libido dominandi* (the lust to dominate),[3] and
this is precisely what has seized the heart of Amnon.

How often it is the case that the sinner will find someone
to aid and abet his sin: "Now Amnon had a companion named
Jonadab...who was very clever" (2 Sm 13:3). The use of "clever"
in the New American Bible translation is apt, since it calls to mind
the cunning of the snake in the Garden of Eden. Jonadab lays out
the plan that Amnon should play at being sick and then protest to
his father that he will accept nourishment only from the hand of
his half-sister. One is struck by the unlikeliness, even childishness,
of this stratagem, but David falls for it, proving once again that his
failure to act in a disciplinary way is one of his chief faults. In point
of fact, he gives the order to Tamar to go and feed her brother,
thereby unwittingly facilitating the rape of his own daughter. The
narrator allows us to look in on the very vivid scene of Amnon's
seduction/manipulation. As her brother lies on his bed—how like
his father who was presented as lying in bed at the beginning of the
Bathsheba story—Tamar prepares "cakes" (which some translations call "heart-shaped dumplings") for him (2 Sm 13:6–10).[4] One
would have to be naïve in the extreme not to notice the voyeuristic
and sexually charged nature of this scene. When she brings the
food to her brother, Amnon seizes her and says, "Come! Lie with
me, my sister" (2 Sm 13:11), words which closely echo those of the

3. St. Augustine, *The City of God*, trans. Rev. J. J. Smith (New York: Random House, Inc., 1950), I.33, pg. 37; V.19, pp. 171–173.

4. For example, Robert Alter, *The David Story: A Translation with Commentary of 1 and 2 Samuel* (New York: W.W. Norton, 1999), 267.

wife of Potiphar to Joseph in the book of Genesis (Gn 39:7). Then, in four different ways, Tamar signals her lack of acquiescence to this demand, culminating in the observation, "Where would I take my shame?" (2 Sm 13:13). Tamar knows that, according to Israelite law and custom, this rape would result in an immediate and permanent reduction in her status. Here the comparison with Bathsheba fails to obtain, for even after being violated by David, Bathsheba became a queen, whereas Tamar knew that in the wake of Amnon's attack, she would be a pariah.

Utterly indifferent to her plea and her plight, Amnon, in the blunt words of the Scriptures, "overpowered her and abused her, and bedded her" (2 Sm 13:14), the three transitive verbs in rapid succession imitating the thrusting force of Amnon's crime. I can't help but *feel* a connection here to the numerous stories we have heard in the last twenty years of powerless children and young people who were aggressed and shamed by sexually abusive priests. And then we hear of a weird reversal: "Then Amnon felt an intense hatred for her, which far surpassed the love he had had for her" (2 Sm 13:15). The psychological perceptiveness of the author is on evidence throughout the Samuel cycle, but perhaps no more conspicuously than here. How often it is the case that those who aggressively pursue someone out of lustful intention lose all interest in the person once the conquest has been made. Completely reversing the words he had used earlier, "Come lie," Amnon shouts, "Get up, leave!" (2 Sm 13:15). The curtness and directness of the command conveys the brutality of an unbalanced man. Tamar immediately senses the precariousness of the situation. A lively option would have been that, having had relations with her, Amnon would petition David for her hand. Though this scenario might have been repugnant to her, it at least would have covered her shame and restored her social status. In sending her away so peremptorily, Amnon was closing out this option, thereby exposing her to ridicule and condemning her to social exile and a permanently unmarried state. The author provides the poignant detail of the "long tunic" that Tamar wore (some translations have "ornamental"), as did all the virgins of David's household (2 Sm 13:18). Putting ashes on her head, the young woman tore the tunic and walked away, "crying loudly" (2 Sm 13:19). Every bit of that description hammers home her humiliation and hopelessness. How disturbingly familiar all of this sounds to us, who have heard hundreds of accounts of those who had been sexually abused by priests.

At this point in the narrative, Absalom, Tamar's brother, comes on the scene. Outraged at the violation of his sister, he plots his revenge on Amnon (2 Sm 13:22). Meanwhile, David the King has heard about the affair and signals his extreme displeasure (2 Sm 13:21); nevertheless, he fails to act. Once more the sin of Eli—inaction regarding gross injustice—comes to the surface, and it is precisely this inaction on the part of the king that gives Absalom room to maneuver. Two years after the rape of Tamar, Absalom sprang his trap at a shearing festival. While Amnon was "merry with wine" (2 Sm 13:28), Absalom ordered his murder, thereby both avenging his sister's violation and positioning himself to be the next king. Though he was deeply chagrined by what had happened, David, once again, did nothing, allowing Absalom to escape and, in time, to foment a rebellion against his father, which resulted in Absalom's own death and a disaster for the nation (2 Sm 18:9–17). We have certainly seen how often it is the case that sexual sin, unaddressed, gives rise to extraordinary violence and division in its wake.

Jesus the Son of God

Having surveyed a handful of Old Testament narratives treating of various forms of sexual misconduct, I should like to turn to the New Testament and a consideration of Jesus himself. How wonderful that the Gospel of Luke includes a genealogy of Jesus that traces his origins through the roiled and complex history of Israel, all the way back to Noah, Methuselah, Enoch, and Adam. Luke's point is that the story of salvation, which culminates in Jesus, has been carried on precisely through the family and sexuality. As we saw, there is nothing puritanical or Gnostic in the biblical imagination.

Moreover, a baby, a child, is at the center of attention as the Gospel story commences. Cherished by his mother, protected by his foster-father, visited by the shepherds, bestowed with gifts by the Magi, the baby Jesus is, at the same time, threatened by Herod and indeed by all of Jerusalem, who we are told, were "greatly troubled" at his coming (Mt 2:3). Herod's massacre of the innocents mimics

Pharaoh's murder of the male children of the Hebrews at the time of Moses' birth. Once more we are made to see that, in the fallen world, the least powerful can be ruthlessly eliminated in order to satisfy the needs and assuage the fears of the most powerful. Of course, the same Herod who casually ordered the murder of the children of Bethlehem had previously commanded the execution of two of his own sons. As in the Old Testament tales that we considered above, this awful story functions as a vivid picture of what compromised family life looks like. The abuse of young people can and should be analyzed psychologically and sociologically, but biblical people know that, in the final analysis, it is a manifestation of the dysfunction born of sin, Augustine's *libido dominandi*.

We know next to nothing about Jesus' youth and coming of age, but the Gospel of Luke provides one intriguing glimpse— namely, the account of the finding of Jesus in the Temple. This well-loved story teaches a fundamental biblical truth about family life and the proper relation between parents and children. We hear that the boy Jesus had wandered away from his parents while they were journeying, with their wider circle of relatives, from Jerusalem to Nazareth. After they discovered that he was missing, they returned to the capital and searched for him frantically across three days. Finally, they found him in the temple precincts, listening to the elders and asking them questions. Understandably exasperated, Mary asked, "Son, why have you done this to us?" And Jesus replied with devastating laconicism: "Why were you looking for me? Did you not know that I must be in my Father's house?" (Lk 2:48–49). The narrative in many ways echoes the account of Hannah and her son in the first book of Samuel. Though she had, in the course of many years, begged God for a child, Hannah, upon receiving the gift she had so ardently desired, returned him to the temple for service to the Lord. On the scriptural reading, the family is meant to be a place where parents shape their children in the direction of mission. Children are not the means by which parents satisfy their own needs and ambitions; rather, they are ends in themselves, to use the Kantian language, and parents and other elders are meant to suit them for a life of service to God. Can we see the sexual abuse of children by their own relatives and by those who play a fatherly role in their lives as the supreme instance of the reversal of these values? We are told that the child Jesus, upon returning with his parents to Nazareth, "was obedient to them" (Lk 2:51). What should be clear in light of the narrative is that this obedience on his part had not the slightest hint of obsequiousness or slavish acquiescence to arbitrary authority—an important reminder, given the number of children who were coerced into submission by predatory adults, often members of their own families.

Jesus and Children

The eighteenth chapter of Matthew's Gospel commences with a lovely and incisive meditation on the spiritual significance of children and of Jesus' attitude toward them. Exhibiting their customary tendency to miss the point, Jesus' entire company of disciples approached him with the question, "Who is the greatest in the kingdom of heaven?" (Mt 18:1). Their inquiry, of course, is born of a false or fallen consciousness, a preoccupation with honor and worldly power. In answer, Jesus called a little child over and placed him in their midst, which is to say in the focal point, the center (Mt 18:2). By so situating the child, he physically interrupted their jockeying for position and notice. In his innocence and humility, the child exemplifies what the spiritual masters call the 'true self,' which is able to relate simply and directly to reality. The true self is in opposition to the false self, which is so layered over with preoccupations with honor that it gets at reality only haltingly and through a kind of buffer. This is why it is altogether appropriate to associate the true self with humility, drawn from the Latin *humus* (the earth or the rough ground). Though they take on the qualities of the false self soon enough, little children typically exemplify this spiritual alertness precisely in their ability to lose themselves in a game or a conversation or the beautiful facticity of the simplest things.

It was a commonplace in the ancient world to hold up distinguished figures as models: military commanders, religious leaders, and political potentates. What Jesus is doing is turning this tradition on its head, placing in the position of honor a figure of no social prominence, no influence, and no connections. Within the standard societal framework of the time, children were expected to remain silent, and it was assumed that the powerful could manipulate them at will. Jesus reverses this, identifying the socially negligible as the greatest. Indeed, for those who have moved from the false self to the true self, the very meaning of greatness has been adjusted: "Whoever humbles himself like this child is the greatest in the kingdom of heaven" (Mt 18:4). What follows is a remark of rich theological significance: "And whoever receives one child such as this in my name receives me" (Mt 18:5). In the second chapter of Philippians, we find the remarkable hymn that Paul has adapted to his epistolary purposes. It commences with an evocation of the self-emptying quality of the Son of God: "Though he was in the form of God, Jesus did not deem equality with God a thing to be grasped, but rather emptied himself and took the form of a slave, being born in the likeness of men. He was known to be of human estate and it was thus that he humbled himself, obediently accepting even death, death on a cross" (Phil 2:6–8). In short, the child—humble, simple, and self-effacing— functions as a sort of iconic representation of the divine Child of the divine Father. The route of access to Jesus is therefore to move into the spiritual space of a child, to 'accept' him in the fullest sense. This truth becomes especially clear in Mark's version of this story. When the disciples disputed about which of them is greatest, Jesus said, "If anyone wishes to be first, he shall be the last of all and the servant of all" (Mk 9:35). Then he took a child and in a gesture of irresistible poignancy, he placed his arms around him, simultaneously embracing, protecting, and offering him as an example. The clear implication is that the failure to accept, protect, and love a child, or what is worse, the active harming of a child, would preclude real contact with Jesus.

And this helps to explain the vehemence of the statement that immediately follows: "Whoever causes one of these little ones who believe in me to sin, it would be better for him to have a great millstone hung around his neck and to be drowned in the depths of the sea" (Mt 18:6). Mind you, this from the mouth of the same Jesus who, just a few chapters before, had urged the love of enemies! I don't think for a moment that the earlier teaching is being repudiated, but I do indeed think that the extraordinary gravity of the offense is being emphasized. There is no other sin—not hypocrisy, not adultery, not indifference to the poor—that Jesus condemns with greater passion than this: "Woe to the world because of things that cause sin! Such things must come, but woe to the one through whom they come! If your hand or foot causes you to sin, cut it off and throw it away. It is better for you to enter life maimed or crippled than with two hands or two feet to be thrown into eternal fire. And if your eye causes you to sin, tear it out and throw it away. It is better for you to enter into life with one eye than with two eyes to be thrown into fiery Gehenna" (Mt 18:7–9). It cannot possibly be accidental that Jesus mentions Gehenna in the context of condemning those who attack children, for Gehenna was the place where children, through-out much of the Old Testament period, were sacrificed to Moloch (2 Kgs 23:10).

This extraordinary peroration concludes with an evocation of the angels: "See that you do not despise one of these little ones, for I say to you that their angels in heaven always look upon the face of my heavenly Father" (Mt 18:10). This is far more than pious decoration. The abuse of children is a function of the objectification of children, turning them, as we saw, into mere means. In reminding his listen-ers that every child is assigned a supernatural guide who is, in turn, intimately linked to God, Jesus is insisting upon the incomparable dignity of those whom society—then and now—is likely to disregard or undervalue. The central tragedy of the clergy sex abuse scandal is that those who were ordained to act *in persona Christi* became, in the most dramatic way, obstacles to Christ.

In the following chapter of Matthew's Gospel, we find another beautiful icon of Jesus in relation to children. The chapter com-mences with a pointed discussion between Jesus and the Pharisees concerning marriage and divorce. Hearkening back to the book of Genesis, Christ reminds his interlocutors, "Have you not read that from the beginning the Creator 'made them male and female' and said, 'For this reason a man shall leave his father and mother and be joined to his wife, and the two shall become one flesh'… There-fore, what God has joined together, no human being must separate" (Mt 19:4–6). Lest anyone miss the implication of the two becom-ing one flesh, this discourse segues neatly into the account of Jesus blessing little children. One of the marks of our time, of course, is precisely the tendency to separate copulation from procreation, to drive a wedge between the pleasure of sexual congress and the moral demand of raising children. As one American journalist put it, we no longer want to see the link between sex and diapers.[5] At any rate, in the Gospel story, people bring youngsters to Jesus for a blessing, and the Lord's disciples rebuke them. As we saw, this was in line with the social conventions of the time, according to which children should never be permitted to bother a prominent adult. But Jesus is having none of it: "Let the children come to me, and do not prevent them; for the kingdom of heaven belongs to such as these" (Mt 19:14). The reign that Jesus speaks of, the new order of things brought about by his appearance in space and time, involves a turning upside down of the false order of the fallen world. Now humility, nonviolence, guilelessness, and service are the marks of prominence, and hence children are the living icons of the new world.

Conclusion

It is perhaps best to conclude with the image of Jesus laying his hands upon the children in blessing, for it sums up so much of what I have wanted to communicate in this reflection. The God of the Bible is the God of creation, which is to say, the God who cherishes matter and fosters the teeming of life. Family, sexuality, sensual pleasure, and the joy and responsibility of raising children—all of it is, from the beginning, blessed by God. The corruption of these, therefore, is one of the surest indicators of the reign of sin. The rapists of Sodom and Gomorrah, Eli and his wicked sons, David in his abuse of Bathsheba, and Amnon in his cruel manipulation and rape of his sister are all standing athwart the purposes of the Creator God. Jesus, the divine child, who welcomes the young with joy and places his hands on them in blessing, is the beginning of the great restoration of a devastated creation.

According to Catholic ecclesiology, the Church is not simply a collectivity of like-minded people, not just the 'Jesus of Nazareth Society.' Rather, it is a mystical body, made up of interconnected cells, molecules, and organs. It is, in the language of the Church Fathers, the prolongation of the Incarnation across space and time.

---

5. E. J. Graff, "What is Marriage?" *The Boston Globe*, Focus section (July 21, 1996). Cited in *About Philosophy*, Eight Edition, edited by Robert Paul Wolff, 208–210 (Upper Saddle River, NJ: Prentice Hall, 2000), 209.

Therefore, its task, up and down the ages, is to be Christ to the world and to do what Christ did. It is meant to foster what God wants to foster and to bless what God wants to bless. This is precisely why the abuse of children at the hands of priests is such an outrage, such a violation and contradiction, and why it stirs in the hearts of all decent believers a sense of disgust and an ardent desire to set things right. We have, justly enough, suffered, but how wonderful that we can find, in the Scriptures themselves, such a rich source of information, inspiration, and renewal.

CHAPTER 11

OPTATAM TOTIUS AND THE RENEWAL OF THE PRIESTHOOD

Optatam Totius, Vatican II's document concerning the formation of priests, was approved by an overwhelming majority of the Council Fathers (2318 to 3) and promulgated by Pope Paul VI on October 28, 1965. The massive support for this relatively brief statement would seem to indicate that its recommendations were rather straightforward and uncontroversial. However, in the years following its publication, a crisis in the priesthood has unfolded, especially in the West. In the immediate wake of Vatican II, priests in the United States and Western Europe left the active ministry in droves, and in relation to the growing population of Catholics, the number of priests worldwide has, over the past fifty years, dropped dramatically.

There are, of course, many reasons for this decline—including enormous cultural shifts, the sexual revolution, loss of confidence in established institutions, and the clergy sex abuse scandal—but what is particularly interesting for our purposes is that the crisis in the priesthood has conduced, over the past fifty years, toward an intense focus upon the priesthood and the training of priests. Accordingly, the reception of *Optatam Totius* is complex and includes, to mention just a few of the most prominent, the following documents: *Ratio Fundamentalis Institutionis Sacerdotalis* from the Sacred Congregation for Catholic Education; Paul VI's encyclical letter *Sacerdotalis Caelibatus*; *The Directory for the Ministry and the Life of Priests* from the Congregation for the Clergy; John Paul II's remarkable series of Holy

Thursday letters to priests,[1] as well as his yearlong Wednesday audience catechesis on the priesthood in 1993, and most importantly, his Apostolic Exhortation *Pastores Dabo Vobis*; Benedict XVI's letter proclaiming a year for priests; and, in the American context, the *Program for Priestly Formation* (now in its fifth edition) issued by the United States Conference of Catholic Bishops. There is, obviously, an embarrassment of riches here, and in the context of this brief article, we could never cover all of this material adequately. Thus, I have decided to concentrate on what I take to be the most important 'moments' in the reception process of *Optatam Totius*—namely, *Pastores Dabo Vobis* and the *Program of Priestly Formation*. Drawing on my own experience as rector of the largest Catholic seminary in the United States, I should also like to include some of my own ruminations on how *Optatam Totius* might best be applied in the present ecclesial situation.

Optatam Totius

Before considering the reception of *Optatam Totius* over the past half century, it will be useful to provide a brief overview of the document itself. The first significant observation that the Council Fathers make is that the duty of fostering vocations is incumbent upon the entire Church and is not the responsibility of priests and bishops alone.[2] Congruent with *Lumen Gentium*'s stress on the universal call to holiness and the priesthood of all believers, *Optatam Totius* wants to cultivate a culture of vocations throughout the life of the entire Christian community. John Paul II would echo this theme in *Pastores Dabo Vobis*, especially in his call for the family to be the "first seminary," and it would provide the theological foundation for the innumerable societies for the promotion of vocations that have flourished in the Church around the world since Vatican II.[3] *Optatam Totius* also calls

---

1. Pope John Paul II, *Holy Thursday Letters to My Brother Priests* (Princeton, NJ: Scepter Publishers, 1994).

2. *Optatam Totius*, §2, in *Decrees of the Ecumenical Councils*, vol. 2, ed. Norman Tanner, SJ (London: Sheed and Ward, 1990), 948.

3. Pope John Paul II, Post-Synodal Apostolic Exhortation *Pastores Dabo Vobis* (Washington, DC: United States Conference of Catholic Bishops, 1992), §41.

upon priests themselves to recruit vocations through their "apostolic zeal" and the joyfulness of their lives.[4] Though this might sound like something of a velleity, it has been shown over and over again in more recent years that priests are in fact among the happiest people.[5] Oddly, this state of affairs, though established with remarkable consistency, has not impressed itself on the popular consciousness. A common though demonstrably false perception is that priests are lonely, bored, and unhappy, and unfortunately for vocational recruitment, the general attitude seems more influential than the truth on the ground.

Continuing in the tradition established by the Council of Trent, *Optatam Totius* clearly affirms the importance of major seminaries for the formation of priests.[6] In these "seed-beds,"—and not in universities or mere houses of formation—seminarians should be shaped according to the mind of Christ, who is priest, prophet, and shepherd.[7] In using that famous triplet, *Optatam Totius* suggests its indebtedness to the thought of John Henry Newman, who had borrowed and adapted the priest, prophet, and king motif from the thought of John Calvin.[8] It also demonstrates continuity with *Presbyterorum Ordinis*, which uses the same figure to articulate the nature of the priesthood.[9] In accord with both *Lumen Gentium* and *Presbyterorum Ordinis*, *Optatam Totius* maintains that the primary focus of the seminary should be training in the proclamation of the Word of God. This emphasis is a function of a strict theologic: if faith is the door

---

4. *Optatam Totius*, §2.

5. See Stephen Rosetti, *The Joy of Priesthood* (Notre Dame, IN: Ave Maria Press, 2005), 24, 25–26, 91, 168, 205.

6. H. J. Schroeder, *Canons and Decrees of the Council of Trent* (St. Louis, MO: B. Herder Book Co., 1941), XXIII Session, Ch. XVIII, 175.

7. *Optatam Totius*, §4.

8. See John Calvin, *Institutes of the Christian Religion*, trans. Henry Beveridge (Peabody, MA: Hendrickson Publishers, Inc., 2008), Bk. 2, Ch. 15, "Three Things Briefly to be Regarded in Christ—i.e., His Offices of Prophet, King, and Priest," 317–322; John Henry Newman, "Sermon 5: The Three Offices of Christ," in *Sermons Bearing on the Subjects of the Day* (London/New York/Bombay: Longmans Todd, and Co., 1902), 52–62. Accessed at *Newman Reader — Works of John Henry Newman* Copyright © 2007 by The National Institute for Newman Studies.

9. *Presbyterorum Ordinis*, §13, in *Decrees of the Ecumenical Councils*, 1060.

to the spiritual life, and if, furthermore, faith only comes from hearing, the first and most important pastoral task, the *primum officium*, is indeed the ministry of the Word. Hence, apprenticing to Christ in his prophetic mode is fundamental in the seminary.

Therefore, *Optatam Totius* called for a revision of ecclesiastical studies in seminaries. Its first recommendation is that the students be grounded in the humanities as well as in the physical sciences, so that they might be able to facilitate a dialogue between the ancient faith and contemporary culture. It also called for a keen promotion of the teaching of Latin, so that the treasures of the theological tradition might be unlocked more easily, and Greek and Hebrew, so that the Bible might be more thoroughly understood.[10] Further, it strongly promoted the study of philosophy, more specifically a consideration of the issues of "humanity, the world, and God."[11] And this investigation ought to be carried out, it argued, according to "that philosophical tradition that is of permanent value," meaning apparently the great *philosophia perennis* (perennial philosophy) stretching from the ancients to the scholastics of the high Middle Ages.[12] At the same time, it recommended that the intellectual formation of seminarians ought to be supplemented by contemporary forms of thought, especially those that are dominant in their respective countries. The authors of *Optatam Totius* hope that the study of philosophy helps future priests to understand the mysteries of the faith more profoundly but also to sense the limitations of human knowledge.

In regard to theology, *Optatam Totius* stresses, first, the intimate link between doctrine and spirituality. The dogmas of the Church ought to be presented in such a way that they are not simply data for the mind but signposts on the spiritual itinerary. Secondly, it wants theology to inform a healthy and culturally engaged apologetics, so that future priests can defend the faith in a public setting. Thirdly, it wants Sacred Scripture to be taught in such a way that the students appreciate the Bible as the "soul of theology."[13] This last suggestion, of course, is congruent with the renewal of scriptural study called

---

10. *Optatam Totius*, §13

11. *Optatam Totius*, §§14 and 15.

12. *Optatam Totius*, §15.

13. *Optatam Totius*, §16.

for by *Dei Verbum*. Dogmatic theology ought to be arranged so that biblical themes come first and then the meditations of the Church Fathers, both East and West. It is not difficult to see the influence of the *ressourcement* tradition in this manner of laying out the starting points for dogmatics. Having taken in the scriptural and patristic foundations, the seminarians are then to be instructed in the theology of St. Thomas: "Let the students learn, with the aid of speculative reason under the guidance of St. Thomas, to penetrate them (the mysteries of the faith) more deeply and see their connection."[14] We will return later to this vexed issue of the use of Thomas Aquinas in the intellectual formation of seminarians; for the moment, we will observe only that *the formula used by Optatam Totius* —"*Thoma magistro* (with Thomas as master)"—was meant to mollify both those who wanted Thomism strongly emphasized and those who felt that only the method and not necessarily the content of Aquinas's theology should be recommended.

In line with the instincts of the liturgical movement and the strong Vatican II stress on the Sacred Liturgy, the document suggests that liturgy ought to be a privileged interpretive lens for the understanding of Christian dogma. This represented a significant shift from the prior relegation of liturgy to the arena of pastoral practice. Also, one of the most important and seminal recommendations of *Optatam Totius* is that moral theology ought to be radically renewed: "its scientific presentation ought to be more based on the teaching of Scripture."[15] This turning away from the rationalistic and purely deductive moral calculus of neoscholastic moral theology has been slow in coming but has emerged in the last two decades as an extremely significant development.

Finally, *Optatam Totius* insists that all of seminary formation be geared toward pastoral formation: "Therefore, all the methods used in training—spiritual, intellectual, and disciplinary—are to be coordinated by joint action towards this pastoral purpose."[16] In the sixth section of *Optatam Totius*, the Council Fathers specify the focus of this pastoral instruction: "The pastoral concern which should inspire

---

14. *Optatam Totius*, §17.

15. *Optatam Totius*, §16.

16. *Optatam Totius*, §4.

the whole training of students also requires that they be instructed in matters especially concerning the sacred ministry: that is, in catechesis and preaching, in the liturgy and the administration of the sacraments, in works of charity, in the duty of helping those in error and unbelievers, and in all other pastoral tasks."[17] Relatedly, seminarians should be encouraged to cultivate those virtues that "favor dialogue with people," including "the capacity of listening to others, and of opening their hearts in a spirit of charity to the various circumstances of human need."[18] We will see how thoroughly this last point is developed, under the rubric of "human formation," by both John Paul II and the authors of the *Program for Priestly Formation*.

Reception

It is really quite remarkable how these suggestive but sketchy observations have inspired such a rich tradition of interpretation and reception. No one read this text with greater care than Karol Wojtyła, the man who was an active participant in the Council proceedings and who later became the Pope most responsible for providing the Council with a definitive interpretation. In his 1992 Apostolic Exhortation *Pastores Dabo Vobis*, Pope John Paul II offered a textured reading and application of *Optatam Totius*, which has provided the framework for thinking through seminary formation in the postconciliar era.

In John Paul's document, we find the extremely influential schema of the "four pillars" of seminary education—namely, human, spiritual, intellectual, and pastoral.[19] The last three of these correspond rather clearly to *Optatam Totius*'s stress on forming seminarians who imitate Christ as priest, prophet, and shepherd. In fact, John Paul specially emphasizes the pastoral dimension, agreeing with *Optatam Totius* that all of seminary formation tends toward pastoral integration and repeating over and again throughout *Pastores Dabo Vobis* that the priest is meant to be configured to

---

17. *Optatam Totius*, §19.

18. Ibid.

19. Pope John Paul II, *Pastores Dabo Vobis* (March 15, 1992), §§43–59.

Christ, "head and shepherd of his people."[20] This seems to be John
Paul's way of articulating the difference between the manner in
which all the baptized participate in the kingly office of Christ and
the manner in which ordained priests do so. While all the faithful
exercise certain types of leadership within the context of the Mystical Body, ordained priests assume the principal responsibility of
ordering the charisms within the community toward the upbuild-
ing of the Kingdom of God. The overall purpose of the seminary
is to produce shepherds willing and able to give their lives in order
to feed, protect, and direct their flocks.

What is new in John Paul's adaptation of *Optatam Totius* is the
stress on human formation as a fourth pillar of formation. This has
its roots in the earlier document's brief evocation of certain human
qualities necessary to effective priestly ministry, but it comes too from
John Paul's deep grounding in the thought of Thomas Aquinas, one
of whose key principles is the tight relationship between nature and
grace: "*Gratia praesupponit et perficit naturam*" ("Grace presupposes and
perfects nature").[21] Since God's grace works on and transfigures a
nature that is receptive to it, corruptions in nature can effectively
compromise the effectiveness of grace. This is why, in fact, John Paul
goes so far as to say that human formation is the foundation for the
other three.[22] Another source for the Pope's preoccupation with the
human dimension of seminary formation is undoubtedly his training
in the philosophical anthropology of the phenomenological movement. From his work on Max Scheler's ethics, through his trenchant
study of moral agency in *The Acting Person*, to his meditations on sexuality in *Love and Responsibility*, Karol Wojtyła had long been interested
in the nature of human choice and identity. Thus it is not surprising that this philosopher of human nature would want the seminarians of the world to be healthy and integrated human beings. Here
John Paul echoes an adage attributed to Cardinal Albert Meyer of

20. *Pastores Dabo Vobis*, §12.

21. This scholastic dictum derives from two tenets expounded by Aquinas: *gratia
non tollat naturam, sed perficiat* in *Summa theologiae*, I, q. 1, a. 8, ad. 2; and *Sicut enim gratia
praesupponit naturam, ita oportet quod lex divina praesupponat legem naturalem* in *Summa theologiae*,
I-II, q. 99, a. 2, ad. 1.

22. *Pastores Dabo Vobis*, §43.

Chicago, a major player at Vatican II: "First we want to form gentlemen, then disciples, and finally priests." Employing an evocative
trope, John Paul says that the humanity of the priest must function
as a bridge between Christ and his people, a sort of Jacob's ladder on
which the angels of God can ascend and descend.[23]

Now what are the characteristic marks of an integrated humanity? A first, says John Paul, is the capacity to be a person of communion, which means the ability to relate to others sincerely, hospitably,
and affably. It entails freedom from arrogance and self-regard and
a willingness to reach out to those trapped in loneliness. Another
dimension of a healthy humanity is what the Pope calls "affective
maturity," which amounts to an ordering of the emotions so as to
make real love possible.[24] In his encyclical *Redemptor Hominis*, John
Paul had specified that "Man cannot live without love"; the affective
maturity he discusses in *Pastores Dabo Vobis* is the condition for the
possibility of exercising a true gift of self.[25] Essential to this emotional integration is a disciplining of the emotions in the direction of
authentic love and the living out of the nuptial meaning of the body,
which is to say, the body's potential to become a vehicle of self-giving
love for the sake of another.

The *Program for Priestly Formation* heartily embraces John Paul's
vision for human formation and amplifies it. The American bishops
speak of the movement from self-knowledge to self-acceptance and
finally to self-gift.[26] In line with the recent stress in moral theology
on virtue ethics, the *Program for Priestly Formation* emphasizes the cultivation of the classical cardinal virtues of prudence, justice, temper-
ance, and courage, and it calls as well for the future priest to practice
"humility, constancy, sincerity, patience, good manners, truthfulness,
and keeping his word."[27] It also insists that a seminarian is "a man

---

23. *Pastores Dabo Vobis*, §43; for a similar idea, see Fulton J. Sheen, *The Priest is
Not His Own* (San Francisco: Ignatius Press, 2004), 31–35, esp. 31.

24. *Pastores Dabo Vobis*, §43.

25. John Paul II, *Redemptor Hominis*, §10.

26. United States Conference of Catholic Bishops, *Program for Priestly Formation*,
5th Edition (Washington, DC: United States Conference of Catholic Bishops, 2006),
§80, pg. 33.

27. *Program for Priestly Formation*, §76, pg. 30.

who respects, cares for and has vigilance over his body,"[28] for a physically unhealthy priest will not be able to carry the burdens of the priesthood. Finally, it recommends that the seminarian cultivate a simple lifestyle and that he become "a good steward of material possessions."[29] John Paul II argued that the implementation of the Church's social teaching is an essential aspect of the New Evangelization, and central to that teaching is the conviction that the use of private property must always be for the common good. Priests and seminarians, above all, ought to witness to this healthy detachment.

One of the principal features of human formation—stressed by both John Paul II and the *Program for Priestly Formation*—is preparation for celibacy. Congruent with his customarily positive approach to the spiritual life, John Paul says that celibacy is the giving of "one's love and care to Jesus Christ and to his Church."[30] It is, above all, a mode of love and not a negation. Having said that, however, John Paul knows that the living out of celibate love depends upon a remarkable asceticism: "Freedom requires the person to be truly master of oneself, determined to fight and overcome the different forms of selfishness and individualism that threaten the life of each one, ready to open out to others, generous in dedication and service to one's neighbor."[31] A seminary must be the place where such asceticism is cultivated. The *Program for Priestly Formation* specifies that the physiological and psychological dimensions of celibacy must be presented but that, more importantly, the theological and spiritual rationale of the discipline must be brought forward, "so that it is made clear how it pertains to the logic of the ordained priesthood."[32] The scandals in the Church over the past twenty years have made painfully clear how necessary are this training and this discipline.

After delineating the main features of human formation, John Paul turns to spiritual formation, the shaping of a candidate according to the priestly character of Jesus. An anthropology unhampered by the contemporary secularist ideology understands that the human

---

28. *Program for Priestly Formation*, §76, pg. 31.

29. Ibid.

30. *Pastores Dabo Vobis*, § 44.

31. *Program for Priestly Formation*, §44, pg. 21.

32. *Pastores Dabo Vobis*, §79.

being is naturally ordered to transcendence, to becoming, in Christian language, a son or daughter of God. This configuring to God takes on a special coloring in the context of priesthood, for the priest is called to friendship with Christ, head and shepherd of his Church, as John Paul II writes: "Those who are to take on the likeness of Christ the priest by sacred ordination should form the habit of drawing close to him as friends in every detail of their lives," precisely so that they can then draw others into that same intimacy.[33] The erstwhile disciples of John the Baptist asked Jesus, "Where are you staying?" and the Lord answered, "Come, and you will see" (Jn 1:38–39). This conversation represents a permanent dynamic in the Christian spiritual life, for the religious seeker is meant, finally, to come to the house of Jesus and to remain with the Lord, learning his mind, his ways, and his style of life. The seminary should be construed as a disciplined 'staying' with Jesus so as to cultivate friendship with him.

What does this 'remaining' with Jesus look like? John Paul explicitly cites *Optatam Totius*'s "triple path" of "faithful meditation on the word of God, active participation in the Church's holy mysteries, and the service of charity to the 'little ones.'"[34] One of the very best methods, he continues, for fostering the meditation on the Word is the classic practice of *lectio divina*, which involves both listening to the Word of God and responding to it prayerfully. In fact, he argues, this attention to the Scriptures is indispensable to the work of the New Evangelization. The active participation in the mysteries is prayer in the fullest sense of the term. For the seminarian, this means the Liturgy of the Hours, prayed in its entirety, the frequent celebration of the sacrament of reconciliation, adoration of the Blessed Sacrament, the Rosary, and above all, the Eucharist on a daily basis. John Paul specially stresses the sacrament of penance for seminarians growing up in a culture that is fast losing a sense of sin and is marked by "subtle forms of self-justification."[35] The *Program for Priestly Formation* also recommends retreats and days of recollection, ascetical practice, obedience to one's superiors, simplicity of life, solitude, and regular spiritual direction, meaning at least once

---

33. *Pastores Dabo Vobis,* §45.

34. *Pastores Dabo Vobis,* §46; *Optatam Totius,* §8.

35. *Pastores Dabo Vobis,* §48.

a month. Signaling its central importance, John Paul returns to a consideration of celibacy in this context of spiritual formation. He brings out the spousal profile of the discipline, showing how celibacy conforms a man to Christ, who is bridegroom of his bride the Church. Just as a husband pledges exclusive fidelity to his wife, so the priest pledges exclusive fidelity in love to his bride, the Church. And just as a husband's chaste love brings forth children in the biological order, so the priest's chaste love brings forth new spiritual children for the Church.[36]

The third pillar that John Paul discusses is intellectual formation, the training of prophets. He notes first that this academic formation is tightly linked to the pillars of spiritual and pastoral formation. On the one hand, the drive toward intellectual perception is deeply ingrained in human nature, and on the other, spirituality, which is tantamount to friendship with Jesus, naturally seeks understanding. Further, in our time, argues John Paul, theological and philosophical acuity is especially requisite for the successful exercise of the New Evangelization. To a culture growing increasingly skeptical of religion in general and Catholicism in particular, we need priests who can sharply give reasons for the hope that is within them: "The present situation…strongly demands a high level of intellectual formation, such as will enable priests to proclaim, in a context like this, the changeless Gospel of Christ and to make it credible to the legitimate demands of human reason."[37]

Following *Optatam Totius* and his own instincts as a trained philosopher, John Paul observes that instruction in philosophy is crucial to the formation of seminarians. He subscribes to the standard justification for such study—namely, that there is a profound link between the kind of questions entertained by the philosophers and those analyzed by theologians in the light of faith—but he adds a rationale more precisely for our time. Seminarians in the postmodern period are coming of age at a time when the very notion of objective truth is in doubt. Philosophy in its classical form should help convince future priests that there is a firm foundation for their own commitment and for their preaching: "If we are not certain about the truth, how can

---

36. *Pastores Dabo Vobis*, §50.

37. *Pastores Dabo Vobis*, §51.

we put our whole life on the line, how can we have the strength to challenge others' way of living?"[38] John Paul's successor would speak famously of "the dictatorship of relativism,"[39] which has come to hold sway over much of the high culture in the West, and John Paul himself would bemoan the "culture of death" that flows precisely from this skepticism and indifferentism at the epistemological level. In order to battle these poisonous states of affairs, he wants seminarians who are grounded in the *philosophia perennis* and who embrace thereby "the cult of truth," which is to say, a deep devotion to objective truth in both the metaphysical and moral orders.[40] The *Program for Priestly Formation* lays out this very concrete curriculum: "The philosophy program must include the study of logic, epistemology, philosophy of nature, metaphysics, natural theology, anthropology, and ethics."[41] It further specifies that the thought of Thomas Aquinas in these areas should be "given the recognition that the Church accords it," noting *Optatam Totius*'s qualified endorsement of Thomism.[42]

Of course, one of the most remarkable developments in regard to the study of philosophy in a seminary context has been the emergence of programs of pre-theology throughout the Church. Since the majority of candidates approach the seminary without the requisite formation in philosophy, the bishops of the United States and a number of other countries have implemented two-year programs that include a heavy dose of philosophy, as well as courses in spirituality, basic religious studies, and the humanities.

But the intellectual formation of future priests is predicated principally on the study of theology or sacred doctrine. Taking a clear position on an issue much debated in the postconciliar period, John Paul argues that authentic theology "proceeds from the faith and aims at leading to the faith."[43] He has no truck with the view that nonbelievers can practice theology in the proper sense of the term,

38. *Pastores Dabo Vobis*, §52.

39. Joseph Ratzinger, *Mass Pro Eligendo Romano Pontifice: Homily of his Eminence Card. Joseph Ratzinger, Dean of the College of Cardinals* (April 18, 2005).

40. *Pastores Dabo Vobis*, §52.

41. *Program for Priestly Formation*, §156, pg. 59.

42. *Program for Priestly Formation*, §157, pg. 60–61.

43. *Pastores Dabo Vobis*, §53.

though they might be engaging in religious study or sociology of religion. In this context, he cites Thomas Aquinas to the effect that faith is, as it were, the *habitus* of theology, the permanent principle of its operation. Thus, the theologian is, first and foremost, a believer, but a believer who stubbornly "asks himself questions about his own faith," seeking a deeper understanding.[44] John Paul wants these two aspects to remain intimately connected and intertwined in the hearts of seminarians. Since faith brings about a relationship with Jesus Christ in his Mystical Body (the Church), true theology must have both Christological and ecclesiological dimensions. The seminarian is meant to take on the mind of Christ and to think according to the intuitions and instincts of the Church (*sentire cum ecclesia*). Moreover, theology is meant to lead to spirituality and spirituality to theology in a mutually enhancing cycle. Here, John Paul II quotes St. Bonaventure: "Let no one think that it is enough for him to read if he lacks devotion, or to engage in speculation without spiritual joy, or to be active if he has no piety, or to have knowledge without charity."[45]

Theology, says John Paul, moves in two directions, the first toward the Word of God and the second toward the human person who receives that Word. Concurring with the conciliar tradition, John Paul affirms that Sacred Scripture must be the soul of theology, informing all of its branches. But he also insists that theology must look carefully at the one who is called "to believe, to live, to communicate *to* others the Christian faith and outlook."[46] This anthropological focus should be present as well in all aspects of theology, including dogmatics, morals, canon law, and pastoral theology. Theology has always been interested in the relationship between faith and reason, but this issue is of particular importance today, given the extreme valorization of scientific reason in the wider culture. Accordingly, John Paul urges that fundamental theology be given special emphasis in the seminary curriculum. Throughout his papacy, John Paul was preoccupied with the problem of the relationship between magisterial teaching and theological speculation. Ideally, the two work in concert, the former articulating the fundamentals of the apostolic

---

44. Ibid.

45. Ibid.

46. *Pastores Dabo Vobis*, §54.

faith and the latter teasing out the implications and applications of
that faith for the present cultural situation. But in the postconciliar
period, the two often appeared as enemies, and theologians sometimes seemed to propose themselves as a second magisterium. John
Paul wants seminarians to be clear that a rival magisterium would
radically compromise the unity and missionary effectiveness of the
Church. A second major concern is the wedge that is sometimes
driven between "high scientific standards in theology and its pastoral aim."[47] Especially when it is taught in a university setting, theology can become abstract, *wissenschaftlich* (scientific), and can come to
lose its essential relationship to evangelization and pastoral praxis.
John Paul wants seminarians trained according to serious 'scientific'
methodology, but he doesn't want them thereby to lose the feel for
how theology must be applied in the pastoral setting. A third area
of interest today is the inculturation of the faith, often in cultures
that are inimical to it. In accord with the incarnational principle, the
Church holds that the unchanging Word of God must become 'flesh'
in a wide variety of different cultures. Even as it avoids all forms of
relativism and syncretism, the Church confirms that the Gospel takes
on a variety of forms and colorations as it implants itself in the many
cultures. John Paul wants seminarians to have a keen sensitivity to
the tricky dynamics of this process.

Finally, reacting to some of the extreme activist interpretations
of the faith that came to the fore in the postconciliar period, John Paul
holds strong against all forms of anti-intellectualism in the Church:
"It is necessary to oppose firmly the tendency to play down the seri-
ousness of studies and the commitment to them."[48] Especially now, he
argues, when the Church is facing such a stern challenge from ideological secularism, a sturdy intellectualism is a desideratum.

The fourth pillar that John Paul considers corresponds to the
shepherding or kingly office of the priest. From one point of view,
this training is one aspect among many, but in a larger sense, it is
the organizing principle of the whole of seminary formation. John
Paul enthusiastically cites *Optatam Totius* to the effect that "the whole
training of the students should have as its object to make them true

---

47. *Pastores Dabo Vobis*, §55.

48. *Pastores Dabo Vobis*, §56.

shepherds of souls after the example of our Lord Jesus Christ."[49] The study of theology ought to conduce, finally, to the pastoral task of preaching and catechizing; the study of worship and spirituality ought to lead, finally, to doing the work of salvation through the Eucharist and the other sacraments; and human formation ought to make the candidate a suitable bridge between the people and Christ. All of pastoral instruction is animated by and ordered to the pastoral charity of Christ himself, and seminary instruction in this area ought not to be simply making a candidate familiar with various pastoral techniques, but rather a real apprenticeship to Christ, an initiation into "the sensitivity of being a shepherd."[50] What does this look like concretely? John Paul specifies: "The conscious and mature assumption of responsibility, the interior habit of evaluating problems and establishing priorities and looking for solutions on the basis of honest motivations of faith and according to the theological demands inherent in pastoral work."[51] It is said that when, as Archbishop of Krakow, he was presented with a pastoral challenge, Karol Wojtyła would typically ask two questions: "What is the truth of faith that sheds light on this problem?" and "Whom can we get—or train—to help?"[52] This approach was born of the cultivation of the pastoral *habitus* just described.

John Paul hopes that seminarians are sent for their pastoral internships, first, to parishes, and their priority should be the care of "the sick, immigrants, refugees, and nomads," as well as those "sunk in inhuman poverty, blind violence, and unjust power."[53] Whatever power the seminarian exercises should be congruent with pastoral charity toward the weakest and most vulnerable. Of fundamental importance is that the seminarian develops his pastoral sensitivity in tandem with an awareness of the Church as mystery, communion, and mission. The work of the Church is, primarily, the work of the

---

49. *Pastores Dabo Vobis*, §57.

50. *Pastores Dabo Vobis*, §58.

51. Ibid.

52. George Weigel's interview with Bishop Stanisław Smoleński (April 9, 1997), as cited in George Weigel, *Witness to Hope: The Biography of Pope John Paul II 1920–2005* (New York: Harper Perennial, 2001), 187–188.

53. *Pastores Dabo Vobis*, §58.

Holy Spirit, and the Church prospers only under the influence of the Spirit. When he loses sight of this, the seminarian or priest falls prey to a worldly activism. The Church is not a collectivity of individuals, but rather a mystical body, a communion. Cognizant of this, the seminarian can "carry out his pastoral work with a community spirit, in heartfelt cooperation with the different members of the Church: priests and bishop, diocesan and religious priests, priests and lay people."[54] A healthy pastoral attitude excludes any sort of individualist messianism. The priest does his work as a cell in a complex organism—under the bishop, in fellowship with his brother priests, in collaboration with laity and religious, and for the sake of the people of God. Lastly, the pastorally alert seminarian knows that the Church does not *have* a mission; the Church *is* a mission.[55] Any pastoral field is a missionary field, especially in the fast-secularizing West, and the seminarian today has to be aware of the many tools available to him for proclamation and evangelization, including and especially the media of communication. The missionary attitude also involves a willingness on the part of the priest to go wherever his bishop sends him, even beyond the borders of his diocese or his country.

In its attempt to specify even further these recommendations in *Pastores Dabo Vobis*, the *Program for Priestly Formation* first discusses the proclamation of the Word, which *Presbyterorum Ordinis* famously teaches to be the *primum officium* of the priest.[56] The American bishops maintain that such proclamation is "aimed at the conversion of sinners."[57] Given the general cultural prejudice against being 'negative' in matters spiritual, this might strike us as a bit surprising, but even the most casual acquaintance with the preaching of Jesus would indicate that the bishops are in line with deep Christian sensibilities. In his inaugural address in the Gospel of Mark, Jesus says, "The kingdom of God is at hand. Repent, and believe the gospel" (Mk 1:15). The assumption of the entire New Testament is that every human being has fallen into shadow and needs to turn to the light.

---

54. *Pastores Dabo Vobis*, §59.

55. Pope Paul VI, Apostolic Exhortation *Evangelii Nuntiandi* (December 8, 1975), §§14–15.

56. *Presbyterorum Ordinis*, §4.

57. *Program of Priestly Formation*, §239, pg. 77.

Therefore, the matrix of every homily ought to be *metanoia*, turning around, conversion. Practically every Gospel presents a confrontation between Jesus and a sinner. The proclaimer of the Gospel ought, therefore, to consider a number of key questions: What are the dynamics of their conversation? How does Jesus move a given sinner to consider the offer of grace? What happens when that grace breaks through? More generally, the *Program for Priestly Formation* continues, the preacher ought to be able to affect the delicate balance between exegeting the Bible and interpreting the signs of the times. Preaching in fact is one of the privileged places where all four of the pillars come naturally together.

Next, the *Program for Priestly Formation* turns to a consideration of the sacramental ministry of the priest. Precisely because the priesthood is a type of spiritual fatherhood, it is connected intimately to the sacraments, which are the principal means by which Christ's life is communicated to his people. Baptism initiates the divine life; reconciliation restores it when it is lost; the Eucharist nourishes and sustains it; confirmation strengthens it; marriage and holy orders give it vocational focus; and the sacrament of the sick heals it and prepares it for transfiguration in a higher order. Therefore, a spiritual father has to be utterly at home with the theology and practice surrounding the sacraments. Eagerly following the lead of John Paul II, the American bishops insist that every seminarian should have "sustained contact with those who are privileged in God's eyes," which is to say, "the poor, the marginalized, the sick, and the suffering."[58] They cultivate, thereby, the preferential option for the poor, and they are also prompted to understand the "social contexts and structures that can breed injustice."[59]

Drawing on years of experience since the Council, the American bishops recommend a number of venues for the pastoral training of seminarians. These include field education placements, pastoral quarters or sustained internships during the seminary years, clinical pastoral education, which usually takes place in a hospital setting, and diaconate internships. In all of these settings, the seminarian should be under the guidance of an experienced supervisor or spiritual father who provides practical feedback and clear direction. And

---

58. *Program for Priestly Formation*, §239, pg. 81.

59. Ibid.

all of these pastoral experiments should be followed by a focused and disciplined theological reflection that "provides an opportunity for personal synthesis, the clarification of motivations, and the development of directions for life and ministry."[60] Especially in these practical settings, the seminarians should develop leadership skills, including administration and the management of the physical and financial resources of a parish or institution. Increasingly, one hears from young priests the concern that they did not receive sufficient training in this regard while in seminary. To be sure, seminaries cannot do everything, but more needs to be done in this area, especially since the majority of young priests become pastors within a few years of ordination.

Application of *Optatam Totius* Today

What draws together *Optatam Totius*, *Pastores Dabo Vobis*, and the *Program for Priestly Formation* is a stress on evangelization. John Paul II's "New Evangelization" is grounded firmly in the Vatican II documents, especially *Lumen Gentium, Gaudium et Spes, Presbyterorum Ordinis*, and *Optatam Totius*. Throughout his pontificate, John Paul emphasized the notion and unfolded its various aspects; it is clearly the master idea behind both *Pastores Dabo Vobis* and the directives of the *Program for Priestly Formation*. Accordingly, the very best way to apply *Optatam Totius* in the situation of the early twenty-first-century Church is to shape seminary programs in the light and for the purpose of the New Evangelization.

In the remainder of this paper, I should like to lay out a number of qualities that ought to characterize priests of the New Evangelization and to make at least some tentative suggestions as to how a seminary might inculcate them. First, an evangelizing priest must be deeply and personally in love with the Lord Jesus Christ. Christianity is not primarily an ideology or a program; it is, instead, a relationship with the person of the God-man. And evangelization is not the propagation of a set of ideas; it is the sharing of that relationship. Therefore, unless a person is already a friend of Jesus, he cannot offer friendship with the Lord to anyone else: *nemo dat quod non habet* (no one can give

---

60. *Program for Priestly Formation*, §239, pg. 80.

what he does not have). To be a true evangelist, the priest must not (to use the overworked cliché) just know about Jesus; he has to *know Jesus*. Therefore, the spiritual, pastoral, and academic programs of the seminary should help the student find the center and stay close to the fire. Kierkegaard said that a saint is someone whose life is about "one thing."[61] He didn't mean that the saint's life is monotonous; he meant that it is, in all of its variegation, focused on Christ alone. When a young man presents himself for admission to a Benedictine monastery, he is asked a simple question, "What do you seek?" If he is seeking anything other than God—security, the approval of others, escape from the world, or anything else—he is encouraged to turn away. The spiritual program of the seminary ought to compel the student, first, to ask and answer that same question, and if the response is in the affirmative, it ought to move him through a series of exercises—including contemplative prayer, Eucharistic adoration, *lectio divina,* the Liturgy of the Hours, mental prayer, and the Mass—designed to order the whole of his life to Christ.

Secondly, priests of the New Evangelization ought to know the story of Israel. The Good News (*euangelion*) that the first Christians shared concerned the resurrection of Jesus Christ from the dead, and that event represented the fulfillment of the promises made to the people Israel. The first evangelists consistently read the risen Jesus through the lens of the history of salvation, *kata ta grapha* (according to the Scriptures). In his resurrection from the dead, they saw the establishment of Yahweh's kingship precisely through the human kingship of a son of David, and this king, they insisted, must reign as the ruler of the world. Hence the watchword of the early Church was *Iesous Kyrios* (Jesus is Lord), a clear provocation in a culture that acknowledged Caesar as Lord. When Jesus is proclaimed in abstraction from Israel, therefore, he is diminished. In our cultural framework, he becomes a guru or a teacher of timeless spiritual truths, rather than the new king to whom final allegiance is owed. N. T. Wright has lamented that much of the Christology of the past two hundred years, both Protestant and Catholic, has

---

61. Søren Kierkegaard, *Purity of Heart is to Will One Thing: Spiritual Preparation for the Office of Confession,* trans. Douglas V. Steere (New York: Harper and Brothers Publishers, 1948), 31.

been largely Marcionite in form—that is to say, formulated without substantive reference to the Jewishness of Jesus.[62] This means that seminarians who want to declare the kingship of Jesus must be immersed in Israel, and implies that they be men of the Bible. As *Optatam Totius* and its interpretive tradition have insisted, the Bible must take pride of place in the academic program of the seminary, and Scripture must be consistently invoked as the "soul" of theology. This biblical orientation will guarantee that the future priests are filled with the ardor necessary for efficacious evangelization. As Aristotle observed in his *Rhetoric*, audiences finally listen only to an excited speaker. When the contemporary evangelist is convinced of the resurrection and furthermore appreciates the resurrection as the climax of the story of Israel, he will have the same excitement and enthusiasm evident in the first evangelists and in the authors of the New Testament.

One practical observation I would make in this context is that seminary formation in the Bible ought to put special stress on the canonical reading of the Scriptures. One unfortunate consequence of a strict application of the historical-critical method is a tendency to break the Bible into its constitutive parts and lose a sense of its narrative integrity. Another way to put this is that an exclusive use of the historical-critical method, given its preoccupation with discovering the intention of the human authors of the various biblical books, can lead to an obscuring of the purposes of the properly divine author of the entire Bible. Consequently, seminarians trained for the New Evangelization should be keenly aware of how the various biblical books relate to one another, echo one another, and contribute together to the telling of a great story, which culminates in the resurrection of Jesus Christ.

Thirdly, seminarians preparing for the New Evangelization ought to be deeply and critically conversant with the contemporary culture. John Paul stressed that the New Evangelization ought to be new in ardor, but he also insisted that it be new in expression.[63] This means

---

62. N. T. Wright, *Jesus and the Victory of God*, vol. 2 of *Christian Origins and the Question of God* (Minneapolis: Fortress Press, 1996), 25–27.

63. John Paul II, "Address to the Assembly of CELAM" (March 9, 1983), §3: *AAS* 75 (1983), 778.

that seminarians concerned with announcing Jesus Christ to the world today have to know the culture well enough to formulate articulations of the faith that will be resonant with a contemporary audience. Here especially the study of philosophy is paramount. Again and again in today's Western cultural context, one hears echoes of Nietzsche's philosophy of the *Übermensch* and of Sartre's existentialism, by which I mean the valorization of self-creation and the setting aside of objective values, both epistemic and moral. It is crucially important that future evangelists understand this dynamic and have the intellectual resources to confront it. Another key theme in the contemporary culture is an atheism born of the suspicion that God represents a threat to full human flourishing. This notion, with its roots in Feuerbach, Marx, and Freud, is born of a fundamental misconception of God as a supreme being alongside of other beings. A supreme being would indeed compete with other conditioned things in the measure that they would all occupy together the same metaphysical space. But the God presented by classical Catholic philosophy is not one being, however supreme, among many, but rather is the sheer act of to-be itself, *ipsum esse subsistens*, in Aquinas's pithy formulation.[64] This distinction is pivotal, for it implies that God and creatures are not caught in a desperate zero-sum game, whereby the more God is glorified the more creatures are denigrated, and vice versa. Rather, as St. Irenaeus has it, "The glory of God is a human being fully alive."[65]

Still another dominant philosophical motif in the contemporary West is what Charles Taylor calls "the disenchanted world," which is to say, the understanding of the universe as self-sufficient, self-contained, and with no real reference to the supernatural.[66] The philosophical anthropology that corresponds to this metaphysic is, again

---

64. Aquinas, *Summa Contra Gentiles: Book Three, Providence, Part 1*, trans. Vernon J. Bourke (Notre Dame, IN: University of Notre Dame Press, 1975), III.19; *Summa theologiae*, I, q. 4, a. 2; q. 11, a. 4. For more on this point, see chapter three, "Thomas Aquinas and the New Evangelization," 48–51.

65. St. Irenaeus of Lyons, *Against Heresies*, IV.20.7. In *Irenaeus on the Christian Faith: A Condensation of* Against Heresies, trans. and ed. James R. Payton, Jr. (Eugene, OR: Pickwick Publications, 2011), 116.

66. Charles Taylor, *A Secular Age* (Cambridge, MA: The Belknap Press of Harvard University Press, 2018), 25–27, 28–42.

to borrow Taylor's terminology, that of the "buffered self."[67] Along
with many other postmodern philosophers, Taylor finds numerous
warrants for the reintroduction of a keen sense of supernaturality
and a concomitant embrace of the "porous self," a subjectivity open
to transcendence.[68] Seminarians training to be new evangelists in our
time have to be formed philosophically in such a way that they can
spy and name these indicators of transcendence, what the Church
Fathers called *semina verbi* (seeds of the Word). In regard to all of
these issues, a knowledge of what *Optatam Totius* calls "a philosophical
patrimony that is perennially valid" is indispensable.[69]

I would make a final recommendation concerning formation.
Priests of the New Evangelization should have the hearts of missionaries. Everyone knows the disturbing statistics dealing with the
decline in church attendance in most Western countries. Even the
most positive reading of the situation in the United States reveals
that more than 60% of Catholics do not attend Mass regularly,[70]
which means that the majority of Catholics are avoiding what Vatican II called "the source and summit of the Christian life."[71] This
implies that the United States—indeed most Western countries—
constitute mission territory. Seminarians today should be deeply
bothered by this situation and should burn with a passion to set it
right. They cannot succumb to the indifference and religious relativism that dominates so much of the culture. And hence they must
be immersed in the beauty of the Catholic tradition. Dietrich von
Hildebrand famously distinguished between the merely subjectively
satisfying and the objectively valuable.[72] The first is a function of
one's private tastes and experiences, but the latter overthrows and

---

67. Taylor, *A Secular Age*, 27, 37–42.

68. Taylor, *A Secular Age*, 37–42.

69. *Optatam Totius*, §15. Translation slightly amended from the official Vatican version.

70. See Lydia Saad, "Catholics' Church Attendance Resumes Downward Slide,"
Gallup (April 9, 2018). https://news.gallup.com/poll/232226/church-attendance-
among-catholics-resumes-downward-slide.aspx.

71. Vatican Council II, Dogmatic Constitution of the Church *Lumen Gentium* (November 21, 1964), §11.

72. Dietrich von Hildebrand, *Christian Ethics* (New York: David McKay Company, Inc., 1953), 34–63. For more on this point in von Hildebrand, see chapter two,
"Evangelizing the Nones," 24–25.

transforms subjectivity, imposing itself with an undeniable authority. The *Divine Comedy*, *The Canterbury Tales*, Chartres Cathedral, the
Sistine Ceiling, and the stories of Flannery O'Connor are not things
that we like or don't like, according to our individual taste. They are
instances of the Good, objective values, to which subjectivity must
accommodate itself. And the truly beautiful, as Balthasar argued, not
only stops us in our tracks (aesthetic arrest) but sends us on mission.[73]
If seminarians are to be true missionaries, therefore, they have to
be connoisseurs of Catholic beauty, for it is especially the encounter
with the objectively valuable that will convince them that their lives
are not about them.

Conclusion

Sadly, the mass exodus of priests in the sixties and seventies of
the last century was closely followed by the clergy sex abuse scandal, the worst crisis in the history of the American Church. The
last several decades have been, it is fair to say, a bleak season for
the priesthood. Yet within that period, very real rays of light have
appeared. Among these are *Optatam Totius*, *Pastores Dabo Vobis*, the
Program of Priestly Formation, and most remarkably, the heroic priesthood of John Paul II himself. One is reminded of the narrative told
at the beginning of the first book of Samuel concerning Eli and his
wicked sons, Hophni and Phineas. Eli was a sort of high priest, and
his sons were priests. Hophni and Phineas were using their authority to abuse the people they were meant to serve, but when complaints were brought to their father, he did nothing.[74] The result of
this wickedness and indifference was disastrous for Israel: the Philistines routed the Israelite army, killing 30,000 soldiers and making
off with the Ark of the Covenant. When Eli heard the news of the
death of his sons, he himself fell over dead. But in anticipation of
this calamity, Yahweh had quietly stirred the heart of Hannah to

---

73. Hans Urs von Balthasar, *The Glory of the Lord: Theological Aesthetics*, vol. 1,
Seeing the Form, trans. Erasmo Leiva-Merikakis (San Francisco: Ignatius Press, 2009),
312–313. See also the discussion in chapter five, "How Von Balthasar Changed My
Mind," 74–75.

74. For more insight for our present situation from the story of Eli and his sons,
see chapter ten, "Examining the Sexual Abuse Scandal with Biblical Eyes," 155–157.

beg for a son, and that child, Samuel, would come of age as one of the most powerful figures in Israelite history, setting the nation back on course and anointing David as King. God never gives up on his people, and he never tires of renewing the priesthood. The adoption of *Optatam Totius* and its rich implementation over the past fifty years represents one of the clearest signs of that renewal.

CHAPTER 12

IMAGO DEI AS PRIVILEGE AND MISSION

Reflections Offered for the 2015 World Meeting of Families

That we human beings have been made in the image and likeness of God is one of the best-known doctrines of the Bible, but I don't think that even devout Christians and Jews have begun to unpack the full significance of this claim. There is no philosophy, no religion, no social theory, no ideology that has ever proposed a more thoroughgoing affirmation of the human being than the Bible has. Neither ancient programs of perfectibility, nor Renaissance humanism, nor modern progressivism, nor Marxism, nor the contemporary valorization of freedom have come close to holding up the human person as high as do the Scriptures. For the biblical authors' claim is that the human being is marked, in every aspect of his existence, by a likeness unto God, that he has been endowed with a distinctive mission from God, and that he is ultimately destined for life on high in union with God.

Atheism, both old and new, is predicated upon the assumption that God poses a threat to human flourishing. Thus, Ludwig Feuerbach, the founder of modern atheism, is known for the idea that "the No to God is the Yes to man!"[1] Karl Marx, an ardent disciple of

---

1. This paraphrase of Feuerbach comes from Walter Kasper, *The God of Jesus Christ* (New York: Continuum Books, T&T Clark International, 2012), 29; see also Walter Kasper, *Der Gott Jesu Christi* (Mainz: Matthias-Grünewald-Verlag, 1982), 45.

Feuerbach, could characterize religion as the "opium of the people" (*die Religion ist das Opium des Volkes*).[2] And Sigmund Freud, moving down the same avenue of thought, could argue that religious faith is an infantile fantasy, a dream from which an enlightened humanity should wake.[3] Mikhail Bakunin, the father of collectivist anarchism, proposed the syllogism, "If God is, man is a slave; now, man can and must be free; then, God does not exist."[4] Finally, Christopher Hitchens could propose a book with the simple title *God is Not Great: How Religion Poisons Everything*. All of these atheists take for granted that divinity and humanity are caught in a desperate zero-sum game, whereby the more glory God gets, the less glory we receive, and vice versa.[5]

The Bible consistently proposes a completely opposing vision, best summed up in an image from the third chapter of the book of Exodus. While tending his flock on the slopes of Mt. Sinai, Moses spied a peculiar sight: a bush that was on fire but not consumed. And from that bush came the voice of the God who identified himself as the One Who Is, "I am who I am" (Ex 3:14). The point is this: the closer the true God comes to his creation, the more beautiful and radiant that creation becomes. The drama of human life consists in realizing the full implications of this noncompetitive relationship with the living God. The French spiritual master Leon Bloy reminded us a century ago that the only real sadness in life is not to be a saint—that is to say, not fully to become the image of God that each of us is meant to be.[6] What I should like to do in the course of this chapter is to explore the meaning of the *imago Dei* and to search out the many ways that baptized Christians are summoned to embody it.

2. Karl Marx, *A Contribution to the Critique of Hegel's Philosophy of Right: Introduction*, trans. Annette Jolin and Joseph O'Malley (Cambridge: Cambridge University Press, 1970), 131.

3. Sigmund Freud, *The Future of an Illusion*, trans. Gregory C. Richter (Ontario: Broadview Editions, 2012), 92–95, 98–100.

4. Mikhail Bakunin, *God and the State*, trans. Benjamin Tucker (New York: Mother Earth Publishing Association, 1916), 25.

5. For more on this subject, see chapter three, "Thomas Aquinas and the New Evangelization," 35–38.

6. Léon Bloy, *Pilgrim of the Absolute*, trans. John Coleman and Harry Lorin Binsse (New York: Pantheon Books Inc., 1947), 301.

Back to the Beginning

Let us begin our investigation by returning to the endlessly suggestive story told in the opening chapters of the book of Genesis. Most of the controversies surrounding the Genesis account of creation as an alternative 'science' are exercises in missing the point. The key to understanding the initial moves in the Bible is theological and, more precisely, liturgical. We should notice, first, the difference that obtains between the scriptural story and the myths of origin found in practically every other ancient culture. In those latter accounts, the order of creation follows upon some primordial act of violence, usually a battle between rival gods, resulting in the victory of one and the dismembering of the other.[7] But there is none of this in the book of Genesis, according to which God creates, not through violence against a rival force or the aggressive shaping of some pre-existing stuff, but rather through a sheerly peaceful act of speech: "Let there be light, and there was light" (Gn 1:3).

The theological tradition has described this process with the phrase *creatio ex nihilo* (creation from nothing), implying that, quite literally, nothing stands between the Creator God and the creatures whom he brings, from moment to moment, into existence. The being of the latter is not "over and against" the being of the former; instead, creation is, in Thomas Aquinas's remarkable language, *nihil est aliud realiter quam relatio quaedam ad Deum cum novitate essendi* ("nothing but a relation of the creature to the Creator together with a beginning of existence").[8] On the biblical reading, the most fundamental truth of things is nonviolence, continuity, co-operation.

Next we should notice how all of the elements of creation, as they flow forth harmoniously from God, form a sort of stately liturgical procession: the light, followed by the waters above the heavens, followed by the sea and dry land, followed by the plants, and followed by the animals. It is not the least bit incidental to observe that all of those

---

7. For more detail on this subject, see chapter ten, "Examining the Sexual Abuse Scandal with Biblical Eyes," 151–152.

8. St. Thomas Aquinas, *On the Power of God (Quaestiones Disputatae de Potentia Dei)*, trans. English Dominican Fathers (Westminster, MA: The Newman Press, 1952), q. 3, a. 3, *respondeo*. For more on this theme in Aquinas, see chapter three, "Thomas Aquinas and the New Evangelization," 47–48, and chapter seven, "The One Who Is, The One Who Gives," 101–102.

realities were, at one time or another in the ancient world, worshipped as gods. The author of the book of Genesis is effectively dethroning and desacralizing them but also giving them their proper place as liturgical actors: all of creation is designed to praise the Creator.

Coming at the very end of the liturgical procession (which position signals the most important player) is the human being, whose task it will be to give voice to the praise of all creation, to worship God on behalf of the entire universe. This is why the Jewish scriptural interpreters of the intertestamental period as well as the Fathers of the Church consistently presented Adam as the first priest and the Garden of Eden as a sort of primordial temple. Walking in easy fellowship with the Lord and with all of his faculties aligned to God, Adam, prior to the Fall, is in the stance of *adoratio* (mouth to mouth) vis-à-vis the Creator. This is precisely what authentic worship entails: not something for the benefit of God—for how could God possibly benefit from what he has made in its entirety?—but rather something for our benefit. We become rightly ordered in the measure that we place God at the center of our concern. Humans as priests of creation.

In the second account of creation, we hear that God wanted to make a suitable partner for the first man and so brought forth a variety of animals whom Adam named. The Church Fathers loved this image, for it signaled, they thought, the scientific and philosophical vocation of human beings. It is crucially important to note that Adam named the animals not arbitrarily but rather *kata logon*, according to the *logos* or inherent intelligibility placed in them by the Creator. Joseph Ratzinger and many others have argued that the modern physical sciences emerged when and where they did, precisely because of certain properly theological assumptions; namely, that the world is not God and that the world, in every detail, is marked by intelligibility.[9] If the world were construed as divine—as it is in most forms of nature mysticism—it would not be a fit object of investigation, analysis, and experimentation. By the same token, if the universe were not imbued, in every nook and cranny, with intelligibility, it would not be sought out by inquiring minds. Both of these assumptions are, as I suggested, theological in nature, for both

---

9. Joseph Ratzinger, *Introduction to Christianity*, trans. J. R. Foster and Michael J. Miller (San Francisco: Ignatius Press, 2004), 152–155.

are corollaries of the doctrine of creation. What we see here is the prophetic or truth-telling dimension of the *imago Dei*. Just as human beings are designed to praise God on behalf of all creation, so they are intended to name the truth of things, so that, through them, the universe might come to understand itself aright.

At the close of the first creation narrative, God says to Adam and Eve, "Be fertile and multiply; fill the earth and subdue it. Have dominion over the fish of the sea, the birds of the air, and all the living things that move on the earth" (Gn 1:28). These verses have, of course, proven controversial in recent years, since they seem to signal that humans are given an exploitative lordship over the rest of creation. But that is not what is meant here. The sense of the biblical term "dominion" is stewardship, a lordship indeed, but according to God's nonviolent and loving purpose. The human being is meant to tend and protect the Garden, preserving it as a place where God's Lordship is in evidence. Stamped with God's image, human beings are the Lord's viceroys, governing the beautiful creation in God's name.[10] To exploit, to take advantage of, or to dominate through violence would be utterly opposed to God's nature, as that nature is revealed in the act of creation itself.

If we follow the prompts of some of the early Jewish readers of Genesis, Adam, having properly governed Eden, is then charged with 'Edenizing' the world—that is to say, establishing the good order of the Garden everywhere. What I have been describing is the properly kingly dimension of the *imago Dei*. In a word, the human being's vocation is to lead all of creation in right praise, to name and understand things *kata logon*, which is to say, as they are, and finally rightly to order things so as to preserve the integrity and beauty of what God has made. Could God have accomplished all of this on his own? Well, certainly. But he desired to give his human creatures the privilege of participating in his governance of the world.

So much attention over the centuries has been paid to the forbidden fruit that we easily enough overlook the extraordinary divine permission given to our first parents: "You are free to eat from any of the trees of the garden except the tree of knowledge of good and bad"

---

10. N. T. Wright, *Paul and the Faithfulness of God* (Minneapolis: Fortress Press, 2013), 686.

(Gn 2:16–17). The Church Fathers interpreted the ranginess of Adam in the Garden as evocative of the human cultivation of science, philosophy, literature, politics, conversation, and art—all of the endeavors that make life worth living. St. Irenaeus's magnificent phrase is apposite here: "The glory of God is a human being fully alive."[11]

What I hope is eminently clear is that this vocation cannot be construed as merely private. It is, by its very nature, a vocation for the world, on behalf of the world. I will return to this theme a bit later in the text, but allow me to signal at the outset that so much of the momentum of public opinion is in the direction of privatizing religious obligation and vocation. This might be in line with contemporary sensibilities, but it is distinctly unbiblical. Therefore, a fundamental scriptural affirmation is that we have been made in the image and likeness of God. This is our pride, our joy, and our vocation. However, a balancing scriptural assertion is that we have fallen from grace and that the image in us has, accordingly, been compromised. This means that our capacity to function as priests, prophets, and kings is attenuated.

Let's look at the Fall first in terms of priesthood. When Adam and Eve grasped at the forbidden fruit, they were arrogating to themselves what is a unique prerogative of God—namely, the determination of good and evil. In so doing, they effectively turned themselves into gods, and this led to their expulsion from the Garden, for it conduced automatically to a suspension of right praise. When anything other than God is the object of worship, the individual worshipper disintegrates, and around him the family, society, and culture tend to disintegrate. In the strict sense, orthodoxy (right praise) is always the central issue: when we worship errantly, trouble ensues.

The grasp at godliness also entails the loss of the prophetic identity, for it involves a move into intellectual arbitrariness. When they seize at the knowledge of good and evil, they commence automatically to name things according to their own whims and private preferences, rather than *kata logon* (according to reason), and this in turn conduces toward a corruption of philosophy and science. The great twentieth-century Jesuit philosopher Bernard Lonergan pointed out,

---

11. St. Irenaeus of Lyons, *Against Heresies*, IV.20.7. In *Irenaeus on the Christian Faith: A Condensation of* Against Heresies, trans. and ed. James R. Payton, Jr. (Eugene, OR: Pickwick Publications, 2011), 116.

over and again, how the fallen mind, turned in upon itself, is insufficiently "attentive, intelligent, reasonable, and responsible."[12]

Finally, following the suggestion of the serpent is a function of
bad kingship. Though they are supposed to be good stewards of the
Garden, Adam and Eve allow the snake to hold sway, going so far as
to submit to his direction and insinuation. Those who are intended
to be the viceroys of the Creator God become, instead, lackeys of a
wicked ruler—and the result is a disaster for the Garden and a suspension of the program of 'Edenizing' the world.

Israel, Christ, and the Church

So what does God do? He sends a rescue operation. A basic biblical
truth is that God never delights in sin or the suffering of the sinner.
Rather, he burns to set things right. All scriptural references to the
anger or wrath of God should not be interpreted along emotional
lines, as though God falls in and out of snits; they should instead be
read as poetic evocations of God's passion for justice.

The means that the Lord chose for his work of salvation was a
people Israel, a family formed after his own mind and heart. By the
integrity of their worship and their moral life, they would become a
beacon to the rest of the world, drawing everyone back into union
with their Creator. Notice how God sends a series of priests, prophets, and kings—anointed figures—whose purpose is to shape Israel
once again according to the pattern of Adam before the Fall.

The priests—including Noah, Abraham, Moses, David, and the
myriad officials of the Jerusalem Temple—instructed Israel in right
praise. The Temple, adorned inside and out with depictions of plants,
animals, sun, moon, and the planets, was designed to be a recapitula-
tion of the Garden, the place where the whole of creation gathered to
praise the Lord. The prophets—including Elijah, Elisha, Isaiah, Jeremiah, and Ezekiel—were sent in order to align the mind of Israel
with the mind of Yahweh. The Bible is clear that sin has affected not
only the will but the mind as well, thus preventing us from seeing the
world according to the patterns of grace. It was precisely due to this

---

12. Bernard Lonergan, *Method in Theology*, in *Collected Works of Bernard Lonergan*,
vol. 14 (Toronto: University of Toronto Press, 2017), 273.

fallenness of the mind that the prophets were, almost without exception, seen as strange and marginal figures, out of step with mainstream thought, and why many of them were persecuted. Finally, God sent a line of kings—from Saul and David to Solomon, Josiah, and Hezekiah—whose task was to restore the lost order of Eden, to govern the nation according to the purposes of God, and to protect it from threats both internal and external. Now just as the temple leadership became corrupt and the prophets were ignored or killed, so the kings of Israel tended not to live up to their calling. Even David, Israel's greatest king, was a murderer and adulterer, and Solomon, the wisest of all the nation's leaders, succumbed to idolatry.

And therefore Israel's mission went off the rails, and the family covenant was unfulfilled. The most heartbreaking and theologically challenging moment in Israelite history was the destruction of Jerusalem, the burning of the Temple, and the forced exile of the cream of the society, affected by the Babylonian invaders in 587 BC. This demonstrated, in the minds of the most theologically alert, that Israel's identity and purpose were seriously compromised. This is why Israel began to dream of a Messiah, a new David, a new Moses, who would fulfill the covenant, restore the integrity of the Temple, deal with the enemies of the nation, unite the tribes, and ultimately rule as Lord of the world.[13] We can discern the job description of the anointed one easily enough by consulting the Psalms and the Prophets. How wonderful and illuminating, therefore, that the first Christians referred to Jesus of Nazareth as *Maschiach*, rendered in Greek as *Christos*. In so naming him, they were acknowledging Jesus as precisely the figure for whom the heart of Israel longed.

Was Jesus a priest? Definitively so! In reference to himself, he said, "Something greater than the temple is here" (Mt 12:6), implying that his own person is now the privileged place where divinity and humanity are reconciled. And on the cross, he performed the final priestly act, offering his body as an oblation to the Father.

Was he a prophet? Unsurpassably so! Not only did he preach the truth, but he was, as St. John so clearly argues, the Truth in person, so that every gesture of his was also an illuminating word (Jn 14:6). We

---

13. N. T. Wright, *The New Testament and the People of God*, vol. 1 of *Christian Origins and the Question of God* (Minneapolis: Fortress Press, 1992), 280, 300.

notice how central to his teaching were nonviolence, forgiveness, and compassion, the very values that restore the lost order of Eden.

Was he a king? Absolutely! He did battle with the powers, both religious and secular, that held Israel captive, and he fought not with the weapons of the world but with the weapons of the spirit. That battle came to a head on the cross, when all of the forces of sin and dysfunction met him and found themselves swallowed up in the divine mercy: "Father, forgive them, for they know not what they do" (Lk 23:34). How appropriate, therefore, was Pilate's placing of a sign over the cross of Jesus, designating the crucified one as "King of the Jews" (Jn 19:19–21).

As priest, prophet, and king, Jesus became, not simply the founder of a new community, but the organic head of a new body. Grafted onto him, the Church takes on the task and responsibility of Israel and Adam: to 'Edenize' the world and to restore creation to its integrity. As Vatican II so clearly taught, all of the members of the Mystical Body, therefore, have priestly, prophetic, and kingly orders. All of the baptized are meant to be vehicles of sanctification, instruction, and right governance.

In accord with the subjectivism of our culture, many Christians think of their spiritual lives in an essentially individualist way, as the cultivation of their personal friendship with God. But this is to overlook something that the New Testament authors took for granted—namely, that Christians exist not for themselves but for the world. Jesus compared his followers to salt, which is designed to preserve and enhance something other than itself, and to light, whose purpose is to be set on a stand in order to illumine what is around it (Mt 5:13–14). Pope Paul VI articulated the same truth: the Church doesn't have a mission; the Church *is* a mission.[14]

The *Imago Dei* in the Life of the Church

Priestly Office

So let us see how the priestly, prophetic, and kingly offices play themselves out in the life of the Church today. We will look first at the

---

14. Pope Paul VI, Apostolic Exhortation *Evangelii Nuntiandi* (December 8, 1975), §§14–15.

priestly dimension of the *imago*. If the Scriptures are right, the single greatest problem today is what it has always been throughout human history: lack of orthodoxy, a suspension of right praise. Like the woman at the well, most of us are looking for love in all of the wrong places. Like the priests of Ba'al, most of us hop around the altars to gods that cannot, even in principle, satisfy us. Following the prompt of Thomas Aquinas, we might imagine that well and those altars to the Ba'als as symbolic of our quest for the four great substitutes for God—namely, wealth, pleasure, power, and honor.[15] The more we order our infinite longing for God toward one of these finite objects, the more addicted we become, even to the point of doing damage to ourselves, which is powerfully suggested by the priests of Ba'al slashing themselves as they supplicate their false gods (1 Kgs 18:28). The elegant liturgical formula "Glory to God in the highest and on earth peace to people of good will" functions a sort of prescription: in the measure that our worship is rightly directed, order obtains both in ourselves and in the wider society.[16]

This is precisely why the great theologians of the Liturgical Movement and the Fathers of Vatican II called for a revival of the Mass, including the full, conscious, and active participation of the laity. Awakening the people of God to a keener awareness of right worship would, they wagered, shape Catholics more fully for their work of mission and evangelization. As Benedict XVI commented in *Sacramentum Caritatis*, the concluding words of the Mass, *Ite, missa est,* "succinctly express the missionary nature of the Church."[17] Dorothy Day and Peter Maurin, the cofounders of the Catholic Worker Movement, never tired of saying "cult, culture, cultivation," or, in other words, that cult (liturgy and prayer) cultivates the culture.[18] When he came to Gethsemani Abbey for a Holy Week retreat in 1941, the young Thomas Merton said, "This is the only real city in

---

15. Aquinas, *Summa theologiae*, I-II, q. 2; Aquinas, *Summa Contra Gentiles* III, 25–37.

16. *Roman Missal* © 2010 International Commission on English in the Liturgy Corporation. Cf. Lk 2:14.

17. Pope Benedict XVI, Apostolic Exhortation *Sacramentum Caritatis* (February 22, 2007), §51.

18. Peter Maurin, "Building Churches," in *Easy Essays* (Eugene, OR: Wipf and Stock Publishers, 2003), 28–29.

America—in a desert. It is the axle around which the whole country blindly turns."[19] Any remaking of the culture undertaken without reference to rightness of praise will founder.

But how have Catholics been doing in this regard since the Council? The statistics tell a disturbing story. In the United States, over 60% of baptized Catholics regularly stay away from what Vatican II called "the source and summit of the Christian life," and the numbers in Australia and Europe are far worse.[20] Moreover, the numbers of Catholics who are having their babies baptized or who seek out marriage in the Church are plummeting. If you had told Romano Guardini, Henri de Lubac, Yves Congar, or Reynold Hillenbrand—all great leaders of the preconciliar liturgical movement—that in 2015, the overwhelming majority of Catholics in the West rarely attend Mass, they would have seen their work as a failure.

But this is not what the Vatican II Fathers wanted! They wanted a revitalized liturgy to give rise to great Catholic lawyers, great Catholic physicians and nurses, great Catholic business leaders and investors, great Catholic writers and journalists, and great Catholic parents. One wonders whether one of the factors contributing to the emergence of a secularist ideology today is the withdrawal of so many Catholics from the sacraments and hence, *as properly formed Catholics*, from the secular arena.

St. Pope John Paul II urged us to see the family as an *ecclesiola* (a little church), which is to say, a place where people learn to pray and to make God the absolute center of their lives. The rosary, morning and evening prayers, blessings of children as they go off to bed, regular attendance at Mass and participation in the other sacraments of course—through all these practices, families develop as schools of prayer.[21] One cannot help but think in this context of the manner in which Karol Wojtyła's father, by his quiet but consistent piety, shaped his son to be the saint who would, in time, transform the face of the earth.

---

19. Thomas Merton, *Run to the Mountain: The Story of a Vocation*, ed. Patrick Hart (San Francisco: Harper San Francisco, 1995), 333.

20. Lydia Saad, "Catholics' Church Attendance Resumes Downward Slide," *Gallup* (April 9, 2018). https://news.gallup.com/poll/232226/church-attendance -among-catholics-resumes-downward-slide.aspx.

21. Pope John Paul II, Apostolic Exhortation *Familiaris Consortio* (November 22, 1981), §§59–62.

But the secularist ideology today is telling especially our young people that they can be perfectly happy through the worship of wealth, pleasure, honor, and power.[22] In this situation, those who share in the priesthood of Jesus Christ cannot be content to exercise their worship in private. The prophet Elijah was not content simply to worship the true God in the right way; rather, he actively challenged the false worship practiced by King Ahab and his wife Jezebel. When Ahab responded in anger, Elijah took on the 450 priests of Ba'al on Mt. Carmel. (As has been true from ancient times to the present day, the avatars of the false gods are always thick on the ground.) How deliciously Elijah mocked the advocates of errant worship: "When it was noon, Elijah taunted them, 'Call louder, for he is a god; he may be busy doing his business, or may be on a journey. Perhaps he is asleep and must be awakened'" (1 Kgs 18:27).

Recall, too, John Paul II's visit to Warsaw in June of 1979. In the capital city of one of the principal nations of the Soviet bloc, surrounded by officials of the Communist government, hemmed in on all sides by spies and informers, the Pope spoke to the people of God, of human rights and dignity, of creation, salvation, and eternal life. And the hundreds of thousands took up a chant: "We want God! We want God!" On and on it went, "We want God!" for over fifteen minutes.[23] Prescient political observers at the time realized that this was the beginning of the end of the Communist regime in Poland. Canny theological observers knew that they were witnessing a late twentieth-century reiteration of Elijah and the priests of Ba'al. Christians must, in the manner of Elijah, publicly expose, even mock, the myriad forms of false worship that obtain in our society. This is precisely why the tendency in the West to reduce religious liberty to freedom of worship in private is unacceptable to serious Christians.

Prophetic Office

As we have seen, the New Israel of the Church is also called to be a prophetic people, which means a people who boldly witness to the

---

22. *Summa theologiae*, I-II, q. 2; Aquinas, *Summa Contra Gentiles* III, 25–37.

23. George Weigel, *Witness to Hope: The Biography of Pope John Paul II 1920–2005* (New York: Harper Perennial, 2001), 293, 295.

truth of things. One of the dimensions of the original sin of Adam and Eve is the skewing or setting aside of truth for the sake of protecting the ego. Once they grasp at the tree of the knowledge of good and evil, making themselves thereby the criterion of truth, they will no longer 'catalogue' reality, but rather name it according to their own whims and for the suiting of their needs.

Many have commented how this 'grasping' tendency manifests itself today especially in regard to the body and sexuality. In the Gnostic mode, the body is seen as an infinitely malleable substance that can be twisted, stretched, and redefined according to our desire for self-creation. I call this impulse Gnostic because it is predicated upon a dualist anthropology according to which the spiritual dimension of the human being (mind and freedom) hovers sovereignly over the material and manipulates it. We find something similar in Nietzsche's will to power philosophy,[24] as well as in Sartre's insistence that "existence precedes essence," which means that arbitrary freedom determines the nature of reality.[25] Should you think that this is all just abstractly philosophical, peruse the famous decision of the US Supreme Court in the matter of *Casey v. Planned Parenthood*. Articulating what amounts to an existentialism more radical than anything proposed by Sartre, the justices declared that it belongs to the nature of liberty to determine the meaning of one's own existence and indeed of the universe itself![26] But all of this is repugnant to a biblical vision. On the scriptural reading, the body has its own integrity and moral intelligibility, which constitutes an objective datum and that informs the mind and constrains arbitrary freedom. In a word, we can discern finalities and purposes within the structure of matter—and this provides the ground for a moral discourse that can be undertaken even by representatives of differing religious systems.

---

24. Friedrich Nietzsche, *Thus Spoke Zarathustra*, trans. Adrian Del Caro (Cambridge: Cambridge University Press, 2006), I, Prologue 3–5; Nietzsche, *Beyond Good and Evil*, trans. Judith Norman (Cambridge: Cambridge University Press, 2002), 42–44, 88–90, 112–115; 22–23, 36, 48, 106, 153.

25. Jean-Paul Sartre, *Existentialism is a Humanism*, trans. Carol Macomber (New Haven, CT: Yale University Press, 2007), 22, 24, 29.

26. Casey v. Planned Parenthood of Southeastern Pennsylvania, 505 U.S. 833 (1992), no. 851.

The Gnostic anthropology that we have been criticizing is in tight correlation to a typically modern construal of freedom. The Dominican moral theologian Servais Pinckaers famously distinguished between the "freedom of indifference" and the "freedom for excellence."[27] The former, with its roots in the speculation of William of Ockham, is freedom understood as choice and self-determination, an arbitrary hovering of the will above the yes and the no. The latter, on display in both classical philosophy and the Bible, is liberty as the disciplining of desire so as to make the achievement of the good first possible and finally effortless. Think of the manner in which a young man comes to play the piano freely or a young woman to master the intricacies of the game of golf. Each becomes free in the measure that he or she internalizes the relevant objectivities that govern the disciplines in question. On this more classical interpretation, law is not the enemy of freedom but rather the very condition for its possibility. One thinks of King David dancing ecstatically before the Ark of the Covenant, which contained the Ten Commandments (2 Sm 6:13–16). It would be difficult indeed to imagine even the most passionate advocate of law in our society dancing before a municipal tax code! And this is precisely because the freedom for excellence has been almost thoroughly trumped by the freedom of indifference, so that law is appreciated as, at best, a sort of necessary evil.

Based upon the objective truth grounded in the nature of things, the Church makes bold to speak of moral obligation. It knows that the purpose of an open mind is like that of an open mouth (as G. K. Chesterton said)—namely, to close down on something solid and nourishing.[28] Openness to all points of view and radical 'nonjudgmentalism' might be the cultural vogue of our time, but they are repugnant to the Gospel and to the mission of the Church. Moreover, the Church is in the business of making saints, not moral mediocrities. The culture might be satisfied with producing nice people, but the Church wants to make us holy: "be perfect, just as

---

27. Servais Pinckaers, OP, *Sources of Christian Ethics*, 3rd ed., trans. Sr. Mary Thomas Noble (Washington, DC: The Catholic University of America Press, 1995), 329.

28. G. K. Chesterton, "Illustrated London News" (October 10, 1908), in *Collected Works*, vol. XXVIII (San Francisco: Ignatius Press, 1987), 196; Chesterton, *Autobiography* (New York: Sheed & Ward, 1936), 229.

your heavenly Father is perfect," says the Lord (Mt 5:48). This is why the moral demand of the Church is strong, uncompromising, and abundantly clear. It does indeed recognize certain acts—such as abortion, racial discrimination, and the sexual abuse of children—as intrinsically evil and warns that we can never do such things, for any reason. But especially when its convictions and principles are applied to the sexual arena, the Church comes in for massive criticism. It is characterized as unrealistic, harsh, overbearing, insensitive, and unmerciful. But we cannot abandon our fundamental mission.

At the same time, the extreme demand of the Church is coupled with an equally extreme mercy, and one ought not to drive a wedge between the two. To the woman at the well, Zacchaeus, the good thief, the woman caught in adultery, and Mary Magdalene, Jesus demonstrates a mercy that can only be called extravagant. But in every one of those cases, he makes a concomitant moral demand. Following the example of the Lord, the Church, even as it calls her sons and daughters to spiritual heroism, lavishes upon them mercy upon mercy. If the very worst of sinners comes to confession in an attitude of true repentance, he receives forgiveness. Period. When someone falls, even to the very bottom, the Church picks her up and gives her a second chance, a third chance, a fourth chance, and so on.

Chesterton commented that a mark of the Catholic Church is a holding together of opposing elements in creative tension: asceticism and sensuality, divine immanence and divine transcendence, procreation and celibacy.[29] This characteristic style is grounded in the great paradox of the Incarnation, which is a coming together of divinity and humanity "without confusion or change, without division or separation."[30] The Church, Chesterton concluded, likes to have "two strong colors, red and white.... It has always had a healthy hatred of pink."[31] So it presents an extreme, even exaggerated, moral demand *and* an extreme, even exaggerated, mercy.

---

29. G. K. Chesterton, *Orthodoxy* (New York: Image Books, 1959), especially 90–99.

30. Heinrich Denzinger, *Enchiridion symbolorum definitionum et declarationum de rebus fidei et morum: Compendium of Creeds, Definitions, and Declarations on Matters of Faith and Morals*, 43rd ed., ed. Peter Hünermann (San Francisco: Ignatius Press, 2012), no. 302, pg. 109.

31. Chesterton, *Orthodoxy*, 99.

Kingly Office

Finally, we sons and daughters of Adam and Eve, we members of the Mystical Body of Jesus, are meant to be kings, which is to say, defenders of the garden and propagators of its good order. Human beings, the stewards of creation, are not meant to hunker down behind the walls of the garden; rather they are sent on mission to 'Edenize' the world.

One of the most significant challenges to this mission is a secularist ideology that would privatize religion and hence exclude religiously motivated people from the public conversation, allowing, perhaps, for freedom of worship but not a truly free exercise of religion. To be sure, Christians should never enter the public arena violently, aggressively, or in meanness of spirit, for such a move would undermine the very principles we are endeavoring to propagate. But we should do so boldly and confidently, for we are not announcing a private or personal spirituality but rather declaring a new King under whose lordship *everything* must fall. If Jesus is truly Lord, then government, business, family life, the arts, sexuality, and entertainment all come properly under his headship.

The great biblical image for this right ordering of the whole of life under the leadership of Jesus is found in the book of Revelation. The seer envisions the New Jerusalem coming down from heaven, and he notices that there is no temple in the holy city (Rv 21:22). This peculiar arrangement signals that the whole of the city has come so completely under the aegis of Christ that every aspect of its life is ordered to proper praise (orthodoxy). As such, no temple is necessary, for the entire city has become a temple. Kings operate in the time between the coming of Christ and the descent of the New Jerusalem, doing all that they can to make their world a place where God is consistently praised. The story of Elijah and the priests of Ba'al taught us that authentic priests are always thin on the ground compared to the avatars of the false gods; St. Augustine, likening the City of God to a tiny Noah's Ark bobbing up and down on the stormy waters of the sinful world, taught us that authentic kings are always dramatically outnumbered by the princes of the earthly city.[32]

---

32. St. Augustine, *The City of God*, ed. Marcus Dods (New York: Random House, 1950), XV.26, pg. 516.

This should not discourage us, but at the same time we ought not to be naïve about it.

Now what does this kingly mission look like concretely? It is a commonplace of Catholic Social Teaching that the family is the building block, the most fundamental unit, of civil society.[33] This is meant in far more than an arithmetic or sociological sense. If the society as a whole is meant to be a new Eden or a new Jerusalem, then the family is meant to be the place where the virtues and practices required for that transfiguration are cultivated. Within the family, one learns, first, that every member of the family is to be cherished and respected for his or her own sake. Kant's second formulation of the categorical imperative is apposite here: never treat another human being as a means merely but always as an end.[34] In a healthy family, one learns that children, parents, grandparents, and brothers and sisters unborn are all precious, none is expendable. Without that discipline, it is remarkably easy to fall into the conviction that the unborn, the elderly, the sick, the mentally ill, and even the troublesome can be shunted aside or put to death. If you doubt me, read the works of some of the leading ethicists in the academy today or witness the social practices of many countries in the so-called developed world.

Furthermore, in the family, a child learns the disciplines of obedience, fraternal correction, mutual encouragement, goal setting, self-control, appropriate punishment, and creative problem-solving. Take away the family or radically change its form, and these practices and virtues never adequately develop. To cite but one instance, many social theorists in recent years have drawn an undeniably clear correlation between the breakdown of the family—most notably the absence of fathers—and a plethora of social maladies, from unemployment and gang activity to violence and rampant substance abuse. Broken and dysfunctional families conduce to broken and dysfunctional neighborhoods and societies. Further, as an ethical relativism

---

33. See *Catechism of the Catholic Church*, 2nd ed. (Washington, DC: United States Conference of Catholic Bishops, 2000), §§2202, 2207, and 2209–2211.

34. Immanuel Kant, *Groundwork of the Metaphysics of Morals: A German–English Edition*, trans. Mary Gregor and Jens Timmermann (Cambridge: Cambridge University Press, 2011), IV, 429.20, pg. 87.

has come increasingly to hold sway in the West, the only values that remain for the determination of individual worth are power and wealth. Once we have consigned virtues such as integrity, generosity, chastity, courage, and justice to the realm of the subjective, people are compelled to measure themselves against the debased standards of dominance and money—and this has led to nothing but mischief both personally and societally. Once more, the family is the place where the objective virtues are taught and cultivated and from whence morally informed people go forth for the reworking of the culture. When this kingly responsibility is abdicated, other kings, one can be assured, will step into the breach.

Finally, I would like to emphasize how the family provides a training ground in the practice of creative nonviolence. In both the animal kingdom and among human beings, two standard responses to violence can be discerned: flight or fight. In the face of threats or injustices, we tend either to run away or to fight back using the very methods employed by those who are oppressing us. As many have pointed out, Jesus indicates, in the Sermon on the Mount, a third way, beyond fleeing or fighting, a way of engaging the wicked so as to move them to conversion. To turn the other cheek, accordingly, is not acquiescence or surrender (Mt 5:38–40); rather, it is a mirroring technique, which compels the aggressor to see his aggression. In the martial art form called Aikido, the warrior does not aggress his opponent, but rather uses his opponent's weight and momentum against him. As one proponent of this method explained once to me, the purpose of the Aikido warrior is not to injure or kill his counterpart, but instead to leave him laughing on the floor. I would suggest that what Jesus proposes in the Sermon on the Mount is a kind of spiritual and moral Aikido, a creative and nonviolent way to engage the violence of the world. There is, it seems to me, no better place for learning the ways of creative nonviolence than the family. Though it is sadly the case that people sometimes use violence against family members or simply flee from tensions within the family, normally, brothers, sons, sisters, and parents realize that they have to find another way to resolve their conflicts. Consequently, they commence to explore nonviolent means: forgiveness, loving confrontation, honest speech, and prayer. Outside of the family structure, it becomes remarkably easy, when faced with negativity, either to flee or to fight.

One of the principal ways that we will fulfill our kingly mission to Edenize the world is to practice creative nonviolence, and the privileged *locus* for training in that subtle art is the family.

Conclusion

I hope that at least one thing has become clear in the course of this chapter: the *imago Dei* is not simply a privilege in which we delight; it is a mission we are called to undertake. Marked with the image of God, we are like viceroys or representatives of a king who carry documents embossed with the sovereign's seal. We go forth, therefore, with God's authority and empowered for his work. Accordingly, the *imago Dei* is something like the talents that the master entrusted to his servants before going on a long journey (Mt 25:15–30). They were not meant to be hoarded or protected, but rather risked on the open market, given away so that they might increase. When we stand before the judgment seat of Christ, he will ask whether we have risked the *imago Dei*, whether we have taught the world how to praise, how to reverence the truth, and how to go out vigorously on campaign.

CHAPTER 13

GREATNESS OF SOUL

Remarks for the 2019 Commencement Exercises at
Thomas Aquinas College

I t is indeed a high honor for me to be speaking to the 2019 gradu-
ating class of Thomas Aquinas College, an institution that I have
admired for decades and that is situated, I am proud to say, within
the borders of my own Santa Barbara Pastoral Region.[1] I am deeply
grateful to President Michael McLean, as well as to the board and
faculty of this wonderful college. I want to offer a word of sincere
and hearty congratulation, of course, to the class of 2019 but also
to the parents of these gifted young people. It is your love that has
sustained them over the years, and this day belongs to you as much
as to them.

I distinctly remember my first visit to this beautiful campus five
years ago. I had been invited to speak to the community and had
brought a fairly serious academic paper. After the long plane trip
from Chicago and the surprisingly arduous car journey from LAX to
Santa Paula (I wasn't yet accustomed to southern California travel),
I was fairly worn out, and I was convinced that my dense presentation would bore the students—and probably myself—to tears. With
some trepidation, I made my way through the text and then, to my

---

1. The California campus of Thomas Aquinas College is located in Santa Paula,
California, within the Archdiocese of Los Angeles.

delighted surprise, entertained smart and challenging questions for the next hour and three quarters. As I remember, President McLean had to intervene to bring things to a close, even as dozens of hands remained in the air. In my wildest imagination, it would never have occurred to me that night that I would one day be the bishop presiding over this region, but I must say that one of the particular joys of my current assignment is that I can make frequent visits to this college and experience again the thrill of that initial encounter with the bright and delightfully feisty students here.

Magnanimity

How could I not take as my point of orientation today some thoughts from the patron of this school? I would like to draw your attention to a fairly obscure section of St. Thomas's *Summa theologiae*—namely, question 129 of the *Secunda Secundae*, wherein the master considers the virtue of *magnanimitas* (magnanimity), which is to say, the quality of having a great soul.[2] There is an intriguing etymological link, by the way, between the term *magna anima* in Latin and the Sanskrit title famously ascribed to Mohandas Gandhi: *Mahatma*, which means precisely the same thing, 'great soul.'

So how does Thomas elaborate upon the notion? Here is the beginning of his *respondeo* to article one of question 129: "Magnanimity by its very name denotes stretching forth of the soul to great things (*extensio animi ad magna*)."[3] And this has to do, primarily, with great moral acts, or acts for which one would expect to be honored. Thomas is quick to clarify that the magnanimous person is not interested in honors for their own sake, for such an obsession would amount to *vana gloria* or vainglory; rather, he or she is interested in doing those things that rightly deserve honor. Following Aristotle, Thomas further specifies that true magnanimity is ordered to high honor, which is another way of saying to the performance of those moral acts that are particularly hard to perform. Here is part of the *respondeo* to article five of question 129: "Accordingly it is clear that magnanimity agrees with fortitude in confirming the mind about

2. St. Thomas Aquinas, *Summa theologiae*, II-II, q. 129.

3. *Summa theologiae*, II-II, q. 129, a. 1, *respondeo*.

some difficult matter."[4] And this is from article six of the same question: "Magnanimity is chiefly about the hope of something arduous" (*magnanimitas proprie est circa spem alicuius ardui*).[5] But what is the ground for such hope? It is, says Thomas, in the moral and intellectual character of the one who knows himself capable of attaining to high, difficult, and great things. Were one not in possession of the capacity for greatness, it would be presumptuous and proud to strive toward excellence.

Some further light can be shed on our theme by considering the opposite of magnanimity—namely, pusillanimity (literally, small-souledness), and this Thomas does in question 133 of the *Secunda Secundae*. If presumption makes one strive beyond one's capabilities, pusillanimity "makes a man fall short of what is proportionate to his power, by refusing to tend to that which is commensurate thereto."[6] In light of this clarification, we see why some translators choose to render *pusillanimitas* as "faintheartedness," for it amounts to a fear of attempting the moral excellence of which a person is capable. In article two of question 133, Thomas makes the contrast unmistakably clear: "For just as the magnanimous man tends to great things out of greatness of soul, so the pusillanimous man shrinks from great things out of littleness of soul" (*ex animi parvitate*).[7] And what causes this shrinking of the soul? Thomas says, "ignorance [on the part of the intellect] of one's qualifications and on the part of the appetite the fear of failure in what one falsely deems to exceed one's ability."[8]

I trust by now it has become plain why I chose to take us on this brief tour of a usually overlooked corner of Thomas's masterpiece. It seems to me that the entire purpose of the programs here at Thomas Aquinas College is to produce magnanimous people, young women and men of great souls, capable of high moral achievement, willing and able to undertake arduous tasks for which they will rightly merit great honor. Thomas Aquinas College has no interest in giving

---

4. *Summa theologiae*, II-II, q. 129, a. 5, *respondeo*.

5. *Summa theologiae*, II-II, q. 129, a. 6.

6. *Summa theologiae*, II-II, q. 133, a. 1, *respondeo*.

7. *Summa theologiae*, II-II, q. 133, a. 2, *respondeo*.

8. Ibid.

rise to pusillanimous graduates, men and women with small souls, who would shrink from the difficult moral challenge of the present time. Given what you have learned here through strenuous effort in the classroom, given how your souls have been shaped by steady exposure to people of exemplary virtue, given the formation that has inevitably come from the Mass and the sacraments, none of you graduates should feel unqualified, either intellectually or morally, to seek the most honorable course. God knows that the world is filled with moral mediocrities, not to mention the craven and the wicked, but you have been made of sterner stuff. Thomas tells us that one of the principal marks of the magnanimous person is confidence; we send you forth today as confident men and women, ready for the high adventure of the spiritual life.

Two Challenges

Now sufficient challenges certainly rise to meet the confidence of the magnanimous today, and many of those who have preceded me in this role of commencement speaker have articulated them: materialism, ideological secularism, moral relativism, and the fruit of these three—namely, a culture of self-invention, a Nietzschean voluntarism, which has emerged as the dominant philosophy of our time. But I would like, in the short compass of this speech, to focus on two particular challenges that call forth heroic moral excellence: corruption in the Church and the massive attrition of our own Catholic people, especially the young.

There is no need to rehearse the sickening details regarding the sexual abuse of young people by priests these last several decades. Suffice it to say that attacks on the bodies and souls of the most vulnerable members of the Catholic community precisely by those ordained by Christ to be their shepherds and guardians constitutes the gravest scandal in the history of the Church in the United States. Compounding the problem, of course, has been the tragic misman-agement of the crisis on the part of some bishops and religious supe-riors. Far more concerned with the reputation of the institution than with the safety of God's people, too many ecclesial leaders allowed the rot to spread. If you seek distant historical mirrors of the present troubles, take a look at St. Peter Damian's writings in the eleventh century or the story of Eli and his wicked sons Hophni and Phineas from the first book of Samuel in the Old Testament.[9] Wicked priests and clueless religious superiors are, sadly, nothing particularly new in the life of God's people. Undermining the work of the Church in practically every way, the clerical sex abuse catastrophe has been the devil's masterpiece, and I realize that, in the wake of these revelations, many Catholics are tempted to abandon ship. In fact, in a very recent poll, fully 37% of Catholics said that they are seriously considering leaving the Church because of its corruption.[10]

But it is my conviction that this is not the time to leave; this is the time to fight. And here I call upon every magnanimous graduate sitting here before me today. Fight by entering the priesthood or religious life and live up to the dignity of your calling; fight by your very holiness of life, becoming the saint that God wants you to become; fight by doing a Holy Hour every day for the purification of the Church; fight by calling for real reform; fight by insisting that the guilty be held accountable; fight by doing the corporal and spiritual works of mercy; fight by evangelizing in your everyday life; fight by ordering your life according to the virtues; fight by playing your priestly role in the sacrifice of the Mass. And more to it, fight by sanctifying your family, your workplace, the market, the political arena, the world of high finance, even the realms of sports and entertainment. In other words, be what the Church is supposed to be in the world. In the second book of Samuel, we hear that David's corruption with Bathsheba commenced precisely when the King, instead of going on campaign as was his wont, lingered at home, indulging his private desires (2 Sm 11:2).[11] As Pope Francis has often reminded us, when the Church fails to go on campaign, when it turns in on itself, corruption is never far behind. Don't wait for other reformers to arise; this is your moment to meet this crucial moral challenge.

---

9. See chapter ten, "Examining the Sexual Abuse Scandal with Biblical Eyes," 155–157, for a more thorough discussion of the similarity of 1 Samuel and the sexual abuse crisis.

10. Jeffrey M. Jones, "Many U.S. Catholics Question Their Membership Amid Scandal," *Gallup* (March 13, 2019). https://news.gallup.com/poll/247571/catholics -question-membership-amid-scandal.aspx.

11. See chapter ten, "Examining the Sexual Abuse Scandal with Biblical Eyes," 158–159, for more analysis of this story of David and its implications for the Church today.

And no pusillanimous people need apply.

The second great crisis to which I will draw your attention is the rise of the 'nones' or the religiously unaffiliated. When I was a child, in the early 1970s, roughly 3% of our country identified as nonreligious. By the early 1990s, that figure had doubled to 6%, but still, in terms of absolute numbers, the overwhelming majority of the nation was still religious. However, today, nearly 25% of Americans surveyed claim no religious affiliation, and the situation is even direr when we focus on young people. Among those under thirty, fully 40% claim the status of 'none.' [12] And among Catholics under thirty, 50% are no longer practicing the faith.[13] Any way one looks at these statistics, one must conclude that we are hemorrhaging young people from religion in general and Catholicism in particular. In point of fact, one of the most damning figures is the ratio between those who join the Catholic Church and those who are leaving. It stands at 1:6.5—that is to say, for every one person who enters our Church, six are going out the door.[14]

I call on the magnanimous graduates sitting before me, rise to meet this challenge! And may I say that as alumni of Thomas Aquinas College, you will be uniquely positioned to do so. Numerous studies have indicated that a major reason that people are leaving the Church is that they no longer believe the doctrines put forward by classical Christianity.[15] Though many commentators are tempted to say that the mass exodus is prompted largely by the scandals, this in fact is not true. When queried why they have left the practice of the faith, most people, especially the young, tell us that they have

12. Robert P. Jones, Daniel Cox, Betsy Cooper, and Rachel Lienesch, *Exodus: Why Americans are Leaving Religion—and Why They're Unlikely to Come Back* (Washington, DC: Public Religion Research Institute, 2016).

13. Pew Research Center, "America's Changing Religious Landscape: Chapter 2" (May 12, 2015). https://www.pewforum.org/2015/05/12/chapter-2-religious-switching-and-intermarriage.

14. David Masci and Gregory A. Smith, "Seven Facts about American Catholics," *Pew Research* (October 10, 2018). https://www.pewresearch.org/fact-tank/2018/10/10/7-facts-about-american-catholics.

15. E.g., Nicolette Manglos-Weber and Christian Smith, *Understanding Former Young Catholics: Findings from a National Study of American Emerging Adults* (Notre Dame, IN: University of Notre Dame Press, 2014), 15.

done so because faith and science are implacable enemies, because God is an unnecessary hypothesis, because Jesus is one questionable mythic character among many, because the Bible is a collection of prescientific, Bronze Age fairy tales, and so on. In a word, they find Christianity intellectually untenable. You who have had the incomparable privilege these past four years carefully and critically to read Aristotle, Plato, Cicero, Newton, Thomas Aquinas, Descartes, Kant, Hegel, and Bertrand Russell are specially qualified for the arduous task of engaging the army of skeptics who have wandered from the Church. The contemplation of the great intellectuals is indeed an intrinsic good, but may I stress that especially at this moment in the Church's life, such contemplation can and should give rise to active evangelization and compelling apologetics. So, become university professors of theology, college and high school teachers of religion, catechists at the parish level, and online evangelists—and know that the moment you exit any Catholic church in America you have entered mission territory. And may I suggest to those who have a particular interest in the physical sciences that you will be in the front lines of this battle for souls. In survey after survey, many young people report that the supposed conflict of faith and science is a major intellectual obstacle to remaining a believer.[16]

Conclusion

For many years, I lived and worked at Mundelein Seminary outside of Chicago. A blend of extraordinary natural beauty and extremely fine Georgian architecture, the Seminary is one of the most striking places in the American Catholic world. Cardinal Mundelein, who actively presided over its design and construction, said that he wanted the splendor of the seminary to give the future priests an idea of heaven, so that they would never lose sight of the ultimate goal of their pastoral work among the people. This place, with its own distinctive blend of natural and man-made beauty, has always reminded me a bit of Mundelein. And indeed, this campus, where

---

16. Pew Research Center and Michael Lipka, "Why America's 'Nones' Left Religion Behind" (August 24, 2016). https://www.pewresearch.org/fact-tank /2016/08/24/why-americas-nones-left-religion-behind.

liturgy, prayer, fellowship, and deep communion with the saints and geniuses of the Catholic tradition are on steady offer, is something of a Catholic heaven on earth, an anticipation even now of the splendor of life on high with God and the saints. But just as the students at Mundelein were not meant to stay on the grounds of the seminary, so you are not meant to stay at this lovely place. Rather, you are meant to go forth, carrying what you have received and cultivated here in order to sanctify our suffering world.

Is this an arduous task? Yes! But magnanimous people like arduous tasks, for they are ordered to the moral work that will give the highest honor. Are these choppy seas? Yes! But only pusillanimous people are afraid of choppy seas. Your four years here have given you great souls. Let them be unleashed! God bless you all.

Part 4
RENEWING OUR **CULTURE**

CHAPTER 14

EDUCATION IN VIRTUE, LOVE, AND MISSION

A Reflection on Chapters Seven, Eight, and Nine of
Amoris Laetitia

It is my happy responsibility today to explicate the final three chapters of Pope Francis's Apostolic Exhortation, *Amoris Laetitia*. As all the world knows, there has been an extraordinary emphasis on the controversial sections of chapter eight, dealing with the pastoral outreach to those in irregular marital situations. Accordingly, though I will not overlook chapter eight completely, I will attend especially to the underappreciated riches in the chapters that precede and follow it. Pope Francis's focus in chapter seven is on the moral formation of young people, and his insights in this regard are not only extraordinary in themselves but also in the measure that they provide an interpretive key to the much-discussed following chapter. The final chapter of *Amoris Laetitia*, a marvelous reflection on the spirituality of marriage, is replete with both theoretical wisdom and practical recommendations, which are of enormous benefit both to those endeavoring to live out Christian marriage in its fullness as well as to those involved in ministry to couples and families.

Amoris Laetitia, Chapter Seven: Toward a Better Education of Children

Formation in Virtue

What concerns the Pope in this pivotal chapter is not so much education in the intellectual sense of the term, but rather moral and spiritual formation, the process by which parents draw their children into the dynamics of the Christian life. Though schools can be entrusted with instructing children academically, the shaping of character is, primarily, the responsibility of parents.[1] The first and indispensable condition for the possibility of this endeavor, the Pope insists, is the unconditional quality of the love that mothers and fathers show to their children.[2] Without a fundamental trust in their parents, the young people will never take in the requisite moral lessons and will encounter "deep hurt and many difficulties" along their path.[3]

But how precisely is a child formed in virtue? Showing himself the faithful disciple of both Aristotle and St. Thomas Aquinas, the Pope opines that moral formation is primarily a matter of inculcating certain habits and only secondarily a matter of teaching abstract ethical norms.[4] Like his great Greek forebear, Francis holds that "without the conscious, free, and valued repetition of certain patterns of good behavior, moral education does not take place."[5] We recall that Aristotle departed from Plato's theory that intellectual illumination would translate automatically into correct behavior, the so-called 'Socratic fallacy.' Aristotle knew that rational clarity plays a role in moral formation but that the heart of the matter is habituation, the placing of moral goodness in the bodily moves of the agent, something in the manner of an apprentice musician learning to play the violin. In paragraph 267, we find a pithy definition: "Virtue is a conviction that has become a steadfast inner principle of operation."[6]

---

1. Pope Francis, Post-Synodal Apostolic Exhortation *Amoris Laetitia* (March 19, 2016), §260.

2. *Amoris Laetitia*, §263.

3. Ibid.

4. *Amoris Laetitia*, §264.

5. *Amoris Laetitia*, §266.

6. *Amoris Laetitia*, §267.

There has been, in the last twenty-five years or so, a revival of the Aristotelian approach to ethics, especially in the writings of Alasdair MacIntyre, James William McClendon Jr., and Stanley Hauerwas. These so-called 'virtue ethicists' often compare the learning of the moral life to the picking up of a trade or the playing of a game. Hauerwas, for instance, famously proposes a comparison with the art of bricklaying.[7] It seems clear that Pope Francis has been a student of this tradition. How does one learn the moral life? Through "ideas, incentives, practical applications, stimuli, rewards, examples, models, symbols, reflections, dialogue, and a constant rethinking of our way of doing things."[8] This is classic virtue ethics language and not the language of an ethics of rules or abstract norms.

Though it appears counterintuitive to say, habits and virtues actually contribute to freedom, authentically construed. On the more modern reading, freedom is liberty from constraint, either interior or exterior. It is doing what one wants, arbitrarily determining the direction of one's life. The Dominican theologian Servais Pinckaers characterizes freedom in this modern sense as *liberte de indifference* ("freedom of indifference"), a sort of hovering indifferently over the possibilities of yes or no. And he contrasts this notion of freedom with a more classical one, which he describes as *liberte de qualite* ("freedom for excellence").[9] This is not so much arbitrary choice but rather the disciplining of desire so as to make the achievement of the good first possible and then effortless. Think here of the way in which someone becomes, in time, a free speaker of her language. It is not through a sovereign and arbitrary exercise of will that this occurs but rather through habituation to certain disciplines, practices, and norms. Hence, as Pope Francis puts it: "The virtuous life thus builds, strengthens, and shapes freedom, lest we become slaves of dehumanizing and antisocial inclinations."[10]

In paragraph 273, we find a remarkably clear presentation of the Pinckaers's distinction. In Francis's terms, this is the demarcation

---

7. See Stanley Hauerwas, *A Community of Character: Towards a Constructive Christian Social Ethic* (Notre Dame, IN: University of Notre Dame Press, 1981).

8. *Amoris Laetitia*, §267.

9. Servais Pinckaers, OP, *Sources of Christian Ethics*, trans. Sr. Mary Thomas Noble, 3rd ed. (Washington, DC: The Catholic University of America Press, 1995), 329.

10. *Amoris Laetitia*, §267.

between the authentically free and the merely voluntary.[11] Someone can, without external pressure, choose something that is objectively bad for him, and this choice will be, in the casual sense of the term, 'free'; this just means that it was the result of a person's unconstrained choice. But this, the Pope says, has little to do with real spiritual freedom, which is always a matter of choosing, easily and without internal tension, what is in fact the good. Thus, Francis reminds us, in regard to addicts, "It makes no sense to 'let them freely choose,'"[12] for such ersatz freedom will only bring harm. Again, how starkly this stands in contrast to the culture of self-creation that holds sway in so much of the West. Precisely as an "expert in humanity," to use Pope Paul VI's words, the Church has enormous resources for the formation of rightly-ordered freedom. [13]

What should be clear from this characterization is that virtue formation is never an entirely positive process; indeed, it often involves punishment, correction, and the pointing out of faults. No pianist ever became a great player without being corrected, even sharply so, and no footballer ever became a master of his game without enduring the harsh interventions of some tough coaches. And therefore, within the school of virtue that is the family, something like 'tough love' ought to obtain: "Children who are lovingly corrected feel cared for; they perceive that they are individuals whose potential is recognized."[14] Under this aegis, the Pope addresses an issue that has come to the fore in many sociological and psychological studies of the rising generation—namely, the tendency to overindulge children, to make, as Francis puts it, "everything revolve around the child's desires."[15] There is little question that today's culture tends to encourage, in young people, an attitude of entitlement and a sense of victimization, both of which conduce toward self-preoccupation. The Pope observes, "Such children will grow up with a sense of their rights but not their responsibilities."[16]

---

11. *Amoris Laetitia*, §273.

12. Ibid.

13. Pope Paul VI, *Address of the Holy Father Paul VI to the United Nations Organization* (October 4, 1965).

14. *Amoris Laetitia*, §269.

15. *Amoris Laetitia*, §270.

16. Ibid.

Another distinctly Aristotelian feature of the Pope's teaching on moral formation is his stress on ethical exemplars. When asked how to determine the right thing to do, Aristotle replied, in essence, 'Find a good man, watch him in action, and then imitate him.'[17] This is remarkably similar, of course, to the advice that a master practitioner might give to his apprentice: 'Stay with me; learn my manner of life; do what I do.' Pope John Paul II understood this principle in his bones, which is precisely why he put such great stress on the exemplary quality of the saints—and why he canonized more saints than all of his predecessors combined.[18] But Francis adds a characteristic twist to this scenario, emphasizing that even those who are less than perfect in the moral order can function as models: "Adolescents should be helped to draw analogies: to appreciate that values are best embodied in a few exemplary persons, but also realized imperfectly and to different degrees in others."[19] I think here of how some Catholic literary artists have used far less than perfect characters to exemplify some dimension of the Christian life. Consider, for example, Graham Greene's 'whiskey priest' from *The Power and the Glory* or even of the deeply compromised but still noble Sebastian from Evelyn Waugh's *Brideshead Revisited*.[20]

In paragraph 274, we find this wonderful summary statement: "The family is the first school of human values, where we learn the wise use of freedom."[21] I deeply appreciate how bracingly unsentimental that statement is! The family is not so much the place where warm feelings are cultivated (though the Pope has nothing against warm feelings) but rather the place where both parents and children are trained in virtue. This is a particularly helpful concretization of a key dictum of the Church's social teaching—namely, that the family

---

17. Aristotle, *Nicomachean Ethics*, trans. C. D. C. Reeve (Indianapolis: Hackett Publishing Company, Inc., 2014), II.7, pp. 29–32.

18. George Weigel, *Witness to Hope: The Biography of Pope John Paul II 1920–2005* (New York: Harper Perennial, 2001), 446–449.

19. *Amoris Laetitia*, §272.

20. Graham Greene, *The Power and the Glory* (New York: Penguin Books, 1990); Evelyn Waugh, *Brideshead Revisited* (New York: Back Bay Books/Little, Brown and Company, 1973).

21. *Amoris Laetitia*, §274.

is the building block of the wider society.[22] Pope Francis is clarifying that if the family breaks down, the most powerful school of virtue breaks down, and if virtue is not successfully taught, the political order founders.

Communication Technology

It is worth noting that the first specific recommendation that Pope Francis makes in chapter seven is in regard to the new means of social communication, and it is not a word of praise but rather an admonition. Francis tells mothers and fathers what they must resist if they want their children to develop Christian values: "Parents need to consider what they want their children to be exposed to, and this means being concerned about who is providing their entertainment, who is entering their rooms through television and electronic devices, and with whom they are spending their free time."[23] Though the Pope himself does not often use the devices associated with social media, he has proven to be, time and again, deeply sensitive to their prevalence and to their potential dangers. According to the Fathers of the Church, one of the fundamental tasks of Adam was the cultivation, protection, and extension of the Garden, and hence, on their reading, the original sin could be construed as a failure to exercise this charge, allowing the dark power to have sway where he should not.[24] Similarly, the kings of Israel are called upon to protect their people, though they, like Adam, typically fail. At the commencement of chapter seven, Pope Francis is summoning parents to precisely this kingly responsibility of protecting the Garden.

Now the manner in which they accomplish this task is articulated according to one of the Pope's favorite principles, borrowed from the theologian Romano Guardini—namely, that "time is greater than space."[25] This means that discipline in this arena does not amount to

22. *Catechism of the Catholic Church*, 2nd ed. (Washington, DC: United States Conference of Catholic Bishops, 2000), §§2202, 2207, and 2209–2211.

23. *Amoris Laetitia*, §260.

24. For a longer discussion on this subject, see chapter ten, "Examining the Sexual Abuse Scandal with Biblical Eyes," 151–153.

25. *Amoris Laetitia*, §261.

a tyrannical control over the domestic space but rather to a process of drawing children, gradually but firmly, toward responsible autonomy. A patient formation in discriminating between the good and the bad in the digital world is preferable to an aggressive censorship. Very much in line with Pope John Paul II's doctrine that every moral act shapes the character either for weal or for woe, Pope Francis says that this training "involves forming persons who readily understand that their own lives…are in their hands, and that freedom is itself a great gift."[26]

Crucial to the right use of social media is a formation in the virtue of hope. Pope Francis worries that all of our gadgets and communication technology promote a culture of immediate gratification, information, and entertainment. Anything that young people want can be attained, or so it seems, at the push of a button. But the best things in life—friendship, love, aesthetic beauty, a relationship with God—have to be waited for. They arrive in their own way and according to their own timetable. One of the earliest critics of modern science was the great German sage Johann Wolfgang von Goethe. He argued that Newtonian science, predicated upon an aggressive, intrusive, almost bullying rationality, yields up some data about the world, but that only a patient, observant, humble type of science actually discloses the deepest truths concerning nature.[27] For all of their power, the new technologies encourage a much more Newtonian than Goethian attitude—and this, for Francis, is a shame.

Another virtue that the Pope emphasizes in this context is socialization, because "[the family] is where we first learn to relate to others, to listen and share, to be patient and show respect, to help one another and live as one."[28] Along with an army of other social commentators, Francis worries that the new media encourage an inward-looking attitude on the part of the young and a tendency to live stubbornly in a virtual space, several steps removed

---

26. *Amoris Laetitia*, §262.

27. Hermann von Helmholtz, "The Scientific Researches of Goethe: A Lecture Delivered before the German Society of Königsburg in 1853," in *Selected Writings of Hermann von Helmholtz*, ed. Russell Kahl (Middletown, CT: Wesleyan University Press, 1971), 65, 67–68, 73. See chapter five, "How Von Balthasar Changed My Mind," 72–74, for a longer discussion of this difference.

28. *Amoris Laetitia*, §276.

from concrete reality. The American psychologist and sociologist Jean Twenge recently penned a book called *iGen*, a careful study of the effects of social media on the rising generation. She shows that those born after 1999 have indeed turned in on themselves, proving far less capable than their forebears of relating to others, socializing, and reading interpersonal cues. Moreover, they are growing up much more slowly than their generational predecessors, preferring to stay at home, delaying the acquiring of a driver's license, remaining averse to "adulting," as they put it.[29] Pope Francis appreciates the family as the privileged place where young people learn that their lives are not about them.[30] Many times, in his sermons and popular talks, he bemoans families that appear to have succumbed to the values of the social media space, with each family member sitting around the dinner table absorbed in his or her own mobile device.[31] In paragraph 278, we find this helpful summary remark: "It is clear that these media cannot replace the need for more personal and direct dialogue, which requires physical presence or at least hearing the voice of the other person."[32]

Education in Sexuality

Commencing in paragraph 280 of chapter seven, Papa Francesco broaches the sensitive topic of education in the area of sexuality, a theme strongly emphasized at Vatican II. He clearly indicates that in our instruction of children on this score, we should be willing to use the findings of the "psychological, pedagogical, and didactic sciences,"[33] but that these are never enough. Very much in line with the Thomistic conviction that grace builds on nature, Francis insists that

29. Jean M. Twenge, *iGen: Why Today's Super-Connected Kids are Growing Up Less Rebellious, More Tolerant, Less Happy—and Completely Unprepared for Adulthood (And What That Means for the Rest of Us)* (New York: Atria Books, 2017), 17–47.

30. *Amoris Laetitia*, §276.

31. See Pope Francis, *Message of His Holiness Pope Francis for the 53rd World Communications Day: We Are Members One of Another (Eph 4:25): From Social Network Communities to the Human Community* (January 24, 2019).

32. *Amoris Laetitia*, §278.

33. *Amoris Laetitia*, §280; Vatican Council II, Declaration on Christian Education *Gravissimum Educationis* (October 28, 1965), §1.

the use of these insights must be supplemented by a proper training in the virtues surrounding sexual expression, especially "an education for love, for mutual self-giving."[34] The Pope knows how thoroughly commodified and objectified sex has become in our culture, just one more means of attaining pleasure, one more 'contact sport.' But he also knows that the great biblical and theological tradition teaches that sex, like all things human, needs to be brought under the discipline of love, which is to say, willing the good of the other. And so the Church and the family must stand athwart the regnant culture and propose a more persuasive type of education in sexuality.

A first particular issue he discusses is the prevalence of pornography.[35] Though pornographic images have been available for many years, the Internet and mobile devices have made even hardcore erotic films readily available to the widest possible public. Numerous studies have indicated that the use of pornography, especially among men, is pervasive and that the earliest exposure to it typically takes place at the age of ten or eleven.[36] In very recent years, researchers have furthermore indicated that the constant use of these images have produced a generation of young men with a severely distorted sense of sexuality, a marked tendency to objectify women, and, tellingly, the inability to perform sexually with real partners. That parents should do all they can to combat this scourge—even prohibiting private use of computers—goes without saying. Another practical recommendation that Francis makes is to recover (and teach) the virtue of modesty. Though customarily mocked today as a prim Victorian preoccupation, Francis presents it as a means of empowerment, especially for women: modesty, he says, "is a natural means whereby we defend our personal privacy and prevent ourselves from being turned into objects to be used."[37]

The Pope next helpfully observes that much sex education in the West has to do with "protection" through the practice of "safe

---

34. *Amoris Laetitia*, §280.

35. *Amoris Laetitia*, §281.

36. See Matt Fradd, *The Porn Myth: Exposing the Reality Behind the Fantasy of Pornography* (San Francisco: Ignatius Press, 2017).

37. *Amoris Laetitia*, §282.

sex."[38] An initial problem with such language, he says, is that it gives
the strong impression that the procreation of children is a problem
that has to be solved, or worse, a disease that has to be prevented.
A second and more fundamental difficulty is that it promotes a sort
of narcissism, whereby one is preoccupied with protecting oneself
rather than with holding oneself open to novelty and surprise, even
to a state of affairs that might upset one's plans.[39]

As I hinted above, the ultimate purpose of all sex education,
for Pope Francis, is to teach young people how to make their bodies
and their sexuality a gift, both to their spouses and eventually to their
children. In a manner powerfully reminiscent of John Paul II, Francis speaks of "the language of the body," which "calls for a patient
apprenticeship in learning to interpret and channel desires in view
of authentic self-giving."[40] The phrase "language of the body" is
especially good, since it includes both a technical, biological understanding of the sexual organs, but also a sense of how the body com-
municates—especially through sexual intimacy—deep psychological
and spiritual truths. Over and against the cheapening and flattening
out of that communication that happens in our pornography-soaked
culture, the family offers a nuanced instruction in the bodily grammar of love.

In this same context of sexual education, Pope Francis makes
some of his strongest statements regarding the culture of self-invention
and the rise of a sort of "neo-Gnosticism." By these terms, the Pope
means the attitude, dominant throughout Western culture and with
its roots in the speculations of many modern and postmodern philosophers (including Nietzsche, Sartre, and Foucault) that human beings
essentially invent themselves through sovereign acts of freedom. As
Sartre put it pithily enough, "existence precedes essence,"[41] implying
that one's freedom comes first and then, on the basis of that freedom
alone, one determines what one's life should mean and which values one should seek. Pope Francis speaks out of the ancient Catholic

---

38. *Amoris Laetitia*, §283.

39. Ibid.

40. *Amoris Laetitia*, §284.

41. Jean-Paul Sartre, *Existentialism is a Humanism*, trans. Carol Macomber (New
Haven, CT: Yale University Press, 2007), 22, 24, 29.

tradition when he observes that objective values exist, one of which is the body itself, which carries an intrinsic intelligibility and finality.[42] The good life is not a matter of indulging in self-invention, but rather in submitting oneself to these objective goods. The Gnostic quality of the dominant cultural perspective becomes especially clear when we see how control over the body is so highly valued. The Pope, on the other hand, excoriates this tendency to think that "We enjoy absolute power over our own bodies," which conduces toward "thinking that we enjoy absolute power over creation."[43]

Relatedly, over and against the dominant gender ideology today, which construes gender simply as a malleable social construct, Pope Francis teaches that, "An appreciation of our body as male or female is also necessary for our self-awareness in an encounter with others different from ourselves."[44] Lest we think that this last comment is a one-off remark, note that it is perfectly congruent with what Francis has said on many occasions around the world, and indeed in paragraph 56 of *Amoris Laetitia*: "Yet another challenge is posed by the various forms of an ideology of gender that denies the difference and reciprocity in the nature of a man and a woman and envisages a society without sexual differences."[45] And this, also from paragraph 56: "Let us not fall into the sin of trying to replace the Creator. We are creatures and not omnipotent. Creation is prior to us and must be received as a gift."[46] There is a link, by the way, that I think is too often overlooked between this observation regarding gender ideology and the critique of the throwaway culture that is so central to *Laudato Si'*.[47] In both cases, the Pope is putting his finger on our tendency to 'play God,' to assert our lordship over creation, rather than to exercise our stewardship. Neither the earth itself nor the human body is a plaything to be manipulated according to our whim.

---

42. *Amoris Laetitia*, §285.

43. *Amoris Laetitia*, §285; Francis, Encyclical Letter *Laudato Si'* (May 24, 2015), §155.

44. *Amoris Laetitia*, §285; Francis, *Laudato Si'* (May 24, 2015), §155.

45. *Amoris Laetitia*, §56.

46. Ibid.

47. Francis, *Laudato Si'*, §§16, 20–22, 43.

Having made these forceful assertions, Pope Francis, as is his wont, offers a balancing perspective. Though gender is not fluid, he says, gender roles, nevertheless, are not entirely a function of biology. Instead, they are conditioned to a large degree by culture, history, and geography, and hence we should not accept an overly rigid characterization of these categories. "Taking on domestic chores or some aspects of raising children does not make a man less masculine or imply failure," nor is it "not very feminine to exercise leadership."[48]

After his fairly thorough discussion of sex education, the Pope brings chapter seven to a conclusion with a brief but powerful reflection on the passing on of the faith.[49] In accord with the mainstream of the Catholic tradition, Francis holds that the family is the single most important vehicle for the communication of the faith.[50] One thinks here of the admonition given to Catholic parents at the baptism of their children: "You are the first and best educators of your child in the ways of faith." University of Notre Dame sociologist Christian Smith, who has focused his research on the spiritual lives of young people, has said that the surest indicator that a child will keep the faith into adulthood is the vibrant practice of religion in his family of origin.[51] This means not only Mass on Sunday but also prayers and devotions at home and, perhaps most importantly, frequent conversation about religion and Catholicism within the family circle. The Pope confirms this: "Moments of family prayer and acts of devotion can be more powerful for evangelization than any catechism class or sermon."[52] Once more in line with the instincts of Pope John Paul II, Francis insists that, even within the family, the faith is never imposed but only proposed.[53] Not through aggression and threats, but rather through symbol, actions, stories, and attractive testimonies, parents should draw their children into the world of Catholicism.

---

48. *Amoris Laetitia*, §286.

49. *Amoris Laetitia*, §§287–290.

50. *Amoris Laetitia*, §287.

51. Nicolette Manglos-Weber and Christian Smith, *Understanding Former Young Catholics: Findings from a National Study of American Emerging Adults* (Notre Dame, IN: University of Notre Dame Press, 2014), 20.

52. *Amoris Laetitia*, §288.

53. Ibid.

Amoris Laetitia, Chapter Eight

As I mentioned at the outset, I will not spend a great deal of time on this controversial chapter of *Amoris Laetitia*, since it has already been so thoroughly analyzed by so many. What I should like to do is to place this chapter in dialogue, as it were, with the preceding chapter, for in many ways chapter eight is a meditation on education in the moral order, more precisely, the process of leading the faithful toward embracing the fullness of the Church's teaching in regard to sex and marriage.

I want to be eminently clear, as I commence this analysis, that Pope Francis is not the least interested in negating or dialing down the expectations of the Church in this arena. The Church's fundamental task, after all, is not the encouragement of spiritual and moral mediocrity, but rather the making of saints, people of heroic virtue. I would be hard-pressed to find anywhere in the magisterial tradition a clearer articulation of the Christian ideal of marriage than this from paragraph 292, "Christian marriage...is fully realized in the union between a man and a woman who give themselves to each other in a free, faithful, and exclusive love, who belong to each other until death and are open to the transmission of life."[54]

That said, it is equally clear that the Pope is extremely sensitive to the difficulties that people face in living up to the high ideal. His attitude puts me vividly in mind of Cardinal Francis George, who was a mentor to me. Speaking to the assembled seminarians at Mundelein Seminary many years ago, long before Francis became Pope, the Cardinal said, "I have great admiration for you members of the John Paul II generation, since you are so clear and enthusiastic in presenting the truth of the Church's teaching. But remember, it is never enough simply to drop the truth on people and then walk away, satisfied that you have done your job. No! Having given them the truth, you now must commit yourself to walking with them and helping them bear the burden." I know, too, having worked closely for many years with John Paul II generation seminarians, that they often struggle with their own weakness. When they failed to live up to the heroic ideal of John Paul, they sometimes didn't know what to do and discouragement set in.

---

54. *Amoris Laetitia*, §292.

Pope Francis sees the process of moral education according to his familiar principle that "time is greater than space." "Although she constantly holds up the call to perfection…the Church must accompany with attention and care the weakest of her children…by restoring in them hope and confidence, like the beacon of a lighthouse."[55] Patient guidance, education across time, growth in the spirit, cultivation of the seed—these are his images, his watchwords. And it is in this context that we best understand Pope Francis's re-appropriation of John Paul II's "law of gradualness."[56] As both Popes clarified, this has nothing to do with relativism or the compromising of moral absolutes but rather is a function of the conviction that "the human being 'knows, loves, and accomplishes moral good by different stages of growth.'"[57] Given the effects of the fall, our natural limitations, and the pressures of societal consensus that run counter to our moral ideals, it is almost impossible to imagine that one would embrace the full moral program in regard to marriage effortlessly. And this is why the Church has consistently embraced, as Francis puts it, "the way of mercy and reinstatement," not casting someone away.[58] Like a mother, she waits, watches, and encourages; and like a field hospital, she receives the wounded and cares for them.[59] Pope Francis, like St. Paul, is exquisitely sensitive to the ways that the moral law can be used not as a positive lure or a healing balm but as a weapon, a means of judgment and exclusion.

Amoris Laetitia, Chapter Nine: The Spirituality of Marriage and the Family

The Family as Temple

The brief final chapter of *Amoris Laetitia* functions as a sort of poetic coda to the entire text, a prayerful summation of its principal theme,

---

55. *Amoris Laetitia*, §291.

56. Pope John Paul II, Apostolic Exhortation *Familiaris Consortio* (November 22, 1981), §34.

57. *Amoris Laetitia*, §295; citing John Paul II, *Familiaris Consortio*, §34.

58. *Amoris Laetitia*, §296; Francis, "Homily at Mass Celebrated with New Cardinals" (February 15, 2015): AAS 107 (2015), 257.

59. *Amoris Laetitia*, §291.

which is the spirituality of marriage and family. The Pope commences this closing reflection with a look back to the Second Vatican Council and its insistence that a distinctively lay form of spirituality must take "its particular character from the circumstances of married and family life."[60] If the call to holiness is truly universal, then a spirituality peculiar to the laity would have to emerge.

The Pope's master image in this chapter is that of the Temple. "Today we can add that the Trinity is present in the temple of marital communion."[61] This is an extremely pregnant image, for the Temple, in ancient Israel, was the place of right praise, where human beings realized their deepest identity and vocation—namely, to give praise to the Lord on behalf of all creation. According to both the rabbis and the Church Fathers, Adam, prior to the Fall, was in the stance of *adoratio* (*ad-ora*, meaning 'mouth-to-mouth') with God. All of his energies and powers were aligned to God. In this attitude, he represented humanity at its best. Therefore, the original sin might be construed as a form of bad praise, adoring creatures rather than the Creator. On the biblical reading, human beings are rightly ordered when they praise God aright, and they become corrupt when their praise becomes misdirected. Think here of Israel "going after other gods" (Dt 6:14).

Hence, to say that the family is (or at least ought to be) a Temple is to say that the family is most itself when it is a place where God is consistently praised, where the honoring of his will is the paramount concern. Pope Francis puts it this way: "[God] dwells deep within the marital love that gives him glory."[62] There is, finally, no perspective on the family more clarifying and more important than this. One recalls Archbishop Fulton Sheen's book *Three to Get Married*, in which the great evangelist argues that a healthy marriage is a play between three lovers: husband, wife, and the Creator God.[63] Sheen relies on the Aristotelian/Thomistic notion of the transcendent third, which

---

60. *Amoris Laetitia*, §313; Decree on the Apostolate of the Laity *Apostolicam Actuositatem* (November 18, 1965), §4.

61. *Amoris Laetitia*, §314.

62. *Amoris Laetitia*, §314.

63. Fulton J. Sheen, *Three to Get Married* (New York: Scepter Publishers, 1996), 40–67.

is to say, that a relationship—be it a friendship, a partnership, or a marriage—will succeed only in the measure that the two persons fall in love not so much with one another but together with a value that transcends them both. Thus two friends are bonded more tightly together if they are both in love with their country, or with the truth, or with God. Without the transcendent third, the friendship will likely devolve into shared egotism. And so, a marriage will thrive inasmuch as husband and wife together are in love with God and God's purposes. And the same dynamic should obtain in regard to children. Parents should not love their children simply for their own sake but rather should love them in and for God. Pope Francis expresses this principle with admirable economy in paragraph 320: "There comes a point where a couple's love attains the height of freedom and becomes the basis of a healthy autonomy. This happens when each spouse realizes that the other is not his or her own, but has a much more important master, the one Lord." And he brings out a dimension of this principle that is rarely highlighted, speaking of a certain holy disillusionment, to "stop expecting from one's spouse something which is proper to the love of God alone."[64] In other words, precisely in the measure that spouses don't seek their ultimate happiness in one another, they will have a happy marriage!

We speak often of family values, but truly biblical family values might strike most people as fairly surprising. Consider, for example, the story of Hannah and Samuel. After begging the Lord incessantly for a child, Hannah becomes pregnant. But she promises that she will dedicate her much-desired son to the Lord's service. And so, once the child is weaned, she dutifully brings him to the Temple and gives him to Eli the priest. We find a fascinating echo of this narrative in the story of the finding of the child Jesus in the Temple: when confronted by his distraught mother, Jesus blithely says, "Did you not know that I must be in my Father's house?" (Lk 2:49). In both cases, the love of God is more important than any sentimental bond between mother and child. And in the preaching of Jesus, the same theme emerges. When a prospective disciple says that he wants to follow the Lord but would first like permission to bury his father, Jesus says, baldly enough, "Follow me, and let the dead bury their

---

64. *Amoris Laetitia*, §320.

dead" (Mt 8:22). This does not indicate that Jesus is antifamily, but it does indeed indicate that he feels the love of family must be subordinated to a higher and more expansive love.

Thus, "marital spirituality is a spirituality of the bond, in which divine love dwells."[65] It is not simply the bond, for that would be true of the marriage of purely secularized people, but rather the bond in which the divine love is operative. This sacred contextualizing makes all the difference.

Conclusion: Family Life in Christ

Now, at this point, we feel obliged to ask the typically Franciscan question: What does all of this look like on the ground, *in concreto*? The Pope says that if a family is centered on Christ, then the Lord will illumine every aspect of its shared life. Thus those inevitable moments of pain and difficulty "will be experienced in union with the Lord's cross, and his closeness will make it possible to surmount them."[66] Loss, struggle, failure, the breakdown of relationship, the inability to forgive, hurt feelings, sickness, the death of loved ones— none of it is simply dumb suffering but rather redeemed suffering. It is pain that has been elevated into a higher context of meaning. By the same token, "moments of joy, relaxation, celebration, and even sexuality" can be appreciated as a participation in the power of the Resurrection.[67] Similarly, when parents pass on the faith, they are embodying the work of Christ the teacher; when they bring comfort to their children, they are in the image of Christ the healer.

The best way to strengthen and deepen this sensibility is family prayer.[68] Pope Francis shows his indebtedness to Fr. Patrick Peyton when he says that the family that prays together stays together.[69] This is true, of course, precisely because prayer is the privileged route of access to the transcendent third. A few moments of prayer

---

65. *Amoris Laetitia*, §315.
66. *Amoris Laetitia*, §317.
67. Ibid.
68. *Amoris Laetitia*, §318.
69. *Amoris Laetitia*, §227.

or devotion each day can work, Francis tells us, a world of good.[70] And this communal spiritual journey culminates in the sharing of the Eucharist, especially on Sunday.[71] The Mass is the *locus* where the priestly role of the laity is most fully realized; it is the place where spiritual sustenance is found; it is the moment when the family is best shaped as a domestic church. For all of these reasons, it is especially tragic that Mass attendance, at least in the West, has declined so precipitously in recent decades. The Fathers of Vatican II wanted a revival of interest in the Mass, and when the great conciliar texts emerged in the mid-sixties of the last century, Mass attendance in Europe and America was anywhere from 40 to over 60%.[72]

Pope Francis teaches that the total self-gift involved in married love is a prime sacramental image of the divine love, which is utterly generous: *bonum diffusivum sui* (the good is diffusive of itself).[73] How easy it is for relationships to waver, for commitments to fade away. But in the face of innumerable difficulties, faithfully married men and women remain dedicated to one another in the manner of the God of Israel, who maintained fidelity to his covenant despite the steady infidelity of his people. I would like to make a connection between this teaching and a situation that did not obtain when Pope Francis wrote *Amoris Laetitia*—namely, the #MeToo movement. What has legitimately roused the anger and indignation of women all over the world in recent years is the use of sexuality as an expression of pure power and domination, in a word, the divorce between sex and anything even vaguely resembling fidelity, commitment, and love. Women have quite rightly objected to being treated as objects for manipulation or as mere means to an end. The best and most thorough answer to this moral outrage is the very spirituality of marriage that the Pope is speaking of.

---

70. *Amoris Laetitia*, §318.

71. Ibid.

72. For the United States, Lydia Saad, "Catholics' Church Attendance Resumes Downward Slide," *Gallup* (April 9, 2018). https://news.gallup.com/poll/232226/church-attendance-among-catholics-resumes-downward-slide.aspx. For some examples in Europe and more statistics on the United States, see Stephen Bullivant, *Mass Exodus: Catholic Disaffiliation in Britain and America since Vatican II* (Oxford: Oxford University Press, 2019), 141, 196–201.

73. *Amoris Laetitia*, §290.

In the famous interview granted toward the beginning of his pontificate, Pope Francis compared the Church to a field hospital, a place where those suffering from life-threatening spiritual wounds are treated.[74] As he brings *Amoris Laetitia* to a close, he observes that the family is the "nearest 'hospital,'"[75] which is to say, the place where God's mercy is shared most immediately, where the existential wounds of the human race are most promptly addressed. Hence, "all family life is a 'shepherding' in mercy."[76] Or to put the same idea in different words, each member of a family looks to the others with the eyes of Christ. The Pope says that whenever Christ encountered someone, he would meet that person's gaze directly and lovingly: "No one felt overlooked in his presence, since his words and gestures conveyed the question: 'What do you want me to do for you?' (Mk 10:51)."[77] So each member of the family merits the complete attention of the others, since all are subjects of infinite dignity.

The final observation that Francis makes in regard to a spirituality of the family—and the remark that brings the entire letter to completion—is that the family is, necessarily, missionary in purpose and orientation. In a word, the family is meant to go out from itself. Having been formed according to the mind and will of Christ, it now acts for the transformation of the world. What Pope Francis has said often of the Church as such, he reiterates in regard to the *ecclesiola* of the family: it is meant not to turn in on itself but to go out, even to the peripheries, and to tell the Good News. I'll give the Pope himself the last word: "All of us are called to keep striving toward something greater than ourselves and our families, and every family must make this its constant impulse."[78]

74. Antonio Spadaro, "Interview with Pope Francis" (August 19, 23, and 29, 2013).

75. *Amoris Laetitia*, §321; Pope Francis, "Catechesis (June 10, 2015)," *L'Osservatore Romano* (June 11, 2015): 8.

76. *Amoris Laetitia*, §322.

77. *Amoris Laetitia*, §323.

78. *Amoris Laetitia*, §325.

CHAPTER 15

LIBERALISM AND CATHOLICISM—
WHY THE DISCONNECT?

An Address to Members of Congress, Washington, DC, 2019

The topic proposed to me for this presentation is "liberalism and Catholicism: why the disconnect?" I was delighted to accept it, for I believe that the option so presented names a key fault line in the cultural conversation today. I fully realize that 'liberalism' is a famously slippery and multivalent term, but I will use it in this talk to designate the worldview that emerged from the thinking and praxis of the European Enlightenment. And, with your permission, I will broaden my focus, using 'Catholicism' to indicate not simply Roman Catholicism, but the *Weltanschauung* (worldview) that arises from the Bible. So characterized, the 'liberal-Catholic' divide is one that runs right through the heart of the American experience, from colonial times until the present day. Our dual identity, as children of both the Enlightenment and biblical revelation, has been a constant source of tension, creative and otherwise, throughout our history. A visit of a Catholic bishop to the United States Capitol seemed an apt opportunity to explore some of the complexities of this venerable debate.

One of my operating assumptions today is that we tend to focus this conversation around a group of hot-button issues, largely dealing with sexuality and self-determination, but touching on

many other matters as well. The advocates of a more liberal view-
point stand on one side and more biblically-minded people on the
other, the two camps more or less talking past one another. What I
should like to do in this presentation is to bracket those particular
matters and consider the wider horizon, the deeper philosophical
assumptions that undergird the discussion but that remain typically
unexamined. My hope is that this assumption of this higher point
of vantage might make our arguments more fruitful and common
ground easier to find.

What is Liberalism?

As I observed above, liberalism is an overarching view of the whole
that came up out of the Enlightenment of the seventeenth and eighteenth centuries. Though this perspective is richly complex, we might
isolate two major strains within it—namely, the epistemological and
the political. The Enlightenment made possible the emergence of
the physical sciences, informed by a method that has proven itself
extraordinarily powerful, practical, and predictive. Descartes, Pascal,
Leibniz, Newton, and many others affected the shift from the more
deductive Aristotelian method of classical philosophy to the induc-
tive, empirically oriented, and experimental science with which we
are familiar. Almost from the moment of its emergence, this new
natural science gave rise to technologies of tremendous practical
value. Our own Benjamin Franklin showed himself a key player in
this process. And the continuing pragmatic success of modern physics, chemistry, biology, and astronomy has only served to ratify the
legitimacy of the Enlightenment era epistemological shift.

What is the relationship between this strain of Enlightenment
thinking and religion? I know practically no one in our society who
would seriously want to go back to the time prior to the emergence
of the modern sciences and their attendant technologies. Hardly any
serious religious person would question the value of what the great
Enlightenment scientists and their successors have accomplished.
Moreover, the supposed conflict between science and religion is, for
the most part, a chimera, the result of a profound misinterpretation
of certain biblical texts, which were never intended to be read as
exercises in physics or cosmology. This genre confusion conduced

toward a completely unnecessary clash between finally incommen-
surate systems of thought. However, the undoubted beauty of the
modern scientific accomplishment does carry the shadow of what
we might call 'scientism,' which is to say, the tendency to reduce the
whole of knowledge to the scientific form of knowledge. So massively successful has modern science been that people commence to
question whether nonscientific methods can ever produce authentic
knowledge. And this leads to a diminution of the value of the arts,
philosophy, ethics, and religion, or to the temptation to interpret
those disciplines only in scientific terms. There is, obviously, much
more that can be said about this dimension of the Enlightenment,
but for our purposes here, I should like to focus my attention on the
second great stream—namely, the political.[1]

If I might be permitted to simplify matters a bit, I would say
that the crucial ideals behind the liberal political revolutions of the
eighteenth and nineteenth centuries were equality, the rights of the
individual, and freedom. Democracy, republican forms of polity,
freedom of the press and assembly, the conviction that no one is
above the law, tolerance for a variety of religions, the end to cruel
and unusual punishment, and the banishment of the institution of
the monarchy—all were undergirded by the three great principles
just mentioned. So dramatic was this political upheaval that the avatars of the liberal political revolution, in our country at least, saw
their work not simply as a needed reform but as the commencement
of a new era. If you doubt me on this score, I would invite you to
take a dollar bill out of your wallet and examine the Latin motto on
the reverse side: *novus ordo seclorum* ("a new order of the ages"). And
then allow your eye to drift to the all-seeing eye hovering above a
pyramid, suggestive of divine providence, and notice the confident
annuit coeptis ("he nods toward these new beginnings"). And to give
these founders (one of the most impressive congregations of great
minds and hearts in history) their full due, most thoughtful people
of the time felt that political liberalism was, if not the beginning of
a new world, at least a supremely needful thing. That we in the West
today take these reforms for granted should not blind us to their

---

1. For a more thorough discussion on scientism, see chapter two, "Evangelizing
the Nones," 28–29.

novelty in history or their enduring importance. We rightly rejoice when regimes across the world move in the direction of adopting these changes.

The Biblical Roots of Political Liberalism

Now on both sides of the Atlantic, but more clearly in France than here, there were extreme advocates of the liberal revolution who saw religion in general, and the Catholic Church in particular, as the enemies of their project. A relatively mild expression of the conviction can be found in John Adams's famous letter that describes the sensuous power of the Mass and rejoices that rational Protestants had found a way to wriggle free from its influence.[2] A stronger statement of it is on offer in Thomas Paine's writings,[3] and the fiercest of all is the infamous adage of Jean Meslier, "that all the rulers of the earth and all the nobles be hanged and strangled with the guts of priests."[4] One need not go nearly as far as Meslier to acknowledge that, to a degree, the churches stood athwart what was legitimate in the liberal perspective. As a churchman, I would grant, humbly and gratefully, that in the wake of the eighteenth century revolutions, Christianity was forced to come to terms with some of its own moral failings and to accept certain institutional and cultural restrictions.

However, I want vigorously to contest the sweeping claim that the biblical worldview is directly repugnant to political liberalism; and I want, in point of fact, to argue that each of the three great principles informing the liberal revolution emerged precisely from a biblical matrix of thought and practice. They represent, not so much a repudiation of a biblical *Weltanschauung*, but rather a reassertion of key elements within the biblical view that had been lost or undervalued.

---

2. John Adams, *Revolutionary Writings 1755–1775*, ed. Gordon Wood, The Library of America Adams Family Collection, no. 213 (New York: Adams Family Collection, 2011), "Visiting a Catholic Church to Abigail Adams," October 9, 1774, 324–325.

3. Thomas Paine, *The Age of Reason*, in *Collected Writings*, ed. Eric Foner (New York.: The Library of America), 666.

4. Jean Meslier, *Testament: Memoir of the Thoughts and Sentiments of Jean Meslier*, trans. Michael Shreve (Amherst, NY: Prometheus Books, 2009), Ch. 2, 37. A French priest but a closet atheist who published his thoughts anonymously, Meslier attributes the quote to a common Frenchman.

Equality

I should like to begin by examining what is perhaps the fundamental liberal principle—namely, equality. It is instructive to note that none of the great political philosophers of the ancient world—many of whom are rightly considered fathers of democracy—took equality very seriously. On the contrary, the acknowledgement of our radical inequality—in strength, beauty, moral excellence, virtue, courage, and nobility—provided the foundation for their theorizing. Plato, for example, held that the rightly-ordered society is predicated upon the acceptance of the undeniable difference between three types of people: guardians, auxiliaries, and workers or producers.[5] To confound the difference between them, to imagine that an equality obtains among them, is to guarantee that a deep injustice reigns in the city. Plato's pupil Aristotle was convinced that only a small percentage of the population of a *polis* should be engaged in public life. The overwhelming majority of the inhabitants—including women, children, the enslaved, the unintelligent, and prisoners of war—ought permanently to be consigned to the private concerns of the household.[6] Similar assumptions are made by Cicero and other great Roman political theorists as well.

What has always struck me as a fascinating question is this: How could something that appeared self-evidently false to some of the smartest figures in the ancient world suddenly appear self-evidently true to political thinkers of the eighteenth century? Though many factors were undoubtedly at work in producing this change, one very significant influence was biblical Christianity, which had, by then, soaked its way into the minds and hearts of Western people. The scriptural sense of equality is grounded in the fact that all of us, despite the enormous differences among us at practically every discernible level, are equally

---

5. Plato, *The Republic*, in *The Complete Works*, ed. John M. Cooper, trans. G. M. A. Grube and C. D. C. Reeve (Indianapolis: Hackett Publishing Company, Inc., 1997), pp. 1013–1016 (Bk. 2, 374e–376d); pp. 1022–1024 (Bk. 3, 386a–387d); pp. 1032–1033 (Bk. 3, 394e–395d); pp. 1040–1041 (Bk. 3, 403e–405b); pp. 1048–1050 (Bk. 3, 412b–414b); pp. 1051–1052 (Bk. 3, 415e–416e); pp. 1052–1058 (Bk. 4, 419a–425e); pg. 1064 (Bk. 4, 433a–433d); pp. 1077–1094 (Bk. 5, 449a–466e).

6. Aristotle, *The Politics of Aristotle*, trans. Peter L. Phillips Simpson (Chapel Hill: The University of North Carolina Press, 1997), pp. 8–20 (Bk. 1, 1252a–1255b37).

children of God. In light of this clarification, Thomas Jefferson's perhaps overly-familiar words take on a new resonance: "We hold these truths to be self-evident that all men are *created* equal…" In Jefferson's mind, being created and being equal are correlative states of affairs.

Individual Rights

Something very similar holds in regard to the second prime value of political liberalism—namely, human rights. Again, if we cast a glance backward to the ancient world, we find little indication of an acknowledgement of universal human rights; in fact, just the contrary. Plato, Aristotle, Cicero, and their many colleagues taught that a few privileged people enjoyed political prerogatives and protections within the society, but the vast majority of people decidedly did not. But once more, something of rather massive importance intervened between ancient times and the eighteenth century, for the founders of political liberalism took the universality of rights as self-evident. Let us return to Jefferson and his frank acknowledgment of that influence: "…that they are endowed by their Creator with certain inalienable rights, that among these are Life, Liberty, and the pursuit of Happiness."[7] What is rather clearly on display here is at least the remnants of a biblical anthropology. Precisely in the measure that all human beings are beloved children of the Creator God, they are in possession of those protections and prerogatives that we call 'rights.' And one notices in Jefferson's formulation that the inalienability of these rights flows from their groundedness in the fact of creation. Our great founding father knew that if these rights were construed as the gift of government or of the civil society, they could be rescinded as easily as they are granted. Their permanence is a function of their correlation to the permanence of God's manner of being. The dignity of the individual, upon which committed liberals continue to insist to this day, is rooted, finally, in the fact of creation. Indeed, pay careful attention to what happens to human dignity and natural rights in societies that systematically militate against belief in God.

---

7. Thomas Jefferson, "The Declaration of Independence," in *Basic Documents in American History*, ed. Richard B. Morris, The Anvil Series (Malabar, FL: Krieger Publishing Company, 1965), 27.

Freedom

And finally let us consider the third of the major values of political liberalism—namely, freedom. Even the most cursory analysis reveals that freedom is a major biblical motif, from the story of Exodus to Paul's ecstatic declaration, "It is for freedom that Christ has set you free" (Gal 5:1). Escaping from forms of enslavement, literal and spiritual, is an essential and unifying theme of the biblical narrative. Even the word "redemption," so sacred to the New Testament writers, implies the paying of a ransom so as to set free a kidnapped prisoner. Moreover, freedom of choice, the capacity to determine oneself, is seen by both the biblical authors and the theologians of the great Christian tradition, as one of the distinctive marks of the *imago Dei* (the image of God) in us.[8] Typically, theologians and biblical commentators have identified intellect and freedom of the will as the two constitutive elements of this likeness. In his account of divine providence, Thomas Aquinas says that God indeed infallibly directs human affairs, but not in the manner of a tyrant constraining creaturely liberty, but as a lure, awakening and engaging our freedom.[9]

This deep congruence between the Bible and the ideals of liberalism explains why a rapprochement between the two worldviews has been, from the beginning of the American experiment, a lively possibility. One has only to think of the many reflections of our founding fathers on the theme of the necessity of finding a religious grounding for democracy, or of Alexis de Tocqueville's still compelling analysis of the central role that religion plays within an officially secular state,[10] or of Abraham Lincoln's frequent correlations between American political ideals and biblical convictions,[11]

---

8. For more on the *imago Dei*, refer to chapter twelve, "*Imago Dei* as Privilege and Mission," 201–211.

9. St. Thomas Aquinas, *Summa theologiae* I, qq. 22–23.

10. Alexis de Tocqueville, *Democracy in America*, vol. 2, trans. Harvey C. Mansfield and Delba Winthrop (Chicago: The University of Chicago Press, 2000), Part 1, Ch. 5, 417–424.

11. For example, see Abraham Lincoln, *Speeches and Writings: 1832–1858*, The Library of America 48 (Washington, DC: The Library of America, 1989), 271, 426; Fred Kaplan, *Lincoln: The Biography of a Writer* (New York: HarperCollins Publishers, 2008), 173, 195–196, 223, 270, 273, 278, 279–280, 339.

or of Martin Luther King's sermon/speech on the steps of Lincoln's Memorial or his letter from the Birmingham City Jail, which explicitly references St. Thomas Aquinas's theory of the divine sanction for just civil law.[12] All of these indicate how biblical insights and values can deeply inform the American experiment in political liberalism.

The Disconnect

So how do we explain the disconnect assumed in the topic upon which I was invited to speak? Why does a biblical vision seem at odds with the ideals of liberalism? We might get a clue by glancing at a recent sociological study. In her book *iGen*, which analyzes the coterie of people born after the turn of the millennium, sociologist Jean Twenge comments that, increasingly, young Americans are neither religious nor spiritual. She means that they are not only less likely to be adepts of particular religious organizations, but they are also less likely to hold to the existence of God, the immortality of the soul, or the inspiration of the Bible.[13] This is a good example of Will Herberg's "cut flower" theory, according to which certain values produced by religion will endure for a time, like flowers in a vase, but that they will, sooner or later, fade once they are uprooted from their natural soil.[14] I am indeed concerned that as our society becomes increasingly hostile to religion and religious institutions, we are in danger of losing those political values dear to liberalism that in fact grew from the soil of a religious consciousness.

It might be useful to re-examine the three principles that we have identified as central to the liberal program and to see how they are construed apart from a religious context. As we saw, freedom is strongly affirmed in the biblical tradition, but it is a freedom of a very particular kind. The Dominican moral theologian Servais Pinckaers

---

12. Martin Luther King, Jr., *A Testament of Hope: The Essential Writings and Speeches of Martin Luther King Jr.*, ed. James M. Washington (New York: HarperOne, 1991), 293.

13. Jean M. Twenge, *iGen: Why Today's Super-Connected Kids are Growing Up Less Rebellious, More Tolerant, Less Happy—and Completely Unprepared for Adulthood (And What That Means for the Rest of Us)* (New York: Atria Books, 2017), 119–142.

14. William Herberg, *Judaism and Modern Man: An Interpretation of Jewish Religion* (New York: Meridian Books, Inc., and The Jewish Publication Society of America, 1951), 91–92.

made an extremely illuminating distinction between two understand-
ings of freedom, the first more biblical in form, which he calls *liberte
de qualite* ("freedom of excellence") and the second more modern and
secular, which he calls *liberte de indifference* ("freedom of indifference").[15]
The second mode, with its roots in the late medieval and early modern
period, is freedom as choice and self-determination. On this reading,
one hovers, as it were, above the yes and the no, and on the basis of no
coercion, either from within or without, decides for one or the other
option. But the first mode, "freedom for excellence," is not so much
liberty of choice but rather the disciplining of desire so as to make the
achievement of the good first possible and then effortless. We might
think of the process by which someone becomes an increasingly free
player of the piano, or speaker of a language, or swinger of a golf
club. She is not simply choosing according to her whim; rather, she is
subjecting herself to a series of objective demands, laws, and practices
by which the skill in question works its way into her body and her
mind. In regard to freedom of indifference, law is, at best, a necessary
evil, for it limits the range of free choice; but in regard to the freedom
for excellence, law is a great boon, for it is the condition for the possibility of such freedom. One might even say that authentic liberty is
tantamount to the perfect internalization of the law.

What I hope is clear is that in the measure that freedom of
indifference comes to hold sway, God and his law will appear as especially threatening. Anarchist Mikhail Bakunin showed that he was
operating out of a thoroughly freedom-of-indifference perspective
when he summed up his philosophy: "If God is, man is a slave; now,
man can and must be free; then, God does not exist."[16] But in the
measure that a freedom for excellence perspective obtains, God and
his law will be seen, not as threats, but as a great gift. At the time of
our nation's founding, the two views of freedom that I have described
were both present, but enough of the biblical understanding was
on offer to make the compatibility of God and human freedom the

---

15. Servais Pinckaers, OP, *Sources of Christian Ethics*, 3rd ed., trans. Sr. Mary
Thomas Noble (Washington, DC: The Catholic University of America Press, 1995),
329.

16. Mikhail Bakunin, *God and the State*, trans. Benjamin Tucker (New York:
Mother Earth Publishing Association, 1916), 25.

cultural default position. What has happened in the past fifty years, especially through the influence of postmodernism, is that the freedom-of-indifference model has asserted itself with such compelling force that a culture of self-invention largely holds sway. How often do we hear especially young people taunt anyone who would lay out a program to inform their freedom: "Who are you to tell me how to think or how to behave?" For many in our culture today, ancient traditions of behavior, inherited patterns of meaning, and especially religious values and intuitions appear simply as arbitrary impositions on the self-legislating and self-inventing ego. This reconfiguration of the notion of freedom is one reason for the disconnect between biblical people and liberalism.

The emergence of freedom for self-invention as a default position has also had a distorting influence on the other two great values of political liberalism. As we saw, human rights were classically seen as grounded in God and, at least implicitly, ordered to God, since the Creator presumably granted them for a divinely-sanctioned purpose. But now, under the aegis of the freedom of indifference, human rights are more often than not interpreted as the privilege to do what one wants with one's life, free of outside interference. The value of equality, too, has suffered a similar fate. Once we were seen as equally children of God and hence equally subjects of dignity and respect, but now equality tends to be construed as a warrant for any type of self-assertion: since you're no better than I, who are you to tell me what I can do or who I can be? In other words, equality among persons seems to imply that all desires and aspirations are equally valid. The consequence of this shift is that the classical relationship between freedom and truth collapses. How often we hear, especially on our campuses, the Foucault-inspired assertion that truth claims have no objective validity but are only thinly disguised assertions of power.[17] What has been lost—and it is a principal reason for the disconnect between liberalism and a biblical worldview—is the subtle relationship between equality in personal dignity and inequality in claims to moral value.

---

17. Michel Foucault, *Power/Knowledge: Selected Interviews and Other Writings 1972–1977*, trans. Colin Gordon, Leo Marshall, John Mepham, Kate Soper (New York: Pantheon Books, 1980), 114–115, 118, 132.

 A further implication of the transition to freedom as self-invention is the tendency, frequently on display within political liberalism today, to privatize religion, treating it as a kind of hobby or a practice peculiar to a particular group and legitimately expressed only within it. It is difficult to deny that the theorizing of Jürgen Habermas and John Rawls has been influential in this regard. Both philosophers deliberately exclude religious people, qua religious, from the table of public conversation, allowing only forms of purely rational speech to hold sway in that forum.[18] But this sort of aggressively antireligious liberalism would have disallowed the public speech, marked through and through by religious conviction, that was practiced by Lincoln and King. The sequestering of religious discourse to the private sphere is hence another reason for the disconnect between the liberal and biblical view today.

Thomas Hobbes and the Common Good

As I bring these remarks to a conclusion, allow me to consider, however briefly, the role played by Thomas Hobbes in the development of the liberal view of politics. It is difficult to overstate the importance of Hobbes and his social contract theory to the political revolutions of the eighteenth century. In his *Leviathan*, Hobbes breaks with the tradition of political philosophy running from Aristotle to Thomas Aquinas and argues that human beings are not by nature political or social. Rather, by nature we are bundles of self-interested desire. This condition leads ineluctably to conflict, which is why Hobbes's "state of nature" is identical to the "state of war," where life is, famously, "nasty, brutish, and short."[19] As a result of this intolerable situation, we enter, as a sort of necessary evil, into a contract by which we surrender our rights to a sovereign who is charged with protecting us from one another. Now this rather blunt and reductive view was indeed softened and nuanced by Rousseau,

---

18. For example, see Jürgen Habermas, "Political Liberalism: A Debate with John Rawls," in *The Inclusion of the Other: Studies in Political Theory* (Cambridge, MA: The MIT Press, 1998), 49–73.

19. Thomas Hobbes, *Leviathan*, XIII, 9. *Revised Student Edition* edited by Richard Tuck (Cambridge, UK: Cambridge University Press, 1996), pg. 89.

Locke, Jefferson, and others, and as I have been arguing, the liberal project did retain many elements of the biblical view. However, liberalism has remained, as it were, haunted by Hobbes from the very beginning.

If we look again at the prologue to the Declaration of Independence, we find the purpose of government spelled out in the Hobbesian manner: "In order to secure these rights, governments are instituted among men…" The end of government is, if I may put it this way, protective rather than directive. Notice, too, how Jefferson effectively mutes any sense of a truly common good by bracketing a consideration of the nature of happiness and speaking only of the right to pursue happiness as each individual sees fit. It seems not to be government's business to direct us to a common end but only to protect us from one another as we seek our particular ends. Now as de Tocqueville and many others have insisted, this Hobbesian quality of the liberal form of government positively calls out to a robustly active religion, which would provide the necessary moral direction and spiritual uplift to society.[20] And this uplift, as I have been arguing, has been on display in American history from abolitionism to the battle for civil rights, both of which campaigns were directed principally by people with a strong religious sensibility.

My fear, to state it simply, is that the withdrawal of religion from the public square and the concomitant rise of an aggressive secularism permit the Hobbesian element within liberalism to reassert itself powerfully. And is this not apparent in the dramatic breakdown of civil discourse and in the disheartening balkanization of our public life? Has the loss of a sense of the common good, which has been one of the gifts of religion to our civil society, not conduced to a sort of Hobbesian state of perpetual war? At its best, liberalism finds an extraordinary amount of common ground with a biblical view of the world, but when liberalism's Hobbesian dimension comes to the fore, the two perspectives tend, to their mutual detriment, to fall into conflict.

---

20. Alexis de Tocqueville, *Democracy in America*, vol. 2, trans. Harvey C. Mansfield and Delba Winthrop (Chicago: The University of Chicago Press, 2000), Part 1, Ch. 5, 417–424.

CHAPTER 16

RELATIVISM AND ITS DISCONTENTS

D uring the General Congregations preceding the papal conclave of 2005, Cardinal Ratzinger, elected at that conclave as Benedict XVI, famously spoke of a "dictatorship of relativism."[1] He meant that the relativist philosophy—namely, the view that there is no absolute truth, but only truths conditioned by time, space, and culture—was being, ironically enough, imposed as an absolute norm on Western society. That this dictatorship has only intensified in the ensuing years goes without saying. The Church, the Cardinal insisted, had to resist this view, since it speaks, across the centuries, absolute truths regarding God, Jesus, the human condition, morality, and eternal life and salvation. Pilate's cynical question "What is truth?" (Jn 18:38) seems, he argued, the leitmotif of our time, but the Church ought stubbornly to follow its Master who referred to himself, quite emphatically, as the Truth (Jn 14:6). I must say that I encounter the sort of relativism of which Ratzinger spoke practically every day in my evangelical work, and I recognize both how entrenched it is and how debilitating to the project of announcing the Gospel.

What I should like to do in this brief presentation is to explore some of the theoretical roots of the relativism that bedevils us today, to explicate why it poses perhaps the greatest threat to the work of the Church, and finally to explore ways that we might engage it and

---

1. Joseph Ratzinger, *Mass Pro Eligendo Romano Pontifice: Homily of his Eminence Card. Joseph Ratzinger, Dean of the College of Cardinals* (April 18, 2005).

outmaneuver it. Far from a merely philosophical exercise, this sort of investigation should be of interest to anyone charged with preaching, teaching, catechizing, or evangelizing today.

Genealogy of Relativism

When searching out the theoretical and practical sources of relativism, we could go back a long way indeed, but it might be best to begin with medieval voluntarism. This view, consistently opposed by Thomas Aquinas and the Dominican intellectual tradition but embraced to varying degrees in the Franciscan intellectual tradition, holds that the divine will trumps the divine reason. God's power is so absolute that it determines the truth of things. Thus, on the voluntarist reading, 2+2=4 because God so willed. It might be the case that 2+2=6 if God changed his mind. Similarly, adultery, murder, and rape are crimes because God has determined so. Once again, he could change his mind and turn them into virtues through the exercise of his sovereign freedom.

Aquinas resisted this interpretation of the divine will as arbitrary by insisting on the identification of God's intellect, will, and act of being. Precisely because God is the sheer act of 'to-be,' the unique reality in whom essence and existence coincide, his mind and will can never fall into conflict, and hence what God wills is identical to the good that God is. Thus, though he is correctly described as utterly free, God cannot sin, which is to say, fall out of union with his own perfection. Further, whatever exists in the realm of creatures does so through an act of participation in God. Therefore, whatever is good and true in created reality is a reflection of the supreme goodness and truth of God's 'to-be.' Thus it is absurd to suggest, for example, that adultery could, through a sovereign exercise of freedom, become something other than wicked or that 2+2 could be 5 if God so desired. In a way, Aquinas felt, we are simply being misled by a peculiarity of our language if we think that such observations amount to a limitation on God's freedom or power.

Though Aquinas and the Dominican intellectual tradition held to this counter position, the voluntarist construal of God's power proved persuasive to many in the later Middle Ages, especially through the influence of William of Ockham. It is absolutely no accident, by the way, that a voluntarist understanding of the will was coincident with Ockham's nominalist epistemology, for both are radically subjectivist in orientation. Now the nominalist-voluntarist strain was passed from the later Middle Ages to the early modern period and was enthusiastically adopted by the leading Reformers of the sixteenth century, most especially Luther and Calvin. A voluntarist account of God's freedom is on clear display in Luther's *Bondage of the Will*[2] and in Calvin's doctrine of double predestination.[3] So powerfully did the Reformers emphasize the sovereignty of God's will, that God became a rather frightening, arbitrary Lord.

As many historians of ideas have pointed out, the triumph of voluntarism in regard to God tended to awaken in the modern mind an answering and challenging assertion of will on the part of human beings.[4] The many Deist and quasi-Deist accounts of God that came to characterize modern philosophers from Descartes to Newton effectively pushed God off the stage, permitting a relatively untrammeled exercise of freedom on the part of human agents. And the pantheist theologies of Spinoza and Hegel, which turned God into an abstraction, effectively accomplished the same thing. In time, this competitive understanding of the God-human interaction evolved into an explicit rejection of God on the part of the atheists. From Feuerbach through Sartre, they affirmed their atheism as authentic humanism: "the no to God is the yes to man."[5]

As we continue to seek out the theoretical roots of contemporary relativism, we should also attend to Cartesian subjectivism. In order to find absolute truth, Descartes famously retired to a heated room in the German town of Ulm and resolved not to emerge until

---

2. Martin Luther, *The Bondage of the Will*, trans. Henry Cole (Peabody, MA: Hendrickson Publishers, Inc., 2008), 31–62. For secondary literature, see Harry J. McSorley, *Luther: Right or Wrong? An Ecumenical–Theological Study of Luther's Major Work, "The Bondage of the Will"* (New York: Newman Press, 1969).

3. John Calvin, *Institutes of the Christian Religion* (add citation).

4. For example, see Servais Pinckaers, OP, *The Sources of Christian Ethics*, 3rd ed, trans. Sr. Mary Thomas Noble (Washington, DC: The Catholic University of America Press, 1995), 341.

5. This paraphrase of Feuerbach comes from Walter Kasper, *The God of Jesus Christ* (New York: Continuum Books, T&T Clark International, 2012), 29; see also Walter Kasper, *Der Gott Jesu Christi* (Mainz: Matthias-Grünewald-Verlag, 1982), 45.

he had found his treasure.[6] His method was systematically to doubt all that can be doubted. What he found, of course, was the *cogito*, the terra firma of both epistemology and metaphysics. It is important to note that Descartes was by no means a relativist in regard to truth—just the contrary. But his introverted and individualistic approach to truth—bringing all of objective reality before the bar of subjectivity for adjudication—opened up the characteristically modern way of getting at truth. This Cartesian path leads rather directly to Kant and Hegel, both of whom have had a massive impact on the modern consciousness. For Kant, the mind no longer revolves around reality, but rather vice versa,[7] and for Hegel, the Cartesian ego, which was already implicitly deified, now becomes explicitly deified as Absolute Spirit coming to full self-consciousness through the mind of the philosopher.

The coming together of the voluntarist and the Cartesian strains provides the breeding ground for contemporary relativism: the subject's assertion of truth through a sovereign act of the will. The greatest theoretician of this confluence was Friedrich Nietzsche. In his master texts *Beyond Good and Evil, Thus Spoke Zarathustra*, and *On the Genealogy of Morals*, Nietzsche dismisses all of classical morality as a sort of bourgeois invention and affirms the primacy of the will to power of the individual strong man (*Übermensch*). The will of this figure trumps any attempt to constrain it through appeals to objective truth or morality. The "slave morality" or the morality of the camel is what everyone inherits.[8] This produces resentment and sparks the awakening of the will to power. The *Übermensch* invents himself and creates his own values, even if that means embracing what is traditionally held to be ugly or ignoble.

The founder of existentialism, Jean-Paul Sartre, was the Nietzsche of the twentieth century. His philosophy bears its name

---

6. René Descartes, *Discourse on Method and Meditations on First Philosophy*, trans. Donald A. Cress (Indianapolis: Hackett Publishing Company, 1998), Part Two, 6–7.

7. Immanuel Kant, *Critique of Pure Reason*, trans. Paul Guyer (Cambridge: Cambridge University Press, 1998).

8. Nietzsche, *Beyond Good and Evil*, 153–156; Nietzsche, *Thus Spoke Zarathustra*, trans. Adrian Del Caro (Cambridge: Cambridge University Press, 2006), 16–17.

because its central tenet is that "existence precedes essence,"[9] whereby Sartre means the primacy of freedom over value and self-definition. First, we are free; then we determine who we are and what we are to do. As in Nietzsche, the inherited morality has to be overthrown, and the prime representative of that morality—namely, God—has to be put to death. Sartre's philosophy can be summarized by Bakunin's quote cited above: "If God is, man is a slave; now, man can and must be free; then, God does not exist."[10] This is a coldly syllogistic expression of Nietzsche's ecstatic: "We are all his murderers… God is dead!… And we have killed him!"[11]

Still another extremely influential figure in the development of this line of thought should be mentioned: Michel Foucault. When I was a doctoral student in Paris twenty-five years ago, Foucault's owlish face looked out from practically every bookstore window. He was Sartre's successor as the most prominent public intellectual in France. Foucault was, quite consciously, a disciple of Nietzsche, especially in his stress upon the role that power relationships play in the determination of what a given society considers true or good. The appeal to objective truth or goodness almost always masks, according to Foucault, a particular regime's attempt to control things. For the details of his theories, read through his admittedly fascinating studies of madness, sexuality, and imprisonment in Western societies.

What was once bandied about only in rather high philosophical circles has now become the standard view of young people in high schools and universities across the West. Subjectivism and voluntarism, brought together powerfully by Nietzsche, Sartre, and Foucault, have become, for many people in our society, especially the young, a sort of default position. Through an assertion of one's will, one has the right to define the meaning of one's own existence. If that language sounds familiar, it is because I took it directly from the Supreme Court ruling in 1992 in the matter of *Casey v. Planned*

---

9. Jean-Paul Sartre, *Existentialism is a Humanism*, trans. Carol Macomber (New Haven, CT: Yale University Press, 2007), 22, 24, 29.

10. Mikhail Bakunin, *God and the State*, trans. Benjamin Tucker (New York: Mother Earth Publishing Association, 1916), 25.

11. Friedrich Nietzsche, *The Gay Science*, trans. Josefine Nauckoff (Cambridge: Cambridge University Press, 2001), 120.

Parenthood: "At the heart of liberty is the right to define one's own concept of existence, of meaning, of the universe, of the mystery of human life."[12] That absolutely outrageous statement, which would have struck Aristotle or Thomas Aquinas as absurd, was made possible by the confluence outlined above.

The Dangers of Relativism

Having explored, in a necessarily cursory way, some of the roots of the relativism that holds sway today, I would like now to make plain why this philosophical approach is a formidable obstacle to the Church's work of evangelization. A first great danger that this contemporary Nietzscheanism poses is that it frustrates the mind's deep hunger for the truth. Voluntarism, as we saw, is a kind of swallowing up of mind by will, and this means that the intellect never attains what it is designed to attain—namely, truth—which the classical tradition defines as the *adequatio rei et intellectus*, the coming together of mind and reality.[13] Notice that this is a coming together that is not dependent upon one's feelings about reality, not a function of one's resentments or expectations, not conditioned upon one's desires about the way things ought to be, but rather grounded in the objective nature of things. Until the mind finds this objective truth, it is restless. In fact, as Christian philosophers from Augustine to Lonergan have maintained, it will search until it discovers the horizon of all that can be known, that which, objectively speaking, is infinitely intelligible.[14] Denying this quest is to sequester oneself within the confines of what Charles Taylor has termed "the buffered self,"[15] which is to say, the ego that has cut itself off from any lively connection to the transcendent. And this isolation produces a deep frustration of mind and soul—evident widely in our culture today, especially among the young.

---

12. Casey v. Planned Parenthood of Southeastern Pennsylvania, 505 U.S. 833 (1992), no. 851.

13. *Summa theologiae*, I, q. 16, a. 1; q. 79, a. 11, ad. 2.

14. *Summa theologiae*, I, q. 2, a. 3.

15. Charles Taylor, *A Secular Age* (Cambridge, MA: The Belknap Press of Harvard University Press, 2018), 27, 37–42.

A second fundamental problem is that Nietzschean relativism fosters radical individualism and hence produces division. Though it is frequently excoriated today as a tool of oppression, objective truth is one of the forces that draws people together. Precisely because truth is one, it brings those who seek it and find it into unity. When each individual is herself the criterion of truth, this unity breaks apart. A dictum of Aristotle that I first encountered when I was nineteen has stayed in my mind and governed my activities and decisions ever since. The great philosopher said that a friendship will endure only when the two friends love not so much each other but rather together love a transcendent third.[16] When together, they love their country or a particular cause or the will and purposes of God, they will, paradoxically, remain strong as a pair.[17] On a purely relativist and subjectivist reading, there can be no truly transcendent values, no goods that stretch beyond the self-inventing power of the ego. Hence, no enduring unity will obtain.

Moreover, relativism leads to a kind of spiritual laziness. What gives a river its verve and energy is the firmness of its banks. Knock down the banks in the name of liberty, and the river opens up into a lazy, undefined lake. People might float on this lake, but they have no energy or sense of purpose. This is an apt metaphor for our society wherein toleration of each individual's program of self-invention is the supreme moral ideal. We put up with each other as we float on our separate air mattresses on the lazy lake, but we have no purpose that unites us in a common effort.

A final and related consequence of subjectivism and voluntarism is violence. When reason has been put to the side and truth construed solely as a game of power, then all that remains is force. When tensions arise, we can no longer argue; we have to fight. This could take very explicit form, but it can also be expressed more indirectly through censorship, the aggressive shutting down of one's opponents. There is, in many quarters, increasing concern about the hypercharged political correctness that has gripped our campuses

16. See the discussion in chapter fourteen, "Education in Virtue, Love, and Mission," 237–238.

17. Aristotle, *Nicomachean Ethics*, trans. C. D. C. Reeve (Indianapolis: Hackett Publishing Company, Inc., 2014), VIII.3–4, 1156a–1157b, pp. 138–141.

and other forums of public conversation. Even great works of literature and philosophy—from *Huckleberry Finn* and *Heart of Darkness* to, believe it or not, Kant's *Critique of Pure Reason*—are now regularly accompanied by 'trigger warnings' that alert prospective readers to the racism, sexism, homophobia, or classism contained therein. And popping up more and more at our colleges and universities are 'safe spaces' to which exquisitely sensitive students can retreat in the wake of jarring confrontations with points of view with which they don't sympathize. My favorite example of this was at Brown University where school administrators provided retreat centers with Play-Doh, crayons, and videos of frolicking puppies to calm the nerves of their students *even before a controversial debate commenced!*[18] Apparently even the prospect of public argument sent these students to an updated version of daycare. Again, as I've argued, the paradoxical concomitant of this exaggerated sensitivity to giving offense is a proclivity to aggressiveness and verbal violence; for once authentic debate has been ruled out of court, the only recourse contesting parties have is to some form of censorship or bullying.

Nowhere is this dynamic clearer than in regard to religion. When it comes to ultimate things, there appear to be today only two options—namely, either bland toleration or violent imposition. Since we are deathly afraid of the latter, we tend toward the former. But what this binary option rules out is constructive intellectual engagement of religious questions in the public forum. What it renders impossible is, in a word, argument, which is none other than a nonviolent way to adjudicate disputes concerning matters of truth and falsity.

Engaging Relativism

So given all of this, what is the best strategy for moving forward? Is there a way to engage this pervasive philosophical perspective so inimical to the proclamation of the Gospel? I believe that there is, and I believe, furthermore, it is essential that the Church not lose its nerve in the face of this overwhelming cultural consensus. We have faced similar challenging cultural default positions before.

---

18. Judith Shulevitz, "In College and Hiding from Scary Ideas," *New York Times* (March 21, 2015).

I would recommend that we might commence with Dietrich von Hildebrand's distinction between the merely subjectively satisfying and the objectively valuable.[19] Before delving into this distinction and its implications, it might be worthwhile to draw attention, if only for a moment, to Hildebrand himself, who stood bravely athwart a nefarious cultural consensus of his time and place, the Nazi ideology.[20] When even many of the intelligentsia had gone over to National Socialism (Heidegger for one), von Hildebrand stood his ground. His personal witness gives us hope. According to Hildebrand, there is indeed the phenomenon of the merely subjectively satisfying—that is to say, something that gives one pleasure at the personal level.[21] I have, for example, a taste for Italian food, more precisely for pizza, but I would never endeavor to claim any greater range for this preference, to force it on anyone else. The subjectively satisfying fits into a pre-existing and receptive subjectivity. It is, as it were, tamed and domesticated by the subjective.

However, over and against this category, there is what Hildebrand calls "the objectively valuable." A value (*Wert* in his German) appears phenomenologically as powerful, unquestionable, and objective.[22] It does not fit into a pre-existing subjectivity, but rather challenges and rearranges subjectivity. It presents itself not as something that can be controlled but as something overwhelming, demanding, insisting upon itself. When one hears the final movement of Beethoven's Ninth Symphony, for example, one knows oneself to be in the presence of an objective value. To say, having heard that piece, 'Well, I just don't like it' or 'It's not to my taste' would be altogether inappropriate. One's subjectivity doesn't judge the Ninth Symphony; it is judged by the Ninth Symphony. We would say something very similar regarding the Sistine Chapel Ceiling, Sainte Chapelle, Bach's *St. Matthew's Passion*, Dante's *Commedia*, or Eliot's *The Wasteland*. Along with these aesthetic

---

19. Dietrich von Hildebrand, *Aesthetics*, vol. 1, trans. Fr. Brian McNeil (Steubenville, OH: The Hildebrand Project, 2016), 18–19, 26–27, 127–129, 438. For more on this point in von Hildebrand, see chapter two, "Evangelizing the Nones," 24–25.

20. See von Hildebrand, *My Battle Against Hitler: Faith, Truth, and Defiance in the Shadow of the Third Reich*, trans. John Henry Crosby (New York: Image, 2014).

21. Von Hildebrand, *Christian Ethics*, 34–63.

22. Von Hildebrand, *Christian Ethics*, 129–139.

values, Hildebrand would also point to objective ethical values: Maximilian Kolbe's self-sacrifice, the ministry of Mother Teresa, and the courage of the martyrs, to name just a few examples. To say that such acts were not to one's taste—or that some might appreciate them but I don't—would be, obviously, absurd. Hildebrand argued that the objective values that appear in the world are, finally, echoes of the supreme value that brought them into existence—namely, God. God is properly recognized as the creative ground of the objective truths, values, and beauties that obtain in our experience.

What is happening in our culture today—if we were to express it in Hildebrandian terms—is the reduction of the objectively valuable to the category of the merely subjectively satisfying. And this renders the very best things in life flat, mundane, and harmless. It precludes the possibility of the soul really catching fire. The Church ought to be in the business of cultivating, propagating, and celebrating the realm of the objectively valuable. I have spoken often of the importance of leading evangelically with the beautiful. In our postmodern time, when truth and goodness are both seen as oppressive ('Who are you to tell me what to think or how to behave?'), the third transcendental might offer a more winsome way into the realm of the objectively valuable. And thanks be to God, the Church is a treasure trove of the beautiful. The tendency in the years following the Second Vatican Council to set the beautiful aside in our architecture, our liturgy, and our pious practices and to opt, in an exaggerated way, for the works of social justice, has led to a real impoverishment of our ecclesial life. One way to break through the buffered self is to let the beautiful shine again.

But we ought also to hold up sublime examples of moral excellence. These too will cut through the carapace of subjective self-regard and reorder the ego. This is not the time, I would insist, to dial down our moral ideals—just the contrary. The mitigation of moral ideals serves, in fact, a subjectivizing purpose—and this is not the needful thing at the moment. A splendid balance obtains in the Church between the intensity of our moral demand and the extravagance of our offer of mercy.[23] We are not content to call people to spiritual mediocrity, for our purpose is to cultivate sanctity; and at

---

23. See chapter twelve, "*Imago Dei* as Privilege and Mission," 206–207, for more on this point.

the same time, we are lavish in our offer of the divine forgiveness. When these two extremes are construed as mutually exclusive or in tension one with the other, something of crucial importance is lost. In point of fact, both extreme demand and extreme mercy can function as Hildebrandian objective values.

Thirdly, we should put a stress on common mission. Hans Urs von Balthasar said that the truly beautiful (and here he was very much like Hildebrand) stops us, rearranges our subjectivities, and then sends us on mission.[24] The beautiful works a sort of evangelical power within the soul. When you sense the objectively valuable, you want to be a missionary on its behalf. One of the most compelling accounts of this process is the strand scene in James Joyce's *Portrait of the Artist as a Young Man*. Stephen Daedalus spies the lovely girl standing just off-shore. After taking in her beauty, he looks with her out to the open sea, invoking the Diotima speech from Plato's *Symposium*.[25] He then cries "Heavenly God,"[26] signaling that the girl's very particular beauty has triggered an awareness of the source of beauty. But what Joyce most wants us to appreciate is that Stephen's vocation to become a reporter of epiphanies flowed directly from that experience of being seized by the objectively beautiful. For the last couple of hundred years—at least since the time of Friedrich Schleiermacher—religion has taken a subjective and experiential starting point.[27] This has encouraged the individualism that I complained of above. Beginning with the beautiful and the objectively valuable turns the momentum in another direction.

One thinks also in this context of Gerard Manley Hopkins's advice to a young man who was struggling with unbelief: "Give alms."[28] A key way to engage and combat relativism is to encour-

24. Hans Urs von Balthasar, *The Glory of the Lord: Theological Aesthetics*, vol. 1, *Seeing the Form*, trans. Erasmo Leiva-Merikakis (San Francisco: Ignatius Press, 2009), 312–313.

25. Plato, *Symposium*, in *Complete Works*, ed. John M. Cooper, trans. Alexander Nehamas and Paul Woodruff (Indianapolis: Hackett Publishing Company, 1997), 211a–212c, pp. 493–494.

26. James Joyce, *A Portrait of the Artist as a Young Man*, Oxford World's Classics (Oxford: Oxford University Press, 2000), 144.

27. See chapter five, "How Von Balthasar Changed My Mind," 69–71, for an in-depth analysis of Schleiermacher.

28. Gerard M. Hopkins, *The Letters of Gerard M. Hopkins*, ed. Claude Colleer Abbott (London: Oxford University Press, 1955), 60, 64.

age mission on behalf of Christ's poor. The very radicality of the Church's moral commitment had a powerfully evangelical influence in the earliest centuries of its life. "Look how they [the Christians] love one another" was Tertullian's summary of the pagan reaction to the service that Christians offered to their own and even to those outside their circle.[29] We see much the same thing in the work of St. Antony of the Desert and St. Benedict. The withdrawal from the world and the embrace of poverty, simplicity, care for the poor, and trust in God's providence galvanized the imagination of people in the late Roman period. This happened again in the Middle Ages through the witness of Francis and Dominic. What these men were displaying was objective moral value, and it had a powerful evangelical impact.

A fourth major area of engagement is around the question of freedom. Liberty is the value most correlative to subjectivism in our culture. If existence truly precedes essence,[30] then freedom has to come first and must be unhindered. What is, consequently, most resented in our cultural context is the presumption that someone can or should interfere with an individual's freedom to determine the meaning of his own life. One sees this perhaps most clearly in the arena of gender issues today. Even if one's entire body points in one direction, no one can tell the sovereign self that it can't point in the opposite direction.

But this view of freedom is rooted in certain moves that occurred in the late Middle Ages and then became hardened during the modern period. Scotus and especially Ockham speculated that freedom amounts to a person's will hovering indifferently above two choices. On the basis of no coercion, either interior or exterior, this sovereign will then makes a choice. As many have pointed out, this completely atomistic view of human freedom was an extrapolation from the totally sovereign view of divine freedom that came to the fore through Nominalism. The contemporary Dominican theologian Servais Pinckaers has characterized this Ockhamist conception as "the freedom of indifference." This is a radically "pro-choice"

---

29. Tertullian, *Apology*, trans. T. R. Glover, The Loeb Classical Library (London: William Heinemann Ltd, 1931), 39.7, pg. 177.

30. Cf. Jean-Paul Sartre, *Existentialism is a Humanism*, trans. Carol Macomber (New Haven, CT: Yale University Press, 2007), 22, 24, 29.

understanding of liberty, and it has come to hold sway in most Western cultures today. To this understanding, Pinckaers contrasts what he calls "freedom for excellence."[31] This is the view that dominated through most of the classical period and that is on clear display in the Bible. On this reading, freedom is not so much indifferent, self-determining choice, but rather the ordering of the will so as to make the achievement of the good first possible and then effortless.

To understand this principle, one has only to think of the process whereby someone learns to play the piano, swing a golf club, or speak a language. When I was in the process of learning French many years ago, I felt dramatically unfree, for I knew precisely what I wanted to say but couldn't articulate it. When I play golf, I typically feel unfree, for I can't do what the game requires. On the first interpretation of freedom, law is, at best, a 'necessary evil,' for it restricts freedom of choice. It is accepted in order to allow for a greater good, but in a perfect world, it wouldn't obtain. But on the second interpretation of freedom, the freedom for excellence, law is not the enemy but rather the condition for the possibility of real freedom. It is the interiorization of the law that allows for free expression in speech, in sports, in music, or in the moral order. I found considerable traction evangelically with the observation that most people, in regard to areas of life they take seriously, stop being subjectivists in short order. No serious golfer would ever say to a beginner, "Just swing any way you want. Who am I to tell you how to play?" No serious musician would encourage a beginner to pick up the guitar and play according to his lights. Both would lead their disciples through a careful apprenticeship, gradually placing the relevant laws in their minds and bodies.

In light of this distinction, we can understand the psalmist who cries out, "How I love your law, Lord! I study it all day long" (Ps 119:97). Within the framework of a freedom-of-indifference interpretation, one might indeed tolerate law as a necessary evil, but one would scarcely be tempted to meditate upon it day and night or, in the manner of King David, to dance with joy before it. Those who would aspire to be evangelists must convince people today that the objective law is not the enemy of their subjectivity and their freedom.

---

31. Pinckaers, *The Sources of Christian Ethics*, 329.

Another way to engage the relativists more positively is to present Cardinal Newman's notion of the development of doctrine and its attendant perspectivalism. What seems to irk many people today is the insinuation that someone simply has the truth. Period. For confirmation, take a look at sociologist Christian Smith's recent work on why young Catholics are leaving the faith. One of the principal reasons they give is that claims to absolute truth are exclusive and aggressive.[32] Newman opined, "The idea which represents an object or supposed object is commensurate with the sum total of its possible aspects."[33] Anticipating Husserl's phenomenology by several decades, Newman teaches that an idea does not present itself univocally and one-sidedly. Rather, it discloses itself gradually and through the process of lively thought and conversation. It is a bit like a diamond that is thrown repeatedly in the air, allowing various aspects to present themselves. Thus, the idea of the Incarnation, to give one example, was at least *in nuce* (in seed form) given to the apostles of Jesus, but it has required two millennia of conversation, debate, disagreement, and compromise to make the fullness of this idea appear—and that process is indeed ongoing. This notion of doctrinal development not only allows for but positively demands steady dialogue, debate, and openness to new perspectives. I believe that this Newmanian approach actually includes what is best in the dialogic and conversational models so eagerly embraced by the defenders of relativism, even as it steers quite clear of the epistemological anomalies of relativism.

A Model for Cultural Engagement

In closing, I should like to propose a model for the creative, intelligent, and nonviolent presentation of religious ideas. Whereas today we tend to see in regard to religion only the binary option of aggressive imposition or permissive relativism, there was a time when a

---

32. Nicolette Manglos-Weber and Christian Smith, *Understanding Former Young Catholics: Findings from a National Study of American Emerging Adults* (Notre Dame, IN: University of Notre Dame Press, 2014), 24.

33. John Henry Cardinal Newman, *An Essay on the Development of Christian Doctrine*, 6th ed (Notre Dame, IN: University of Notre Dame Press, 1989), I.I.2, pg. 34.

very lively third option existed—namely, public argument. The
period I have in mind is neither classical Greece nor early modern
Europe, but rather the High Middle Ages, the time when the university system as we know it was born. And to illustrate the medieval
method of disciplined conversation there is no better candidate than
St. Thomas Aquinas.

The principal means of teaching in the medieval university
was not the classroom lecture, which became prominent only in the
nineteenth-century German system of education; rather, it was the
quaestio disputata (disputed question), which was a lively, sometimes
raucous, and very public intellectual exchange. Though the written
texts of Aquinas can strike us today as a tad turgid, we have to recall
that they are grounded in these disciplined but decidedly energetic
conversations. If we consult Aquinas's masterpiece, the *Summa theologiae*, we find that he poses literally thousands of questions and that
not even the most sacred issues are off the table, the best evidence of
which is article three of question two of the first part of the *Summa*:
"*Utrum Deus sit?*" (Whether there is a God).[34] If a Dominican priest is
permitted to ask even that question, everything is fair game; nothing
is too dangerous to talk about.

After stating the issue, Aquinas then entertains a series of
objections to the position that he will eventually take. In many cases,
these represent a distillation of real counterclaims and queries that
Aquinas would have heard during public *quaestiones disputatae*. But for
our purposes, the point to emphasize is that Aquinas presents these
objections in their most convincing form, often stating them better
and more pithily than their advocates ever did. In proof of this,
we might note that during the Enlightenment, rationalist *philosophes*
would sometimes take Thomistic objections and use them to bolster
their own antireligious positions. To give just one example, consider
Aquinas's devastatingly convincing formulation of the argument
from evil against the existence of God: "If one of two contraries
be infinite, the other would be altogether destroyed. But the word
God means that He is infinite goodness. If, therefore, God existed,
there would be no evil discoverable; but there is evil in the world.

---

34. *Summa theologiae*, I, q. 2, a. 3.

Therefore God does not exist."[35] Aquinas indeed provides a telling response, but, as stated, the objection is a darn good argument. Might I suggest that it would help our public discourse immensely if all parties would be willing to formulate their opponents' positions as respectfully and convincingly as Aquinas did.

Having articulated the objections, Aquinas then offers his own magisterial resolution of the matter: *Respondeo dicendum quod...* ("I respond that it must be said..."). One of the more regrettable marks of the postmodern mind is a tendency endlessly to postpone the answer to a question. Take a look at Jacques Derrida's work for a master class in this technique. And sadly, many today, who want so desperately to avoid offending anyone, find refuge in just this sort of permanent irresolution. But Aquinas knew what Chesterton articulated, that an open mind is like an open mouth—that is, designed to close finally on something solid and nourishing.[36] Finally, having offered his *respondeo*, Aquinas returns to the objections and, in light of his resolution, answers them. It is notable that a typical technique of Aquinas is to find something right in the objector's position and to use that to correct what he deems to be errant in it. How much more civil our religious conversation would be if each side were willing to practice that technique in regard to his opponent's position?

Throughout this process, in the objections, *respondeos*, and answers to objections, Aquinas draws on a wide range of sources: the Bible and the Church Fathers, of course, but also the classical philosophers Aristotle, Plato, and Cicero, the Jewish scholar Moses Maimonides, and the Islamic masters Averroes and Avicenna. And he consistently invokes these figures with supreme respect, characterizing Aristotle, for example, as simply "the Philosopher" and referring to Maimonides as "Rabbi Moyses." It is fair to say that, in substantial ways, Thomas Aquinas disagrees with all of these figures, and yet he is more than willing to listen to them, to engage them, and to take their arguments seriously. Again, we might see a parallel with Chesterton, who famously remained friends with those with whom

---

35. *Summa theologiae*, I, q. 2, a. 3, obj. 1.

36. G. K. Chesterton, "Illustrated London News" (October 10, 1908), in *Collected Works*, vol. XXVIII (San Francisco: Ignatius Press, 1987), 196; Chesterton, *Autobiography* (New York: Sheed & Ward, 1936), 229.

he radically disagreed. He and George Bernard Shaw—as unlike in ideology as could be imagined—nevertheless were lifelong friends.

What this Thomistic method produces is, in its own way, a 'safe space' for conversation, but it is a safe space for adults and not timorous children. Might I modestly suggest that it wouldn't be a bad model for our present discussion of the most serious matters? And might I further suggest that it would be an excellent method for engaging and overcoming the relativism that so bedevils us today?

CHAPTER 17

CHRIST IN CINEMA

The Evangelical Power of the Beautiful

Even as a secularist ideology comes increasingly to dominate the culture of the West and as the mainstream Christian denominations (at least in Europe, Canada, the United States, and Australia) continue to lose members and institutional focus, Jesus of Nazareth appears to be alive and well in contemporary cinema. Even the most casual devotee of film will notice a plethora of 'Christ figures' in the movies of the last few decades, including Aslan in the *Narnia* series, Randle Patrick McMurphy in *One Flew Over the Cuckoo's Nest*, Lucas Jackson in *Cool Hand Luke*, John Coffey (notice the initials) in *The Green Mile*, the charming alien in *ET: The Extraterrestrial*, Neo in *The Matrix*, Daniel in *Jesus de Montreal*, Clark Kent in the most recent *Superman* films, Frodo, Aragorn, and Gandalf in the *Lord of the Rings* series, and, for a comic variation on the theme, the Dude—with his long hair, beard, robes, laid-back attitude, pacifism, and, in one scene, a carpenter's belt—in *The Big Lebowski*. Alongside of these more indirect and symbolically evocative presentations, there are also a number of films explicitly about the figure of Jesus, including Franco Zeffirelli's multi-part *Jesus of Nazareth*, Martin Scorsese's *The Last Temptation of Christ*, Pier Paolo Pasolini's *The Gospel According to St. Matthew*, George Stevens's *The Greatest Story Ever Told*, and most controversially and lucratively, Mel Gibson's *The Passion of the Christ*. That the person and story of Christ are deep in the cultural DNA of the West goes without saying, but the frequency with which film directors and producers turn to Jesus is one of the clearest indications that Jesus remains disturbingly relevant to our postmodern consciousness.

I have chosen to submit for the reader's consideration three films that include a particularly strong Christ figure: *Babette's Feast*, *The Shawshank Redemption*, and *Gran Torino*. Out of the many I could have picked from, I chose these three for a variety of reasons. First, they are all excellent movies—well-directed, beautifully photographed, and featuring fine acting and writing; second, they all exhibit Christ figures that sneak up on the viewer, asserting themselves subtly; and thirdly, they each illumine a somewhat underexplored theological dimension of the person of Jesus.

Babette's Feast

Gabriel Axel's 1987 film adaptation of Isak Dinesen's short story "Babette's Feast" is about many things—friendship, loss, religious devotion, and sensual delight—but above all it is about the power of Jesus Christ to heal and illumine. The figure of Jesus in this movie is a curious one indeed: a French chef who finds herself living among fiercely puritanical Lutherans in late nineteenth-century Denmark.

The film is set in a remote village nestled at the foot of a mountain at the edge of a Danish fjord, where two sisters—Martine and Philippa—preside over the remnants of a religious community that had been founded by their father, a prim and devout pastor known as "the Dean." In a series of flashbacks, we learn that Martine and Philippa were, in their youth, extremely beautiful and had been courted by any number of young men, whose overtures were met with a firm refusal from the girls' father. When Martine was eighteen, she was sought out by a dashing young military officer named Lorens Löwenhielm, but the romance came to nothing, for Lorens knew he could never break through the carapace of piety and otherworldliness that Martine had constructed around herself. And Philippa had been pursued by an even more distinguished suitor, Achille Papin, one of the most celebrated opera singers of his time. While sojourning on the Danish coast, Papin had wandered into the Dean's church and heard Philippa sing. Ravished by the beauty of her voice, Papin commenced to coach the young woman in the hopes of preparing her for the musical stage in Paris. While practicing the "seduction duet" from Mozart's *Don Giovanni*, Papin took his disciple in his arms and kissed her. Afterward, Philippa asked her father to inform Papin that she would take no further lessons, and the great singer returned, heartbroken, to France.

Some fifteen years later, the sisters were shocked to find a pale and frightened woman on their doorstep, with a note from Achille Papin introducing her. Babette Hersant had been a *petroleuse* during the recent communard uprising in Paris, had lost both her husband and her son, and was now unable to remain in France. Would the kind sisters, whom Papin had known years before, be willing to take her in? In great generosity of spirit, the sisters took in this forlorn character, and in time, Babette became their trusted and beloved servant. Because the sisters were suspicious of French cooking (the French, they had heard, ate frogs), they taught Babette how to prepare their customary meal of split cod and ale-and-bread soup. Given their austere religious commitments, they explained, their food had to be as plain and unappetizing as possible.

Returning to the present day, we learn that the sisters want to celebrate the upcoming centenary of their father's birth. Even as they contemplate this glad anniversary, they are saddened that the spirit of the Dean seemed to have faded among his aging followers. Strife, jealousy, and division had replaced the kind fellowship that he had cultivated among them. As the sisters were considering how best to mark the great day, a letter arrived from France for Babette, containing the improbable news that she had won ten thousand francs in the national lottery. The loyal servant begged her mistresses to be allowed to prepare a sumptuous gourmet meal for them and their community in honor of the Dean. Though they were moved by the generosity of the offer, the sisters were reluctant to acquiesce, for they saw only spiritual danger in such a sensual affair. But Babette stepped forward and with tremendous resolve said, "Ladies, I have never in twelve years asked you for a favor…because I have had nothing to pray for. But tonight, I have a prayer to make from the bottom of my heart." The sisters gave in and agreed to the dinner.

A month before the feast, Babette went on a journey (her first in twelve years), and upon her return, she announced that the goods necessary for the festivities were on their way. In the course of the next several days, the food, drink, and other accoutrements commenced to arrive, and the villagers were flabbergasted, for they never imagined that such culinary extravagance was even possible. But their astonishment was complete when a primeval-looking turtle arrived, poking his snake-like head out of a greenish-black shell. Concerned that they had countenanced a witch's sabbath, Martine, Philippa, and the other disciples of the Dean agreed that they would eat the meal, out of deference to Babette, but that they would neither speak of it nor take any pleasure in it.

The great dinner took place on Sunday, the Lord's Day. The first guest to arrive was ancient Mrs. Löwenhielm, who long ago had lost most of her hearing and sense of taste and who thus functioned as an apt embodiment of the community's puritanism. The old lady brought as a guest her nephew, General Löwenhielm, the military officer who, so many years before, had courted Martine. Though he had fulfilled all of his professional aspirations, the General was bored and depressed and came to the dinner only with reluctance. In time, the other members of the Dean's congregation arrived and, after singing two hymns, the diners came to the table. The General, the only member of the company who had not taken a vow against enjoying the dinner, could barely believe it when he sipped his first glass of wine: "Amontillado! And the finest Amontillado that I have ever tasted." When he took his first spoonful of the soup, he exclaimed, "The best I have ever had!" But his puzzlement and delight reached their apex when he tasted the main course. He told his fellow diners that, years before, at the Café Anglais in Paris, he had eaten "an incredibly *recherché* and palatable dish" called *Cailles en Sarcophage*, which was the invention of the culinary genius who was the chef of that establishment. Looking about at everyone around the table, he eagerly exclaimed, "But this is *Cailles en Sarcophage!*" As the delicious concoctions were consumed and as the fine wine flowed, the conversation became freer, the laughter readier. Old resentments seemed to melt away and broken friendships were being repaired. So moved was he by the entire experience that General Löwenhielm rose and addressed the assembly: "In our human foolishness and short-sightedness, we imagine that grace is finite. Grace, my friends, demands nothing of us but that we shall await it with confidence and acknowledge it in gratitude…Grace takes us all to its bosom and declares general amnesty." In the wake of this extraordinary oration, the entire place seemed suffused with the very grace of which the General spoke. All during the dinner, a steady snow had fallen, so that when the guests were taking their leave, the entire countryside was blanketed in white. As they set out, they staggered and wavered on their feet, some slipping down or falling forward, so that their elbows, backsides, and knees were covered in snow, making them look, for all the world, like gamboling little lambs.

But the film does not end on this gentle note, all things simply reconciled through the mystical power of a meal. The filmmaker shifts our attention to the kitchen, so that we can see the price that was paid to make the grace-filled repast possible. Babette sits exhausted and pale in the midst of myriad unwashed and greasy pans. More precisely, she sits on the chopping block, where she had butchered the various animals that the happy company had just consumed. Then the one who had, for so many years, maintained silence about her past, spoke up: "I was once cook at the Café Anglais." This meant little to the sisters, but Babette continued, laying out to them the full extent of her sacrifice. Not only had she lost her husband and son in the uprising, but she had also lost her job, since the gentlemen and aristocrats who had frequented the Café Anglais disappeared after the revolution. Further, she said, "I have no money." When the sisters protested that Babette had won ten thousand francs in the lottery, the former master chef explained that she had spent every centime of her winnings on the magnificent dinner.

Christology must always convey a theory of salvation—that is to say, some account of what is fundamentally wrong with humanity and how Jesus saves us from that condition. For the director of *Babette's Feast*, the problem is lifelessness produced by a tragic divorce between body and soul, sensuality and spirituality. And the solution is a figure who comes from a world that has not experienced such a divorce and who willingly sacrifices herself so as to allow those in the fallen world a taste of higher things. Babette, accustomed to the highest and finest, arrived in the forlorn Danish village as an alien, a visitor from another realm. But she freely entered into their lives, emptying herself even to the point of suppressing her skills so as to prepare the simplest and least appetizing meals. Paul said that Christ became poor for our sake so that by his poverty we might become rich (2 Cor 8:9). Babette will indeed affect a transformation in the village, but she does not do so right away. Rather, in the manner of Jesus, her saving work is preceded by a long period of preparation during which she humbly identified herself with those she is destined one day to lift up. During these 'hidden years,' she was readying herself and her community for the moment of transfiguration.

It is a biblical commonplace that God desires to express his intimacy with his people through a festive meal. In the book of Genesis, God gives the first humans practically free rein in the Garden, permitting, even inviting, them to eat of all the trees save one (Gn 2:16–17). In the book of Exodus, God commands his people to celebrate a sacred meal on the eve of their liberation from slavery and then to repeat that meal as an emblem of their shared identity (Ex 12). In the book of the prophet Isaiah, we hear that the Lord will host a feast on the summit of his holy mountain, where there will be "juicy, rich food and pure, choice wines" (Is 25:6). And in the book of Proverbs, divine Wisdom is pictured as a Jewish mother spreading a sumptuous banquet before her people (Prv 9:1–6). It is absolutely no accident that Jesus, who is personally identified with the divine Wisdom, picks up and gives radical expression to this theme, offering table-fellowship to all, saints and sinners alike. At the climax of his life, Jesus sat down in table-fellowship with his intimate followers and there spread before them a meal of his own Body and Blood, effecting thereby the most radical union possible between divinity and humanity (Mt 26:17–29). In John's account of the Last Supper, Jesus tells his table fellows: "I have told you this so that my joy may be in you and your joy may be complete" (Jn 15:11). By means of these sacred meals, the God of Israel has been consistently luring his fallen people back to life and communion.

However, in a world gone wrong, there is no communion without sacrifice. An off-kilter state of affairs can only be set right through a painful reconfiguring. This is why Isaiah imagines the savior of Israel to be a suffering, rejected figure. In the Gospel narratives of the Last Supper, there is always a link between the meal that Jesus offered and the sacrifice he would make on the cross the following day: "This is my body, which will be given for you" (Lk 22:19) and "for this is my blood of the covenant, which will be shed on behalf of many for the forgiveness of sins" (Mt 26:28). In a world without sin it might be otherwise, but, in the actual world, the festive union of God and humanity could take place only through an act of sacrificial love. And so it goes with Babette and her fallen community. She did indeed use a festive meal to bring them together with God and one another, but she paid an enormous price: her many years of humble self-effacing service, her weeks' long labor to prepare the meal, her exhausting evening's labor to cook and present it, and ultimately her expenditure of all the money she had. All of this was summed up in her taking a seat on the chopping block, just as Jesus' was summed up in his being nailed to the cross.

The Shawshank Redemption

Frank Darabont's *The Shawshank Redemption*, a 1994 film adaptation of Stephen King's novella, has proven to be one of the most beloved and carefully analyzed movies of the past thirty years. In an interview, Darabont and two of the lead actors—Tim Robbins and Morgan Freeman—opined that *Shawshank* is, at bottom, a story of the liberating power of hope. It is certainly that. But it is also a most compelling presentation of the story of Jesus. Like many other 'Christ figure' films in recent years—*The Green Mile, One Flew Over the Cuckoo's Nest,* and *Cool Hand Luke* come most readily to mind—*The Shawshank Redemption* is set in a prison. These films see the fundamental problem as one of spiritual imprisonment, and they powerfully recover the idea of Jesus as redeemer, which carried in the ancient world the overtone of paying a ransom to buy back the freedom of a hostage (Mk 10:45). The Council of Trent teaches that sin is a predicament that has implicated the entirety of the human race, a shared dysfunction.[1] It is so pervasive that it amounts to an incarceration. What is required, therefore, is not simply a teacher who can shed light on our suffering but a liberator, someone powerful enough to foment a general prison break. The well-known hymn text expresses the idea with admirable laconicism: "O come, O come, Emmanuel, and ransom captive Israel."

---

1. H. J. Schroeder, *Canons and Decrees of the Council of Trent* (St. Louis, MO: B. Herder Book Co., 1941), Session V, no. 2, 21.

The first clue that Andy Dufresne is a Christ-character (besides his initials, AD) is that he is an innocent man who finds himself unjustly thrown among criminals. John's Gospel describes Jesus as a light shining in the darkness and as the divine Word that has pitched its tent in the midst of a deeply compromised human condition (Jn 1:5, 14). And all four Gospels present the baptism of Jesus by John (Mt 3:13–17; Mk 1:9–11; Lk 3:21–22; Jn 1:29–34). Since the Baptist was offering a ceremonial cleansing from sin, Jesus' first great public act was to stand in the muddy waters of the Jordan, in solidarity with the guilty. But his purpose was not simply to express compassion but rather to get people out of their dreadful condition: "Behold the Lamb of God, who takes away the sin of the world" (Jn 1:29). What we see in the course of the *Shawshank Redemption* is the process by which the innocent Andy opens up a path to freedom for his fallen brothers. Andy's difference is signaled his first night at Shawshank. As his fellow "freshmen" inmates collapse in anguish, anger, and despair, Andy, despite the desperation and profound injustice of his own situation, and to the infinite surprise of the veteran prisoners, maintains a Zen-like calm, not uttering a sound. Red, the narrator of the story, remarks that, from the beginning, "He [Andy] had a quiet way about him, a walk and a talk that just weren't normal around here. He strolled, like a man in a park, without a care or worry. Like he had on an invisible coat that would shield him from this place." In Shawshank but not of it.

Andy's transcendence of the normal patterns and attitudes appeared in connection with the tarring of the roof of the license plate factory on the prison grounds. A number of inmates, including Andy and Red, were chosen by lottery, and they happily took the opportunity to work outside. After hours of laboring in the sun, however, they were exhausted. In the meantime, one of the bored guards was discussing with his fellows how he was being cheated out of an unexpected inheritance through confiscatory taxation. Violating one of the most sacred rules of Shawshank, and taking his life in his hands, Andy approached the guards without being invited. They stiffened and pulled their guns, but Andy stood his ground. The head man grabbed Andy by the shirt and dangled him over the edge of the roof, threatening to drop him to his death, but the prisoner (who had been a banker in his previous life) coolly explained that he knew a way for the man legally to keep the entire inheritance. Intrigued, the guard pulled him back, and Andy explained the entire situation, asking in recompense for this invaluable financial advice only that his "coworkers" could be allowed to take a break and share some beers. Red comments, "We sat and drank with the sun on our shoulders, and felt like free men. We coulda been tarring the roof of one of our own houses. We were the Lords of all Creation." Andy himself didn't partake, but only sat against the wall that surrounded the roof and smiled. Like Nurse Ratched and her minions in *One Flew Over the Cuckoo's Nest*, the prison guards represent all of those structures that maintain the integrity of the dysfunctional system, all of those persons, habits, and institutions that keep the fallen world fallen. And like McMurphy in *Cuckoo's Nest*, Andy Dufresne is the courageous and canny fellow who manages, through wit and subtle manipulation, to outmaneuver the keepers of the system. It is very common in contemporary Christology to present Jesus as the wily opponent of the political and religious establishment, the one who, through clever speech and provocative gesture, managed to expose the hypocrisy of the scribes and Pharisees and to undermine the brutality of the Roman occupiers. A direct confrontation of the Shawshank power structure would have been useless, but Andy employed a kind of Aikido, the martial art that uses the momentum of one's opponent against him. This was consistently Jesus' strategy in his struggle with the dark powers that hemmed him in.

Later, Andy petitioned the warden, a hypocritical fundamentalist Christian named Norton, to allow him to write to the state government to provide funds for a library at Shawshank. In a prison setting, freedom matters most of all, and knowledge is a path to spiritual freedom. Norton gives him leave to write, and Andy, over the course of many years, inundates the government with letter upon letter. Finally, to general astonishment, the legislature granted him some money to buy books, magazines, and recordings. When the cache arrived, Andy unpacked the boxes and found, among many other treasures, Mozart's *Le Nozze di Figaro*. Hungry for the music, he immediately turned on the phonograph and played one of his favorite pieces, the duet between Susanna and the Contessa. Then, knowing full well that he would be punished severely for doing so, he locked the door of his cubicle and brought the PA microphone over

to the tiny phonograph speaker and the glorious duet commenced
to echo all over Shawshank. In the prison yard, the inmates froze in
their places and, with mouths agape, simply took in the impossibly
beautiful music. Red summed up their feelings: "I have no idea to this
day what them two Italian ladies were singing about. Truth is, I don't
want to know. Some things are best left unsaid. I like to think they
were singing about something so beautiful that it can't be expressed
in words, and makes your heart ache because of it... It was like some
beautiful bird flapped into our drab little cage and made these walls
dissolve away, and for the briefest of moments—every last man at
Shawshank felt free." Jesus spoke some of the most lyrical and compelling words ever uttered, and his speech has, across the centuries,
set the souls of his listeners free from the constraints of general opinion: *was man sagt* ("what are they saying"). And he famously upbraided
the scribes and Pharisees for storing up knowledge for themselves and
allowing no one else access to it (Lk 11:52). The Andy who unleashed
the power of *Le Nozze di Figaro* in the hopeless gray of Shawshank
prison is showing this profile of the Christ figure.

One of the consistent themes in *The Shawshank Redemption* is the
way in which the prisoners become so accustomed to their lives, so
institutionalized, that they cannot imagine a form of life beyond the
walls of the prison. Nowhere is this theme more fully on display than
in the likeable but tragic character of Brooks, memorably played
in the film by the veteran character actor James Whitmore. Acting
utterly out of character, Brooks holds a knife to the throat of one of
his friends. When he is finally disarmed, he explains, through tears,
that he was trying to do something that would guarantee he could
stay in prison. The parole board had informed him that he would
be released, and Brooks simply couldn't bear the prospect of living in the world outside of Shawshank. Once freed, Brooks tried to
make his way at a halfway house and a small grocery store where he
served as a bagger, but he found himself frightened and disoriented.
Finally, in despair, he hanged himself from one of the rafters in his
tiny room. Years later, Andy spoke to Red of the power of hope,
and Red reacted angrily: "Hope is a dangerous thing. Drive a man
insane. It's got no place here. Better get used to the idea." The one
who demonstrates an entirely new way of thinking and acting is a
threat not only to the keepers of the established system but also to

most people who are victimized by that system. This helps to explain why the proclaimer of the Kingdom of God was not only harassed and eventually eliminated by the powers that be but also abandoned by the vast majority of his followers, and why the Israelites, liberated from slavery, still hankered after Egypt.

In the course of many years, Andy had also been helping the warden with his taxes and finances. At the prompting of the corrupt Norton, Andy had moved into shadier territory, setting up a series of tax shelters and bank accounts under assumed names, which permitted the warden to siphon off huge amounts of cash with impunity. If he indicated an unwillingness to continue in this vein, the warden would threaten him with brutal retaliation. But Andy was, all this time, contriving a way to undermine and outmaneuver the lord of Shawshank. His plan hinged on successful escape. Many years before, Red had secured a small rock hammer for Andy so that his friend could pursue his hobby of shaping and polishing stones. But Andy had been using that hammer to dig a tunnel from his cell to a sewer pipe, which emptied out five hundred yards from the prison. One stormy night, when the tunnel was complete, Andy made his move, breaking through the sewer pipe with a stone and then, in Red's words, crawling "through five hundred yards of shit-smelling foulness I can't even imagine. Or just don't want to." When he emerged from the awful pipe, after his half-mile crawl, Andy spilled into a drainage ditch, pulled off his prison clothes, spread his arms out, and cocked his head to the sky in triumph. For years, Andy had been addressing issues on the surface of life at Shawshank, but finally he entered into the very bowels of the place, into the grime and mud at the foundational level, and worked his way through it to freedom. Christ Jesus brought grace, freedom, and beauty to an imprisoned humanity, but at the end he had to enter into the deepest foundations of the dysfunctional world, which is to say, into death and the fear of death. He did not eschew what is darkest and most painful in the human condition, but rather moved through it to resurrection on the far side. Awash in baptismal water after his journey through the foul tunnel, his arms spread out in the attitude of crucifixion, and looking up to heaven, Andy is an image of the Christ of the Paschal Mystery, the Lord who crawled all the way through sin and death to resurrection.

The Christian imagery becomes even more striking in the scenes depicting the events of the next morning. Roll is called as usual, and the prisoners line up outside their cells, but Andy Dufresne is not there. Annoyed, the guards call out to him, and when he doesn't respond, they inspect his cell directly. To their astonishment, the tiny space is empty; the bird had flown. The infuriated warden arrived, looked in, and saw no sign of the escapee. In his frustration, he threw one of Andy's polished stones at a large poster of Raquel Welch, which was affixed to one of the walls of the little cell. The rock went right through, revealing the tunnel that Andy had spent twenty years hollowing out. The camera looks back through the tunnel to the consternated, delighted, and puzzled faces of the warden, the guards, and the other prisoners who had crowded in to see what was happening. We see thereby what the faces of the Roman guards, Mary Magdalene, John, and Peter must have looked like when they peered into the empty tomb on Easter morning.

Andy's aikido-like outmaneuvering of the oppressive forces of Shawshank then came to its fullest expression. Wearing the warden's suit and shoes, and armed with all of the information pertaining to the numerous hidden accounts that Norton had established, Andy made the rounds of a dozen banks in the area and emptied out the funds. Not only did he escape from the penitentiary, but he disempowered the keeper of the place. We will explore this theme much more fully in our discussion of *Gran Torino*, but Andy's action is an evocation of the patristic doctrine of the *Christus Victor*, the Christ who released the imprisoned human race and despoiled the devil at the same time.

While he was still behind the walls of Shawshank, Andy dreamed of establishing a new life in the tropical beauty of Zihuatanejo, Mexico. Sometime after Andy's escape, Red received a blank postcard that was postmarked from a small town on the Texas-Mexican border, the place, Red concluded, where Andy had crossed into Mexico. When Red was finally paroled, he sought out a rock that Andy had told him about years before, a rock tucked away near a stone wall in a Maine hayfield. Under that rock was a box in which were a note from Andy and enough cash to allow Red to travel to Mexico. Paul describes Jesus as the "first fruits of those who have fallen asleep" (1 Cor 15:20), implying that Christ's resurrection is not simply a boon for him but rather a signal that those who follow him will experience a like resurrection. The closing of *The Shawshank Redemption* is one of the most beautiful scenes in recent cinema. Having made his way across the United States and through Mexico, Red walks the beach at Zihuatanejo. He spies Andy, dressed all in white, working on a boat along the seashore. The two friends smile and then, as the camera pans back to provide a godlike perspective, we see Red dropping his suitcase and enveloping Andy in an embrace. In Matthew's account of the resurrection appearances, an angel speaks to the holy women who have come to the tomb: "Then go quickly and tell his disciples, 'He has been raised from the dead, and he is going before you to Galilee; there you will see him'" (Mt 28:7). By the shore of the Sea of Galilee, Jesus met and called his first followers; and Galilee—beautiful and splendid—becomes the place of encounter with the risen Lord. Dressed in white, working on a boat by the sea, at an infinite remove from the gloominess of Shawshank Prison, Andy is a symbol of the risen Christ who, having liberated his friends, invites them to share his life forever.

Gran Torino

Certainly one of the most surprising Christ figures in recent cinema is Walt Kowalski in Clint Eastwood's 2008 film *Gran Torino*. I say surprising, for Walt is probably best known for the scene in which he aims a shotgun and snarls to a group of delinquents: "Get off my lawn!" Nevertheless, this character, beautifully played by the seventy-eight-year-old Eastwood himself, is an extraordinarily complete embodiment of Christ in his role as conqueror of sin.

The film opens at the funeral of Walt's wife, and the old man is surveying the scene skeptically and critically. Upon seeing his granddaughter exposing her belly button ring, Walt's eyes narrow, and he utters what is only his second line of the film: "Jesus Christ." After the choir sings the beatitudes, young Fr. Janovich rises to speak, and he delivers himself of a series of banalities. Disgusted, Walt mutters (and it is his third line of the film), "Jesus." A church, the liturgy, the beatitudes, a priest, and two mentions of the sacred name suggest the fundamentally religious theme and purpose of the movie.

At the reception following the funeral, we learn that Walt still lives in a Detroit neighborhood that once had been filled largely with Poles and other whites but that has now gone into economic decline. The formerly tidy and well-kept homes have slid into disrepair, and the Poles have been replaced by Hispanics, Blacks, and Hmong people from Laos and Cambodia. Next door to Walt is a particularly lively Hmong family, one of the younger denizens of which is a teenager named Thao. In one tightly written scene, we discover that Thao is a decent kid but is dominated by several of the women in the family. He means well, but he hasn't found his voice, his manhood. Some of the Hispanic gang members in the neighborhood purposely humiliate him, stealing his bicycle and leaving him helpless on the ground. Learning of this, a Hmong gang, led by one of Thao's cousins, decides to recruit him, turning him into a man on their terms. One of the gangbangers addresses Thao: "Spider told me how everyone thinks you're a pushover, how everyone walks over you and shit. I mean, look at you out here, working in the garden like a woman." Despite the vocal opposition of Thao's sisters and in the face of the boy's own reluctance, the gang draws Thao in, and for his initiation, they give him the assignment to steal the pristine 1972 Gran Torino that is Walt's pride and joy. While rummaging awkwardly and noisily through Walt's garage late one night, Thao is accosted by the old man and runs away.

In the meantime, Walt had managed to become something of a hero among the Hmong, since he had stood up to some obnoxious gangbangers who had threatened Thao's family. And this gave him a certain entrée to the Hmong world. In the wake of the attempted robbery, Thao's family commanded the young man to give himself to Walt as a sort of servant, and thus began the unlikely master-disciple relationship that stands at the heart of the film. One of the master's first moves is to help Thao with women. While attending a Hmong gathering—at which he appears a complete fish out of water—Walt notices that a pretty young woman is eyeing Thao. But the young man does not respond and allows her to leave with three other suitors. Walt says, "I got the greatest woman who ever lived to marry me. I had to work at it, but I got her. And it was the greatest thing that ever happened to me... But you? You just sit there and watch..." After this bit of romantic instruction, Walt has Thao work around his house, re-attaching gutters, digging up stumps, scraping paint, hanging a screen door. He even has his disciple paint a neighbor's house. Soon, others in the area catch on and approach Walt to get Thao to do things for them. The young man who had been more or less adrift now finds himself an extremely useful contributor to his community, and with satisfaction, Thao looks down at the callouses forming on his hands. When his last day of indentured servitude arrives, Thao eagerly asks Walt what the old man wants him to do and is sincerely disappointed when his master says, "Take the day off; you've done enough."

Even after his official time of servitude is up, Thao continues to follow Walt and soak up his wisdom. Like an eager apprentice, Thao asks Walt about the myriad tools in his garage, and like a patient master, the old man names and spells out the purpose of each one: "Post pole digger, hand spade, tack hammer, putty knife, wire stripper, dry wall saw, tile spacers." A key moment in the apprenticeship occurs when Walt invites Thao to help him move a large freezer out of the basement of one of Walt's children's house. The old man gives instructions as they place the appliance on a dolly, and then Walt says that he will take the heavy weight on top while Thao pushes from the bottom. When Thao objects to this arrangement, Walt answers with a dismissive slur, but the young man holds his ground: "You listen, old man. You came and got me because you needed help, so let me help you. Either it's top or I'm out of here." Walt can barely suppress a smile of satisfaction, as he realizes that the shy, pampered boy is becoming a man.

The funniest episode in the apprenticeship process occurs in a barbershop. Walt is friendly with the neighborhood barber and, for laughs, the two men converse exclusively through outrageous insults and slurs. The master brings in his apprentice in order to teach him how to talk like a man. After demonstrating the process a bit more fully, Walt invites Thao to go out and come back in again and greet the barber properly. Imitating Walt to a tee, the boy re-enters the shop and insults the man. The barber lowers a shotgun barrel in Thao's face and shouts, "Get out of my shop!" Thao stiffens with terror, while Walt and the barber throw their heads back and laugh.

From the very beginning of his public ministry, Jesus gathered disciples (*mathetai*, learners) around him. They lived with him at close quarters, watching his moves and listening to his speech. Often, they displayed a gross, even comical, misunderstanding of what Jesus wanted to convey, and the Lord sometimes expressed a profound impatience with their obtuseness: "how long will I be with you and endure you?" (Lk 9:41; compare Mt 17:17 and Mk 9:19). But all the while, Jesus was shaping their minds and bodies to become the bearers of his way of life. In the Gospel of John, two *mathetai* of the Baptist approach Jesus. The Lord turns on them and asks, "What do you seek?" Answering a question with a question, they say, "Where do you stay?" And he replies, simply enough, "Come, and you will see" (Jn 1:39). That little exchange discloses the essential dynamic of spiritual apprenticeship. Spiritually immature men come to live in intimacy with a master and thereby absorb his manner of living through their bodies. They "stay" with the teacher, discovering the source of his spiritual energy. All of this is echoed in the master/ disciple relationship between Walt and Thao: a learner comes to see how a master lives, withstands much abuse and sharp correction, and then becomes conformed to his teacher.

But Walt's configuring to Christ becomes especially clear in the last part of the film, when the old man realizes that teaching and modeling will not be enough to save his charge, but rather an act of radical sacrifice. The Hmong gangbangers who had tried to recruit Thao earlier had not given up. Just as the young man, with Walt's help, was settling into a job, they approached him and demanded that he join their company. When Thao resisted, they burned his cheek with a cigarette, and upon seeing the wound, Walt went into a rage, invading the home of one of the gang members, dragging him out of his house and onto the front porch and beating him. This in turn led to a retaliatory act. The gang members sprayed machine gun bullets through the front window of Thao's family's home and raped his sister. At this point, Walt realized that the enraged Thao was in serious danger of losing his life. Giving vent to his anger, he would either be gunned down directly or drawn into a cycle of violence from which he would never escape. So after some intense meditation, Walt hatches a plan, which is subtle, ingenious, and very dangerous.

His opening move is, through trickery, to lock Thao in the basement for his own protection. Then he confronts the Hmong gang. Standing in front of the duplex where they live, he calls them out. Though they wave their guns and threaten him, he stands his ground, and the young men are disconcerted by his utter lack of fear. Walt makes sure that all of the gang members are present and accounted for, and he waits until a large contingent of bystanders have assembled. That Walt is played by Clint Eastwood matters enormously at this point, for practically every Eastwood movie comes to its climax with such a scene. Clint the cowboy or Clint the cop faces down a posse of bad guys who have him hopelessly outnumbered, and he manages to gun them down. Walt reaches into his coat pocket and mumbles the beginning of the Hail Mary, and the gangbangers, convinced that he is going for a pistol, open fire, and strike Walt down, in full view of the bystanders. He dies in the attitude of the crucified Jesus, and when the camera comes in on his right hand, we see that it is gripping not a gun but a cigarette lighter. In one great act of self-sacrifice, Walt had saved Thao from the cycle of violence and disempowered those who made that cycle possible.

In the Christology of the Church Fathers, Jesus' salvific act on the cross is understood, not so much in Anselm's substitutionary sense but rather as an act of liberation for sinners and victory over dark powers.[2] The Fathers construe the devil as one who has claimed authority over the human race and Christ as the more powerful agent who has managed to wrest this authority from the dark spirit. What is fascinating for our purpose here is that these early theologians interpret Jesus as a kind of trickster, one who outfoxes the devil, drawing him out by providing an attractive target. In one version of this theory, Jesus' humanity is compared to a tasty bait wrapped around the hook of his divinity. When the devil bites (arranging for the death of Jesus on the cross), he is "caught" by the Lord's divinity. In another variation, the devil is seen as a kidnapper who holds the human race in his arms. Jesus offers his perfect humanity in exchange for all the human souls the devil holds. The wicked one willingly surrenders every sinner in order to have this one splendid prize, but when he grasps at Jesus' humanity, he is wrestled to the ground by Jesus' divine power. Walt Kowalski identified the forces that held Thao and indeed the entire neighborhood in their grasp. He then offered himself as a target for their fury, drawing them out into the open, exposing their wickedness. In giving away his life, he

---

2. See St. Athanasius, *On the Incarnation*, trans. John Behr, Popular Patristics Series, vol. 44B (Yonkers, NY: St. Vladimir's Seminary Press, 2011), §§28–29, pp. 78–79.

was stripping them of power and offering freedom to Thao. In this, he is a splendid contemporary icon of the *Christus Victor*.

Conclusion

In the postmodern context, so marked by deconstruction and relativism, it is often difficult to commence an evangelical presentation of the faith with either the true or the good. If we tell people in the contemporary West that they are thinking incorrectly or acting incorrectly, they will typically react with extreme defensiveness, for they are in the grip of what Joseph Ratzinger called "the dictatorship of relativism."[3] However, beginning with the beautiful can be much more promising, since the third transcendental is less threatening than the other two. Just look, the evangelist might say, at the Sistine Ceiling or the Sainte Chapelle or the work of Mother Teresa's sisters. The very beauty of those forms can then lure someone toward the good (what is the style of life that made them possible?) and the true (what are the doctrines that undergird such things?). This is why films—the distinctive art form of our time—can prove so evangelically effective. Just look at Babette, at Andy Dufresne, at Walt Kowalski. In doing so, you are, willy-nilly, looking into the face of Christ.

---

3. Joseph Ratzinger, *Mass Pro Eligendo Romano Pontifice: Homily of his Eminence Card. Joseph Ratzinger, Dean of the College of Cardinals* (April 18, 2005). See chapter sixteen, "Relativism and Its Discontents," for a full discussion of relativism.

Works Cited

All Vatican documents, including papal writings, in this list are available at vatican.va unless otherwise noted.

Adams, John. *Revolutionary Writings 1755–1775*. Edited by Gordon Wood. The Library of America Adams Family Collection 213. New York: Adams Family Collection, 2011.

Alter, Robert. *The David Story: A Translation with Commentary of 1 and 2 Samuel*. New York: W.W. Norton, 1999.

Ambrose, St. *Hexaemeron, Paradise, and Cain and Abel*. Translated by John J. Savage. The Fathers of the Church: A New Translation 42. Washington, DC: The Catholic University of America Press, 1961.

Aquinas, St. Thomas. *Expositio super librum Boethii De Trinitate*. Translated by Rose E. Brennan. St. Louis: Herder Books, 1946.

———. *On the Power of God (Quaestiones Disputatae de Potentia Dei)*. Translated by English Dominican Fathers. Westminster, MA: The Newman Press, 1952.

———. *In Librum de Causis*. Edited by H. D. Saffrey. Fribourg: Société Philosophique, 1954.

———. *Summa Contra Gentiles: Book One, God*. Translated by Anton C. Pegis. New York: Hanover House, 1955.

———. *Summa Contra Gentiles: Book Two, Creation*. Translated by James F. Anderson. Notre Dame, IN: University of Notre Dame Press, 1956.

———. *Treatise on the Separate Substances*. Translated by Francis J. Lescoe. Carthagena, OH: The Messenger Press, 1963.

———. *On Being and Essence*, 2ⁿᵈ ed. Translated by Armand Maurer. Toronto: Pontifical Institute for Mediaeval Studies, 1968.

———. *Summa Contra Gentiles: Book Three, Providence, Part 1*. Translated by Vernon J. Bourke. Notre Dame, IN: University of Notre Dame Press, 1975.

———. *Summa theologiae Prima Pars 1–49*. Translated by Fr. Laurence Shapcote. Latin/English Translation Series. Lander, WY: The Aquinas Institute for the Study of Sacred Doctrine, 2012.

———. *Summa theologiae Secunda Secundae 1-91*. Translated by Fr. Laurence Shapcote. Lander, WY: The Aquinas Institute for the Study of Sacred Doctrine, 2012.

———. *Summa theologiae Tertia Pars 1–59*. Translated by Fr. Laurence Shapcote. Lander, WY: The Aquinas Institute for the Study of Sacred Doctrine, 2012.

———. *Summa theologiae. Supplementum*. Translated by Fr. Laurence Shapcote. Latin/English Edition of the Works of St. Thomas Aquinas 21. Steubenville, OH: Emmaus Academic Press, 2017.

Arendt, Hannah. *The Origins of Totalitarianism*. New York: Schocken Books, 1996.

Aristotle. *The Politics of Aristotle*. Translated by Peter L. Phillips Simpson. Chapel Hill: The University of North Carolina Press, 1997.

———. *Nicomachean Ethics*. Translated by C. D. C. Reeve. Indianapolis: Hackett Publishing Company, Inc., 2014.

Aron, Raymond. "Bureaucratie et fantisme." *La France Libre* III, no. 13 (1941).

Athanasius, St. *On the Incarnation*. Translated by John Behr. Popular Patristics Series 44B. Yonkers, NY: St. Vladimir's Seminary Press, 2011.

———. "Life of Antony." In *Early Christian Lives*. Translated by Carolinne White. London: Penguin Books, 1998.

Augustine, St. *The City of God*. Edited by Marcus Dods. New York: Random House, Inc., 1950.

———. *Confessions*, 2ⁿᵈ ed. Translated by F. J. Sheed. Indianapolis: Hackett Publishing Company, Inc., 2006.

———. *Essential Sermons*. Translated by Edmund Hill. The Works of Saint Augustine: A Translation for the 21st Century. Part III-Homilies. Hyde Park, NY: New City Press, 2007.

———. *The Trinity*. Translated by Stephen McKenna. The Fathers of the Church Series: A New Translation 45. Washington, DC: The Catholic University of America Press, 2002.

Bakunin, Mikhail. *God and the State*. Translated by Benjamin Tucker. New York: Mother Earth Publishing Association, 1916.

Barron, Robert. *The Strangest Way: Walking the Christian Path*. Maryknoll, NY: Orbis Books, 2002.

———. *Bridging the Great Divide: Musings of a Post-Liberal, Post-Conservative Evangelical Catholic*. Lanham, MD/Oxford: Rowman & Littlefield Publishers, Inc., 2004.

———. *The Priority of Christ: Toward a Postliberal Catholicism*. Grand Rapids, MI: Brazos Press, 2007.

———. *Exploring Catholic Theology: Essays on God, Liturgy, and Evangelization*. Grand Rapids, MI: Baker Academic, 2015.

———. *Letter to a Suffering Church: A Bishop Speaks on the Sexual Abuse Crisis*. Park Ridge, IL: Word on Fire, 2019.

Barth, Karl. *Barth in Conversation*. Vol. 3, *1964-1968*. Edited by Eberhard Busch. The Center for Barth Studies. Louisville, KY: Westminster John Knox Press, 2019.

Benveniste, Émile. *Dictionary of Indo-European Concepts and Society*. Translated by Elizabeth Palmer. Chicago: Hau Books, 2016.

Benedict XVI, Pope. *Sacramentum Caritatis*. Apostolic Exhortation. February 22, 2007.

Bergsma, John and Brant Pitre. *A Catholic Introduction to the Bible*. Vol 1, *The Old Testament*. San Francisco: Ignatius Press, 2018.

Bloy, Léon. *Pilgrim of the Absolute*. Translated by John Coleman and Harry Lorin Binsse. New York: Pantheon Books Inc., 1947.

Bonaventure, St. *The Soul's Journey into God*. In *Bonaventure: The Soul's Journey into God, the Tree of Life, and the Life of St. Francis*. Translated by Ewert Cousins. Mahwah, NJ: Paulist Press, 1978.

Borghesi, Massimo. *The Mind of Pope Francis: Jorge Mario Bergoglio's Intellectual Journey*. Collegeville, MN: Liturgical Press, 2018.

Buckley, Michael J. *At the Origins of Modern Atheism*. New Haven, CT: Yale University Press, 1987.

Bullivant, Stephen. *Mass Exodus: Catholic Disaffiliation in Britain and America since Vatican II*. Oxford: Oxford University Press, 2019.

Burrell, David B. *Aquinas: God and Action*. Notre Dame, IN: University of Notre Dame Press, 1979.

Calvin, John. *Institutes of the Christian Religion*. Translated by Henry Beveridge. Peabody, MA: Hendrickson Publishers, Inc., 2008.

Caputo, John D. *The Prayers and Tears of Jacques Derrida: Religion without Religion*. Bloomington: Indiana University Press, 1997.

Catechism of the Catholic Church, 2nd ed. Washington, DC: United States Conference of Catholic Bishops, 2000.

Chaigne, Louis. *Paul Claudel: The Man and the Mystic*. Translated by Pierre de Fontnouvelle. New York: Appleton-Century-Crofts, Inc., 1961.

Chenu, Marie-Dominique. *Toward Understanding St. Thomas*. Translated by A.–M. Landry and D. Hughes. Chicago: Henry Regnery Company, 1963

Chesterton, G. K. *Autobiography*. New York: Sheed & Ward, 1936.

———. *Orthodoxy*. New York: Image Books, 1959.

———. *Collected Works*. Vol. XXVIII. San Francisco: Ignatius Press, 1987.

Dawkins, Richard. *The God Delusion*. Boston: Houghton Mifflin Company, 2006.

Denzinger, Heinrich. *Enchiridion symbolorum definitionum et declarationum de rebus fidei et morum: Compendium of Creeds, Definitions, and Declarations on Matters of Faith and Morals*, 43rd ed. Edited by Peter Hünermann. San Francisco: Ignatius Press, 2012.

Derrida, Jacques. *Dissemination*. Translated by Barbara Johnson. London/New York: Continuum, 1981.

———. *Parages*. Paris: Galilée, 1986. [English translation (with same title) edited by John P. Leavey. Stanford University Press, 2011.]

———. *Given Time*. Vol. 1, *Counterfeit Money*. Translated by Peggy Knauf. Chicago/London: The University of Chicago Press, 1992.

———. *Aporias*. Translated by Thomas Dutoit. Stanford University Press, 1993.

Descartes, René. *Discourse on Method and Meditations on First Philosophy*. Translated by Donald A. Cress. Indianapolis: Hackett Publishing Company, 1998.

Duns Scotus, Blessed John. *On Being and Cognition*. Edited and translated by John van den Bercken. New York: Fordham University Press, 2016.

———. "Six Questions on Individuation from His *Ordinatio* II. d. 3, part 1, qq. 1–6." In *Five Texts on the Mediaeval Problem of Universals*. Translated and edited by Paul V. Spade. Indianapolis: Hackett Publishing Company, Inc., 1994.

———. *Ordinatio II*. In *Opera Omnia: Opera Theologica*. Vol. 3, part 1. Edited by Giovanni Lauriola. Bari, Italy: A.G.A. Arti Grafiche Alberobello, 2001.

Ferré, Alberto Methol. "Grandes orientaciones pastorales de Pablo VI para América Latina." Buenos Aires, October 10–11, 2000. In *Pablo VI y America Latina: Jornadas de studio*. Rome: Istituto Paolo VI–Studium, 2002.

Ferré, Alberto Methol and Alver Metalli. *El Papa y el Filósofo*. Buenos Aires: Editorial Biblos, 2013.

Fessard, Gaston. *La main tendue? Le dialogue catholique-communiste est-il possible?* Paris: Éditions Bernard Grasset, 1937.

———. *France, prends garde de perdre ton âme*. Cahiers du témoignage chrétien 1. St. Etienne: St. Etienne, 1941.

———. *France, prends garde de perdre ta liberté*. Paris: Éditions du Témoignage chrétien, 1946.

———. "Le christianisme des chrétiens progressistes." *Études* 260 (January 1949): 65–93.

———. *La dialectique des Exercices Spirituels de Saint Ignace de Loyola*. Paris: Éditions Aubier-Montaigne, 1956; Vol. 2, *Fondement-Péché-Orthodoxie*. Paris: Éditions Aubier-Montaigne, 1966; Vol 3, *Symbolisme et historicité*. Paris/Namur: Éditions Lethielleux/Culture et Vérité, 1984.

———. *De l'actualité historique*. Vol. 1, *À la recherché d'une méthode*. Vol. 2, *Progressisme chrétien et apostolat ouvrier*. Paris: Desclée de Brouwer, 1960.

———. *Eglise de France prends garde de perdre la foi!* Paris: Éditions Julliard, 1979.

———. *La philosophie historique de Raymond Aron*. Paris: Julliard, 1980.

———. *Hegel, le christianisme et l'histoire: textes et documents inédits présentés par Michel Sales*. Paris: Presses universitaires de France, 1990.

Feuerbach, Ludwig. *The Essence of Christianity*. Translated by George Eliot. New York: Harper & Row Publishers, 1957. First published in German in 1841, in English in 1854.

Foucault, Michel. *Power/Knowledge: Selected Interviews and Other Writings 1972–1977*. Translated by Colin Gordon, Leo Marshall, John Mepham, and Kate Soper. New York: Pantheon Books, 1980.

Fradd, Matt. *The Porn Myth: Exposing the Reality Behind the Fantasy of Pornography*. San Francisco: Ignatius Press, 2017.

Francis, Pope. *Chrism Mass: Homily of Pope Francis*. March 28, 2013.

————. *Address of Pope Francis to Participants in the Pilgrimage from the Diocese of Brescia*. June 22, 2013.

————. *Evangelii Gaudium*. Apostolic Exhortation. November 24, 2013.

————. *Laudato Si'*. Encyclical Letter. May 24, 2015.

————. "Homily at Mass Celebrated with New Cardinals" (February 15, 2015): AAS 107 (2015).

————. "Catechesis (June 10, 2015)." *L'Osservatore Romano* (June 11, 2015): 8.

————. *Amoris Laetitia*. Post-Synodal Apostolic Exhortation. March 19, 2016.

————. *Gaudete et Exsultate*. Apostolic Exhortation. March 19, 2018.

————. *Message of His Holiness Pope Francis for the 53rd World Communications Day: We Are Members One of Another (Eph 4:25): From Social Network Communities to the Human Community*. January 24, 2019.

Freud, Sigmund. *The Future of an Illusion*. Translated by Gregory C. Richter. Ontario: Broadview Editions, 2012.

Garnett, Jane. "Joseph Butler." In *The Oxford Handbook of John Henry Newman*, edited by Frederick D. Aquino and Benjamin J. King, 135–153. Oxford: Oxford University Press, 2018.

George, Cardinal Francis. *The Difference God Makes: A Catholic Vision of Faith, Communion, and Culture*. New York: The Crossroad Publishing Company, 2009.

————. *A Godly Humanism: Clarifying the Hope that Lies Within*. Washington, DC: The Catholic University of America Press, 2015.

Gillis, Hugh. "Gaston Fessard and the Nature of Authority." *Interpretation* 16, no. 3 (1989): 445–463.

Gilson, Etienne. *The Christian Philosophy of St. Thomas Aquinas*. Translated by L. K. Shook. New York: Random House, 1956.

Goethe, Johann Wolfgang von. *The Metamorphosis of Plants*. Cambridge, MA: MIT Press, 2009.

Greene, Graham. *The Power and the Glory*. New York: Penguin Books, 1990.

Griffiths, Rudyard, ed. *Hitchens vs. Blair: Be it Resolved Religion is a Force for Good in the World: The Munk Debates*. Toronto: House of Anansi Press Inc., 2011.

Guardini, Romano. *The Lord*. Translated by Elinor Castendyk Briefs. Chicago: Henry Regnery Company, 1954.

Habermas, Jürgen. *The Inclusion of the Other: Studies in Political Theory*. Cambridge, MA: The MIT Press, 1998.

Hauerwas, Stanley. *A Community of Character: Towards a Constructive Christian Social Ethic*. Notre Dame, IN: University of Notre Dame Press, 1981.

Helmholtz, Hermann von. *Selected Writings of Hermann von Helmholtz*. Edited by Russell Kahl. Middletown, CT: Wesleyan University Press, 1971.

Herberg, William. *Judaism and Modern Man: An Interpretation of Jewish Religion*. New York: Meridian Books, Inc., and The Jewish Publication Society of America, 1951.

Hitchens, Christopher. *God is Not Great: How Religion Poisons Everything*. New York: Twelve/Hachette Book Group USA, 2007.

Hobbes, Thomas. *Leviathan, XIII, 9. Revised Student Edition* edited by Richard Tuck. Cambridge, UK: Cambridge University Press, 1996.

Holmes, Jr., Oliver Wendell. *Holmes-Pollock Letters: The Correspondence of Mr. Justice Holmes and Sir Frederick Pollock 1874–1932*. Vol. 1. Edited by Mark DeWolfe Howe. Cambridge, MA: Harvard University Press, 1942.

Hopkins, Gerard M. *The Letters of Gerard M. Hopkins*. Edited by Claude Colleer Abbott. London: Oxford University Press, 1955.

Ignatius of Loyola, St. *The Spiritual Exercises of St. Ignatius*. Translated by Anthony Mottola. New York: Image Books, 1964.

Index Thomisticus search engine, http://www.corpusthomisticum. org/it/index.age.

Irenaeus of Lyons, St. *Irenaeus on the Christian Faith: A Condensation of Against Heresies*. Translated and edited by James R. Payton, Jr. Eugene, OR: Pickwick Publications, 2011.

Jefferson, Thomas. "The Declaration of Independence." In *Basic Documents in American History*. Edited by Richard B. Morris. The Anvil Series. Malabar, FL: Krieger Publishing Company, 1965.

Jesuit Life & Mission Today: The Decrees of the 31st-35th General Congregations of the Society of Jesus, edited by John W. Padberg. Jesuit Primary Sources in English Translation 25. Saint Louis, MO: The Institute of Jesuit Sources, 2009.

John Paul II, Pope. *Familiaris Consortio*. Apostolic Exhortation. November 22, 1981.

———. "Address to the Assembly of CELAM" (March 9, 1983): *AAS* 75 (1983), 778.

———. *Redemptoris Missio*. Encyclical Letter. December 7, 1990.

———. *Centesimus Annus*. Encyclical Letter. May 1, 1991.

———. *Pastores Dabo Vobis*. Post-Synodal Apostolic Exhortation. Washington, DC: United States Conference of Catholic Bishops, 1992.

———. *Holy Thursday Letters to My Brother Priests*. Princeton, NJ: Scepter Publishers, 1994.

———. *Fides et Ratio*. Encyclical Letter. September 14, 1998.

Jones, Jeffrey M. "Many U.S. Catholics Question Their Membership Amid Scandal." *Gallup* (March 13, 2019). https://news.gallup .com/poll/247571/catholics-question-membership-amid- scandal.aspx.

Jones, Robert P., Daniel Cox, Betsy Cooper, and Rachel Lienesch. *Exodus: Why Americans are Leaving Religion—and Why They're Unlikely to Come Back*. Washington, DC: Public Religion Research Institute, 2016.

Joyce, James. *A Portrait of the Artist as a Young Man*, Oxford World's Classics. Oxford: Oxford University Press, 2000.

Kant, Immanuel. *Religion within the Limits of Reason Alone*. New York: Harper Torchbooks, 1960.

———. *Critique of Pure Reason*. Translated by Paul Guyer. Cambridge: Cambridge University Press, 1998.

———. *Groundwork of the Metaphysics of Morals: A German–English Edition*. Translated by Mary Gregor and Jens Timmermann. Cambridge: Cambridge University Press, 2011.

Kaplan, Fred. *Lincoln: The Biography of a Writer*. New York: HarperCollins Publishers, 2008.

Kasper, Walter. *Der Gott Jesu Christi*. Mainz: Matthias-Grünewald-Verlag, 1982.

———. *The God of Jesus Christ*. New York: Continuum Books, T&T Clark International, 2012.

Kierkegaard, Søren. *Purity of Heart is to Will One Thing: Spiritual Preparation for the Office of Confession*. Translated by Douglas V. Steere. New York: Harper and Brothers Publishers, 1948.

———. *Philosophical Fragments: Johannes Climacus*. Translated by Howard V. Hong and Edna H. Hong. Princeton, NJ: Princeton University Press, 1985.

King, Jr., Martin Luther. *A Testament of Hope: The Essential Writings and Speeches of Martin Luther King Jr*. Edited by James M. Washington. New York: HarperOne, 1991.

Kojève, Alexandre. "Communisme et christianisme." *Critique* 3–4 (1946): 308–12.

Lewis, C. S. *Mere Christianity*. New York: Macmillian Publishing Co., Inc., 1952.

———. *God in the Dock: Essays on Theology and Ethics*. Grand Rapids, MI: William B. Eerdmans Publishing Company, 1970.

———. *The Collected Letters of C.S. Lewis*. Vol. 2, *Books, Broadcasts, and the War, 1931–1949*. Edited by Walter Hooper. New York: HarperCollins Publishers, 2004.

Lincoln, Abraham. *Speeches and Writings: 1832–1858*. The Library of America 48. Washington, DC: The Library of America, 1989.

Lindbeck, George. *The Nature of Doctrine*. Philadelphia, PA: The Westminster Press, 1984.

Lonergan, Bernard, SJ. *Method in Theology*. Toronto: University of Toronto Press, 2003. First published 1971.

———. *Insight: A Study of Human Understanding*. Vol. 3 of *Collected Works of Bernard Lonergan*. Edited by Robert Doran and Frederick Crowe. Toronto: University of Toronto Press, 1992.

———. *Method in Theology*. Vol. 14 of *Collected Works of Bernard Lonergan*. Toronto: University of Toronto Press, 2017.

Long, D. Stephen. *The Perfectly Simple Triune God: Aquinas and His Legacy*. Minneapolis: Fortress Press, 2016.

Luther, Martin. *The Bondage of the Will*. Translated by Henry Cole. Peabody, MA: Hendrickson Publishers, Inc., 2008.

———. *Tischreden*. Edited by K. Aland. Stuttgart: P. Reclam, 1981.

Manglos-Weber, Nicolette and Christian Smith. *Understanding Former Young Catholics: Findings from a National Study of American Emerging Adults*. Notre Dame, IN: University of Notre Dame Press, 2014.

Marion, Jean-Luc. *God Without Being*, trans. Thomas A. Carlson. Chicago: The University of Chicago Press, 1991.

Maritain, Jacques. *Three Reformers: Luther—Descartes—Rousseau*. New York: Charles Scribner's Sons, 1934.

Marshall, Bruce D. *Trinity and Truth*. Cambridge Studies in Christian Doctrine 3. Cambridge, U.K.: Cambridge University Press, 2000.

Marx, Karl. *A Contribution to the Critique of Hegel's Philosophy of Right: Introduction*. Translated by Annette Jolin and Joseph O'Malley. Cambridge: Cambridge University Press, 1970.

Maurin, Peter. *Easy Essays*. Eugene, OR: Wipf and Stock Publishers, 2003.

Mauss, Marcel. *The Gift: Expanded Edition*. Translated by Jane I. Guyer. Chicago: Hau Books, 2016.

McCabe, Herbert, OP. *God Still Matters*. London: Continuum, 2005.

McSorley, Harry J. *Luther: Right or Wrong? An Ecumenical–Theological Study of Luther's Major Work, "The Bondage of the Will."* New York: Newman Press, 1969.

Meier, Hans, ed. *Totalitarianism and Political Religions*. Vol. III, *Concepts for the Comparison of Dictatorships—Theory & History of Interpretations*. Translated by Jodi Bruhn. London: Routledge, 2008.

Menges, Matthew C. *The Concept of Univocity Regarding the Predication of God and Creature According to William Ockham*. St. Bonaventure, NY: Franciscan Institute, 1952.

Merton, Thomas. *Run to the Mountain: The Story of a Vocation*. Edited by Patrick Hart. San Francisco: Harper San Francisco, 1995.

Meslier, Jean. *Testament: Memoir of the Thoughts and Sentiments of Jean Meslier*. Translated by Michael Shreve. Amherst, NY: Prometheus Books, 2009.

Newman, John Henry. *The Letters and Diaries of John Henry Newman*. 32 volumes. Oxford: Clarendon Press/Oxford University Press, 1961–2008.

———. *Apologia Pro Vita Sua*. Edited by Martin Svaglic. Oxford: Clarendon Press, 1967.

————. *An Essay in Aid of a Grammar of Assent.* Edited by I. T. Ker. Oxford: Clarendon Press, 1985.

————. *An Essay on the Development of Christian Doctrine*, 6th ed. Notre Dame, IN: University of Notre Dame Press, 1989.

————. *Fifteen Sermons Preached Before the University of Oxford Between A.D. 1826 and 1843.* Edited by James David Earnest and Gerard Tracey. Oxford: Oxford University Press, 2006.

————. *Sermons Bearing on the Subjects of the Day.* London/New York/Bombay: Longmans Todd, and Co., 1902. Accessed at *Newman Reader — Works of John Henry Newman* Copyright © 2007 by The National Institute for Newman Studies.

Nicholas of Cusa. *Nicholas of Cusa on God as Not-Other: A Translation and Appraisal of* De Li Non Aliud. Translated by Jasper Hopkins. Minneapolis: The Arthur J. Banning Press, 1983.

Nietzsche, Friedrich. *The Gay Science.* Translated by Josefine Nauckoff. Cambridge: Cambridge University Press, 2001.

————. *Beyond Good and Evil.* Translated by Judith Norman. Cambridge: Cambridge University Press, 2002.

————. *Thus Spoke Zarathustra.* Translated by Adrian Del Caro. Cambridge: Cambridge University Press, 2006.

Ockham, William of. *Scriptum in Librum Primum Sententiarum: Ordinatio (Dist. XIX-XLVIII).* In *Opera Theologica.* Vol. IV. St. Bonaventure, NY: The Franciscan Institute, 1977.

Otto, Rudolph. *The Idea of the Holy: An Inquiry into the Non-Rational Factor in the Idea of the Divine and its Relation to the Rational.* Translated by John W. Harvey. London: Oxford University Press, 1970.

Paine, Thomas. *The Age of Reason.* In *Collected Writings.* Edited by Eric Foner. New York.: The Library of America/Penguin Books, 1995.

Paul VI, Pope. *Address of the Holy Father Paul VI to the United Nations Organization.* October 4, 1965.

————. *Evangelii Nuntiandi.* Apostolic Exhortation. December 8, 1975.

Petrache, Ana. *Gaston Fessard, un chrétien de rite dialectique?* Paris: Les Éditions du Cerf, 2017.

Pew Research Center. "'Nones' on the Rise." (October 9, 2012). https://www.pewforum.org/2012/10/09/nones-on-the-rise.

————. "America's Changing Religious Landscape: Chapter 2." (May 12, 2015). https://www.pewforum.org/2015/05/12/chapter-2-religious-switching-and-intermarriage.

Pew Research Center and Michael Lipka. "Why America's 'Nones' Left Religion Behind." (August 24, 2016). https://www.pewresearch.org/fact-tank/2016/08/24/why-americas-nones-left-religion-behind.

Pew Research Center, David Masci, and Gregory A. Smith. "Seven Facts about American Catholics." (October 10, 2018). https://www.pewresearch.org/fact-tank/2018/10/10/7-facts-about-american-catholics.

Pew Research Center. "In U.S., Decline of Christianity Continues at Rapid Pace: An Update on America's Changing Religious Landscape." (October 17, 2019). https://www.pewforum.org/2019/10/17/in-u-s-decline-of-christianity-continues-at-rapid-pace.

Philo of Alexandria. *On the Creation of the Cosmos According to Moses*. Translated by David T. Runia. Philo of Alexandria Commentary Series 1. Leiden: Brill, 2001.

Plantinga, Alvin. *Does God Have a Nature?* The Aquinas Lecture Series. Milwaukee, WI: Marquette University Press, 1980.

Plato. *The Complete Works*. Edited by John M. Cooper. Translated by Alexander Nehamas and Paul Woodruff. Indianapolis: Hackett Publishing Company, 1997.

Pinckaers, Servais, OP. *The Sources of Christian Ethics*, 3rd ed. Translated by Sr. Mary Thomas Noble. Washington, DC: The Catholic University of America Press, 1995.

Rahner, Karl. "Eine Antwort." *Orientierung* 14 (1950): 141–45.

———. *The Church and the Sacraments*. New York: Herder and Herder, 1963.

———. *Foundations of Christian Faith: An Introduction to the Idea of Christianity*. Translated by William V. Dych. New York: The Crossroad Publishing Company, 1978.

Ratzinger, Joseph. *Wahrheit, Werte, Macht: Prüfsteine der pluralistischen Gesellschaft*. Frieburg im Breisgau: Herder, 1993.

———. *Introduction to Christianity*. Translated by J. R. Foster and Michael J. Miller. San Francisco: Ignatius Press, 2004.

———. *Mass Pro Eligendo Romano Pontifice. Homily of his Eminence Card. Joseph Ratzinger, Dean of the College of Cardinals*. April 18, 2005.

Rosetti, Stephen. *The Joy of Priesthood*. Notre Dame, IN: Ave Maria Press, 2005.

Russell, Bertrand. *Dear Bertrand Russell: A Selection of his Correspondence with the General Public, 1950–1968.* Boston: Houghton Mifflin Company, 1969. First published 1958.

———. *The Collected Papers of Bertrand Russell.* Vol. 11, *Last Philosophical Testament, 1943–68.* London: Routledge, 1997.

Saad, Lydia. "Catholics' Church Attendance Resumes Downward Slide." *Gallup* (April 9, 2018). https://news.gallup.com/poll/232226/church-attendance-among-catholics-resumes-downward-slide.aspx.

Sartre, Jean-Paul. *Existentialism is a Humanism.* Translated by Carol Macomber. New Haven, CT: Yale University Press, 2007.

Schleiermacher, Friedrich. *On Religion: Speeches to its Cultured Despisers.* Translated by John Oman. New York: Harper and Brothers, 1958 (translation of the third German edition).

———. *The Christian Faith.* Edited by H. R. MacKintosh and J. S. Stewart. Edinburgh: T&T Clark, 1986.

———. *On Religion: Speeches to Its Cultured Despisers.* Translated by Richard Crouter. Cambridge: Cambridge University Press, 1988.

———. *The Christian Faith.* Vol. 1. Translated by Terrence N. Tice, Catherine L. Kelsey, and Edwina Lawler. Louisville, KY: Westminster John Knox Press, 2016.

Schroeder, H. J. *Canons and Decrees of the Council of Trent.* St. Louis, MO: B. Herder Book Co., 1941.

Sheen, Fulton J. *Three to Get Married.* New York: Scepter Publishers, 1996.

———. *The Priest is Not His Own.* San Francisco: Ignatius Press, 2004.

Sokolowski, Robert. *The God of Faith and Reason: Foundations of Christian Theology.* Washington, DC: The Catholic University of America Press, 1995.

Spadaro, Antonio. "Interview with Pope Francis." August 19, 23, and 29, 2013.

Spinoza, Baruch. *Ethics.* Vol. 1 of *The Collected Works of Spinoza.* Translated by Edwin Curley. Princeton: Princeton University Press, 1985.

Steinfels, Peter. *A People Adrift: The Crisis of the Roman Catholic Church in America.* New York: Simon & Schuster, 2003.

Stowe, Harriet Beecher. *Uncle Tom's Cabin.* Oxford: Oxford University Press, 1998.

Stump, Eleonore. "God's Simplicity." In *The Oxford Handbook of Aquinas*. Edited by Brian Davies and Eleonore Stump. Oxford: Oxford University Press, 2012.

Taylor, Charles. *A Secular Age*. Cambridge, MA: The Belknap Press of Harvard University Press, 2018. First published 2007.

Tertullian. *Apology*. Translated by T. R. Glover. The Loeb Classical Library. London: William Heinemann Ltd, 1931.

———. "On Prescription Against Heretics." Translated by Alexander Roberts and James Donaldson. In vol. 3 of *The Ante-Nicene Fathers: The Writings of the Fathers down to A.D. 325*. Grand Rapids, MI: William B. Eerdmans Publishing Company, 1963.

Tillich, Paul. *Systematic Theology*. Vol. 1. Chicago: The University of Chicago Press, 1967. First published in 1951. Vol. 2. Chicago: The University of Chicago Press, 1957. Vol. 3. Chicago: The University of Chicago Press, 1963.

———. *Dogmatik*. Düsseldorf: Patmos Verlag, 1986.

———. *Against the Third Reich: Paul Tillich's Wartime Radio Broadcasts into Nazi Germany*. Translated by Matthew Lon Weaver. Louisville, KY: Westminster John Knox Press, 1998.

Tocqueville, Alexis de. *Democracy in America*. Vol. 2. Translated by Harvey C. Mansfield and Delba Winthrop. Chicago: The University of Chicago Press, 2000.

Torrell, Jean-Pierre. *Saint Thomas Aquinas*. Vol. 1, *The Person and His Work*. Translated by Robert Royal. Washington, DC: The Catholic University of America Press, 2005.

Tornielli, Andrea and Giacomo Galeazzi. *This Economy Kills: Pope Francis on Capitalism and Social Justice*. Translated by Demetrio S. Yocum. Collegeville, MN: Order of St. Benedict, 2015.

Tracy, David. *The Analogical Imagination: Christian Theology and the Culture of Pluralism*. New York: The Crossroad Publishing Company, 1981.

Twenge, Jean M. *iGen: Why Today's Super-Connected Kids are Growing Up Less Rebellious, More Tolerant, Less Happy—and Completely Unprepared for Adulthood (And What That Means for the Rest of Us)*. New York: Atria Books, 2017.

Twomey, Vincent. *Pope Benedict XVI: The Conscience of Our Age*. San Francisco: Ignatius Press, 2007.

United States Conference of Catholic Bishops. *Fulfilled in Your Hearing: The Homily in the Sunday Assembly.* Washington, DC: United States Conference of Catholic Bishops, 1982.

———. *Program for Priestly Formation,* 5th Edition. Washington, DC: United States Conference of Catholic Bishops, 2006.

Vatican Council II. *Lumen Gentium.* Dogmatic Constitution. November 21, 1964.

———. *Optatam Totius.* Decree on Priestly Training. October 28, 1965. In vol. 2 of *Decrees of the Ecumenical Councils.* Edited by Norman Tanner, SJ. London: Sheed and Ward, 1990.

———. *Gravissimum Educationis.* Declaration on Christian Education. October 28, 1965.

———. *Apostolicam Actuositatem.* Decree on the Apostolate of the Laity. November 18, 1965.

———. *Gaudium et Spes.* Pastoral Constitution. December 7, 1965.

———. *Presbyterorum Ordinis.* Decree on the Ministry and Life of Priests. December 7, 1965.

Vedder, Ben. *Heidegger's Philosophy of Religion: From God to the gods.* Pittsburgh: Duquesne University Press, 2007.

Voiss, James K. "Karl Rahner, Hans Urs von Balthasar, and the Question of Theological Aesthetics: Preliminary Considerations." *Louvain Studies* 29, nos. 1–2 (Spring-Summer 2004): 147–165.

von Balthasar, Hans Urs. *Razing the Bastions.* San Francisco: Ignatius Press, 1993.

———. "Geist und Feuer: Ein Gespräch mit Hans Urs von Balthasar." *Herder Korrespondenz* 30, no. 2 (1976): 72–82.

———. *Theo-Drama: Theological Dramatic Theology.* 5 vols. San Francisco, CA: Ignatius Press, 1988–1998.

———. *Explorations in Theology.* Vol. 1, *The Word Made Flesh.* Translated by A. V. Littledale and Alexander Dru. San Francisco: Ignatius Press, 1989.

———. *The Glory of the Lord: A Theological Aesthetics.* Vol. 1, *Seeing the Form.* Translated by Erasmo Leiva-Merikakis. San Francisco: Ignatius Press, 2009.

von Hildebrand, Dietrich. *Christian Ethics.* New York: David McKay Company, Inc., 1953.

————. *My Battle Against Hitler: Faith, Truth, and Defiance in the Shadow of the Third Reich.* Translated by John Henry Crosby. New York: Image, 2014.

————. *Aesthetics.* Vol. 1. Translated by Fr. Brian McNeil. Steubenville, OH: The Hildebrand Project, 2016.

Waugh, Evelyn. *Brideshead Revisited.* New York: Back Bay Books/Little, Brown and Company, 1973. First published in 1945; Waugh made a few edits for the subsequent edition.

Weigel, George. *Witness to Hope: The Biography of Pope John Paul II 1920–2005.* New York: Harper Perennial, 2001.

Wippel, John F. "Thomas Aquinas and the Condemnation of 1277." *The Modern Schoolman* 72, no. 2/3 (1995): 233–272.

Wright, N. T. *The New Testament and the People of God.* Vol. 1 of *Christian Origins and the Question of God.* Minneapolis: Fortress Press, 1992.

————. *Jesus and the Victory of God.* Vol. 2 of *Christian Origins and the Question of God.* Minneapolis: Fortress Press, 1996.

————. *Paul and the Faithfulness of God.* Minneapolis: Fortress Press, 2013.

Index

#MeToo movement, 240

abortion, 207
abuse. *See* sexual abuse crisis.
Abraham, 19, 32, 74, 152,
153–54, 199
Adam, 162, 208, 237; and
dominion, 197–99, 201; and
the Garden of Eden, 228; as
king, 159; and original sin,
205; as priest, 30–33, 152,
196. *See also* Garden of Eden
Adams, John, 245
adoratio, 31, 152, 196, 237
adoration, 178, 187
Albigensianism, 56
Ambrose, St., 31n25, 88
Anselm of Canterbury, St., 57,
66, 88, 287
Aron, Raymond, 133, 134, 138
Aristotle, 12, 218; on friendship, 110, 260; on gift-giving,
108–109; and liberty, 259; on
magnanimity, 213; and mo-
rality, 224, 227; on *phronesis*,
124; and politics, 246, 247,

252; and rhetoric, 188; and
Thomas Aquinas, 47–48, 269
Amoris Laetitia, ix, xiii, 223–41
Antony of the Desert, St., 39, 265
assent, 113–130
Aparecida Document. *See*
Bergoglio, Jorge Mario
Athanasius, St., 39, 287n2
atheism, 4, 5, 13, 37, 141, 189,
256; and Fessard, 146; new,
xii, 28, 38, 39, 49, 193; practical, 146
Augustine, St., 18, 39, 66, 70,
109; and Cain, 32; and the
City of God, 208; on divine
simplicity, 88; on gifts, 108; on
God, 93; and *libido dominandi*,
160, 163; and Newman, 128;
and religion, 7; and restless-
ness, 6, 57, 259
autonomy, 83, 229, 238
Avicenna, 12, 269

Babette's Feast, 272–277
Bakunin, Mikhail, 37, 194, 250,
258n10

Balthasar, Hans Urs von, viii, xi,
26, 74–75, 131; on aesthetics,
191; and Barron, 65–67, 72–
73, 80–84; on bastions, 21;
on beauty, 264; on *capax Dei*,
72; and Christology, 76–78,
80; and Claudel, 23–24; and
Fessard, 142; and Goethe,
73–74; and Guardini, 76; and
Ignatius of Loyola, 79; and
Kant, 72–73; on theo-drama,
19; and transcendentals, 23,
24, 264
baptism, xiii, 60, 185, 234, 281;
of Jesus, 278
Barth, Karl, 58, 72; on Christ,
44; on cultured despisers, 74
beauty, 229, 246; and *Babette's
Feast*, 272; and Catholicism,
25, 190, 191; and cinema,
288; and creation, 197; and
Fessard, 136; and James
Joyce, 25, 264; and Mun-
delein Seminary, 218; and
Newman, 118; and *Shawshank
Redemption*, 281; and von
Balthasar, 23–24, 84
"beige Catholicism." *See* Catholicism
being, 5, 46, 86, 115, 137, 247;
and Christ, 30, 54, 69, 75;
and the Christian, 109; and
creatures, 103; and God, 6,
35–36, 43, 48, 49, 51, 52, 68,
70, 79, 80, 86, 87, 92–95,
100, 101–102, 104–107,
189, 255; human, 20, 29, 30,
38, 44, 48, 52, 53, 80, 96,

142, 152, 175, 177–78, 184,
189, 193, 195, 196–98, 205,
208–210, 232, 236, 237, 252,
256; and Jean-Luc Marion,
104; and the universe, 14,
85–86
Beecher, Harriet Stowe, 116
Bellarmine, St. Robert, 57
Benedict XVI, Pope, and dictatorship of relativism, 254;
and New Evangelization,
21–22; and the Mass, 202;
and *Pastores Dabo Vobis*, 170.
See also Ratzinger, Joseph
Benedict, St., 39, 187, 265
Benveniste, Émile, 98, 111
Bonaventure, St., 57, 181; on
divine simplicity, 88; on God's
Name, 104–05
Bergoglio, Jorge Mario, xiii; and
the Aparecida Document, 22;
and capitalism, 145; and Fes-
sard, 145, 148; and Guardini,
131; and proselytism, 147;
and theology of the people,
144. *See also* Francis, Pope
Borghesi, Massimo, 131
Brideshead Revisited, 24, 227
Brown University, 261
Bultmann, Rudolf, 30
Burrell, David, 52, 80n29, 86

Cain, 32
Calvin, John, 171, 256
causality, 41, 52, 106
Cartesianism, 74, 256, 257
Casey v. Planned Parenthood, 205,
258–259

parable, 80, 159

participation, active, 178, 202; and "experiential expressivism," 82; and the family, 203; and God, 255; and the Resurrection, 239; and Tillich, 9, 138

Pascal, Blaise, 243

Paschal Mystery, 281

Passover, 33

Paul, 74; and the Areopagus, 23, 125, 128; and Christ, 33, 35, 40, 44, 53, 165, 248, 275–76, 282; and the Church, 19, 24, 60, 82; and Fessard, 133, 134, 136, 139, 140; and Pope Francis, 236; and Guardini, 76; and Thomas Aquinas, 89, 102

Paul VI, Pope, 21, 169, 201, 226

Paulsen, Fr. Thomas, 41

peace, 34, 137, 195, 202

perfection: and Christian life, 236; and God, 87, 91–92, 94, 102, 105, 107, 255

person, 126, 161, 279; and Adam, 31; and beauty, 118; and celibacy, 177; and the family, 210; and freedom, 226, 251; and friendship, 238; and God, 15, 29, 88, 91–92, 117, 119, 128; human, 111, 116, 142, 176, 181; and holiness, 56; and Jesus Christ, ix, 29, 38, 54, 77, 79, 83, 95, 110, 130, 137, 200, 241, 271–72, 276; and magnanimity, 213–15; and modernity, 6, 7, 10, 217; and modesty,

231; and priesthood, 166, 186; and Protestantism, 147; and religion, 69–70, 127, 243; and salvation history, 129; and the Scriptures, 193; and spirituality, 143, 201, 208; and subjectivism, 262; and technology, 230; and the Trinity, 104, 107, 108–109; and virtue, ix, 124, 227, 229

Peter, St., 74, 78, 110, 282

Philo of Alexandria, 31n25

philosophy, 9, 261; Catholic, 26; destruction of, 28; and divine freedom, 79–80; and divine simplicity, 85; and the Enlightenment, 243; and existentialism, 257–58; and the Fall, 198; and freedom, 206; and the Garden of Eden, 31, 198; and history, 134–37; and Hobbes, 252; and the human person, 193; and Nietzsche, 205, 215; and relativism, 254; and science, 244; and seminary education, 172, 179–80, 189; and theology, 4–48, 83, 99; and truth, 28–29; and the university, 28; and young people, 14

physics, 8, 16, 18, 243; spiritual, 32, 154

Pincakers, Servais, 79, 206, 225, 249–50, 256n4, 265, 266

Plato, 12, 218, 247; and being, 102; and dialogues, 44–45, 69; and the Diotoma speech, 24–25, 264; and God, 104;

155; and the Lamb of God,
33; and Maximilian Kolbe,
263; and Moloch, 166; and
priesthood, 126, 216; and
Shawshank Redemption, 286, 287

Sacramentum Caritatis, 202

salvation: and Buddha, 77; and
double predestination, 80;
and Fessard, 143; and grace,
36–37; and Israel, 199; and
Jesus Christ, 187, 254, 275;
and John Paul II, 204; and
liberation theology, 144–45;
and Marxism, 140–41; and
Mary, 17–18, 26; and the
priesthood, 61; and Rahner,
68; and reproduction, 152–
53, 162; and theology, 183

Sartre, Jean-Paul, 35, 49,
133; and atheism, 256; and
existentialism, 189, 257–58;
and freedom, 78–79, 205,
232–33, 257–58, 265n30;
and subjectivism, 258

Schelling, Friedrich Wilhelm
Joseph von, 132

Schillebeeckx, Edward, 65

Schleiermacher, Friedrich: and
Christology, 75; and experiential expressivism, 18, 26,
43–44; and faith, 69–71;
and Jesus Christ, 29–30, 44,
76–77; and subjective religion, 264; and von Balthasar,
78, 84

science, 8–9; and creation,
196; and the Enlightenment,
243–44; and the Garden of

Eden, 31, 198; and Genesis,
195; and Goethe, 229; and
indirect/formal process, 124;
and religion, 12–14, 16–17,
27–29, 116, 217, 218; and
revelation, 46; and seminary
education, 172; and sexuality,
230; theology as, 47–48, 83

Scripture: and community, 59;
and God, 90; and the human
person, 193, 201–202; and
Jesus Christ, 187; and moral
theology, 173; and the New
Evangelization, 178; and
secularism, 40; and seminary
education, 172, 188; and
sex abuse crisis, 151, 153,
168; and theology, 181; and
Thomas Aquinas, 48, 89

secularism, 215; and the buffered self, 57, 190; and the
Church, ix, 40, 182; and
liberalism, 253

self(-): alienation, 141; buffered,
57, 58, 259, 263; consciousness, 72, 73, 79, 257; control,
209; creation, 189, 205, 226;
definition, 258; determination, 206, 242, 250, 266; and
the disenchanted world, 189;
emptying, 165; evident, 246,
247, 251–52; giving, 231,
232, 240; interest, 109, 154,
159, 160; invention, viii, xi,
215, 232, 233, 260; justification, 178; and liberalism, 253;
and liberty, 78; and morality,
118; possession, 134–35;

The Catholic University of America Press presents
Faith and Reason for Everyone

If you appreciate Bishop Barron's work, you may enjoy our other works of Catholic theology and philosophy, such as:

The Light of Christ: An Introduction to Catholicism
By Fr. Thomas Joseph White, OP

"The single best introduction to the Catholic faith in print."
—*Matthew Ramage, Benedictine College*

"Thomas Joseph White is one of the brightest and most articulate theologians writing today. This book is an intelligent and spiritually alert introduction to the principal themes of Catholic theology. Both beginners and serious academics will find much to savor in its pages."
—*Bishop Robert Barron*

The God of Faith and Reason: Foundations of Christian Theology
By Msgr. Robert Sokolowski of The Catholic University of America

The Intellectual Life: Its Spirit, Conditions, Methods
By A. G. Sertillanges, OP

John Henry Newman on Truth and Its Counterfeits: A Guide for Our Times (Sacra Doctrina Series)
By Reinhard Hütter of The Catholic University of America

A Catechism for Family Life: Insights from Catholic Teaching on Love, Marriage, Sex, and Parenting
By Sarah Bartel and John Grabowski of The Catholic University of America, editors

"Having visited most US dioceses and taught young adults for decades, I can testify that this book contains the questions Catholics are asking here and now about sex, marriage, and family life, and sourced answers they can trust."
—*Helen Alvare, Catholic Women's Forum*